The Complete Course Solution That Teaches Students How to Listen . . .

Now in its Third Edition, Charles Hoffer's *Music Listening Today* continues its tradition of teaching students to enjoy all types of music while developing their listening skills. Hoffer encourages students to listen to music more perceptively by integrating numerous innovative pedagogical features that clearly illustrate the elements of music and build their knowledge of styles, forms, genres, terminology, and historical contexts.

With 43 concise chapters, this text's modular format allows you the flexibility to pick and choose the topics and chapter materials you wish to assign. The repertoire includes 89 accessible musical selections that have additional interactive step-by-step instruction on how to listen to each piece. And with a core listening program of 32 pieces on two CDs, as well as the groundbreaking multimedia music tool **ThomsonNOW**™—which can be packaged with the text at no additional cost—*Music Listening Today* is a successful, affordable, complete course package in music appreciation.

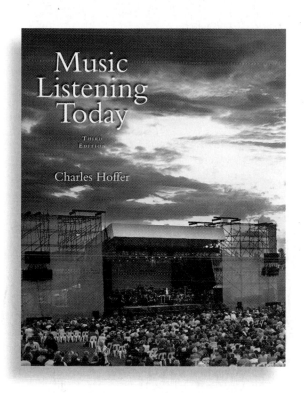

. . . Accompanied by Interactive Music Learning Tools—*At No Additional Cost!*

See pages 4-6 of this Preview for more details on these and other dynamic teaching and learning resources!

THOMSON

SCHIRMER

Dynamic Features That Build Students' Listening Skills

Throughout the text, *Music Listening Today* employs an array of innovative and useful features that help students—regardless of their musical background—learn how to listen to music.

The text begins helping students advance their listening skills as early as Chapter 1, using a Listening Guide for a musical piece that students will recognize and enjoy—the theme from the film *Star Wars*.

▶ **All of the text's 89 Listening Guides provide students with brief descriptive sentences about the music at various points.** Cumulative timings, track-by-track timings, and new, expanded headings provide students with the date of work, as well as reminders about key elements such as genre, form, medium, and tempo, making the text's musical selections easy to navigate.

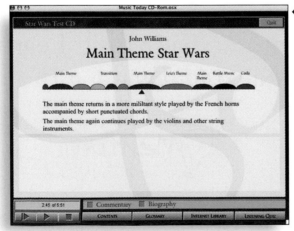

◀ **Each of the text's 89 selections also has a new, downloadable cross-platform Active Listening Guide.** The Active Listening Guides are available on the Book Companion Website and via ThomsonNOW (see pages 4-5).

Walking students step by step through each piece, the Active Listening Guides teach them how to listen to music and identify specific elements. In addition, Active Listening Guides supply students with live access to biographical sketches of composers, musical terms, links to related websites, and interactive "Listening Quizzes" that help students gain greater skill in hearing various aspects of music.

A Fresh Organization That Is Clear, Concise, and Engaging

Music Listening Today also features a reorganization that provides students with a more accessible and logical flow of information. The text's introductory chapters on the elements of music now flow directly into the chapters on Western concert music from Part II through Part VII. The text concludes with a world music section, **Part VIII, Music around the World**. The text also includes eleven new musical selections.

Newly featured music

Rutter: "Open Thou Mine Eyes"

Pérotin: "Alleluia, Diffusa est gratia"

Corelli: Trio Sonata in F, second and third movements

Bach: Brandenburg Concerto No. 5, third movement

Mozart: Piano Sonata No. 11, Rondo alla Turca

Mendelssohn: Symphony No. 4 ("Italian"), fourth movement

Clara Schumann: Scherzo

Crumb: "The moon is dead, dead …" from *Night of the Four Moons*

Hank Williams: "Your Cheatin' Heart"

Japan: "Hakusen no"

In addition, the text now contains separate chapters on early and medieval music. Baroque chapters have been reorganized to group types of music more logically. Program and ballet music, and neoclassism, tone rows, and serialism, are now combined into one chapter each, for a clearer, more concise presentation of each musical style.

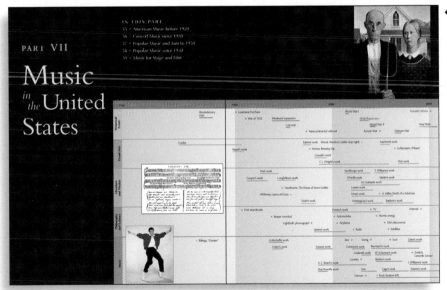

◀ **Parts II-VII contain richly illustrated timelines for each style period.** These timelines introduce students to each musical period, supplying them with a visual representation of the significant historical events of each era. These timelines place the music within its cultural and historical context, further demonstrating the influences on each musical style.

▶ **NEW "Features of" a period's music, in the last chapter for each period,** help to summarize the major changes in the elements of music during each period, providing students with a useful study aid.

Features of Classical Music	
Melodies	Often consist of short, tuneful phrases strung together; usually have a light, elegant quality; statement–answer pattern
Rhythm	Metrical with a steady beat, except in recitatives
Texture	Mostly homophonic
Harmony	Tonal with modulations mostly to nearly related keys; continuo part no longer present
Dynamic levels	Gradual crescendo and decrescendo developed
Performance media	Orchestra; chamber music groups; piano replaces harpsichord; vocal music
Forms	Sonata, theme and variations, rondo, and minuet and trio; forms often contain balanced and symmetrical phrases
Genres	Symphony, solo concerto, sonata, chamber music, opera

A Cutting-Edge Interactive Music Tool for Students and Instructors . . .

Just What Your Students Need to Know NOW!

ThomsonNOW™ for Hoffer's *Music Listening Today, Third Edition*

ThomsonNOW for Hoffer's *Music Listening Today, Third Edition*, is a powerful online learning system that saves instructors time through its automatic grading and easy-to-use gradebook, and provides students with an efficient way to study. Using a variety of technologies to accommodate different learning styles, ThomsonNOW contains quizzing and interactive multimedia tutorials that work with students to build personalized study plans and help them comprehend basic musical concepts.

First, students take a **Pretest** of multiple-choice, true/false, and listening items to assess their proficiency in the material covered in the corresponding text chapter.

Once they have completed the Pretest, students receive a **Personalized Study Plan**, tailored to the specific areas they require the most help with. ThomsonNOW's *Personalized Study Plans* contain links to multimedia tutorials, such as flashcards; summary statements; text pages; interactive demonstrations and lectures on musical elements, features, instruments, and style periods; and much more.

. . . Available With the Text at No Additional Cost!

After working through their *Personalized Study Plan*, students complete a follow-up **Posttest** to assess their mastery of the material. Based on incorrect *Posttest* answers, students receive a *Revised Study Plan*. With ThomsonNOW, students can also choose how they want to read **Music Listening Today**—via integrated digital eBook or by reading the print version. In addition, ThomsonNOW supplies students with access to an *Additional Study and Exploration* section that contains links to the text's downloadable Active Listening Guides, as well as numerous other interactive musical demonstrations and activities that help students grasp essential concepts.

ThomsonNOW is also a powerful and easy-to-use course management tool for Instructors! Using ThomsonNOW, you can manage assignments, grading, and enrollment. You can assign either the whole book or individual chapters, and for each chapter, you can select materials for study and testing. Assigning chapters in ThomsonNOW takes just seconds, and your students' results flow automatically into an online gradebook. Thomson Schirmer offers integration of ThomsonNOW with many course management platforms, including WebCT and Blackboard. Students can log in at their school's course management platform, access all the ThomsonNOW content with no additional login, and see their grades in a single gradebook.

Just What You Need to Do NOW!

ThomsonNOW is also accompanied by a *User Guide* that will help you and your students get up and running quickly, allowing you to take full advantage of its capabilities. And to ensure that you maximize the results you desire, we offer a dedicated service and training program: Thomson Learning Connects. This program includes a 24/7 ThomsonNOW service and support website, a lead teacher program, extensive first day of class services, and more. For details, contact your local Thomson Schirmer representative or visit **http://support.thomsonhighered.com/**.

Student Ancillaries

4-CD Set for *Music Listening Today, Third Edition*
0-495-09429-3

This high-quality CD set provides recordings of the 57 additional pieces not included on the CDs automatically packaged with the text.

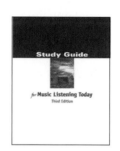

Study Guide for *Music Listening Today, Third Edition*
0-495-09433-1

Coauthored with Dr. Mary Ray Johnson (Santa Fe Community College), this study guide includes reviews of each chapter's main points and terms; part summaries, quizzes, and crossword puzzles; suggestions for writing concert reports; and selected listening scores. Ask your Thomson Schirmer sales representative how to package the Study Guide with this text.

vMentor™

Available with the text at no additional cost, vMentor™ provides students with live, one-on-one, online tutoring help from a subject-area expert. Students may interact with a tutor using two-way audio, an interactive whiteboard for illustrating the problem, and instant messaging. vMentor is accessible free of charge via a link on the Book Companion Website or through ThomsonNOW. Ask your Thomson Schirmer sales representative how to package vMentor with this text.

Music Listening Today, Third Edition, Book Companion Website
http://schirmer.wadsworth.com/hoffer_3e

When you adopt this text, you and your students will have access to a rich array of teaching and learning resources that you won't find anywhere else. This outstanding site features downloadable cross-platform Active Listening Guides that interact with the CD package; chapter-by-chapter online tutorial quizzes, flashcards, and crossword puzzles; a final exam; and more. The Instructor Resources include the Instructor's Manual, Resource Integration Guide, PowerPoint® slides, and chapter outlines.

Multimedia Manager with Instructor's Resources: A Microsoft® Powerpoint® Tool
ISBN: 0-495-09434-X

This Multimedia Manager features the Instructor's Manual, Resource Integration Guide, ExamView® computerized testing, and Microsoft® PowerPoint® slides with lecture outlines and images that can be used as offered or customized by importing personal lecture slides or other material. ExamView allows you to create, deliver, and customize tests and study guides (both print and online) in minutes with its easy-to-use assessment and tutorial system. It offers both a Quick Test Wizard and an Online Test Wizard that guide you step by step through the process of creating tests, while its "what you see is what you get" capability allows you to see the test you are creating on the screen exactly as it will print or display online. You can build tests of up to 250 questions using up to 12 question types. Using ExamView's complete word-processing capabilities, you can enter an unlimited number of new questions or edit existing questions.

Ask your Thomson Schirmer sales representative how to package the Multimedia Manager with this text.

JoinIn™ on TurningPoint®
http://www.joinin.thomsonlearningconnections.com

JoinIn™ on TurningPoint® is the only classroom response software tool that gives you true PowerPoint® integration. With JoinIn on TurningPoint, you are no longer tied to your computer ... you can walk about your classroom as you lecture, showing slides and collecting and displaying responses with ease. There is simply no easier or more effective way to turn your lecture hall into a personal, fully interactive experience for your students. If you can use PowerPoint, you can use JoinIn on TurningPoint!

TextChoice
www.textchoice.com

Let Thomson Schirmer help you create the perfect book for your course through our Custom Solutions program. Here are a couple of simple ways you can customize any of our texts:

- **Rearrange or Delete**. You may want to simply delete chapters you don't use or rearrange chapters to follow your preferred course sequence.
- **Add**. Include your own original material, lecture notes, exercises, or study guides.
- **Combine**. Draw from Thomson's vast content to customize your ideal learning solution.

Ask your Thomson Schirmer sales representative for details or visit us on the web at **www.textchoice.com**

Resource Integration Guide

Chapter 1 — *Music Listening and You*

Class Preparation and Lecture Tools	Testing Tools and Course Management	Study Aids, Tutorials, and Quizzing	Beyond the Book: Research, Writing, Exploration
Instructor's Manual/ Test Bank Includes suggestions for teaching Chapter 1, such as specific teaching activities and test questions	**Instructor's Manual/ Test Bank** Chapter 1 Test questions including multiple-choice and true/false questions.	**Active Listening Guides** Biographical sketches, Listening Quiz, Internet Library, and Glossary for Chapter 1. Active Listening Guide for Main Title from *Star Wars* (John Williams).	**Book Companion Website** Tutorial quiz, flashcards, crossword puzzles for Chapter 1.
Multimedia Manager with Instructor's Resources: A Microsoft® PowerPoint® Tool Chapter 1 Includes ExamView computerized testing, as well as an electronic version of the Instructor's Manual/ Test Bank and PowerPoint Lecture Outlines.	**ThomsonNOW™** An online diagnostic self-study tool, providing Chapter 1 lesson plans customized to students' personal needs, as well as an instructor gradebook.	**CD Set** CD 1.1 Main Title from *Star Wars* (John Williams) **ThomsonNOW™** An online diagnostic self-study tool, providing Chapter 1 lesson plans customized to students' personal needs.	
Book Companion Web Site http://schirmer.wadsworth.com/hoffer_3e Access to the Instructor's Manual and PowerPoints for Chapter 1.		**Study Guide** Review of the main points and key terms of Chapter 1	
JoinIn™ on TurningPoint® PowerPoint® slides are provided that allow you to interact with students by displaying quiz questions, and collecting and displaying responses with ease.		**vMentor™** Live online tutoring for students.	

Music Listening Today

Charles Hoffer

University of Florida

THOMSON

SCHIRMER

Australia • Brazil • Canada • Mexico • Singapore • Spain
United Kingdom • United States

THOMSON

SCHIRMER

Music Listening Today, Third Edition
Charles Hoffer

Publisher: Clark Baxter
Senior Development Editor: Sue Gleason
Editorial Assistant: Emily Perkins
Executive Technology Project Manager: Matt Dorsey
Executive Marketing Manager: Diane Wenckebach
Marketing Assistant: Marla Nasser
Marketing Communications Manager: Patrick Rooney
Project Manager, Editorial Production: Trudy Brown
Creative Director: Rob Hugel
Executive Art Director: Maria Epes
Print Buyer: Judy Inouye

Permissions Editor: Joohee Lee
Production Service: G & S Book Services
Text Designer: Ellen Pettengell
Photo Researcher: Linda Sykes
Copy Editor: Cynthia Lindlof
Autographer: Ernie Mansfield
Cover Designer: Gary Palmatier
Cover Image: R. Ian Lloyd/Masterfile
Compositor: G & S Book Services
Text and Cover Printer: Quebecor World/Dubuque

ExamView® and ExamView Pro® are registered trademarks of FSCreations, Inc. Windows is a registered trademark of the Microsoft Corporation used herein under license. Macintosh and Power Macintosh are registered trademarks of Apple Computer, Inc. Used herein under license.

Library of Congress Control Number: 2005929280

ISBN 0-495-09076-X

Thomson Higher Education
10 Davis Drive
Belmont, CA 94002-3098
USA

For more information about our products, contact us at:
Thomson Learning Academic Resource Center
1-800-423-0563
For permission to use material from this text or product, submit a request online at http://www.thomsonrights.com. Any additional questions about permissions can be submitted by e-mail to thomsonrights@thomson.com.

To Mimi

Brief Contents

Contents

PART III Baroque Music 74

10 • The Baroque Period 76

11 • Oratorio and Cantata 86

12 • Opera in the Baroque 95

13 • Baroque Instrumental Music: Suite and Sonata 102

Preface

A third edition of a book offers an author the chance to keep what seemed effective in the first two editions and to add new works and features to make it even better. The outstanding success of *Music Listening Today* indicates that there is much to retain. But there is always room for improvement.

The third edition

1. *Provides a revised table of contents.* The order of chapters now has a smoother flow of information; in some instances I have combined chapters. Specifically, the Western music chapters now immediately follow the chapters on the elements of music. Separate chapters cover early and medieval music. I have reorganized the Baroque chapters to emphasize the cultural and musical characteristics of the Baroque. An emphasis on grouping topics more logically continues, as Part 4 on Classical music now ends with the piano sonata and "The Symphony and Beethoven." Program and ballet music appear in one chapter, as do neoclassicism, tone rows, and serialism. American music before 1920 has its own chapter, and a section on world music concludes the text.

2. *Presents a solid grounding in Western concert music through a judicious selection of exemplary works.* I have added several new works:

    Rutter: "Open Thou Mine Eyes"
    Perotin: "Alleluia, Diffusa est gratia"
    Corelli: Trio Sonata in F, second and third movements

           Bach: Brandenburg Concerto No. 5, third movement
           Mozart: Piano Sonata No. 11, Rondo alla Turca
           Mendelssohn: Symphony No. 4 ("Italian"), fourth movement
           Clara Schumann: Scherzo
           Crumb: "The moon is dead, dead . . ." from *Night of the Four Moons*
           Hank Williams: "Your Cheatin' Heart"
           Japan: "Hakusen no"

3. *Helps students listen to music more perceptively. Music Listening Today* contains eighty-nine Listening Guides (see left), all keyed to recordings on its six CDs. These guides provide brief descriptive sentences about the music at various points, as well as both cumulative timings and the track-by-track timings that computers and CD players automatically show. Listening Guide headings now provide date of work, as well as reminders about such elements as genre, form, medium, and tempo.

Each work has a downloadable Active Listening Guide that allows students to see a graphic of the music on their computer. The graphic contains an arrow moving in perfect synchronization with the music, as well as pop-up commentary, translations, and music examples. The arrow may be dragged to any point on the line or to one of the colored segments. When students use this program, it is impossible for them to become lost when listening to a work!

This program also includes biographical sketches, a musical glossary, links to related websites, and an interactive "Listening Quiz" for every work on the six CDs. These quizzes will help students gain greater skill in hearing aspects of the music; they are not intended for grading purposes. Students may take the quizzes as often as they wish, for review.

4. *Presents information in a clear, concise, and interesting way.* Several features that allow students to enjoy learning about music and those who make music remain in this edition. The third edition begins in familiar musical territory with music from the *Star Wars* film series. Helpful tips and interesting information also appear in the margins. Enrichment boxes remain, as do the biographical sketches of each composer represented in the Listening Guides and on the CDs. Music terminology is limited to what general students find useful, and key points are highlighted with bullets, numbers, or headings.

New to the third edition are richly illustrated timelines for each style period that place the music within its cultural and historical context. Part 8, on world music, includes a world map that highlights the cultures discussed in that part. New "Features of . . . " charts appear at the conclusion of each style for a review of the key features of the style. Glossary terms now appear in boldface type within the text, for easier recognition.

In short, *Music Listening Today* is user friendly.

5. *Includes representative examples of music from cultures around the world and the United States.* American popular music encompasses two chapters, and another chapter presents stage and film music. Four chapters focus on the music of North and South America. Africa, the Middle East, and Asia.

6. *Provides an interactive study tool to spark student interest and increase understanding of the topics covered in the book.* The new *ThomsonNOW*™ program offers several challenging and interesting features. First, it allows for chapter-by-chapter self-study in which students take a preview quiz to explore their knowledge of the topics presented in the chapter. This quiz is followed by a personalized study plan made up of appropriate flashcards, topic summaries, text pages, and demonstrations—all determined by the student's answers in the preview quiz. A concluding quiz follows, which contains both questions from the preview quiz and general questions about material presented in the chapter.

In addition, *ThomsonNOW* contains a major section presenting interactive experiences with the elements of music, a video of a performance of Britten's *Young Person's Guide to the Orchestra*, several demonstrations of aspects of music that are difficult to describe verbally, interactive explanations relating the information students have acquired to what they hear in musical works, a demonstration of and link to the downloadable Active Listening Guides, and classroom management for instructors.

7. *Contains all these features in a reasonable package.* There is little point in presenting many more works than can be covered in a one-semester course. Therefore, *Music Listening Today* contains only 400 pages, and its information appears in forty-three easily digestible chapters.

ANCILLARY MATERIALS

Music Listening Today suits the needs of traditional classrooms as well as nontraditional online instruction. The basic package consists of the book and two CDs containing a representative sample of its repertoire. Other bundled packages are available including the *Study Guide* and/or four additional CDs.

For Students

CDs KEYED TO DOWNLOADABLE ACTIVE LISTENING GUIDES The two CDs included with the book contain a representative repertoire of works. When combined with the 4-CD collection, every work presented in a Listening Guide in the book is included and is keyed to the downloadable Active Listening Guides described earlier. All the CDs were prepared by Sony BMG Music Entertainment, and the Active Listening Guides are based on the work of Darrell Bailey (Indiana University, School of Informatics, Indianapolis).

THOMSONNOW An online diagnostic self-study tool, providing chapter-by-chapter lesson plans customized to students' personal needs; interactive experiences with the elements of music; a video of a performance of Britten's *Young Person's Guide to the Orchestra*; several demonstrations of aspects of music that are difficult to describe verbally; "Connect the Dots" interactive explanations relating the information students have acquired with what they hear in musical works; a demonstration of and link to the downloadable Active Listening Guides; and classroom management for instructors.

STUDY GUIDE The *Study Guide*, coauthored with Mary Ray Johnson (Santa Fe Community College), includes the following material to help students learn independently:

- Review in outline form of the main points of each chapter
- Reviews of the terms presented in the text, including crossword puzzles
- Sample test questions
- Suggestions for writing concert reports
- A "Listener's Score" of the first movement of Mozart's Symphony No. 40

BOOK COMPANION WEBSITE This outstanding site (at http://schirmer.wadsworth.com/hoffer_3e) features the downloadable program that interacts with the CD package, chapter-by-chapter online tutorial quizzes, a final exam, flashcards, chapter-by-chapter weblinks, flashcards, crossword puzzles, and more. Instructor Resources include the Instructor's Manual, Resource Integration Guide, PowerPoints, and chapter outlines.

vMENTOR Live, one-on-one tutoring for students. When instructors adopt this text packaged with *vMentor*, they give their students access to virtual office hours — one-on-one, online tutoring help from a subject-area expert, at no additional cost. In *vMentor*'s virtual classroom, students interact with the tutor and other students using two-way audio, an interactive whiteboard, and instant messaging. (For proprietary, college, and university adopters only; for additional information please consult your local Thomson Schirmer representative.)

For Instructors

MULTIMEDIA MANAGER WITH INSTRUCTOR'S RESOURCES: A MICROSOFT® POWERPOINT® TOOL Includes the Instructor's Manual, Resource Integration Guide, ExamView® computerized testing, and Microsoft PowerPoint slides with lecture outlines and images that can be used as offered, or customized by importing personal lecture slides or other material. ExamView allows you to create, deliver, and customize tests and study guides (both print and online) in minutes with its easy-to-use assessment and tutorial system. It offers both a Quick Test Wizard and an Online Test Wizard that guide you step by step through the process of creating tests, while its "what you see is what you get" capability allows you to see the test you are creating on the screen exactly as it will print or display online. You can build tests of up to 250 questions using up to twelve question types. Using ExamView's complete word-processing capabilities, you can enter an unlimited number of new questions or edit existing questions.

ACKNOWLEDGMENTS

I wish to thank the following professors for their reviews and suggestions offered for the third edition:

Ann C. Anderson, University of Minnesota, Duluth
Mark Anderson, Foothill College
Charisse Baldoria, Kutztown University of Pennsylvania
Thomas K. Brown, Texas Woman's University
Robert J. Frank, Southern Methodist University
Sara Holtzschue, Kingsborough Community College
Kenneth A. Keeling, Carnegie Mellon University
Luis Sanchez, St. Petersburg College
Anne Thurmond, Tennessee Technological University
Patti Tolbert, Georgia College and State University

Thanks also to the many persons in editorial, production, and marketing who contributed to this third edition: Clark Baxter, Sue Gleason, Julie Yardley, Emily Perkins, Trudy Brown, Matt Dorsey, Diane Wenckebach, Marla Nasser, and Patrick Rooney.

Special thanks are due Gary Palmatier (Ideas to Images) for his excellent cover and to Ellen Pettengell for her beautiful interior design. Many thanks also to Darrell Bailey, who is responsible for the original program for the downloadable Active Listening Guides.

I especially want to thank my wife, Mimi, for her loving patience during the many hours I spent in front of the computer. In addition to coauthoring the *Study Guide*, as an experienced instructor of music appreciation courses she was able to offer many valuable suggestions and was very helpful reading the manuscript and giving encouragement.

Charles Hoffer

PART I

The Nature of Music

1 Music Listening *and* You

Imagine a world without music — no songs to sing, no CDs to listen to, no music to dance to, no sound tracks with music for films, no music at worship services or athletic events. What a depressing thought! The world would certainly be a bleaker and drearier place. No wonder that music has existed in every civilization throughout history and can be found everywhere in the world, even in the remotest places.

Why would the world be a less desirable place? The answer is clear: Music contributes to the quality of life. Music is not the only thing that makes our lives more than physical existence, of course, but it plays a significant role in enriching human expression and feeling.

Do people need music? Not in the sense that they need to eat, sleep, and be healthy. But they do require it in terms of the quality of their lives. Human beings need music, beauty, gentleness, sensitivity to others, and all the civilizing elements that create a meaningful life.

The psychologist Abraham Maslow (1908–1970) identified music as a source of what he termed "peak experiences" in life.

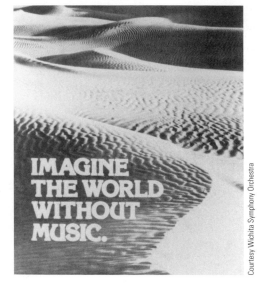

Courtesy Wichita Symphony Orchestra

The hammer and the screwdriver are both useful tools, but they are different from each other. It's like that with types of music.

DIFFERENT TYPES OF MUSIC

Although music can be found throughout the world, it varies tremendously from one culture to another, as you will discover in Part VIII of this book. It differs from place to place, but it also differs greatly in its uses and characteristics within the same culture and society. For this reason, you need to consider also the types and uses of music. Music is used to express feelings while singing or dancing, heighten the drama of a motion picture, provide a "sonic background" while studying, working, or driving a car, and much more. And some of the time, people just listen carefully to music for the intellectual and psychological satisfaction it provides.

Are some uses of music better or more valid than others? Not really. Some music is better for unifying a crowd at a football game, but other music is better for expressing love. Some music is more rewarding to listen to in a contemplative way, and other music is very suitable for dancing. People find or create music that is effective for a particular activity, and what they create differs very much according to its purpose.

"CLASSICAL" MUSIC: MUSIC FOR LISTENING

Crafts such as needlepoint and basket weaving are often referred to as "folk arts."

Music created for the intellectual and psychological satisfaction it provides is referred to as **art music** or **concert music**, or by most people as **"classical" music**. (The term *classical music*, however, actually refers to a particular type of concert music, which is presented in Part IV.) It is usually the kind composed for performance in concert halls and opera houses. It is music with exceptional qualities that people find psychologically rewarding. In fact, the word *art* describes objects that are created with skill and devotion. Often the word **fine** is coupled with **art** to distinguish between objects that can be made by most people and those that demand exceptional skill, effort, and talent.

ORDINARY MUSIC AND EXTRAORDINARY MUSIC

It's true. Concert music is heard far less often and in far fewer places than the various types of popular music we encounter every day. Virtually no performer or composer of concert music makes the millions of dollars that some popular musicians do from the sales of CDs and tickets to performances, and they are given nowhere near the public attention in the media and by the general public. Few people listen to concert music on their radios or CD players, download it, encounter it at parties or other social occasions, or attend concerts at which it is performed. So why is concert music the main (although not the exclusive) fare in music appreciation courses and college music schools? And why is it considered culturally so important?

It comes down to the difference between things that are *ordinary* and things that are *extraordinary*. Most of what we encounter in life is ordinary — the clothes we wear to class, the food we eat, the work we do, the pictures we see in advertisements and magazines, and the music we hear. Usually, we don't give a lot of thought to ordinary things, because they are — ordinary. They are not bad or worthless; they are just easily forgotten or overlooked. If someone asks you what you had for dinner two days ago, you would probably need to think a bit to remember, if indeed you could recall it at all. But suppose you had a dinner at an especially good restaurant and were served something exceptionally delicious, then that experience would be easy to remember. That's why almost all everyday music is "Here today, gone tomorrow," but a lot of concert music is "Here today, here tomorrow."

Fortunately, we don't need to eat extraordinary food at every meal (although that is an attractive thought). Nor do we need to listen only to music of extraordinary quality. But there are times when such experiences are truly enjoyable and psychologically meaningful. It is proper and right that you gain at least a basic level of listening skill and knowledge as part of your college education so that you can understand and value musical works of extraordinary quality. It would be regrettable to acquire a college education and be culturally illiterate about music and the arts.

Because most works of concert music contain more substance in terms of what happens in them, they often require some instruction to be understood and appreciated. They also require a degree of skill in hearing what is happening with the sounds. Both information and listening skill need to be present. The good news is that the efforts at gaining knowledge and listening skill are well worth your time in terms of your enjoyment of music that is more than ordinary.

What did you have for your evening meal two days ago?

Even watching a football or baseball game is dull if you don't understand the game.

"I KNOW WHAT I LIKE"

Everyone likes at least one kind of music. Usually, it is the type of music with which he or she is most familiar — and it is often the only kind the person listens to. The saying *I know what I like* is true. But so is the phrase *I like what I know*. It is not surprising that people feel more comfortable and competent with the music they know. The problem with stopping at this comfort level, however, is that it usually confines them to only a tiny bit of the rich world of music.

Consider this analogy: Suppose you had the chance to advise a person from a foreign country about what to see on a tour of the United States. You might suggest seeing the part of the country where you live, and that would be fine. But is that all a visitor should experience of the United States? What about its other great cities and natural wonders? The analogy with music seems clear. There is a vast and varied world of music out there. Why confine yourself to just one small portion and miss out on other kinds of music that could enrich your life? The more people know about music, especially art music, the more quality they add to their lives.

LEARNING TO LISTEN

You deal with acquiring information in almost every course you take in college. But music is probably the only course that requires listening skill, because hearing what happens to sounds is the very essence of music. For this reason, it is vital to know what to do to improve your ability to perceive musical sounds. The following are suggestions for doing just that.

Realize that hearing and listening are not the same thing. Most people use the word *listen* in a very casual way. When musicians talk about listening, however, they mean an activity requiring concentration. There is a a vitally important fundamental point here: *Listening to music is much more than just hearing its sounds.* Unless you really grasp the basic difference between listening and hearing, chances are you will hear music only superficially and, as a result, will find limited meaning and satisfaction from listening to it. Unless you have a rather strong background in music, listening perceptively is going to require some effort. It doesn't happen automatically.

Adopt the habit of listening for the features of the particular work. Don't just let the sounds wash over you; don't stop with just being aware that some music is playing. Don't day-dream or think about other things or visualize scenes while listening to the music.

Instead, as you listen, decide something about the following:

- The nature of the melodies and themes
- The texture of the music
- The nature of the rhythm and its patterns
- The changes in dynamic levels
- The more important tone qualities
- The forms and other musical practices

At first, this may not be easy to do. But over time you will get better at noticing and describing these aspects of music. Try to determine these six points even if you are not sure your answers are correct. The effort will help you listen better.

Develop different modes of listening. At least three different modes are possible, and each has its place when listening to music. One mode involves listening for the sensu-ous qualities in a musical work, for the physical effect it produces. The chills that run down a listener's spine when an orchestra or choral group reaches a climactic point in a musical work is evidence of music's sensual power.

A second mode of listening centers on the expressive power of music. A musical work may give an impression of sadness, but it does not describe what has caused the feeling. The emotional responses produced by music are general, not specific. The fact that mu-sic does not express definite meanings is one of its virtues. Words are often too conven-tional and inflexible to allow for full expression. Music can be, and often is, a direct route to one's deepest feelings.

A third mode of listening might be called "sheerly musical." It consists of listening for what happens in the music: what notes are being played or sung, at what speed, in what combinations with other notes, on what instrument, with what degree of loudness, and so on. It is also the mode in which you become aware of the skill and imagination that musicians bring to creating interesting combinations of sounds. This mode usually re-quires some education to achieve, something this course, the text and book, and its an-cillaries seek to provide.

The three modes of listening are not mutually exclusive, of course. People switch back and forth among them as they listen. They can feel the rich warmth of a particular chord, then respond to the romantic power of a flowing melody, and also understand that the music uses a certain form.

Develop different expectations about different types of music. Everyday life teaches us not to listen carefully. People learn to ignore the sounds of traffic, clocks ticking, and air con-ditioners turning on and off. People learn to "tune out" music too. They must, because

---

Remind yourself often of this crucial fact as you progress through the course.

Fantasizing may be enjoyable, but it takes your attention away from the music.

All of these musical terms are explained in the following three chapters.

Adopting the habit of listening for specific features applies to all kinds of music from all parts of the world.

Sensuous means "of or appealing to the senses."

Listening perceptively is an active experience. It requires that listeners mentally participate in the process.

music is heard nearly everywhere — in airports, supermarkets, dentists' offices, and cars. Music accompanies almost every activity, from cleaning house to jogging. People would become mentally exhausted if they listened intently to all the music they heard each day.

What's more, most people don't listen carefully to the popular music they hear. Instead, they get most of what it has to offer by "absorbing" it, much as they absorb the impression of the pattern in wallpaper. It is not a question of which kind of music is better! Popular music and concert music simply have different uses, and therefore they have different listening requirements. You should develop a casual style of listening for most of the music you hear in everyday life. You should also learn to listen in a contemplative, thoughtful way to concert music.

And what are those differences?

- Most concert music is not played as loudly as popular music. To a novice listener, concert music must seem pretty pale when heard at its more restrained level of sound.

- Most popular music consists of short pieces that last only a few minutes. The time span of many works of concert music is *much* longer. To someone not used to it, listening to concert music may seem like watching a videotape of a basketball game in slow motion.

- Popular music does not usually contain the development of themes or the other sophisticated musical practices of concert music. Popular music is simpler and doesn't require as much effort to understand.

- With the exception of its use in stage productions, concert music is presented without theatrics, flashing lights, or gyrating performers.

Improve your memory for music. Remembering is absolutely essential for understanding music. At any particular moment, only one millisecond of a piece of music can be heard. What was sounded before that moment exists only in your memory. What will be heard in future moments can only be a guess based on what was heard previously.

It's not like this with what you see. An entire painting or piece of sculpture can be seen in a second or two. If memory were to be made an essential part of looking at a painting, it might be done something like this: An unfamiliar picture is covered except for one thin, vertical opening. You can see the picture only as the opening moves across the painting from one side to the other. Your comprehension of the picture would result from (1) your memory of what you've seen, (2) the portion you could see at the moment, and (3) your guess about what would be revealed by the opening in succeeding moments.

Would this be a difficult way to see a picture? Definitely! But that is the way music is perceived, and that is why memory is so important in listening to music. In the

The careful analysis of an artwork requires more time, of course.

MOST POPULAR MUSIC is heard in situations that focus on activities other than music. The opposite is true for concert music.

Not only is hearing the same work several times a good way to remember it better, it also helps in acquiring positive feelings for the work.

You can't respond to something you don't hear.

foregoing analogy, the more often you see the opening drawn across the picture, the better your recall of the fragments and the more accurate your comprehension of the whole. That is why hearing a musical work several times, especially a complex one, is necessary for understanding it.

Become more sensitive to musical sounds. Each note in a musical work evokes some response *if it is noticed.* A changed rhythm, note in a chord, or the instrument playing a melody affects a listener's response. A sensitivity to what is heard in music is nearly as important as remembering it.

Listening to music with no feeling must be something like watching a soccer game in which the goals have been removed. Likewise, listening to music with no feeling has little point. The psychological involvement is missing, and only a sterile, intellectual experience remains.

How can you become more responsive to musical sounds? It seems simple, but just *trying* to be more sensitive to what you hear is a good first step. Open yourself up to the qualities of music. You can also play a short section of a work, say, five seconds, and then ask yourself, *What kind of response did I have to that portion of the music?*

Use the Listening Guides and downloadable Active Listening Guides to help you gain greater listening skill. The downloadable Active Listening Guides provide you with a visual overview of each work. They provide a graphic representation of the pattern of the work, and an arrow moves in perfect synchronization with the music. Short lines of text and occasional music examples pop up as well. To hear a section again, you can drag the arrow to any point in the music or click on one of the umbrellas. Many other features are contained in the downloadable Active Listening Guides, including a glossary and a connection to selected websites. The Listening Quiz for each work uses a variety of formats to help you practice listening for specific aspects in the music; you may repeat a question or the entire quiz as often as you wish.

The Listening Guides in this book have several features. The elapsed times from the beginning of the work are listed in the left-hand timing column. The timings in the right-hand column are from the preceding track point. These times apply to the recordings on the ancillary CDs for this book. You don't need to follow the time while listening. But because they offer an idea of how much time will pass between features of the work, the timings can be helpful.

The cumulative times in the left-hand column appear on the screen when using the downloadable Active Listening Guides. When the recordings are played on CD players, the times revert to 0:00 with each new track.

A different recording of the same work will not have exactly the same timings but will be approximately the same.

To the right of each track timing is a brief description of a feature of the music. These descriptions may refer to the form of the music, the instruments playing, the quality of the rhythm, or other noticeable elements in the music. The notation for the main themes is sometimes provided as a visual representation of what is heard. It is not expected that you can read music, but the suggestions offered in the enrichment boxes in Chapters 2 and 3 will help you understand notation better.

Listening and Studying

You have a good idea of how to study for most courses: Read a book and take notes in class, and then organize the information in your mind and, if all goes well, remember it. It's somewhat different in a music course because there is an additional element: listening to music.

When beginning to listen to and study an unfamiliar work, you should:

These practice questions could easily be the types of listening questions included on examinations.

1. Listen to it while following the arrow, pop-up text, and music examples, using the downloadable Active Listening Guides on your computer. If you have trouble hearing something described on the monitor, drag the arrow back to that place and listen to that portion again — and again, if necessary. It's also a good idea to go through the Listening Quiz for that work.

2. After you feel comfortable following a work using the computer, listen to it following the Listening Guide in the textbook. When you are able to notice the features as they are being pointed out, then you are ready to move to the next step. If you have trouble

following the music, you should either go back to the computer or try listening again with the Listening Guide.

3. When you are reasonably successful in following the music with the Listening Guide, listen to the work without any visual aids or cues. This is the way one normally listens to music. See if you can hear the aspects of the music that have been presented on the computer and in the Listening Guide.

GETTING STARTED: THE THEME FROM *STAR WARS*

Talking and reading about music are useful up to a point, but then the time comes for listening to examples. The CDs included with this book include the main theme from the *Star Wars* films. Because it is familiar to you, it is a good work with which to begin listening carefully to music.

Although the composer, John Williams, originally created this work to enhance the film, he also succeeded in writing music that people find interesting to listen to apart from the film. In fact, there is much more to this music than can be perceived in just one hearing.

The music is associated with the characters and situations in the *Star Wars* films, so its various sections have different personalities. For example, the music for the beautiful Princess Leia sounds very different from the music for the spaceship.

The main title from *Star Wars* is presented in a simple Listening Guide — simple because it points out only the main sections of the music. Also, it uses as few musical terms as possible because they have not yet been introduced.

No notation is presented in this Listening Guide, however. Notation appears in the Listening Guides from Chapter 2 on.

JOHN WILLIAMS
Main Title from *Star Wars* (1977)
Orchestra

CD 1 Tracks 1–3
5 minutes 47 seconds

0:00	**1**	0:00	Opening fanfare.
		0:08	Main theme played by trumpets and brasses, strings, then entire orchestra.
2:04	**2**	0:00	Battle music begins.
		0:19	Main theme returns in French horns, followed by strings, then entire orchestra.
3:20	**3**	0:00	Princess Leia's theme played by low strings.
		0:48	Main theme returns.
		1:20	Battle music begins in brasses; then music grows slower and softer.
		1:58	Closing section (*coda*) begins in brasses. Music becomes slow and powerful.
		2:33	After drum roll, music concludes decisively.

LISTENING GUIDE

John Williams

© Corbis-Bettmann

BEST-KNOWN WORKS

film scores:

- Star Wars *and its sequels*
- Superman
- Close Encounters of the Third Kind
- Jaws
- The Towering Inferno
- Indiana Jones and the Temple of Doom
- Dracula

John Williams was born in 1932 in New York City, but at the age of sixteen moved with his family to Los Angeles. His father was a musician, so music was a logical career choice for John. He studied at UCLA, intending to become a concert pianist. After three years in the U.S. Air Force, he spent a year at the Juilliard School of Music in New York, still concentrating on piano, and then returned to Los Angeles, where he studied composition with the noted Mario Castelnuovo-Tedesco.

Soon Williams was in demand as a pianist-arranger, starting in television in 1958. He composed music for nearly every kind of TV program, ranging from *Wagon Train* to *Gilligan's Island* to *Mod Squad*. By the 1970s he had become a major composer in American films. His efforts have continued, reaching a total of eighty-one film scores plus twenty-nine television shows and special events such as the Olympic Games.

During his long career Williams has been widely recognized for his composing: five Oscars (forty-one nominations), three Golden Globes (eighteen nominations), seventeen Grammies (forty-seven nominations), and fourteen honorary degrees.

Williams's attention has not been confined to music for television and films, however. From 1980 to 1993, he was conductor of the Boston Pops Orchestra. In addition, he has composed a number of concert works and adapted some of his film music for orchestra.

"CONNECTING THE DOTS"

Being able to listen to a musical work perceptively is essential, but something more is needed: remembering in a general way what you heard and placing it in the right context. It might be thought of as "connecting the dots," because it involves relating what you hear to information about the piece of music. One without the other will limit what you will get out of the course to about half of what's there.

The reasons for learning styles are presented in Chapter 10.

You should also be able to recognize broad, general styles of music according to historical periods, as well as know the types of music. Some of the differences among them can be described verbally, and such descriptions will help you focus attention on what to listen for. But words cannot fully describe a style. You will need to listen carefully to the works presented in the book enough times so that you can recognize a style because it "just sounds like it." A symphony by Mozart simply sounds very different from a symphony by Brahms, even though both are for a symphony orchestra. Knowing if the work is for a solo piano or a jazz band or is from an opera or a chamber music work also helps in perceiving pieces of music.

The ability to remember how music in a particular style and type sounds means that you should try to remember in a general way how each work covered in class and the book sounds. It isn't enough to remember it for a week or two and then forget it once it has been covered on an examination.

ThomsonNOW

ThomsonNOW, for Hoffer's *Music Listening Today,* Third Edition, an online self-study tool, will also give you personalized chapter-by-chapter lesson plans; demonstrations of difficult aspects of music; and "Connecting the Dots" lectures that will help you connect information to listening.

To help you keep the different types and styles of music in mind, downloadable Active Listening Guides also contain a Listening Summary of all the works contained on a particular CD. Clicking on the name of a composer or type of music will play a short segment of a work that you can use for review. In addition, the Study Guide contains a number of practice questions that describe the features of a work and then ask you what type or style of music is being described. By reviewing in these ways, you will be much more able to "connect the dots" between what you hear and what you know.

THE GOALS OF MUSIC APPRECIATION

What are the overall goals of a music appreciation course and this book?

- To increase your ability to listen to music perceptively. Hearing the notes and rhythm and tone colors is what listening to music is all about.
- To acquire basic, useful information about musical styles, forms, terminology, and historical contexts.

The result of achieving these two goals will change your outlook on music, because the more you know and can hear, the greater the chances that your feelings about music will become more positive. It is hoped that with increasing knowledge about music will come an ever-increasing enjoyment that will lead to still greater competence and interest in a continuously growing cycle. Positive attitudes, listening skill, and knowledge can reinforce each another.

CODA

What does music have to do with adding quality to our lives? Perhaps the American patriot and second president of the United States, John Adams, summarized best the value of the arts in a letter he wrote to his wife, Abigail, in 1780 during the hard times of the Revolutionary War:

> I must study politics and war, that my sons may have liberty to study mathematics and philosophy, geography, natural history and naval architecture, navigation, commerce, and agriculture, in order to give their children a right to study painting, poetry, music, architecture, statuary, tapestry, and porcelain.

A **coda** is a closing section of a musical work.

2 Rhythm

The word *rhythm* comes from a Greek word meaning "flow."

Music is a time art. Paintings and pieces of sculpture occupy space, but the "canvas" of music is time. Because all music occupies time, all of it has rhythm, even when it's not a toe-tapping rhythm that makes it easy to mark the time. The term for the orderly flow of music through time is **rhythm.** It is a comprehensive word that includes beat, meter, and tempo.

BEAT: THE MUSIC'S PULSE

Throughout a piece of music, a drum doesn't need to tap the beat, although it often does in dance music and marches.

The **beat** is the regular pulse found in most music. It is what people tap as they listen, and it is most easily heard in marches and dance music when it is marked by the drum sound. Although the beat can be felt most of the time in a musical work, it is not always sounded clearly.

Furthermore, not all music has a beat, although most of the music we hear in the United States today does. It is central to most of the music of the Western world. In fact, our sense of meter depends on the presence of beats.

ThomsonNOW™

See an interactive demo of beat in *ThomsonNOW,* Chapter 2.

Usually, beats are heard and felt in a steady, even succession. If they are erratic, the effect is something like listening to a person who says a few words very rapidly, and then some more words very slowly, and then some words moderately fast, and so on. It is tiring and irritating to listen to someone talk with such changes of speed. The speed with which beats occur in music can change within a piece of music, but usually the changes are gradual and occur by design of the composer and performer.

METER: THE PATTERNS OF BEATS

The human mind has the tendency to seek out patterns in what is heard and seen. It is easier to remember a telephone number such as 555-1212 than 555-2719 because 1212 has a pattern.

When people hear groups of beats, even though the beat may be exactly as strong as one another, their minds tend to group them into twos, threes, or fours; only occasionally are groups larger than four. Instead of beat-beat-beat-beat-beat-beat and so on, the mind tends to perceive **beat**-beat-beat **beat**-beat-beat or **bea**-beat **beat**-beat **beat**-beat. The grouping of the beats (*not* the notes) into patterns is called **meter.**

Whether the meter is perceived in twos or threes depends on the nature of the music.

Meter is very evident in group cheers and rap music. Here is an example of a cheer (the *1* represents the more strongly stressed beat or the **downbeat**):

ThomsonNOW™

Sense the metrical pattern of music in *ThomsonNOW,* Chapter 2.

  1 2 1 2 1 2   1 2

Two bits, **four** bits, **six** bits, a **dol**lar,

  1 2 1 2   1 2   1 2

All for **Den**ver, **stand** up and **holl**er!

Here is an example of meter in a poem, "The Raven," by Edgar Allan Poe:

   ı *U* ı *U* ı *U*   ı *U*

Once upon a **mid**night **drear**y,

   ı *U* ı *U*   ı   *U*   ı *U*

As I **pon**dered **weak** and **wear**y,

The familiar song "Jingle Bells" has an easily felt two-beat meter. The beats are marked with short vertical lines.

Jin - gle bells, jin - gle bells, jin - gle all the way.

Horizontal beams are often used in place of flags when two or more notes occur in the same beat. Beams help the eye group notes when reading music notation.

The Notation of Rhythm

Music existed long before a system for writing it down was devised. In fact, even today most folk music and jazz are rarely written down. In other words, the sounds used in music and the notation of those sounds are two quite different matters. Hearing the rhythm and other elements of music is clearly the more important and valuable of the two. Knowing about the notation of rhythm, however, usually helps in learning and understanding music better.

Although the applications of the system of notating rhythm can be quite complex, the basic system is rather simple: It consists of various combinations of note heads, stems, and flags.

Stem — Flag

Note head

As the combinations progress from an empty oval to a solid head with a stem and flag(s), each note is sounded one-half the length of time that the previous note sounds.

A *whole note* o *usually receives four beats.*
A *half note* ♩ *usually receives two beats.*
A *quarter note* ♩ *usually receives one beat.*
An *eighth note* ♪ *usually receives half a beat.*
A *sixteenth note* ♬ *usually receives a quarter beat.*

And the opposite is also true: As the notes change from solid heads, stems, and flags toward empty ovals, the length of the note played doubles. Therefore, all other things being equal, a passage of music that contains notes with many filled-in heads and flags is going to move quickly.

The notation of silences, called *rests*, uses different symbols:
A *whole rest* ▬ *hangs down from the fourth line of the staff.*
A *half rest* ▬ *is placed on top of the third line of the staff.*
A *quarter rest* ⁊ *has a distinctive shape.*
An *eighth rest* ⁊ *resembles a fancy number 7.*
A *sixteenth rest* ⁊ *looks like an eighth rest but with one more flag.*

As can be seen from looking at the different note lengths, the system for notating rhythm is built on a 2:1 ratio, with note lengths being either one-half or double the length of the other. The 2:1 ratio is even carried over into the use of the dots that are sometimes placed to the right of a note. The dot to the right of a note tells a performer to increase the length of the note by one-half. So a note that is two beats long becomes three beats when a dot is added. Dotted notes are used extensively when the beat is divided into threes instead of twos.

The note with a solid head and a stem ♩ (a quarter note) is most frequently used to represent the beat, although any note can be used for that purpose. For example, the following three lines of notes sound exactly alike when performed, even though they look different from one another. The reason they sound the same is the different numbers at the beginning of each line. This vertical combination is the meter signature or time signature.

The top number of a meter signature usually indicates the number of beats in the measure, and the bottom number usually indicates the type of note that should receive one beat. In the first example above, the eighth note (♪) receives the beat; in the middle example, it is the quarter note (♩); and in the last example, it is the half note (♩). The notation of silences follows the same ratios.

Beats normally follow a metrical pattern. If they don't, the music has not been arranged correctly. For example, the punctuation of the sentence *Every piece of. Music can be enjoyed, for its sounds. And rhythm.* tends to obscure its meaning.

The meter of a piece of music is indicated in notation in two ways. One is by a **meter signature** or **time signature.** Usually, they are placed at the beginning of a work or section. In some contemporary works, however, the meter changes every few measures, so meter signatures are sometimes found within the work.

The other way in which music notation indicates the pattern of beats is by vertical lines that enclose the beats in the pattern. These units of rhythm are called **measures.**

Measures are also called **bars,** possibly because their vertical lines look something like bars on a window.

Music students learn that the first beat of a measure is normally performed more strongly than the other beats in the measure. That is why it is the first beat.

Syncopation

ThomsonNOW™

Learn syncopation firsthand in *ThomsonNOW,* Chapter 2.

Sometimes the emphasis, called **accent,** is deliberately placed off the beat. **Syncopation** happens either by adding the emphasis where it is not expected or by removing the emphasis from where it is expected. Here is an example of syncopation from the song "Dixie."

In the example, the *ie* of *Dixie* and the *ray* of *Hooray* occur halfway through beats instead of on the beat. The syncopation could be removed from the melody and the accent would fall normally, but the song would lose much of its character.

TEMPO: THE SPEED OF BEATS

Tempo means "time" in Italian.

Another important aspect of rhythm is **tempo,** which is the speed of the beats. The tempo of a piece of music can be indicated in two ways. One is by a metronome marking such as ♩ = 84. A metronome is a clocklike device (either windup or electronic) that indicates the beat with audible ticks and/or a flashing light. Metronomes can be set to provide exactly the desired number of beats per minute. With a few exceptions, most tempos in music range between one and three beats per second.

The other way of indicating tempo is through the use of words, which are usually in Italian. These verbal descriptors are general, such as *very fast, moderate,* and *slow.* Because the terms are general, the tempo of a work marked *Allegro* will differ somewhat from one performer or conductor to the next. The words indicating tempo not only provide guidance for performers, they also appear in concert programs and liner notes to identify the large, independent sections, or *movements,* of instrumental works.

ThomsonNOW™

Experiment with different tempos in *ThomsonNOW,* Chapter 2.

The following are the more common terms for tempo.

Largo	Very slow, broad
Adagio	Slow, leisurely
Grave	Very slow, heavy
Andante	"Walking," moderate
Moderato	Moderate

Allegro	Moderately fast, moving briskly
Allegro molto	Much allegro, very brisk
Vivace	Lively
Presto	Very fast
Prestissimo	As fast as possible

Other words are often attached to the indication of tempo. These usually describe the style of the music, not the tempo. Examples of additional words include *con fuoco* (with fire or force), *sostenuto* (sustained), and *con brio* (brusque). Sometimes modifiers such as *meno* (less) and *piu* (more) are added. Two Italian terms affecting tempo that have close parallels in English are *ritardando* (*ritard*, or slow down) and *accelerando* (accelerate, or speed up).

Notes and beats are not the same thing. Although a tempo may be slow, many notes can be played during the beat, giving the impression of much motion. On the other hand, the tempo may be fast but if the duration of the notes is long, the sense of movement is reduced. Of course, all things being equal, more notes are heard when the tempo is fast than when it is slow.

Rhythm in Bizet's *Farandole*

Georges Bizet ("Bee-zay") composed twenty-seven pieces of music to go with the play *L'Arlésienne* (*The Woman of Arles*) by Alphonse Daudet. Later, his friend Ernest Guiraud arranged the music into two suites. *Farandole* is from Suite No. 2.

For the main melody, Bizet chose an old song called "Marche de Turenne" from the Provence region of France. The tune is still sung at Christmastime in English under the title "The March of the Kings."

Bizet's *Farandole* has both a marchlike and a dancelike theme. Notice that the march and the dance have different meters, as you can see from meter signatures of the music

In the world of concert music, it's customary to pronounce names and terms in the language of the particular country. Therefore, the French composer Bizet is pronounced "Bee-zay."

Some marches have been written for processions or coronations, and they are slower. Marches at football games are usually played at a much faster tempo than military marches.

Georges Bizet

Georges Bizet (1838–1875) first learned music from his parents and was admitted to the Paris Conservatory at about the age of ten. By age seventeen he had composed Symphony in C, which was not performed until 1935. He was awarded the Prix de Rome and began composing music mostly for the theater and opera. For a variety of reasons, much of his music was not well received, and he earned his living arranging music and giving piano lessons.

After serving in the national guard in the Franco-Prussian War in 1870, Bizet was commissioned to write incidental music for Daudet's play *L'Arlésienne* (*The Woman of Arles*). The play was not successful, but fortunately Bizet's music survived.

Most of Bizet's fame is the result of his opera *Carmen*. Its plot is built around the gradual decline of Don José, a simple honest soldier, caused by his infatuation

with Carmen, a Spanish gypsy girl who worked in a cigarette factory. The music is filled with one colorful and beautiful work after another. At first it was not well received and was condemned for its "obscene" text. Apparently, the patrons of the Opera Comique, which was something of a family theater, did not enjoy watching Don José's life being ruined by the amoral Carmen.

Today Carmen is perhaps the best-known and best-loved opera in the world.

Bizet had poured enormous effort into *Carmen* and was worn out by months of rehearsal and tension. His sensitive nature was simply unable to tolerate its initial cool reception. He died three months after its premiere.

© Corbis-Bettmann

BEST-KNOWN WORKS

orchestra:
- *Symphony in C*
- *L'Arlésienne, Suites 1 and 2*

opera:
- *Carmen*

A meter signature of ¢ represents "Common Time" or 4/4.

notation in the musical examples. As you listen, try counting the march 1-2-3 1-2-3 instead of 1-2 1-2. You will quickly sense that the music is in two-beat meter, because the three-beat pattern just doesn't seem to fit.

GEORGES BIZET

Farandole from *L'Arlésienne*, Suite No. 2 (1872)

March tempo   4-beat meter   Orchestra

CD 1 Tracks 4–6
3 minutes 7 seconds

0:00 **4** 0:00 Orchestra plays first theme at a march tempo in strong four-beat meter. The first three notes of the theme occur on the beat.

0:33 **5** 0:00 Tempo becomes faster as second theme enters. The first beat of each measure is emphasized. Music grows in intensity.

0:43 Strings play second theme. Tempo remains fast.

0:54 Strings play first theme at a fast tempo.

1:05 Woodwinds play second theme.

1:11 Tempo remains fast, and four-beat meter returns as strings play opening theme.

1:22 Woodwinds take up second theme.

2:18 **6** 0:00 Orchestra combines both first and second themes. Marchlike rhythm of the music continues.

0:50 *Farandole* concludes in a flurry of sound.

POLYRHYTHM

African music has a well-deserved reputation for its exciting rhythms. "Mitamba Yalagala Kumchuzi" is a good example. It comes from the Zaramo tribe of the coastal region near Dar es Salaam in Tanzania in East Africa.

What makes the rhythm of this music exciting is the appearance of several rhythms at the same time, what is referred to as **polyrhythm.** When you hear "Mitamba Yalagala Kumchuzi" for the first time, it may seem like one of the drummers is lost and coming in at the wrong time. Not so. Instead, he is playing a different pattern. As the music progresses, other performers join in with their own particular patterns. Although you might expect rhythmic confusion because of the different patterns occurring at the same time, the effect is exhilarating.

Rhythm is not the only interesting feature of "Mitamba Yalagala Kumchuzi." The recording was made with five goblet drums, four cylindrical drums, and tines rattles. Each

African music is described in Chapter 42.

AFRICAN DRUM ENSEMBLE

AFRICAN MUSIC
"Mitamba Yalagala Kumchuzi"

Polyrhythm   Drums, rattles, vocal

CD 3 Track 1
1 minute 33 seconds

1:33 **1** 0:00 One drummer begins playing two sounds, high and low. Other drummers soon enter. Several different rhythmic patterns are heard at the same time. Rattles enter.

0:44 A singer begins and is answered by other singers. The rhythmic patterns continue in drums and rattles.

1:00 Lead singer exchanges portions of the music with other singers in a call-and-response pattern.

1:33 Although the music continues, often for an hour or more, the recording fades.

LISTENING GUIDE

of the two types of drums has its own distinctive quality of sound, and these different qualities add to the music. The **call-and-response** pattern between the vocal soloist and the group also contributes to the African quality of the music.

CODA

Rhythm is the heartbeat of music. Like the human heartbeat, it is not an intellectual phenomenon. It does not lend itself well to cerebral discussions. Instead, it is learned and understood through listening to and making music.

3 Melody *and* Harmony

It is obvious that most music contains sounds that are higher or lower than others. These differences in high and low sound are the second important element of music.

PITCH: THE HIGH AND LOW OF SOUNDS

In many cultures pitch is described in terms of large/small or masculine/feminine.

ThomsonNOW™
Play different pitches in *ThomsonNOW*, Chapter 3.

As used in music, the word **pitch** refers to the highness or lowness of a sound. It is the result of the number of vibrations made by the sound-making instrument—the human vocal cords, the reed of the clarinet, the string of the violin, and so on. The greater the number of vibrations, the higher is the sound. For example, a sound-producing medium vibrating 440 times per second produces the standard pitch for the note A above middle C. Orchestras tune to this pitch; bands tune to B-flat, which is 456 vibrations per second.

Pitches by themselves are not music. To be useful in music, pitches must meet one of three conditions:

- Be a part of a series of pitches that forms a logical unit of music—melody
- Be a part of two or more logical series of pitches sounded in contrast with each other—counterpoint
- Be a part of several pitches sounded at the same time—harmony

MELODY: PITCHES IN A COHESIVE SERIES

The first of these conditions—a series of pitches that forms a cohesive entity—is referred to as **melody.** The important words here are *cohesive* and *entity.* The pitches must seem to belong together and be a unit—an entity. Not just any sequence of pitches will do.

What causes some melodies to be memorable and emotionally moving and others to seem forgettable and senseless? No one really knows, although from time to time scholars attempt to provide general melodic guidelines. For example, a series made up of the same pitch sounded again and again has little chance of being a melody that anyone will want to sing or listen to; it lacks musical interest and variety. On the other hand, a melody in which the pitches seem to have little relationship to each other won't work either; it lacks a sense of unity. A good melody seems to achieve a balance between unity and variety.

Melodies are what people generally remember in music. The melody is what they whistle, sing, and focus their attention on when listening to music. No doubt you can easily recall the opening melody from *Star Wars.* Some melodies over the centuries have acquired names of their own. In many Protestant churches, the Doxology is sung to a melody named "Old Hundredth." The names of the melodies of hymns are sometimes given in the hymnals just under the title.

Many melodies are known by their words, such as "Take Me Out to the Ball Game" and "Anchors Away!" Some melodies have two or more different sets of words. What we know in the United States as "My country 'tis of thee" ("America") is the national anthem of Great Britain, where its first words are "God save our glorious Queen."

Two other terms are sometimes used as synonyms for *melody.* The word *tune* is a less formal term, the implication being that a tune is less serious and complex than a melody or theme. A **theme** identifies an instrumental melody that plays an important role in a musical work. A theme is of interest both for its musical qualities and for what the composer does with it during the course of the piece. In some cases, quite average themes have become the basis for great musical works. A prime example of this is the famous four-note theme in Beethoven's Symphony No. 5, which is presented in Part IV.

Middle C

The representation of pitch in music notation is partly graphic. The horizontal lines and the spaces between them provide a visual image of the distance from one pitch to another. Both lines and spaces are used to represent pitches.

The five lines and their spaces make up the staff. The higher a note is placed on the staff, the higher it sounds. The clef (French for "key" and meaning the key to the staff) sets the general level of pitch for the five lines. For example, in the treble clef, which is indicated by the symbol 𝄞, the inside curl goes

around the line for G above middle C. In the bass clef indicated by 𝄢, the two dots straddle the line for F below middle C. The relationship between the two clefs can be seen when they are combined, as shown here.

Only the first seven letters of the alphabet are used in music. The notes can be modified by a sharp (♯), raising the pitch one half-step, or a flat (♭), lowering the pitch one half-step. Knowing the names of notes is not essential to appreciating music.

Much as words are read on the page, notes placed one after another in a row are to be performed sequentially. Notes that are aligned vertically on the page are sounded at the same time as a cluster or group, called a *chord*. Chords, too, are read from left to right across the page.

Therefore notation gives you a visual representation of what the music sounds like. It can help you sense and remember what you hear.

Features of Melodies

We can better understand melodies by considering their various dimensions and features.

The topic of how composers work with themes in music is covered in Part IV.

LENGTH Some melodies are short and concise; others stretch out over many measures. The themes in *Star Wars* are clear and to the point, but in contrast, the melody for Joachin Rodrigo's *Concierto de Aranjuez*, discussed in Chapter 4, seems more flowing.

RANGE Some melodies stay within a narrow range of pitches. Others spread out over a wide pitch distance.

STEPS AND LEAPS Some melodies, such as the beginning of "Row, Row, Row Your Boat," move by small steps from one note to the next. Other melodies leap to a note a distance away. As we all know from the occasional strain of singing "The Star-Spangled Banner," it opens with several leaps that carry it over a considerable range:

The word *leap* may seem to be an exaggeration for any note that is not adjacent, but it is the appropriate term.

O ____ say can you see, By___

CONTOUR   Each melody has its own outline, or contour, just as each city has it own sky-line. In fact, melody is often referred to as the "line" or "melodic line." Here is the contour for the first several measures of "The Star-Spangled Banner":

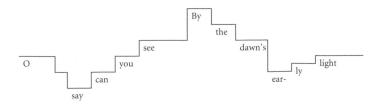

And here is the contour of "America":

We will hear the opposite in decoration in the melody for Rodrigo's *Concierto,* which has many ornamented notes.

DECORATIVE NOTES   In some melodies each note seems solid and unadorned. The Shaker hymn melody is a prime example of a straightforward, undecorated melody. "Simple Gifts" is an American Shaker song from around 1840. Notice that the melody moves in a steplike progression complemented by infrequent leaps.

LISTENING GUIDE

ARRANGED BY AARON COPLAND

"Simple Gifts" (1950)

Strings, piano, vocal

CD 1 Tracks 7–8
1 minute 40 seconds

0.00   **7**   0:00   Short introduction played by strings; then the singer begins:

'Tis the gift to be simple, 'tis the gift to be free,
'Tis the gift to come down where you ought to be.

The melody for the next two lines is very similar to that of the first two:

And when we find ourselves in the place just right,
'Twill be in the valley of love and delight.

0:32   **8**   0:00   Contrasting section begins:

When true simplicity is gained.
To bow and to bend we shan't be ashamed.

0:09   The melody of the second two lines returns, but with new words and a few small changes:

To turn, turn will be our delight,
'Til by turning, turning we come round right.

0:26   Music and words of the opening four lines are repeated exactly.

0:56   Strings play a short concluding section.

1:02   "Simple Gifts" ends with a cadence.

Aaron Copland

Boosey & Hawkes, Inc.: CBS photo

Aaron Copland (1900–1990) was born in Brooklyn, New York, the son of Russian Jewish immigrants. His family had little money, and he took his first music lessons from an older sister. He studied books and scores at the New York Public Library. After graduating from high school, he studied piano and harmony in New York.

In 1921 Copland went to the American School of Music at Fontainebleau in France. The teacher there was a remarkable woman named Nadia Boulanger. (She and her sister, Lili, are discussed in Chapter 31.) He became the first of a long list of young American composers to study with her.

Copland became interested in jazz in the late 1920s, and several of his compositions contain elements of jazz. In the early 1930s, his music tended to be more abstract. He began to be concerned, however, about the gap between the music-loving audiences and contemporary composers. Copland wrote, "It made no sense to ignore them and to continue writing as if they did not exist. I felt that it was worth the effort to see if I couldn't say what I had to say in the simplest possible terms."

———◆———

Copland was an unassuming man who cared much for people.

———◆———

His efforts at greater simplicity were successful, and he was able to retain the interest and respect of trained musicians while at the same time please the general concert-going public. In addition to composing music, he lectured at many universities and wrote several very readable books about music for people who are not musicians.

BEST-KNOWN WORKS

orchestra:
- A Lincoln Portrait
- El salón México

ballet:
- Billy the Kid
- Rodeo
- Appalachian Spring

film scores:
- Of Mice and Men
- The Red Pony
- Our Town

The Shakers were a religious sect that earned their name from the "shaking" they experienced when they felt the spirit of God. They lived a simple, celibate life and developed a number of communities in New England and Kentucky. They are known today for the simple, elegant furniture they designed.

Courtesy of Charles Hoffer

A SHAKER KITCHEN Notice that everything is hung neatly in place from pegs in the upper molding.

What Affects the Impression of a Melody?

Just about everything affects the impression a listener gains of melody.

ACCOMPANYING MUSIC The accompanying music is like a stage setting in that it contributes to the overall effect of a play. Aaron Copland's arrangement of the American

Shaker song "Simple Gifts" demonstrates the skillful creation of accompanying music to enhance the melody. He makes the setting clear and simple, which is in keeping with the simple character of the song and its text.

TONE QUALITIES AND INSTRUMENTS A melody played on a flute gives listeners one impression, whereas the same melody played on a guitar gives another. Some melodies seem more suited for certain instruments than for others; a very decorative melody sounds fine on a violin or flute but would sound cumbersome played by a trombone. Copland used the melody for "Simple Gifts" in his ballet *Appalachian Spring,* which is presented in Part VII. In that music the melody is altered to suit the attributes of the different instruments that play it.

RHYTHM The rhythmic properties of a melody can make a big difference. Imagine singing "Jingle Bells" very slowly. A merry winter song would sound like a funeral dirge. In other cases, average melodies are sometimes successful because of their distinctive rhythmic qualities.

PHRASES You can't exactly see phrases in music as you can in written text, which is punctuated with commas and periods. **Phrases** are there in the logical groupings of notes, which vary in length as much as phrases in language do. For example, in the song "America" the words and notes for "My country 'tis of thee" form a short phrase that is coupled to the next short phrase, "sweet land of liberty," leading to the phrase "of thee I sing" to form a logical musical entity.

STYLE OF PERFORMANCE If you sing a melody such as "America" in short, detached notes instead of in a flowing, singing style, it will seem to be a different song, one you almost certainly will not like as well.

QUALITY OF PERFORMANCE The same piece played by two performers, one who is exceptionally able and another who is mediocre, can leave listeners with very different impressions of the music. Outstanding performers can make what are considered average pieces sound fresh and vital, and less able performers can make exceptional works sound pedestrian.

The word *counterpoint* comes from the time when notes were called "points." The adjectival form of the word is *contrapuntal.*

Canon means "by the rule." When spelled with one *n,* the word has nothing to do with the artillery weapon.

COUNTERPOINT: MELODIES SOUNDED TOGETHER

Melodies can be combined in one of two ways. One is as a *round.* You have known about rounds since you were in elementary school. In a round exactly the same music is sung, but each line starts at a specified time interval. For example, one group of singers sings, "Are you sleeping? Are you sleeping?" and then the second group follows, singing the same melody and words while the first group continues on with "Brother John, Brother John." The process continues with additional groups joining in until the round is sung a given number of times and the last group concludes singing alone.

When one group or instrumental part periodically follows another exactly, it is called **imitation.** When the imitation continues for an entire song or section of music, it is called *strict imitation,* as in a round. The term *round* implies a short song. A **canon** is a somewhat longer and more complex piece than a round in strict imitation.

The second way to combine melodies is to design two different and distinctive lines of music to be performed at the

Round

Counterpoint

same time. The term for this is **counterpoint.** A composer may add a line of counterpoint to an existing melody, or he or she may compose two fresh lines. Usually, the two lines have somewhat different characters; that is part of the reason why counterpoint is interesting to listen to. One line of melody is likely to be more solid and have longer note values than the other.

HARMONY: PITCHES SOUNDED TOGETHER

If melody is the horizontal line in music with its sounds occurring one after another, **harmony** is the vertical line with sounds occurring at the same time. To illustrate this concept, let's return to "The Star-Spangled Banner." Here are the first seven notes in its melody:

F   D   B♭   D   F   B♭   D

Aligned vertically, these same notes form the B-flat major chord, which is the tonic chord in the key of B-flat.

The preceding sentence contains a number of points about harmony that need to be explained.

KEY OR TONAL CENTER Both melodies and harmonies usually have a **tonal center** and are in a **key.** The music tends to move away from and then back to this center. The musical example of "The Star-Spangled Banner" is in B-flat. Like most music we know, our national anthem ends and centers around its tonal center. If "The Star-Spangled Banner" were to end on any note other than B-flat, it would sound incomplete—as if someone had made a mistake.

MODULATION Can the tonal center or key change during a musical work? To use the musical term for changing key, can the music *modulate*? Definitely! Not only *can* it change key, but in works longer than a song, it usually *does*. **Modulations** help make the music sound fresher. If the music goes on too long in the same key, it can become tiring. Most of the music you hear modulates every so often, but usually people aren't aware that the key has changed.

SCALES A **scale** is a series of pitches that goes upward or downward according to a prescribed pattern. Most scales contain seven different pitches, but a five-note scale is often found in Asian music and some folk music. Few melodies contain a complete scale one note after another, but generally scales are the underlying "skeleton" of melodies and harmonies. The scale for "The Star-Spangled Banner" is B-flat C D E-flat F G A B-flat. Although an alteration or two can occur in a song (and there is one in "The Star-Spangled Banner"), most of the notes come from that scale.

CHORDS A **chord** is three or more pitches sounded together. Usually, the notes of chords follow an every-other, checkerboard pattern. For example, the chord for the tonal center in B-flat is B-flat D F, which are the first, third, and fifth notes in that scale. This chord is called the **tonic chord** and is indicated with the Roman numeral I. A chord can be built on each step of a scale, but the I, IV (subdominant), and V (dominant) chords are used more often than the other chords.

Some melodies end on the third or fifth note of the scale, but "The Star-Spangled Banner" is not one of them.

"Joy to the World" is one exception to this statement. Its first eight notes are a descending scale.

The earlier reference to notes forming the tonic chord on B-flat should be clearer now.

ThomsonNOW™
Play different chords in *ThomsonNOW,* Chapter 3.

The note A above middle C vibrates 440 times per second. With each octave higher, the A on the piano vibrates at 880, 1,760, and 3,250. With each descent, the A vibrates at 220, 110, 55, and 27½—the lowest note on the piano.

The limits of human hearing range from about 20 to 20,000 vibrations per second.

ThomsonNOW™

Hear differences between major and minor, consonance and dissonance in *ThomsonNOW*, Chapter 3.

The word *cadence* is also used to describe the pattern played by the drum in a marching band, but this usage is, of course, quite different from the chord patterns discussed here.

ThomsonNOW™

Hear cadences in *ThomsonNOW*, Chapter 3.

Bizet's *Farandole* contains portions in each of these three textures.

ThomsonNOW™

Experience the different textures in *ThomsonNOW*, Chapter 3.

OCTAVES You may have noticed that the B-flat scale mentioned earlier began and ended on B-flat. The second B-flat is an **interval** (the distance between two pitches) of an octave higher than the lower B-flat. An **octave** is eight notes higher or lower than another note with the same name. Each octave has double (if it is higher) or half (if it is lower) the number of vibrations of the other. When sounded, octaves blend very well with one another.

MAJOR/MINOR Two patterns of scales, **major** and **minor,** are traditional in the music of Western civilization. The main difference between the scales is in the third step, which is one half-step lower in the minor scale. The chords based on these scales are also affected by this difference. To listeners, major and minor sound different from one another, but one is by no means better or more pleasing than the other. *Farandole* by Bizet, discussed in the Listening Guide in Chapter 2, has a marchlike theme in minor and a dancelike theme in major. It offers you a chance to listen to their particular qualities.

CONSONANCE/DISSONANCE **Consonance** implies agreement and equilibrium. **Dissonance** implies the opposite—tension and disequilibrium. If you push your hand down on a keyboard, depressing all the keys under your hand, you will get a very dissonant sound. If you press down every other white key, a rather consonant chord will be sounded. There are no clear standards, however, as to what is consonant or dissonant. These two terms are subjective and relative. Therefore, it is more accurate to think in terms of degrees of consonance or dissonance.

HARMONIC PROGRESSIONS AND CADENCES Because music moves through time, so do chords. They have a logic and a sequence, just as notes do in a melody. If you start on C on a keyboard, play the white keys up to B, and then stop without playing the C an octave above where you started, you will be left with an incomplete feeling—somewhat like someone saying to you, "I have a great idea! Why don't we . . . [silence]."

A progression of chords can give listeners the feeling of either conclusion or incompleteness. Certain patterns of two chords have become traditional for "punctuating" music. These patterns are called **cadences.** Usually, they appear at the ends of phrases and they give a sense that the music is going to come to a musical comma or period.

Texture and the Ways Pitches Are Used

In music, the word **texture** refers to the basic approaches in the use of pitches. It does not refer to the smoothness or roughness of a melody. The three terms describing texture are discussed below.

The word for a melody alone, with no other accompanying sounds, is **monophonic.**

The term for a melody with accompaniment is **homophonic.**

Chords

The presence of two or more lines with melodic character creates a **polyphonic** texture.

Homophonic and polyphonic textures are relative, and they are sometimes used at different places in the same work. Often composers include musically interesting patterns in an accompanying part, but these parts lack enough melodic character to be considered another line of music. Occasionally, works that are basically polyphonic include portions containing mostly chords, and vice versa.

Bizet's *Farandole*, explored in the context of rhythm in Chapter 2, also contains many of the musical elements discussed in this chapter: texture, counterpoint, and major and minor scales.

> In the world of concert music, it's customary to pronounce names and terms in the language of the particular country. Therefore, the French composer Bizet is pronounced *"Bee-zay."*

LISTENING GUIDE

GEORGES BIZET
Farandole from *L'Arlésienne*, Suite No. 2 (1872)

March tempo, 4-beat meter   Orchestra

CD 1 Tracks 4–6
3 minutes 7 seconds

0:00 **4** 0:00   Orchestra plays marchlike opening theme (A) in a minor key with simple accompaniment.

         0:16   Strings play A theme in imitation. The texture is polyphonic.

0:33 **5** 0:00   High woodwinds play a faster, lighter theme (B) in a major key with accompaniment. Music slowly grows in intensity.

         0:43   Strings play B theme in major with a homophonic texture.

         0:54   Strings play A theme at a lively tempo. Music returns to minor, and the texture is monophonic.

         1:05   Woodwinds play B theme as texture becomes homophonic.

         1:11   Strings play A theme in minor. The texture is monophonic but changes to homophonic when lower strings add accompaniment.

         1:22   Woodwinds take up B theme in major as texture remains homophonic.

2:18 **6** 0:00   Orchestra plays both A and B themes at a loud dynamic level. The texture is polyphonic, and music remains in a major key.

         0:49   Music concludes with several short chords.

CODA

Melody and harmony give music its shape, its identity. If rhythm is like the heartbeat of music, melody and harmony are the face and body of music. They form what listeners and performers usually notice and remember most about a musical work.

4 Dynamics, Timbre, *and* Organization

Loudness and tone quality have an important impact on how music sounds. Whatever the relative importance of the four basic elements of music (pitch, rhythm, dynamics, and timbre), they amount to little unless they are brought together in an organized way.

DYNAMICS: THE LOUD AND SOFT OF MUSIC

ThomsonNOW

Play with dynamics in *ThomsonNOW*, Chapter 4.

The difference between 100 and 120 decibels may not seem all that much until you consider that the decibel scale is logarithmic; that is, 110 decibels is ten times louder than 100, and 120 decibels is 100 times louder than a subway train.

Every sound has some degree of loudness, or else it could not be heard. The amount of loudness can range from barely audible to earsplitting, although concert music rarely reaches that level of loudness. The term for the levels of loudness in music is **dynamics.** Sometimes the word *volume* is used for dynamics, but technically speaking it is not the correct term.

Loudness can be measured precisely in terms of *decibels*. A food processor reaches a level of 85 decibels, and a New York subway train produces about 100 decibels, which requires shouting over its noise to carry on a conversation. At 120 decibels, rock concerts reach levels louder than those of a jackhammer or a chainsaw.

Dynamic levels in music are indicated only in a general way through the use of terms or symbols representing those terms. The following table lists the commonly used Italian terms and symbols for dynamics.

Term	Symbol	Meaning	Pronunciation
fortissimo	*ff*	very loud	"for-*tis*-si-moh"
forte	*f*	loud	"*for*-tay"
mezzo forte	*mf*	moderately loud	"*met*-zo *for*-tay"
mezzo piano	*mp*	moderately soft	"*met*-zo pee-*ah*-noh"
piano	*p*	soft	"pee-*ah*-noh"
pianissimo	*pp*	very soft	"pee-ah-*nis*-si-moh"

Sfz is an abbreviation for sforzando.

An increase in dynamic level is indicated by the word **crescendo** ("cre-*shen*-doe"), abbreviated **cresc.,** and shown by the sign ◁▭. The opposite of crescendo is **decrescendo** ("*day*-cre-shen-doe"), which is abbreviated **decresc.** and indicated by the sign ▭▷.

Not all changes in dynamics are gradual. Some notes are marked to be accented (>) or suddenly emphasized (*Sfz*). Some changes in dynamic level are to be made suddenly and are indicated by the Italian word *subito*.

Listening to loud music or sounds for several hours causes a temporary partial hearing loss. Doing so often over a period of years can cause a noticeable permanent hearing loss.

Most musical works contain changes in dynamic levels. Such changes are easily heard in virtually every work presented in this book.

TIMBRE: COLOR IN MUSIC

ThomsonNOW

Hear the instruments' different timbres in *ThomsonNOW*, Chapter 4.

The fourth basic element of sound to be presented in this book is its tone quality, its color, which is known as **timbre** ("*tam*-ber"). Timbre in music is as important as color in a picture.

Every musical instrument and every voice have their own particular tone or timbre. If a trombone, clarinet, violin, guitar, flute, and the human voice sound middle C, as all of them can, each will produce it with a different quality. Furthermore, if two or more of them produce the same pitch at the same time, yet another timbre will result.

PAT BENATAR is the national spokesperson for "It's Hip to H.E.A.R." a national initiative whose aim is educating baby boomers about the importance of hearing health. Benatar, shown here wearing ear protectors, says that she knows "firsthand the risks of hearing loss and how it affects your quality of life. Many of my friends have suffered permanent hearing damage, and my husband Neil and I both take proactive steps to protect our hearing health. Unfortunately, many of my peers are in denial."

Why do people and instruments have their own characteristic tone quality? The reason is a bit complicated but worth examining. Almost all musical sounds have pitch (A, D-sharp, G, and so on). But in addition to their fundamental pitch, they also produce small bits and pieces of other pitches, called *partials*, that make up the overtone series for that particular pitch. It's somewhat like getting the accessories (shirt, vest, shoes, cufflinks) that go with a rented tuxedo. The number and the strength of these various partials are what create the timbre of a sound; they make a clarinet sound like a clarinet and a guitar sound like a guitar.

A pitch can be divided in half either by touching the string at half its length or by dividing the air column in half on a wind instrument by opening a key or changing lip tension. Such a division produces a pitch one octave higher than the fundamental. Divide the string or air column into thirds, and a pitch one octave and five notes higher is heard. Divide it into four parts, and a pitch two octaves higher is sounded. The pattern of pitches produced by dividing a string or other sound-producing mechanism into equal parts is called the **overtone series.**

The pattern of the overtone series is exactly the same for every pitch. Here are the first seven overtones for the note C:

> The overtone series is also called the **harmonic series.**

> The importance of the overtone series is described more fully in Chapter 5.

Because the timbre of a sound is determined by the number and strength of the partials, the tone quality of instruments can be reproduced on a tone synthesizer. High-quality synthesizers can come surprisingly close to imitating the authentic timbre of an instrument. They cannot produce foolproof imitations, however, because the sounds they produce are too consistent, too perfect.

The timbre of a pitch played or sung by a human being is not the same from beginning to end. The beginning of a sound may have a distinct hard quality that quickly blends into its basic timbre, which often changes slightly as it is being sustained. In fact, many singers, especially in popular music, make wide changes in timbre as they sing a pitch. These changes usually make the music more interesting and expressive.

Composers and arrangers are very conscious of the different timbres of instruments and voices. They know, for example, that the low notes of the flute are mellow, whereas its high notes are more shrill. They also know that adding French horns to a melody played by cellos will give strength and richness to the sound. The possibilities for combinations of timbres are limitless.

> Because of the subtleties of sound produced by some instruments, technicians make actual recordings (called *samples*) of an instrument's sounds and enter them into a computer for use in electronically produced music.

> Courses in orchestration and arranging are required in university degree programs for composers.

ORGANIZATION: ORGANIZED SOUNDS = MUSIC

Everyone who has taken a psychology course knows this basic principle of Gestalt-cognitive psychology: The whole is greater than the sum of its parts. This principle certainly applies to music. Composers work with a virtually infinite universe of possible combinations of rhythm, pitch, dynamic level, and timbre. But music, which is often defined as *organized sounds occurring in a specified span of time*, is more than just its accumulated total of notes and rhythms and timbres. Something more—and better—is created when they are combined and organized by a skillful composer or improviser. The whole truly becomes greater than the sum of its parts.

Consider again the song "Simple Gifts." It reveals a strong sense of organization. It has a three-part symmetrical pattern, and its phrases have a logical forward motion followed by points of repose. Its chords fit the notes of the melody, and their simple character adds to the thought the song is expressing. The rhythms used in "Simple Gifts" fit the words and are organized into patterns. And, best of all, the musical elements combine into a musically satisfying entity.

The definition of music as organized sound has two implications. One is that any organized group of sounds occurring in a span of time meets the criteria for music. You may or may not enjoy hearing a particular group of sounds, but as long as they are organized, they fulfill the definition of music.

The other implication is that listeners will understand music better if they can consider how sounds are organized. Why? Because the organization of sounds is the very stuff of music. Listening to music carefully and thoughtfully requires listening for what happens in the music, which in turn means listening for how the elements are manipulated by the composer and performer.

Form: Planning in Music

Over the centuries a number of general plans for organizing music have evolved. These general plans are called **forms.**

Forms developed out of the trials and errors of hundreds of composers over hundreds of years. Musicians discovered, for example, that a three-part pattern with the first and third parts almost the same provides a satisfying logic in a musical work. Someone tried it, and other composers and listeners liked it.

Composing a form is not, however, like filling out a job application in which certain specific information must be supplied. They are not molds waiting for composers to fill with notes. Instead, forms in music are usually constructed around one or more of three broad, general considerations: repetition, variation, and contrast.

REPETITION Because music exists in time, the repeating of ideas in music is probably much more important than in the other fine arts. "Simple Gifts," for example, has a three-part form, with the middle part concluding with music similar to the last two lines of the first part. The first melody, the *a* section of the song, begins, "'Tis a gift to be simple . . ."; the contrasting melody, the *b* section, follows, "When, true simplicity is gained . . ."; and the *a* section is repeated by the singer, "'Tis a gift to be simple . . ."

Alphabet letters are used to designate the parts of a work. When the parts are short, the letters are in lowercase. Therefore, the form of "Simple Gifts" is *a b a'*, or what is termed *ternary form*. The prime (') sign is used to indicate that the material is slightly different from its identifying letter. When longer sections of music are repeated, uppercase letters are used.

VARIATION A second broad approach to form is through varying the musical material—to repeat the same basic material but with changes.

CONTRAST A third broad approach is by contrast. In "Simple Gifts" the *b* portion of the song has a different melody and words. The contrasting sections in longer works may have a different melody as well as different tempos, keys, dynamic levels, and instru-

---

Seeing one dot alone has little meaning. But three dots arranged like this

describe a triangle and have more meaning than just three dots.

Ignoring what is taking place in a musical work is a little like watching a football game with no understanding of the action while you sit around waiting for the final score.

Forms were named after they were developed and used often.

ments. Even when a work does not repeat material, it usually contains contrasting sections unless it is quite short.

Because there are many different musical forms, they cannot successfully be discussed in just one chapter. Forms will be presented and discussed at the appropriate places throughout the book.

> Basically, one of three things happens in music: The music you hear can (1) be the same, (2) be somewhat different, or (3) be completely different from what has been sounded.

Genre and Movements

Form in music is largely the result of the pattern in which themes are heard. A **genre** is different. It refers to the type of music—symphony, jazz, chamber music, oratorio, and so on. Think of the word as a synonym for "type of music."

> *Genre* is a French word that is pronounced with a soft *g*.

Many instrumental works are divided into large, independent sections called **movements.** In a sense, they are stand-alone pieces that have been grouped together by the composer to constitute a larger work. Usually, the movements in a multimovement work have a contrasting character in terms of tempo and other musical qualities. Some of the time they are also loosely related by key. These individual movements often follow a particular form.

RODRIGO'S *CONCIERTO DE ARANJUEZ*

An important genre in concert music is the **concerto.** The essential element of a concerto is contrast between a soloist or small group and the remainder of the orchestra. In the case of Rodrigo's *Concierto de Aranjuez,* the solo instrument is a guitar. Many concertos also provide a chance for the soloist to show off his or her technical skill, which Rodrigo's *Concierto* certainly does.

> *Concerto* is pronounced "con-chair-toe."

Only the second of the *Concierto's* three movements is presented here. Usually, second movements are melodious and have a slow tempo, and Rodrigo follows that tradition. Musical works can be examined in terms of how their melodies, rhythms, and timbres are organized. The second movement of *Concierto de Aranjuez* seems especially well suited for such analysis.

> The first and third movements of Rodrigo's *Concierto* have much faster tempos and a more playful quality.

Joaquin Rodrigo

Joaquin Rodrigo (1901–1999) was born in Sagunto, Spain. By the age of three, he was blind. His music studies began at an early age, and they later took him to France, where he studied with the composer Paul Dukas. After his marriage in 1933, Rodrigo returned to Spain, but civil war broke out there in 1936 and lasted three years. During this time he lived in Paris and Germany. He then returned to Spain, and in 1940 his *Concierto de Aranjuez* received a highly successful premiere. He was hailed as Spain's greatest postwar composer. Although he received many honors and continued to compose, none of his works achieved the recognition comparable to that accorded his *Concierto de Aranjuez.*

Events in Rodrigo's personal life are reported to have influenced the second movement. He and his wife, Vickie, lost their first child during childbirth, and it was uncertain whether Vickie would survive. The movement's stormy cadenza is said to express his anger at God, but he finally accepts God's will and is at peace at the end of the movement.

Rodrigo's style did not change over his long life. It is Spanish in character, although he seldom included folk melodies in his music. It also revealed the French influence of his teacher, Paul Dukas. In form, harmony, melody, and rhythms, his music is quite formal and conservative. The dissonances and driving rhythms of other twentieth-century composers seemed not to have affected him. At various times, his music is passionate, colorful, and filled with charm.

Victoria and Joaquin Rodrigo Foundation, Madrid, Spain

BEST-KNOWN WORKS

guitar and orchestra:
- Concierto de Aranjuez
- Fantasia para un gentilhombre

JOAQUIN RODRIGO

Concierto de Aranjuez, Second Movement (1939)

Adagio (slow tempo), 4-beat meter   Guitar, English horn, strings, woodwinds   GENRE: Concerto

CD 1 Tracks 9–12
10 minutes

| 0.00 | **9** | 0:00 | The guitar begins softly strumming four chords. |

0:07   The English horn plays the main theme. It begins with a short, three-note motive followed by a melody with a tender, mournful quality.

0:41   The guitar repeats the theme with decorative notes.

1:14   The English horn plays the theme five notes higher.

1:48   The guitar repeats the theme in a more decorated version.

2:25   The cellos play a contrasting figure, followed by violins and English horn.

2:49   The guitar and woodwinds exchange portions of the theme.

3:56 **10** 0:00   The guitar plays a version of the theme on its low strings. The music grows more stern.

1:02   The oboe plays a fragment of the theme, answered each time by the guitar.

1:37   The flutes and woodwinds play rapidly repeated notes.

5:56 **11** 0:00   The guitar softly begins a cadenza. The theme is embedded in the repeated notes.

0:39   The three-note motive is played four times, each time one octave lower.

1:12   The basic pattern of four notes ascending, then four notes descending, begins. The music slowly becomes more intense and passionate.

1:53   The cadenza climaxes as the orchestra enters with a loud, short chord, followed by the guitar's rapidly repeated chords.

7:57 **12** 0:00   The orchestra plays the main theme passionately, but then ends quietly with the flute, oboe, and guitar.

1:03   The guitar returns, quietly playing a portion of the theme, with two lines that seem to answer each other.

1:44   The movement seems to fade into space as it closes with the guitar and violins playing high, ethereal notes.

MELODY The basic outline of the melody—its "musical skeleton"—consists of a long note, and then the melody moves up two notes before returning to the original long note. Next, the melody ascends for four notes and then works its way down note by note to four notes below where it began. Up to this point, all the melodic movement has been to adjacent notes.

But there is much more than its melodic skeleton. Rodrigo also adds many quick-moving, decorative notes. These notes are especially noticeable when the guitar takes its turn playing the melody. Then three quick, accented notes begin the melody (♪♪♩), something often found in Spanish music. This short melodic figure is heard frequently throughout the music and contributes to the unity of the movement. Such brief figures are called **motives** when they act as a unifying element in a musical work.

The word *motive* has nothing to do with the reasons why the composer wrote the music.

TIMBRE Much of the second movement of the *Concierto* has a tender, melancholy quality, due in large part to the tone qualities of the English horn and the guitar.

HARMONY The quiet, uncomplicated accompaniment adds to the tenderness of the music while allowing the melody to be clearly heard.

RHYTHM The rhythm is slow and steady with four beats to the measure. Because this movement features the melody, its rhythm is not as noticeable as it is in many works, including the other movements of the *Concierto de Aranjuez*.

***Aranjuez* is pronounced "A-*rahn*-hou-ayz." It is the name of the former summer palace of Spanish kings.**

FORM AND ORGANIZATION The movement opens with the melody played by the English horn; then the guitar enters playing a more elaborate version of the melody. The melody returns two more times between contrasting sections and a long cadenza for the guitar. But that's not all. Rodrigo has the music build ever so gradually to a rather lengthy section for the guitar alone. This section also begins quietly but then slowly increases to a truly passionate level of intensity as the orchestra again takes up the theme with its three-note motive. The music just seems to float away as the movement ends.

The section for guitar alone is called the **cadenza.** Cadenzas allow the soloist to play paraphrases of the themes in a free-sounding and often technically stunning style. Cadenzas are almost always featured in one or more movements of solo concertos.

Everything about the second movement of *Concierto de Aranjuez* works. All the elements are organized into a musically satisfying entity. The whole really is greater than the sum of its parts.

CODA

How can you tell if you are really hearing what a musical work has to offer? One way to determine this is by answering these practical questions:

- Does the music seem sensible?
- Does it move along without seeming to be stagnant?
- Do you hear details of form, rhythm, and melody?
- Do you keep your attention on the music most of the time?
- Do you have reactions to the music as you listen to it?
- Are you able to follow the Listening Guide while listening, without getting lost?

If the answer to most of these questions is yes, you are hearing much of what the work has to offer.

5 Orchestral Instruments

Sounds are produced when something causes the molecules in the air to rapidly collide and bounce off one another something like balls on a billiard table. What a musical instrument does is control and shape the vibrations in a particular way. In doing this, instruments provide the element of tone color in music.

Most musical instruments can be examined for their capabilities in doing four things:

1. Producing their characteristic sound
2. Modifying their basic timbre
3. Playing different pitches
4. Starting and stopping their sounds

The instruments used in the symphony orchestra can be grouped into families according to the way they produce sound.

ThomsonNOW™
Learn more about the instruments of the orchestra in *ThomsonNOW*, **Chapter 5.**

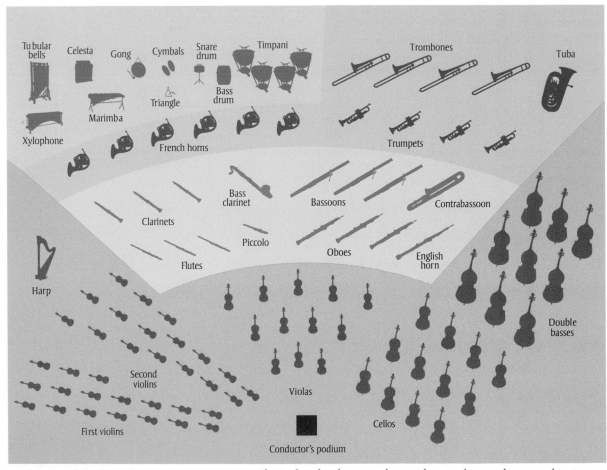

THE INSTRUMENTS OF THE SYMPHONY ORCHESTRA are grouped into four families according to the way they produce sound: strings, woodwinds, brasses, and percussion. This illustration shows a typical seating plan, although exact number and placement of the instruments can vary.

STRING INSTRUMENTS

The difference among the four main string instruments in the orchestra is mostly one of size. The *violin* is the smallest and has the highest pitch. It is held under the chin when played. There is no difference between the instruments used for the first and second violin sections. Only the music written for them differs.

The *viola* ("vee-oh-lah") is somewhat larger than the violin but is still played under the chin. Its general range is five notes lower than that of the violin.

The cello ("*chel*-low," officially known as the *violoncello*) rests on the floor when played and is supported between the player's knees. It is one octave lower than the viola.

The *double bass* has several other names: *bass viol, contrabass,* and *string bass.* Players of the instrument stand or can sit on a high stool when playing. With its sloping shoulders, the shape of its body is slightly different from that of the other string instruments, and its strings are tuned four notes apart.

The *harp* is quite different from the other string instruments. It's a large instrument that sits on the floor with many strings that are strummed or plucked. Its strings are modified to play different pitches through the use of a pedal mechanism.

The strings are the backbone of the symphonic orchestra, with their number equaling that of all the rest of the instruments put together. By far the largest number are violins (about twenty-four to thirty), with at least twelve violas, twelve cellos, and eight basses.

> The guitar is a string instrument, but it is rarely used in symphony orchestras. It is described in the next chapter.

> Sometimes professional string players can be seen tapping the bow against the instrument as a form of applause. Often they are faking it when they do so, because they don't want to hit a $4,000 bow against a $45,000 instrument—a typical price for a fine string instrument.

Sound Production

String instruments produce sounds by vibrating strings. This is done in two ways: by drawing a bow across the string; or by plucking the string with the finger.

The bow was originally slightly arched like the bow used in archery. But over the years, its curve was reduced and then curved slightly inward toward the hair, which allowed for more flexibility in the types of bowing. The hair on a bow is from the tail of a horse. If you look at it through a microscope, you will see hundreds of tiny depressions in it. The uneven surfaces of the hair catch on the string, causing it to vibrate. Usually, players of string instruments apply rosin to the hair to help it catch the string better.

> Pitchers in baseball often apply rosin to their fingers for better control of the ball.

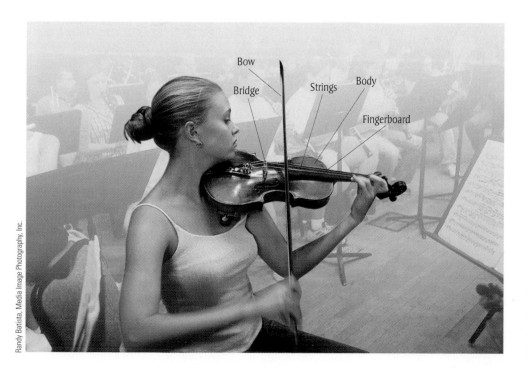

Bow

Bridge   Strings   Body

Fingerboard

Randy Batista, Media Image Photography, Inc.

THE VIOLIN The horsehair bow drawn across the strings sets them vibrating. The vibrations are conducted through the bridge and amplified by the instrument's hollow body. The position of the player's fingers pressing down on the strings on the fingerboard determines the pitches that are played.

A string vibrating by itself doesn't produce much of a sound. The vibrations need to be amplified, which is the purpose of the body of the instrument. The strings are held off the body by a wooden bridge. The vibrations of the strings are conducted through the bridge to the largely hollow body of the instrument.

Modifying Basic Timbre

The timbre of string instruments can be affected in several ways. One is to rock the left hand back and forth in small, rapid motions. This creates a **vibrato** ("vih-*brah*-toe"), which adds warmth to the tone quality by causing small alterations of pitch. All advanced string players use vibrato when playing.

Another way of affecting the timbre of a string instrument is to place a **mute** over the bridge. This small wood or plastic device softens the sound and makes it more mellow.

The timbre of string instruments is also affected by the way the bow is drawn across the string. More pressure on the bow makes the tone more harsh. Several different styles of bowing are used, each of which affects the tone and expressive qualities of the sounds.

Regulating Pitch

Different pitches are achieved on a string instrument (1) by the particular string being played, (2) by the length of string allowed to vibrate, which is regulated by the player, and (3) occasionally by the way the string is fingered. All orchestral string instruments (except the harp) have four strings. The strings each have a different

Some professional-quality double basses have five strings.

THE CELLO Notice the rapid rocking of the left hand to create the small variations in pitch known as *vibrato*.

THE DOUBLE BASS The fingerboard is glued to the neck of the instrument but does not touch the hollow body.

thickness, are made of different materials, and are tuned five notes apart (except for double basses) by tightening or loosening the pegs at the end of the instrument.

As can be seen in the photos, the neck extends from the instrument, and a fingerboard is glued on top of it. The player depresses a string firmly against the fingerboard to shorten the string and thereby makes the pitch higher.

String instruments can also play *harmonics*, which are the notes in the overtone series above the basic pitch. The player can touch the string lightly at various points to create a *natural harmonic* or use a combination of depressed first finger and lightly touching with the little finger to produce an *artificial harmonic*. Both types of harmonics have a high, ethereal sound.

It is possible to sound two or three notes at the same time on string instruments. These combinations of notes are called *double stops* or *triple stops*.

The player's fingers must be placed at exactly the right spot; otherwise, the sounds are out of tune.

Starting and Stopping Sounds

The motion of the bow across the string usually determines how long a sound is produced. String players learn several different styles of bowing. Some styles have abrupt, clear-cut beginnings and endings of the sounds, but others are very smooth with less distinct beginnings and endings. Sounds that are made by plucking with the first finger of the right hand, called **pizzicato,** are short and cannot be sustained. Occasionally, the left hand will pluck an open string in flashy solo works.

WOODWIND INSTRUMENTS

The *flute* used to have a wooden body, but since about 1900 silver–nickel bodies have been universally favored because of their more brilliant sound. The flute generally plays notes higher than those of the reed instruments. It has a smaller cousin, the *piccolo*, which sounds one octave higher.

The *oboe* is made of grenadella wood that has been carefully treated to prevent cracking. The oboe has a distinctive plaintive quality. The English horn is neither English nor a horn. It is basically a large oboe with a bulb-shaped bell. It sounds five notes lower than the oboe.

The *clarinet* has a wide range, but its timbre differs quite a bit from its low notes (very mellow) to its high notes (quite shrill). Clarinets are made from the same wood as oboes. They come in several sizes, including the bass clarinet, which looks like a wooden saxophone.

The *bassoon* has a distinctive appearance, which, with its reddish brown or black finish, looks somewhat like a long bedpost. Like the clarinet, it has a wide range, but it is more than an octave lower in pitch. The *contrabassoon* sounds another octave lower than the bassoon, going almost to the lowest note on the piano.

Saxophones have a metal body and a distinctive **J** shape, except for the soprano saxophone, which has a straight body like that of a clarinet. Saxophones use a single reed clamped on a mouthpiece and come in a variety of sizes.

A symphony orchestra has two flutes and a piccolo, two oboes and an English horn, two clarinets and a bass clarinet, and two bassoons and a contrabassoon. Saxophones are not regular members of the symphony orchestra.

Some special flutes are plated with gold or platinum.

Grenadella is a very heavy wood that comes from the island of Madagascar.

DOUBLE REEDS An oboe reed (top) and a bassoon reed.

Randy Batista, Media Image Photography, Inc.

Sound Production

With the exception of the flute, the woodwinds produce sound through vibrating reeds. The reeds are cut from cane that looks like bamboo. In the case of the clarinet, a single reed is clamped on a mouthpiece. The oboe and bassoon play double reeds, with two reeds being wired together facing each other.

The flute produces sound by the "stopped pipe" principle. It is possible to blow across the top of a bottle or jug and produce a sound. The sound is created by the collision of the air going down into the bottle meeting the air coming back out.

Modifying Basic Timbre

All the woodwinds except the clarinet can be played with a vibrato, especially the flute. Only in jazz is a vibrato used on the clarinet.

Advanced oboists and bassoonists make their own reeds, which is something of an art. The cutting and shaping of the double reed has a noticeable effect on the timbre of the instrument.

No mutes are used on woodwind instruments.

Regulating Pitch

All woodwind instruments regulate pitch by shortening or lengthening the column of air inside the instrument. This is done by *key* mechanisms that open or close holes. Some of the fingerings are quite complicated, however. The closer an open hole is toward the end of the instrument in the player's mouth, the higher the pitch will be—usually.

The qualification is included in the preceding sentence because all the woodwinds can move into a new and higher level of pitch by either overblowing at the octave (as on the flute) or opening a key that causes the instrument to overblow (as on the oboe, clarinet, and bassoon).

Starting and Stopping Sounds

Sounds are usually started when air is allowed to go through the instrument as the player's tongue is pulled off the reed, or away from the upper teeth in the case of the flute. Flute players can also use an action called *double tonguing* to articulate notes very quickly. Flutists can also achieve an effect called *flutter tonguing*.

Randy Batista, Media Image Photography, Inc.

THE FLUTE To generate various pitches, woodwind-instrument players use complex key mechanisms to open and close holes that regulate the length of a column of vibrating air.

Randy Batista, Media Image Photography, Inc.

BASSOONS AND CLARINETS

BRASS INSTRUMENTS

The *trumpet* is the highest-pitched brass instrument. It has three piston valves that change the length of tubing. The *cornet* is similar to a trumpet except that its tubing is more like a cone; the trumpet's tubing is more cylindrical. The configuration of the tubing affects the timbre of the instruments, with the trumpet having a more brilliant quality and the cornet a more mellow timbre.

The *French horn* contains more than sixteen feet of tubing that is coiled so that it can be handled more conveniently. It has three or four rotary valves, which are operated by the player's left hand. Rotary valves turn to open up different lengths of tubing instead of moving up and down as piston valves do. Most of the time, players insert their right hand into the bell of the instrument to modify the timbre.

The most unusual feature of the French horn isn't visible. All the other brass instruments utilize the overtone series starting one octave above the fundamental pitch. The French horn uses the overtone series starting two octaves above the fundamental pitch. This means that the notes with the same fingering are closer together and that much precision is needed to produce the desired pitches. The French horn has a rather wide range, however.

The *trombone* is the only orchestral instrument today that uses a slide to regulate the length of its tubing. It sounds one octave lower than the trumpet. The *bass trombone* is somewhat larger than the more common tenor trombone, and it can play several notes lower.

The *tuba* is the largest and lowest in pitch of the brass instruments. Its role is similar to that of the double bass in the string section in playing the important bass line. The tuba seldom gets to play solos. Like the double bass, however, when played well it has a pleasing quality.

A symphony orchestra usually has three trumpets, four French horns, two trombones and a bass trombone, and one tuba.

FRENCH HORNS Most high-quality French horns are actually double horns, which makes it easier to play the right notes. A valve regulated by the thumb controls which part of the horn is used.

Sound Production

All brass instruments produce sound by the membranes of the player's lips vibrating into a cup-shaped mouthpiece. The buzzing sound is then amplified through a metal tube with a flared bell at the end. For ease of handling, the metal tubing on brass instruments is curled once or twice.

A brass player's lip membranes can vibrate a thousand or more times each second.

BRASS MOUTHPIECES

Trumpet   French horn   Trombone   Tuba

TROMBONES AND TUBA Brass-instrument players can vary pitch by subtle changes in their lips and by mechanical adjustment of the length of the tubing through which vibrating air passes.

It is rather difficult to play the fundamental pitch on a brass instrument, and its quality is not all that satisfying to listen to.

Modifying Sound

All brass instruments occasionally use mutes that are placed in the bell of the instrument to alter the timbres. They come in a variety of shapes and materials, including one resembling a rubber sink plunger and another called a "wah-wah mute." A vibrato can be used when playing brass instruments, especially in solo passages.

Regulating Pitch

The pitches on brass instruments are controlled in two ways. One is by subtle changes in the lips, which produce the different pitches of the overtone series. This phenomenon is best explained by considering the bugle. A bugle has no mechanism for changing pitch. All its different pitches are the result of changes in the tension of the bugler's lips. Only the sounds of the overtone series can be produced, however — the ones heard in bugle calls. All brass instruments can play the "bugle" pitches.

In addition, all brass instruments in an orchestra have either a valve or a slide mechanism that allows the player to change the length of tubing. That means that a new overtone series is made available when the length of the tubing is changed. The various combinations of valves and slide positions therefore make it possible for the player of a brass instrument to sound any pitch within the range of the instrument.

Starting and Stopping Sounds

Brass-instrument players start and stop sounds with their tongue, with the sound beginning as the tongue is pulled back from behind their upper teeth, opening the air stream. They can tongue very rapidly by *double* or *triple tonguing*.

PERCUSSION INSTRUMENTS

XYLOPHONE

The singular of *timpani* is *timpanum*.

The piano is described in Chapter 6.

Percussion instruments can be divided into those that play pitches and those that don't. The *glockenspiel, xylophone, marimba,* and *vibraphone* are all percussion instruments that have metal or wooden bars arranged like the piano keyboard. They are played with sticks. The glockenspiel has metal bars that produce high tinkling sounds. The xylophone has wooden bars and produces dry, brittle sounds. The marimba is like a xylophone except for hollow tubes hanging below each bar that allow the sound to resonate after the bar has been struck. The vibraphone also has tubes, but in addition has an electrically driven device that adds vibrato to the sounds.

Timpani are two or more kettledrums of different sizes tuned to different pitches. Five are used in symphony orchestras today, and three are a minimum for works composed after 1800. The player positions the timpani around him or her in a semicircular arrangement. The sticks used in playing the timpani have round, padded heads. Professional players have several pairs of sticks of differing firmness to fit the needs of the music.

The *celesta* looks like a small piano, but it is more like a glockenspiel that is operated from a keyboard. *Chimes* sound different pitches. The player strikes the top of the metal tube with a wooden hammer.

The *snare drum* is the most prominent percussion instrument that does not sound a definite pitch. It is constructed around two hollow rings that are five or more inches apart. The rings have calfskin or plastic stretched over them. The bottom surface has several strands of wire, called *snares,* that rattle against it. The snares give the drum its characteristic crisp sound. The snare drum is played with a pair of wooden sticks.

The *bass drum* is the largest percussion instrument, sometimes having a diameter of four feet or more. It is placed on its side and hit with a single beater with a round, padded head.

The *cymbals* are large metal disks that are struck against each other with glancing blows. A single cymbal can also be suspended and struck with a stick or a wire brush.

The *triangle* is made of metal and is shaped like a triangle. It is struck with a metal beater while suspended. The *tambourine* has a single calfskin head stretched over a wooden or metal hoop. The rim hoop contains small metal disks that rattle when moved. The player shakes the tambourine or hits it against the heel of the other hand to produce sounds.

Percussion players get to play a number of unusual instruments. For instance, they play something called a *whip,* which is actually two flat pieces of wood that are slapped together. They even get to sound whistles and car horns.

Fortunately for the orchestra's budget, percussionists play more than one instrument, but not at the same time. Orchestras have four regular percussion players and hire extras when needed.

TIMPANI AND BASS DRUM

Sound Production

Percussion instruments make sounds when struck or shaken. None of them can sustain sound, something that all string (except the harp), woodwind, and brass instruments can do. Some percussion instruments are hit together, others are struck with a stick or a beater, and a few are operated from a keyboard.

Modifying Sound

CYMBALS

Sticks and beaters are made from different materials and in different sizes, and each has an effect on the sound produced. Sometimes wire brushes are used, and sometimes beaters with round, padded heads are required. Drumsticks come in a variety of sizes. The manner in which percussion instruments are struck or rattled varies and thus can alter the sound produced.

SNARE DRUM

TRIANGLE

Regulating Pitch

Many percussion instruments do not sound definite pitches. But there are a number of percussion instruments that do. One group has wooden or metal bars arranged in the manner of a piano keyboard. The large kettledrums (timpani) regulate pitch with a foot mechanism or handles at the edge of the drumhead that change the tension in the drumhead.

Starting and Stopping Sounds

Because percussion instruments do not sustain sounds, there is little problem with stopping sounds. An exception involves the ring of cymbals, chimes, and the timpani. Sometimes percussion players must dampen the sound of these instruments immediately after playing them to keep them from ringing too long and intruding on the music that follows.

LISTENING FOR INSTRUMENTS

Being able to identify the timbres of various instruments as you listen helps you understand and enjoy music more. You can learn to do this better by noticing the sounds of instruments as they are pointed out in the Listening Guides, in the CDs and downloadable Active Listening Guides, and in *The Young Person's Guide to the Orchestra* tutorials in ThomsonNOW.

CODA

For nearly two hundred years, the symphony orchestra has been the most important ensemble in instrumental concert music. The particular instruments it comprises therefore have a special place in hearing symphonic music more fully. They provide the palette of musical sounds for composers and listeners alike.

Other Musical Instruments

6

The instruments of the symphony orchestra are often discussed together because they make up a rather standardized musical organization. But these instruments represent only one segment of the instruments used to make music throughout the world. This chapter examines the other important types of instruments.

THE VOICE

It may seem odd to talk about the **voice** as an instrument, although singers often refer to a person's voice as his or her "instrument." But it can be examined using the same categories that were used for orchestral instruments. The reason we don't usually think of the voice as an instrument is that we are born with it. We learn to use it for talking and to some extent for informal singing without any special instruction, something that is usually needed to play most instruments competently.

Sound Production

The voice produces sound through the vibration of the vocal cords in the larynx, or what is commonly called the voice box. Air and enough tension in the cords are required before these cords can produce sound.

> The correct use of breath helps in both speaking and singing, as well as in preserving the voice.

Having enough air for breathing and enough for singing for an audience without the aid of amplification are two quite different matters. Because singing involves sustaining vowel sounds, good singing requires much control over the air. The muscular floor below the lungs, called the diaphragm, must provide a sufficient amount of breath support. The vocal cords must also be tightened; otherwise, no sound can be sustained.

> The lungs are not muscles, hence the importance of the diaphragm.

Modifying Basic Timbre

The timbre of vocal sounds is determined by the shape of the oral and nasal cavities inside the head, as well as the cheeks and tongue formation. Each vowel has its particular formation, which is altered by the placement of the throat and tongue and the shape of the mouth and lips. An infinite number of shadings of timbre are possible.

Regulating Pitch

The pitch of a vocal sound is determined by the amount of tension in the vocal cords in relation to their length and thickness. The shorter the cords and the tighter they are stretched, the higher the pitch.

The difference between men's and women's voices is caused largely by the length of the cords. A man's vocal cords are normally about twice the length of a woman's, and they are also thicker. A larger larynx is required for the male's cords, which explains the more prominent Adam's apple.

Starting and Stopping Sounds

Vocal sounds are controlled by the action of the diaphragm in pushing air through the larynx. Sounds can also be choked off in the throat, but that doesn't sound very attractive, so it is usually avoided in singing.

Types of Voices

Voices in choral singing are traditionally divided into four classifications. The higher, lighter women's voice is called **soprano.** The darker, lower women's voice is called **alto.** In the case of men, the higher voice is called **tenor** and the lower, deeper voice is called **bass** (pronounced "base"). Solo voices are classified using these four basic terms, plus additional modifiers such as *mezzo, dramatic,* and *lyric.* Most of the terms for classifying solo voices are not as well standardized as the four main classifications.

The voice is an instrument in one other way. Training is normally required to achieve the maximum power, beauty, range, and expression. It is, of course, possible to sing simple songs without any formal training. For almost all persons, however, lessons are needed to sing more difficult pieces or to have much power without the aid of a microphone.

It's the same with clothes. College students don't go to class wearing a swimsuit or a tuxedo. Yet both items of apparel are appropriate in other situations.

What people consider singing differs tremendously from popular to concert music and from one part of the world to another. Some singing styles are gentle and smooth, and some are raucous and almost shouted. The style of singing that is typical for one type of music can be very out of place in another style. Because good singing depends very much on the particular type of music, no singing style is inherently superior to another; the styles are just different.

RUTTER'S "OPEN THOU MINE EYES"

Several recordings on the CDs for this book have boys singing the treble parts, including the works by Josquin and Palestrina and Handel's "Hallelujah Chorus."

The choral music tradition in English churches has long been held in high regard among musicians. This tradition is marked by a very polished, refined quality with pitches perfectly in tune. One reason for its beautiful quality is the use of boys with unchanged voices on the soprano and alto parts. When boys are between the ages of about ten to thirteen, their voices have a special brilliance and clarity that disappears once their voices change. The use of boys' voices is developed in England in choir schools in which the students study music extensively as well as their other academic subjects.

John Rutter is one of many excellent composers whose works are largely associated with the English/Anglican choral tradition. Over the years he has written or arranged a number of religious choral works. "Open Thou Mine Eyes" is based on a poem by

John Rutter

Tophan/The Image Works

John Rutter (b. 1945) was born in London and attended the Highgate School. He went on to study music at Clare College, Cambridge University. While there, he published his first compositions and conducted for recordings. Although he has written a wide range of music, he is known mainly for his choral works, including four *Carols for Choir* anthologies with Sir David Willcocks.

From 1975 to 1979 he was director of music at Clare College. He gave up that

position to devote more time to composing and to form the Cambridge Singers, a professional chamber choir that primarily makes recordings. He has conducted or lectured at many universities and concert halls throughout the English-speaking world. He has been honored by Westminster Choir College in the United States and by the Archbishop of Canterbury in England.

BEST-KNOWN WORKS

choral
- Gloria
- Requiem
- Magnificat
- Psalmfest
- Mass for Children

JOHN RUTTER
"Open Thou Mine Eyes" (1980)

GENRE: Church anthem   Unaccompanied voices

CD 1 Tracks 13–14
2 minutes 37 seconds

Form: **a a b a a**

0:00 **13** 0:00   Sopranos sing opening verse.

> *Open thou mine eyes and I shall see;*
> *Incline my heart and I shall desire;*
> *Order my steps and I shall walk*
> *In the way of thy commandments.*

0:29   Altos enter, and sopranos divide into two parts; repeat first verse.

0:58 **14** 0:00   Tenors and basses sing contrasting section.

> *O Lord God, be thou to me a God*
> *And beside thee let there be none else,*
> *No other, nought else with thee.*

0:18   Upper and lower voices combine as a melody returns.

> *Vouchsafe to me to worship thee and serve thee,*
> *According to thy commandments,*
> *In truth of spirit,*
> *In reverence of body,*
> *In blessing of lips,*
> *In private and in public.*

0:57   Opening words and melody sung by sopranos as other voice parts hum accompaniment.

1:40   Music closes quietly with moving notes in alto and tenor parts.

Lancelot Andrewes (1555–1626) and was commissioned by the Texas Choral Directors Association in 1980. It is a beautiful, simple work, one that many choirs are able to sing well and one that listeners can easily enjoy.

WIND BAND INSTRUMENTS

Wind bands vary in size from thirty to more than a hundred players. The wide range in the size of a wind, or *concert*, band indicates that its instrumentation is not as well standardized as that of the symphony orchestra. The larger groups usually produce a more massive sound, and the smaller groups achieve greater clarity. The larger bands also use more players on many of the parts.

As the name indicates, wind bands are composed almost entirely of brasses and woodwinds plus percussion. Some bands include one double bass but no other string instruments.

Wind bands include a number of instruments not usually found in a symphony orchestra. Additional brass instruments include cornets and euphoniums or baritone

The sound of a wind band can be heard on the CD in Sousa's "The Stars and Stripes Forever," which is discussed in Chapter 35.

SCHOOL BANDS are common in the United States, in some provinces of Canada, and more recently, in some schools in Japan and Australia.

horns, which sound one octave lower than a trumpet. Because tubas are difficult to carry while marching, an instrument with the same range and similar timbre was developed in the band of John Philip Sousa. The appropriately named sousaphone is coiled over the player's shoulder and has a large flared bell that faces straight forward.

Wind bands also include saxophones of different sizes: alto, tenor, and baritone. Many times alto and bass clarinets are used in wind bands, and sometimes the low-pitched contrabass clarinet as well.

The wind band is largely an American institution. Bands are seldom found in schools and colleges in the rest of the world. Most bands in other countries are associated with the military. Even in the United States, the most musically recognized professional bands are the armed services bands in Washington, D.C.

TRADITIONAL KEYBOARD INSTRUMENTS

Harpsichord

The *harpsichord* looks something like a grand piano, but it operates quite differently. Often it has two keyboards, called *manuals*, plus knobs that affect the couplings of strings to the keys. Sometimes the pattern of black and white keys is exactly the opposite of what it is on the piano.

The sound of the harpsichord is more delicate and light than that of the piano. Probably for this reason, it fell out of favor with composers after about 1750 because they preferred the more powerful sounds of the piano. It has, however, enjoyed a revival of interest in the twentieth century.

THE HARPSICHORD can be heard on the CD containing Brandenburg Concerto No. 5 by J. S. Bach.

THE PIANO is included on the CD with works by Chopin, Liszt, Rachmaninoff, and Debussy.

Piano

The *piano* is a historically younger instrument than the harpsichord, being first constructed in Italy about 1709. Behind or underneath the strings, depending on the type of piano, is the *soundboard,* which amplifies the vibrations of the strings. Throughout its history, the piano has had a differing number of keys. Today that number is standardized at eighty-eight, although keyboards on most electronic pianos usually have fewer keys.

There are two types of pianos, the upright and the grand. The *grand* piano is long and flat, ranging from five and one-half to nine feet in length. With its longer strings and larger soundboard, the sound of the grand piano is superior to that of the upright piano. Concert music is therefore always performed publicly on a grand piano. The *upright* piano is the type usually seen in homes because of its lower cost and smaller size.

Grand pianos usually have three pedals. One pedal holds the dampers off the strings so that they can ring freely. Another pedal holds the dampers off only certain strings, usually those in the lower half of the keyboard. The third pedal moves the entire mechanism so that the hammers do not strike all the strings for each pitch and thus creates a softer sound. On an upright piano, this pedal moves the hammers closer to the strings, which makes it easier to play the sounds more softly.

Pipe Organ

Although it has a keyboard—usually two or more—the *pipe organ* is a quite different instrument from the harpsichord and piano. Instead of strings, the pipe organ has pipes—hundreds and hundreds of them—into which air is pumped. A piano has a set of strings that produces a uniform timbre. The pipe organ has many sets, or *ranks,* of pipes, each with a large complement of pitches and each with a different timbre. In fact, a large pipe organ can have as many as seventy ranks of pipes; medium-sized organs have forty or so. A rank of pipes is activated when a knob is pulled, and combinations of knobs can be set up in advance to be activated with the hand or foot. The number of combinations of timbres in a high-quality organ is enormous.

A pipe organ has several keyboards or manuals; generally, these keyboards have sixty-one keys. The different manuals make it easier for the organist to change back and forth between ranks of pipes.

A special feature of a pipe organ is the *pedalboard,* which is played with the feet. The pedalboard looks like a series of blond and black wooden slats that have been arranged in the pattern of the keyboard. It sounds many of the low pitches on the organ. Good organists can execute remarkably difficult passages with their feet on the pedalboard. The feet also control pedals for changing dynamic level that look like accelerators on an automobile.

The high cost of professional-quality grand pianos and pipe organs has encouraged the adoption of electronic versions of both instruments. Although electronic organs can sound

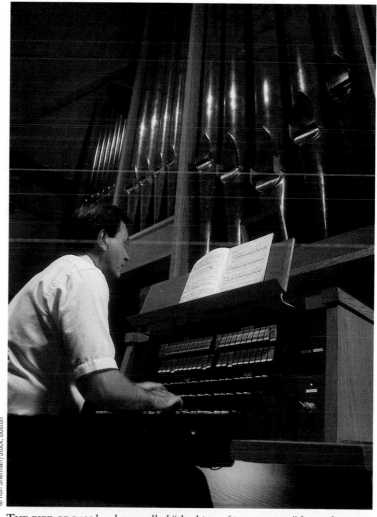

© Ron Sherman/Stock, Boston

THE PIPE ORGAN has been called "the king of instruments." It can be heard on CD 1 in J. S. Bach's *Toccata and Fugue in D Minor.*

quite good, they are also expensive, so cheaper, and therefore less authentic, instruments are often heard.

Sound Production

Keyboard instruments produce sounds in one of three ways: (1) In the case of the piano, a hammer of firmly packed felt strikes a string. (2) In the case of the harpsichord, a plectrum or quill plucks a string. (3) In the case of a pipe organ, air is released into a pipe.

Today, air is pushed through the organ by an electric blower. Until the nineteenth century or so, the air had to be pumped through by an assistant.

Modifying Basic Timbre

It is not possible to make obvious changes in the timbre of the piano or harpsichord. Subtle differences are possible, especially on the piano, by the use of the pedals and the manner in which the keys are depressed. The pipe organ contains many timbres, which are activated by pulling various knobs.

Regulating Pitch

The particular pitches sounded on a piano or harpsichord depend on the keys that are depressed. Unless coupled by some mechanical means, which is possible on larger harpsichords, only the pitch of the depressed key is sounded. The pitch of the strings on the harpsichord and piano depends on how tightly they are stretched. The tension, and therefore the pitch, of a string is regulated by the person tuning the instrument. The tuner twists the tuning pins with a wrench until the correct pitch is achieved.

Many piano duets have been composed, but most of them are for amateurs.

Keyboard instruments also differ from those found in bands and orchestras in that they can easily sound more than one pitch at a time. Therefore, a keyboard instrument can play both a melody and its accompanying part simultaneously. For this reason, keyboard instruments are basically solo instruments; only occasionally are they played in ensembles consisting of only keyboard instruments.

Starting and Stopping Sounds

Sounds on keyboard instruments start when a key is depressed. On the piano and harpsichord, the sounds soon fade or decay; they cannot be sustained, as they can on a pipe organ. Normally, they end as soon as the damper returns to the string. This action can be delayed by holding down the key, or, more commonly, holding down a pedal that keeps all the dampers from returning to the strings. Through the skillful use of the pedal, pianists can affect the impression of the music.

Changing Dynamic Level

The piano's name comes from its capability for making dynamic changes. It was originally called *pianoforte*.

The harpsichord does not allow the player to alter the dynamic level by the amount of finger pressure; in other words, hitting a key harder does not make it sound louder. The only way to change the dynamic level on a harpsichord is to couple the two keyboards so that the sound is doubled an octave higher on the second keyboard. It's different for the pianist. The piano can be played very softly or very loudly, depending on how forcefully the keys are pressed. A person playing the pipe organ can increase or decrease the number of pipes sounding and can also raise or lower a foot pedal to change dynamic level.

FOLK INSTRUMENTS

A vast number of musical instruments have been created around the world. Although each has unique characteristics, folk instruments have been classified into four broad groups according to the way they produce sounds.

Aerophones

This category comprises instruments that are played by blowing. The most common of these are flutes. Some are played sideways, as we are accustomed to seeing today, but many are played straight in front of the player's mouth.

Some reed **aerophones** are also found. Some of these use a double reed like that of an oboe; others have a single reed and mouthpiece like that of a clarinet. The *pungi* played by snake charmers in India is an example of a reed instrument.

Animal horns are simple instruments that approach the buzzing of the lip membranes on brass instruments. They are hollowed out and blown from the small end. The Jewish *shofar* is one such instrument.

One type of flute found among the natives of Oceania and Hawaii is blown through the nose.

Actually, the music is wasted on the snakes, which have no hearing. The snakes respond to the swaying body of the charmer.

Ideophones

These are the percussion instruments other than drums. Bells, chimes, xylophones, and rattles are all examples of **ideophones.**

Membranophones

Membranophones are all the types of drums encountered throughout the world. Drums are constructed from wood, metal, coconut shells, and clay. Some are struck with sticks, others are hit with the hand or fingers, and friction drums are rubbed with a piece of animal hide. Some have straight sides, others taper in, and a few have the shape of an hourglass.

The term *membranophones* is easy to remember because it contains the word *membrane*.

Chordophones

This fourth group includes all string instruments. Most of these are plucked—harps, lyres, and zithers. The strings on some **chordophones** are struck with mallets, and a few are bowed as the violin's.

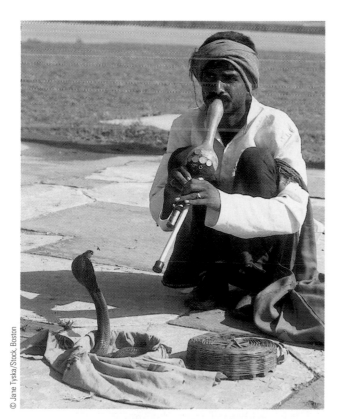

AEROPHONE A snake charmer plays for a cobra.

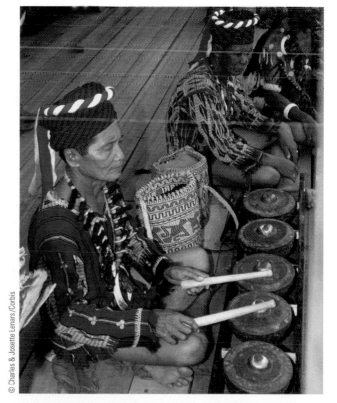

IDEOPHONES Bunaq tribesmen of Borneo play gongs.

A CHORDOPHONE played by a Jordanian bedouin.

It is easy to strum a few chords in G major on the guitar. It is not at all easy to play complicated music on it, however. Rodrigo's *Concierto de Aranjuez*, for example, is a very difficult piece to play correctly.

Unlike orchestral instruments, which are quite standardized, folk instruments lack uniformity. They may be similar to one another, but no two are alike. And they are traditionally taught individually, usually by rote. Because there are few instruction books for learning to play them, the way they are played varies widely.

POPULAR INSTRUMENTS

Guitar

Versions of the *guitar* have existed for hundreds of years in different parts of the world, but it probably originated in the Near East. Actually, the acoustic (nonelectric) guitar of today is not all that different from its ancestors. Some of the older versions had four strings instead of the six used today, and guitars have been constructed in many different sizes.

All guitars produce sounds from the strumming or plucking of the strings by the player. The vibrations of the strings are then resonated by the hollow body of the instrument. The neck of the instrument, where the players place their fingers, has metal strips running across it. These strips, called *frets*, help players find the right place on the fingerboard.

The guitar has two relatives. One is the *banjo*, which has a plastic or parchment head stretched over a hoop and no back. The head gives the banjo a brilliant sound. The other is the *ukulele*, a small four-string guitar.

Accordion

The *accordion* is basically a small organ that the player holds between his or her arms. Air is pushed through the instrument by the in-and-out motion of the player pumping air through the bellows. The sounds are produced by small metal reeds, one for each pitch. The short keyboard is used for playing the notes of the melody, and the chords are sounded by pushing the buttons. One button sounds an entire chord. Expensive accordions can produce several somewhat different timbres.

ELECTRONIC INSTRUMENTS

Electronic instruments are divided into two groups. One group consists of instruments that electronically alter and amplify the sounds of the player. The *electric guitar* is the most prominent of this type of electronic instrument. Unlike the traditional acoustic guitar, the body of the electric guitar is not hollow, even though it is shaped somewhat like a guitar. Instead, it holds the strings and various control knobs, as well as a lever for adding vibrato to the tones. Players still place their fingers on the fingerboard as with the conventional guitar, but there the similarity ends.

The sounds of drums are often altered in popular music by electronic means. As with the electric guitar, electronic drums can produce wider differences in dynamic levels and alter the timbre to some degree.

The other group of electronic equipment is used in creating music. This group includes synthesizers, computers, and tape and disc players. The sky's the limit with such equipment today. Any type of sound and rhythm can be produced. And performances of the music are always flawless! There are no performers in the traditional sense who can affect the musical results—a fact that has both good and bad points.

In the 1950s electronic music was largely confined to the manipulation of magnetic tape. Composers could alter the speed of the tape, splice in other sounds, record different music on two tracks for performance together, and so on.

A generation later technology had moved from analog to digital processing and production. In *analog* music, sounds are recorded in a continuous, uninterrupted form. Dynamic levels, for example, are changed by increasing or decreasing the power.

In *digital* recording, discrete, noncontinuous bits of information, usually in the form of numbers, are produced, sorted, or analyzed. How is this possible? Computers can process these bits of data at an incredible rate of speed. It is the same principle used in motion picture film. The reel of film contains thousands of individual pictures. When they are projected at the rate of twenty-four per second (*much* slower than a computer!), the eye perceives the individual pictures to be a continuous flow.

The complaint about electronically produced music is that it has a certain manufactured quality about it. To overcome this problem, synthesizers can now store recorded samples of the actual complex sounds of instruments and then have them available anytime the composer wants them. The use of recorded samples is, appropriately, called *sampling*. For example, the sound of a snare drum is complex, with its abrupt beginning and ring in the drum after a tap. Technology can come close to imitating it but does not really capture all the nuances of the tap on a drum or the sounds of other instruments. The inclusion of traditional instrumental sounds on the hard drive helps make the electronic music sound more musical.

BLUES ARTIST B. B. KING plays an electric guitar he calls Lucille.

TODAY'S DIGITAL SYNTHESIZERS are compact, sophisticated systems that can produce realistic sounds.

CODA

The past twenty-five years have seen an explosion of interest in the use of images with music through CD-ROM. Multimedia programs can control both sounds and pictures. They offer a real opportunity in the near future for both listeners and composers.

ThomsonNOW
Review Part I in *ThomsonNOW's*
Points to Remember.

PART II

Early, Medieval, *and* Renaissance Music

	1000 BC	1 AD	500
Historical Events	● Early Hellenic civilization ● Greek city-states Golden Age of Athens	Roman Empire ● Birth of Jesus Separation of Eastern and Western Empires ●	Charlemagne Feudalism ● Rome falls
Visual Arts	▲ Parthenon built in Athens (top right) Myron, *Discus Thrower* Colosseum built in Rome		
Literature and Theater	● Homer, *Iliad and Odyssey* Dionysian festivals Sophocles, *Oedipus Rex* Cicero, Virgil, Plutarch		
Philosophy and Science	Socrates, Plato Aristotle		Boethius
Music	Pythagoras discovers acoustical ratios Plato advocates music for all citizens	Pope Gregory codifies liturgy and chant ●	

1100	1450	1500	1550	1600

Papal schism

Copernicus

Council of Trent

Crusades

Universities founded   "Black Death" ●   Exploration of New World   ● Spanish Armada defeated

● Magna Carta signed   Gutenberg invents movable type   ● Luther initiates Reformation

Great cathedrals constructed   Ghiberti   Dürer etchings   ● Leonardo, *Mona Lisa*   St. Peter's built in Rome

● Giotto, *Madonna . . .*   ● Van Eyck, *Arnolfini Marriage*   Michelangelo, *David* (near right) ▶

Donatello   ● Botticelli, *Adoration of the Magi*   Brueghel, *Landscape with Fall of Icarus* ●

Titian, *St. John, the Baptist* ●

Dante, *The Divine Comedy*   Rabelais   ● Ariosto, *Orlando Furioso*

Marlowe, *Essays*

● Boccaccio, *Decameron*

Spenser

● Chaucer, *The Canterbury Tales*   Shakespeare, *Romeo and Juliet* ●

Abelard

Erasmus, *In Praise of Folly* ●

Thomas Aquinas, *Summa Theologica*   Machiavelli, *The Prince* ●

More, *Utopia*) ●   ● Luther, *Ninety-five Theses*

◀ Hildegard, *Ordo virtutum* (left)   Bass voice part introduced
Josquin, *Pange lingua Mass*

Organum develops   ● First music book published

Motets begin at Notre Dame

Palestrina, "Sicut cervus" ●

Weelkes, "As Vesta . . ." ●

7

Early Western Music

There has always been music. Every civilization throughout recorded history and every tribe, even in the remotest parts of the world, had and still have some form of music. We know this because pictures from the various times and places show people singing or playing instruments, and writers have described music and music making. Often, musical traditions have been passed from one generation to another for as long as anyone can determine.

But there is a problem: No one really knows what this music sounded like until the advent of the phonograph and sound recording, which wasn't available until about a hundred years ago. Music notation didn't develop to anywhere near its present state until the fifteenth century, and it has been used mostly for concert and church music, which is part of the reason it receives the greater share of attention in music courses. It's difficult to devote much attention to music that no one is sure how it sounds.

ANCIENT GREEK AND ROMAN TIMES

"Western civilization" is a broad concept consisting of the culture that developed in ancient Greece and then spread throughout Europe and eventually to North and South America. It includes political and religious beliefs, laws, customs, and arts. Traditionally, the contrasts with the Eastern civilizations of the Middle East and Asia were considerable, although they are rapidly being diminished today.

From about 800 BC to the fall of the Roman Empire in AD 476, Western civilization was dominated by various city-states around the Mediterranean Sea. The first were the cities of Greece, especially Athens. Then came the Roman Empire, which dominated most of the known world from the Middle East to England. Although both Greece and Rome were replaced, they left their imprint in architecture, literature, and ways of thinking. In fact, about fifteen hundred years in the future these civilizations would be considered by educated persons as a high point to be greatly admired and copied.

Greek civilization reached its acme in Athens in the fifth century BC. It produced astounding accomplishments for its time. Its architecture can be seen in countless buildings even today. Great works of sculpture were created. Philosophy flourished with Socrates, Plato, and Aristotle, who also is often credited with starting scientific thinking. Great poets such as Homer and dramatists such as Sophocles were active. The ancient Athenians were far ahead of their contemporaries in their type of government, which had the citizens meet and vote in civic matters. Greek religious beliefs revolved around a pantheon of gods and goddesses.

The Greeks, especially those living in Athens during the Golden Age of Pericles, valued music very much. The philosopher Plato (c. 427–347 BC) considered music an essential part of the education of all citizens. One reason for his advocacy of music was his belief that music influenced moral character. The idea that music could influence human behavior largely disappeared with ancient Greek civilization, but remnants of it in various guises are still with us today.

About 555 BC Pythagoras found that the vibrations of certain intervals—the distances from one pitch to another—can be represented in mathematical ratios. As was characteristic of the Greeks at the time, he ascribed philosophical qualities to the ratios, calling those with simple ratios such as 2:1 and 3:2 "perfect." The ancient Greeks also developed several musical instruments. One of these was the harplike lyre, which is often seen as a musical emblem today.

The term *Western music* does not refer to music in the western part of the United States!

The word *democracy* comes from the Greek word *demos*, meaning "people."

Unfortunately, the development of good character cannot be achieved that easily!

Pythagoras is well known for his contributions to geometry and the theorem named for him.

50

THE PARTHENON The Greeks
built this celebrated temple for
the goddess Athena in the fifth
century BC. It defines the classical style still seen in architecture
today.

Music was found in many Greek dramas, too. The chorus did not sing, however; instead, it chanted in a singsong style. Poets such as Homer sang their epic tales in singsong fashion, perhaps accompanied by a simple harplike instrument.

The Roman Republic followed, and the Romans simply took over much of what the earlier Greeks had done. They even adopted and expanded on their religious beliefs, but renamed the gods. Unlike the Athenians, the Romans were militarily strong. They managed an empire that stretched for a thousand or more miles around the Mediterranean Sea. Holding such a huge empire together was quite an accomplishment when there was no communication faster than a man on a horse. But the character and quality of the Roman Empire deteriorated over the centuries, and it collapsed more than it fell to the invading Vandals and Visigoths from the north.

The Romans had music, too. Probably most of it was taken over from the Greeks. The Romans emphasized military music more than the Greeks did.

Zeus, king of the gods, became
Jupiter; and Athena, goddess of
the arts, became Minerva.

THE MIDDLE AGES

With the fall of the Roman Empire in AD 476, Western civilization slipped into what some historians call the "Dark Ages." For more than five hundred years following the fall of Rome, life in the Middle Ages centered around the manor and the monasteries. A system of feudalism bound peasants to the land and to the lord of the manor. People did not place a great emphasis on life, because they thought that either Jesus would come again and bring a new era or they would soon have a better life after they died. It is hard for us living in America today to understand the hold that otherworldly concerns had on many people during that time, but the impact of this attitude was profound. It is difficult for us to imagine how different and arduous life was for people in the Middle Ages. In short, for most people it was grim.

Monasteries dotted the countryside throughout Europe and England. These monasteries preserved the writings and culture of the ancient world. But there was little interest in the civilizations of the Greeks and Romans, which were considered pagan and to be avoided.

MUSIC AND THE ARTS during the Middle
Ages were devoted to the worship of God.
Books were handlettered and decorated by
monks, as shown in this capital C for *Cantate
Domino* ("Sing to the Lord").

MUSIC IN THE MIDDLE AGES

Christianity had no standard musical practices for its first three centuries. It adopted some aspects of Judaism, including daily prayer hours and the reciting of psalms between the leader and congregation. As the Church expanded throughout Asia Minor into Europe, it adopted other musical practices.

Slowly, the Church at Rome became predominant, and the bishop of Rome became the pope. In an effort to bring order to worship practices, about the sixth century Pope Gregory I directed that the Church's worship and music be codified. Although Gregory I was not a musician himself, the music that resulted is known as Gregorian chant. The Church now had a **liturgy**—a body of rites prescribed for worship. The most important and frequent service is the **Mass,** which is described in the enrichment box, "The Mass and Its Music."

The Mass and Its Music

The Mass is central in the Roman Catholic Church. It is a ceremony that reaffirms in a symbolic way the connection between the believers and Jesus Christ through the reenactment of the Last Supper (Eucharist, or Holy Communion) with the sharing of bread and wine and the miracle of that event.

Corbis

The term *Mass* comes from the Latin phrase that ends the service: "Ite missa est." The Mass may be spoken or sung, but in the United States today it is largely spoken.

The Mass contains several parts. Some portions vary according to the particular day in the Church year. These parts are called the **Proper,** because they are proper for a certain day in the Church calendar. Some parts are repeated in each Mass; these are called the **Ordinary,** because they are ordinarily included. The sections of the Ordinary are as follows.

Kyrie This is a short prayer using Greek words instead of the usual Latin. The text means, "Lord, have mercy on us; Christ, have mercy on us."

Gloria This section offers praise to God in Latin with the words, "Glory to God on high."

Credo This rather long statement of belief in Latin ("We believe in one God, . . .") is recited or sung in a reciting style.

Sanctus This follows the consecration of the elements when the priest raises the bread and wine for everyone to see. The Sanctus begins with the words, "Holy, holy, holy."

Agnus Dei This section is based on the Latin words that mean "Lamb of God, who takes away the sins of the world, have mercy on us and grant us peace."

Because the Ordinary appears in all Masses, it has been selected by many composers over the centuries as the text for musical works. Ludwig van Beethoven, Wolfgang Amadeus Mozart, and Franz Joseph Haydn—and Igor Stravinsky in the twentieth century—have composed "concert" Masses not intended for use in worship services. Giovanni Pierluigi da Palestrina and other composers of the sixteenth century composed shorter Masses for worship purposes.

A **Requiem** is a Mass for the dead. It omits the Gloria and Credo but adds a section called **Dies irae** ("Day of wrath"), referring to the day of final judgment.

Until Vatican Council II (1964–1967), the Roman Catholic Church specified the content and words for every service, which are in Latin. Since then, more freedom has been permitted, however, and vernacular (non-Latin) languages are now used. Unfortunately, most chants and music for Masses lose their impact when translated, so much of the inspiring traditional music is no longer heard today.

Gregorian Chant

Gregorian chant is very different from the music you usually hear today. Its features include:

- Nonmetrical rhythm: Although there are groups of notes, you will have no inclination to tap your foot as you hear it.

- Monophonic texture: There is no harmony.

- Smooth contour: Its notes generally move by step to the next note.

- *Modal* scales: The melodies generally do not follow the familiar major or minor scale patterns.

- A reverent and restrained mood: No attempt is made to reach out and grab the listener.

- The texts are in Church Latin, not English.

- The texts are sung only by monks and priests.

Gregorian chant is not concert music. Its goal is to contribute to worship. This it does for persons who understand its attributes.

The music example on these pages is the "Dies irae" from the funeral or Requiem Mass. It is probably the best-known line of chant, especially its first several notes, because of its use to represent death or evil by many composers in the nineteenth century. The music is shown in two versions. One is the traditional four-line staff and square notes of the Roman Catholic Church in medieval times. The other shows the pitches of the chant on a five-line staff.

The fact that the early Church included singing in its worship is recorded in Matthew 26:30, Mark 14:26, and other, non-biblical writings.

Gregorian chant is also known as **plainsong** or **plainchant**.

In 1994 a recording of chant by the monks at the monastery of Santo Domingo de Silos in Spain became the fastest-selling classical CD in history. It sold more than 2 million copies and reached number five on the U.S. pop charts. The monks used the royalties to help the needy in Third World countries and for badly needed repairs to the twelfth-century monastery.

1. Dí - es í - rae, dí - es íl - la, Sól - vet saé-clum in fa - víl-la:

Gregorian musical notation of the Middle Ages

Di - es i - rae di - es il - la Sol - vet sae - clum in fa - vil - la

The same phrase in modern music notation

LISTENING GUIDE

ANONYMOUS

"Dies irae" (opening) (c. 600)

GENRE: Gregorian chant Unaccompanied vocal

CD 1 Track 15
1 minute 2 seconds

Form: *a a b b*

			Latin	English
0:00	**15**	0:00	Dies irae, dies illa Solvet saeclum in favilla, Teste David sum Sibylla.	Day of wrath, that day the world will dissolve into ashes, as witness David and the Sibyl.
		0:14	Quantus tremor est futurus, Quando Judex est venturus, Cuncta stricte discussurus!	What trembling there will be when the Judge shall come; all shall thoroughly be shattered!
		0:28	Tuba mirum spargens sonum Per sepulchra regionem, Coget omnesante thronum.	The wondrous trumpet, spreading its sound to the tombs of all regions, will gather all before the throne.
		0:45	Mors stupebit et natura, Cum resurget creatura Judicanti responsura.	Death will be stupefied, also nature, when all creation arises again to answer to the Judge.
		1:02	Recording fades as "Dies irae" continues.	

Hildegard's *Ordo virtutum*

The Virtues are Knowledge of God, Humility, Discipline, Compassion, Mercy, Victory, Discretion, Patience, Charity, Obedience, Faith, Hope, Chastity, Innocence, World Rejection, and Heavenly Love.

The devil does not get to sing. Instead, he talks.

Most of the creators of Gregorian chant are anonymous. Humility was a virtue in the Middle Ages, especially among the religious men and women. One composer of chant who is known was a remarkable woman named Hildegard of Bingen.

Hildegard's *Ordo virtutum* (*Play of the Virtues*) is a morality play, probably written for the dedication of a convent church. In the play, a soul gives in to the temptations of the devil. The soul is saved through the intervention of the sixteen virtues.

The work contains about eighty chantlike melodies. All the parts were sung by nuns, except the role of the devil, which was played by a priest. Little except the vocal music has survived from most of these medieval plays. Performances today require some creativity in terms of the instruments and staging used.

LISTENING GUIDE

HILDEGARD OF BINGEN

Ordo virtutum, excerpt from Scene 4 (c. 1150)

GENRE: Morality play   Unaccompanied vocal

CD 3 Tracks 2–3
3 minutes 42 seconds

		Latin	English
		Devil	
0:00	**2** 0:00	Que es, aut unde venis?	Who are you, where do you come from?
		Tu amplexata es me, et ego foras eduxi te.	You were in my embrace, I led you out.
		Sed nunc inreversione tua confundis me—	Yet now you are going back, defying me—
		ego autem pugna mea deician te!	But I shall fight you and defeat you!
		Penitent Soul	
	0:22	Ego omnes vias meas malas esse cognovi,	I realize that all my ways were wicked,
		et ideo fugi a te.	so I fled from you.
		Modo autem, o illusor, pugno contra te.	But now, you fraud, I'll fight you face to face.
		Ine tu, o regina Humilitas, tua medicamine	Come, Queen Humility, with your medicine
		adiuva me!	give me aid!
		Humility (to Victory)	
	1:30	O Victoria, que istum in celo superasti,	O Victory, you who once bested this in the heavens.
		curre cum militibus tuis et omnes ligate.	run now, with all your military manner,
		Diabolum hunc!	and all of you, tie up this fiend!
		Victory (to the Virtues)	
2:01	**3** 0:00	O fortissimi et gloriosissimi milites,	Most brave and glorious warriors,
		venite, et adiuvate me istum fallacem vincere.	come, and help me to eliminate this false one.
		The Virtues	
	0:31	O dulcissima bellatrix, in torrente fonte	O sweetest warrior, in the scorching
		torrentqui absorbuit lupum rapacem—	that swallowed up the rapacious wolf—
		o gloriosa coronata, nos libenter	o glorious crowned one, how freely
		militamus tecum contra illusorem hunc.	we will fight at your side against the faker.
		Humility (to the Virtues)	
	1:10	Ligate ergo istum, o Virtutes preclare!	Tie him up then, you shining virtues!
		The Virtues	
	1:27	O regina nostra, tibi parebimus,	O our queen, we obey you,
		et precepta tua in omnibus adimplebimus.	and we will follow your orders completely.
	1:48	Excerpt concludes.	

Hildegard of Bingen

Mary Evans Picture Library

Hildegard of Bingen (1098–1179) was a powerful abbess; she was also a theologian, naturalist, healer, poet, and musician, and she wrote extensively in these fields. She considered herself an instrument through which God spoke in visions. She was born the tenth child of a noble German family. At the age of eight, she was given to a group of nuns and raised in a Benedictine monastery. During her adult life, she led religious communities for women, first at Disibodenberg and later at Rupertsberg near present-day Bingen. Hildegard used her prominent position with the Church to improve both her own position and that of the women in her charge.

Giving a son or daughter to the Church was a common practice at that time.

CODA

During the early years of Western civilization, music was considered valuable for reasons other than something interesting to listen to. It was thought to help with mental health, support drama, and contribute to worship. It was almost all vocal music, but instruments were probably used some of the time in an accompanying role. There was little uniformity from one part of Europe to another. But it was a start, and much would develop from these beginnings.

8

Medieval Music

Change came very slowly in the Middle Ages. The Holy Roman Empire ruled over much of central Europe, but Europe was actually a loose confederation of many small states. People lived mostly in small rural communities, often called manors. Communication and travel were difficult and slow, accomplished on foot or on horseback. So what was true in one place could be unheard of only fifty miles away.

MEDIEVAL TIMES

Although very gradual, changes did take place in society and in music. There were several catalysts toward a more enlightened outlook: increased contacts with the Byzantine civilization to the east, better economic conditions and trade, and the influence of education in the monasteries.

The period from about 1100 to 1450 has come to be known as the medieval, or sometimes the Gothic, period. These centuries were marked by continued progress away from the otherworldly outlook that was so strong during the preceding thousand years. The major intellectual movement of the time was Scholasticism, a highly organized and systematic philosophy culminating in the *Summa Theologica* (*Summary of Theology*) by Saint Thomas Aquinas (1225–1274).

The medieval period rejected the absolute power of kings, a rejection that encouraged the signing of the Magna Carta in England in 1215.

Another feature of the medieval period was chivalry, which glorified women and idealized kindness and refined manners. There was an emphasis on the community—the guild, the Church, or the feudal manor; individualism was not encouraged. Many works of art and music were created by artists who did not attach their names to their creations and whose identities are not known.

The medieval period saw the founding of universities. It was also the time when many of the great cathedrals were built. Literary accomplishments were achieved in this period with the poems of the troubadours, the romantic legends of a Celtic chieftain named Arthur, and *The Divine Comedy* by Dante Alighieri.

Giotto's *Madonna and Child* has a planned, posed look. This work from the fourteenth century was originally part of a polyptych, or series, of paintings. Several points are worth noting about this painting.

First, it was part of a *polyptych*, which contains the same stem word as *polyphony*, a feature of Renaissance music. Second, it has a flat, two-dimensional look; only a little shading was used to outline the figures. Third, the outline of the *Madonna and Child* is in a three-quarter position and creates an elegant Gothic shape broken only by the almost geometric figure. Fourth, the hands and faces are not very lifelike. The Madonna's hand looks as though it could be attached to a mannequin. Fifth, the painting is not very realistic: The Child has a mature face and body for an infant; he is also far too big to be held with one arm. Sixth, the gold background shows the influence of Byzantine or eastern European art. But whatever its limitations, it is nevertheless a compelling work of art.

POLYPHONY

Gregorian chant was monophonic, with only a single line of melody. How did music move beyond that to polyphony? Probably at first the church musicians simply added a second line of music that moved in strict parallel motion with the original line, some-

The use of the word *Gothic* to designate a particular artistic or musical style has little to do with its use in describing a mystery or horror story.

Chivalry perhaps existed more as an ideal in literary works than in real life.

MADONNA AND CHILD by Giotto di Bondone. This early Renaissance painting still contains elements of the Gothic style in its shape and two-dimensional look, but it also foretells intellectual qualities found in the music of Josquin and Palestrina.

what as the two front wheels on a car move exactly parallel to each other. Scholars suspect that initially such parallel lines, called *organum*, were sung without actually being written down. Some of the monks and priests probably tried singing the same line of chant at different pitch levels. Examples of organum began to appear in notation about AD 1000, and at first the added line matched the original chant note for note. But organum in strict parallel motion is not polyphony.

Gradually, the second part of organum began to show more independence, which marks the beginning of polyphony. Sometimes it would move for a note or two in the opposite direction. Over the years the second line became even more independent by having several notes to the one note in the original line.

As the idea of polyphony developed, the notes of original Gregorian chant were made longer, sometimes to the point of sounding almost like a drone. The long note values of the chant became so extended that the chant melody was hardly recognizable, which did not seem to bother the creators of this music. Perhaps they justified this practice because they knew that the music was still based on chant. And the second part, with its several moving notes, certainly did give the music a richer and more interesting quality than

A **drone** is a steady, continuous sound.

that of the original monophonic chant. Shortly before AD 1200 organum became even more interesting when musicians added two lines above the original line of chant. Eventually, a few works included four lines to be sung simultaneously.

Notre Dame means "Our Lady" in Latin and refers to the Virgin Mary.

This more complex organum was developed at the Cathedral of Notre Dame in Paris by two composers whose names are known: Léonin (active from about 1150 to 1201) and his successor, Pérotin (c. 1160–1236). Little is known about them beyond some of the music they composed.

PÉROTIN'S "ALLELUIA, DIFFUSA EST GRATIA"

Many pieces of music were created to express adoration for the Virgin Mary. In this work the chant is presented in the usual monophonic texture of Gregorian chant.

The complete work is longer than can be presented here. The "Alleluia" section comes back twice in the complete work. The word "Alleluia" is sung with several notes for each syllable, which was probably intended to give the sense of spiritual joy. It consists of four phrases. The first, having the most notes, is repeated the first time it's heard. The second phrase reaches the highest pitch level, and the fourth is calmer and has a narrower range.

The organum opens with quite long notes before the upper parts begin singing several notes on each syllable of the word "Diffusa" and the words that follow. The lowest line sounds the notes of the chant in sometimes very long note values. It has become the structure around which the notes of the moving parts are constructed.

The music notation did not contain bar lines. The patterns were indicated by brackets called *ligatures*.

By the thirteenth century another feature had been added to organum: somewhat regular rhythmic patterns. Composers grouped notes into six long-and-short note patterns that are roughly equivalent to the metrical patterns used in analyzing metrical patterns in poetry. For example, ♩♪ is trochaic meter, whereas ♪♩ is iambic meter, and so on. These patterns (called **rhythmic modes**) helped to keep the polyphonic lines of music

PÉROTIN
"Alleluia, Diffusa est gratia" (c. 1190)

GENRE: Organum   Unaccompanied vocal

CD 3 Tracks 4–6
4 minutes 40 seconds

				Latin	English
0:00	**4**	0:00	Chant	Alleluia, Alleluia ——	Hallelujah
0:00	**5**	0:37	Organum	Diffusa, est gratia in labiis tuis; *proterea benedixit te* deus	Grace has been poured upon your lips; therefore, God has blessed you
0:00	**6**	2:37		in aeternum.	eternally.
1:03			Chant	Alleluia, Alleluia	Hallelujah, Hallelujah

Léonin and Pérotin had at least three things in common. One is that we know very little about them. Second, much of what we do know comes from one source, Anonymous IV, who was a student from England at the University of Paris with a particular interest in music. Third, they were tremendously important composers at the Cathedral of Notre Dame in Paris.

Not only are we unsure of when they were born and died but even their names had varied forms. Léonin was also know as Leoninus, Magister Leoninus, Magister Leonius, and Leo. The word *magister* is a title indicating that he had earned a master's degree. He was also a priest, poet, and high-ranking official in the cathedral. He was active there from about 1150 until 1201.

Gargoyle on Notre Dame Cathedral in Paris

Humility was a virtue during medieval times, as was mentioned in the discussion of Hildegard's Ordo virtutum. *Artists and musicians believed that their efforts were for the glory of God. Personal recognition was not considered proper or important. Thus, we know little about them as individuals.*

His book of organum, *Magnum liber organi*, contains about one hundred pieces of two-part organum. He composed this music to make the worship services on special days such as Christmas and Easter more outstanding. This music also provides evidence that sometimes the notes were organized into units of twos or threes — the rhythmic

modes mentioned in conjunction with the presentation of Pérotin's "Alleluia." Although these were not measures as know them today, this was an important first step in organizing rhythm.

Pérotin (c. 1160– c. 1236) was also known as Perrotinus, Perotinus Magnus, and Magister Perotinus. He was probably Léonin's successor at Notre Dame. Anonymous IV names seven compositions by him, but undoubtedly there were many more. Whereas Léonin composed for only two voices, Pérotin wrote for three or four voices, something that had almost never been done before. To keep that many parts together required the further development of rhythm. Although the chant-based tenor part usually retains its long notes, the upper two or three parts follow strict rhythmic patterns. His works tend to be more sectional, with shorter complementary units. The tenor also moves in strict rhythm in some of these short sections.

Léonin, Pérotin, and their colleagues created a huge body of music, probably more than one thousand pieces, which later historians have labeled the "Notre Dame School." The University of Paris attracted many students, who learned not only theology but also the music sung in the cathedral. They then spread its features throughout France and the rest of Europe.

together, as well as add variety to the music. Notice that the "Alleluia" part of Pérotin's organum is sung without a metrical pattern, whereas the word "Diffusa" begins a section with a somewhat steady metrical pattern.

In these early versions of polyphony, pitches an octave apart and four and five notes apart were considered to be consonant. The interval of a third, which has been the basis for most harmony for the past several hundred years, was regarded as dissonant. That interval was, however, found in the secular music of the time, especially in England. It would be nearly 350 years after Léonin before chords containing thirds would be considered consonant enough to appear in the important final chord of a musical work.

These intervals are the same ones Pythagoras considered to be consonant, and they are the most prominent ones in the overtone series.

THE MEDIEVAL MOTET

Medieval religious music, at least as it existed in France, contained a complicated type of polyphony. The **medieval motet** was a musical curiosity. It often contained various languages as well as sacred and secular texts. For example, one motet has two different sets of words for the higher parts: one in Latin, praising the Virgin Mary; and another in

The words are typical of the chivalric writings of the time.

© Scala/Art Resource (Biblioteca Nazionale, Naples)

THE GODDESS MUSIC, seated at center, plays a portable organ accompanied by (clockwise from top center) the "pig snout" psaltery, a mandola, clappers, long trumpets, kettledrums tied around the waist, bagpipe and shawm (both reed instruments), a tambourine-like jingle drum, and a vielle (viol).

These puzzles can be comprehended only by examining the notation, not by hearing the music.

The interval of a sixth is the inversion of a third; for example, C up to A is the inversion of A up to C. The musical effect of both is similar.

French, translated as, "When I see the summer season returning and all the little birds make the woods resound, then I weep and sigh for the great desire I have for fair Marion, who holds my heart imprisoned."

The lower line typically uses a phrase of Gregorian chant, called the **cantus firmus,** or fixed melody. The length of a motet was determined by the length of this phrase, which usually was not very long.

Composers tended to work out each line, but they were not very concerned about how each line might sound when combined with the other parts. Some harsh dissonances were often the result.

Many composers of the medieval period were fascinated with concealed meanings and relationships in their music. They delighted in hiding a phrase of chant in a higher part. Or they set up a complex scheme of rhythmic and melodic patterns so that a rhythmic pattern might appear three times for every two times the melodic pattern was repeated. These intellectual puzzles interested musicians of the time, but they were usually lost on the listeners. Interest in intricate patterns and tricks is revived every so often and can be found in some of the music composed in the twentieth century.

MUSIC IN THE REST OF EUROPE

While the medieval motet was reaching its acme with the compositions of Guillaume de Machaut ("Mah-*show*," c. 1304–1377), interest was waning in this style of music. Medieval motets were developed mainly in France. Composers in other parts of Europe evidently didn't care much for the style or were not advanced enough to attempt composing in it. A blind Italian musician named Francesco Landini ("Lahn-*dee*-nee," 1325–1397) and an English composer named John Dunstable (c. 1385–1453) were writing music that was simpler and easier to listen to. Both men and their successors often used the same text for all parts, which made it possible for the words to be sung about the same time so that they could be understood by listeners.

These composers also avoided harsh dissonances. A significant contribution of Dunstable and other English composers was the use of simultaneous pitches three and six notes apart. These intervals gave the music a richer sound than the fourths and fifths of Léonin and Pérotin. In fact, the musical works of Landini and Dunstable are a pleasure to listen to today, more than six centuries later.

SECULAR MUSIC

Because there were no recordings and only a limited system of notation that was confined to the monasteries and church music, most of the music of the medieval period was lost. In addition to Gregorian chant, there was other music, probably a great deal of it, in the form of songs and dances. Usually, this secular music was in a vernacular language—French, German, English, Italian, or Spanish—rather than the Latin used in the worship services.

The **estampie** was a twelfth-century dance in triple meter and a clear, fast tempo. Only a single line of music was written down, and no instruments were specified. Performers at that time, as well as those today who perform this music, are free to decide which instruments to use for both the melody and the accompanying parts, including a drone, which is heard in the ancillary CD.

Much secular music was performed by wandering musicians who traveled from place to place singing songs, reciting poems, and even exhibiting trained animals. (These entertainers also carried news about what was happening in neighboring areas.) Later, about the twelfth and thirteenth centuries, troubadours and trouvères dominated secular music in France. They were noblemen who were poets and composers, but usually not performers; they hired minstrels to sing their songs.

These songs were for solo voice and may have been sung accompanied by a mandola or similar instrument shown in the *Goddess of Music* painting (page 60) taken from a medieval manuscript. Most of the poems and songs were about an idealized, chivalrous type of love, with a passion more of the spirit than of the flesh. About four thousand such poems and sixteen hundred such melodies have been preserved. Unlike Gregorian chant, they have regular rhythmic patterns and resemble folk melodies.

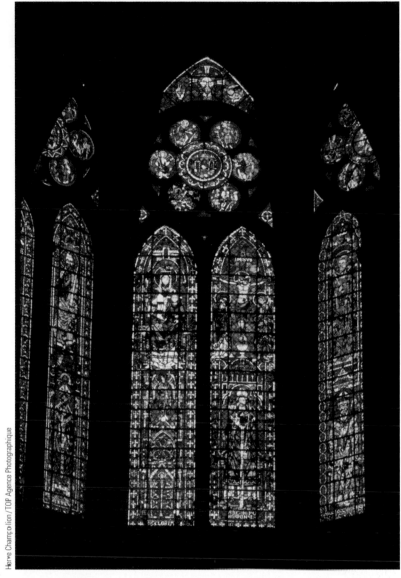

Hervé Champollion / TOP Agence Photographique

The windows of the choir section of the Cathedral at Reims.

ANONYMOUS

Estampie (twelfth century)

GENRE: Dance music   Instruments

CD 3 Track 7
1 minute 14 seconds

Form: *a a a' a*

0:00	**7** 0:00	A simple flute and violin-like instrument play a lively melody as a drone part is plucked by a string instrument.
	0:15	Melody repeated.
	0:47	Varied version of the melody.
	1:00	Opening melody returns somewhat varied.
	1:14	The estampie concludes.

Features of Medieval Music

Melodies	Mostly chantlike within a limited range; some pieces with several short flowing notes on a word or syllable
Rhythm	No definite meter; some pieces use rhythmic modes
Textures	Monophonic and polyphonic
Dynamic levels	Restrained and rather soft
Performance media	Small groups of unaccompanied voices; some in two, three, or four parts; a few solos in secular music Very little instrumental music
Forms	Phrase by phrase; a few pieces in sectional form (e.g., *a a b b*)
Genres	Organum Medieval motet Dance music

CODA

As the 1450s approached, the medieval motet was rapidly disappearing. Gregorian chant continued to play an important role and could also be found in other types of music. Drawing to a close, however, was that long stretch of history called the Middle Ages. The years leading up to 1450 laid the foundation for a new age — the Renaissance — which provided some great literature and architecture as well as beautiful and intricate music.

Renaissance Music

9

The word *Renaissance* means "rebirth" in French. Historically, it referred to a revival of interest in the philosophy and arts of ancient Greece and Rome, although there was much more to it than just the admiration of an earlier civilization. Because music had no ancient models to resurrect, for music the term *Renaissance* refers only to the style that predominated from about 1450 to 1600.

THE RENAISSANCE OUTLOOK

The intense interest of Renaissance artists and scholars in the earlier Greek and Roman civilizations led to a curious mixture of Greek and Christian belief. Michelangelo expressed this union of the pagan and Christian by decorating the ceiling of the Sistine Chapel in the Vatican in Rome with alternating figures of prophets (Christian) and sibyls (pagan). Erasmus, the great philosopher, regarded the ancient Athenian Socrates as a pre-Christian saint.

During the Renaissance certain intellectual viewpoints emerged that are still common in Western civilization today. Among them are optimism, worldliness, hedonism, naturalism, and individualism. But the most important of these is *humanism*, which is an emphasis on the human and natural as opposed to the otherworldly or divine. For example, pride, which was considered a sin in the Middle Ages, was elevated to a virtue.

Hedonism is the belief in the importance of pleasure, especially physical pleasure, for its own sake.

Naturalism is the belief that what is natural is right.

The humanistic view can be seen by comparing the two treatments of the human body shown on these pages. One is a sculpture from the great medieval cathedral at Chartres in France. This figure has a spiritual, otherworldly quality; the head and eyes seem serene, and the position of the body is erect and formal. The proportions of the body are exaggerated to make the figure appear longer; the feet seem to dangle as though they were merely attached to the robes. As with most artworks of the medieval period, the artist is unknown.

Michelangelo's *David*, on the other hand, looks like a magnificent Greek god. Standing about 13½ feet high, the sculpture suggests confidence and an admiration of the human body. David looks natural, almost casual, and free.

With increasing interest in the value of life on earth, there was a corresponding interest in the fine arts. Art was valued for its own sake, not just as a means of religious devotion. The result of this new interest in the arts was a long list of outstanding sculptors and painters: Botticelli, Leonardo, Michelangelo, Dürer, Raphael, Titian, Brueghel, and Tintoretto, to name but a few.

Sandro Botticelli's *Adoration of the Magi* depicts the three wise men or kings paying homage to the infant Jesus. It reveals the fondness of artists of the time for order and balance. A group of figures at the left of the painting is balanced by a group on the right, with the Madonna and Child in the center. The painting has a "staged" look. The converging lines of the Greek and Roman ruins add linear perspective to the painting and indicate a renewed interest in these ancient civilizations. Botticelli gives many of his figures brightly colored clothing. In addition, the sky is bright and clear.

Leonardo's most famous painting is the *Mona Lisa*.

Not only were works of art being enjoyed in a new climate of acceptance but improving economic conditions meant that money was available to hire artists and musicians. The Church sought rich adornment for its buildings, which was one of the practices that led to the Reformation started by Martin Luther in 1517.

MEDIEVAL AND RENAISSANCE INTERPRETATIONS OF THE HUMAN FORM illustrate the advent of humanism, a philosophy that asserts the dignity and worth of humankind and emphasizes secular rather than spiritual concerns.

THE ADORATION OF THE MAGI by Botticelli presents the logical, planned qualities also found in Renaissance music.

An event that affected education, commerce, and religion was Johann Gutenberg's invention of printing from movable type. Printing made possible the wide dissemination of music, beginning with the appearance of the first printed music books in 1501.

The spirit of the time was one of optimism and discovery. The voyages of Columbus, Cabot, Balboa, and Magellan took place during the Renaissance. Copernicus was announcing his discoveries about the universe. Rabelais, Machiavelli, Boccaccio, Montaigne, More, Bacon, and Erasmus were exploring new ideas in literature and philosophy.

Perhaps the Renaissance is best epitomized by Leonardo da Vinci (1452–1519). It seems there was little that this genius did not do extremely well: design weapons and other devices, recite stories, paint, depict human anatomy, plan cities, make maps, and analyze proportions and things mathematical. He was interested in everything and left seven thousand pages of notebooks!

FEATURES AND TYPES OF RENAISSANCE MUSIC

Musically, the Renaissance started in the Netherlands. The composers there had reached a level of achievement that was the envy of Europe. Many were eventually lured away from their homeland to better-paying jobs in Spain, Bohemia, Austria, Germany, and especially the cities of northern Italy.

The style and techniques of the Netherlanders became internationally known and imitated. Many composers became so cosmopolitan that they thought of themselves as musicians first and citizens of a particular country second.

One composer who shaped the period known as the High Renaissance was Josquin Des Prez. Like composers before him, Josquin used the device of *imitation*, in which one line of melody appears in another part a measure or two later, somewhat like a round. But instead of having all parts singing continuously, as composers before him did, he had

A SKETCH FROM LEONARDO'S NOTEBOOKS As can be seen here, Leonardo wrote so that the words read from right to left with the letters reversed. His writing is most easily read using a mirror.

Alinari Archives/Corbis

Josquin Des Prez

The most esteemed composer of the middle Renaissance was **Josquin Des Prez** ("*Jzhoss*-can deh *Pray*"), who lived from about 1440 to 1521. Born in Flanders (now part of Belgium), Josquin was a choir singer in Milan, a musician in the service of the Sforza family, a member of the Papal Choir, a choirmaster, and finally a musician in the service of Louis XII of France. His composing skill was much admired by his contemporaries, including Martin Luther. Josquin composed what and when he wanted, not what his patron wanted, and was known for his chansons and motets. He also demanded a salary much higher than that of most of his contemporaries, which could explain why he changed jobs rather often. He was also very particular about his music and would become angry if singers tried to make any changes in it.

———◆———

A **chanson** *was a French polyphonic song of the Renaissance.*

———◆———

© Corbis-Bettmann

BEST-KNOWN WORKS

choral:
- Missa Ave Maria Stella
- Missa de Beata Virgine

each voice enter one after another. This emphasized the imitation and made the words sung by each entering part easier to hear.

THE RENAISSANCE MASS

It was the custom among composers during the Renaissance to compose music for the Ordinary of the Mass using a phrase from a chant as a cantus firmus. The Mass usually acquired the name of the phrase or chant. For example, Josquin wrote eighteen different settings of the Mass. His *Pange lingua Mass* has many melodies from a Gregorian hymn called "Pange lingua." A portion of both the hymn and the Kyrie section of Josquin's Mass is shown here:

JOSQUIN DES PREZ

Kyrie from *Pange lingua Mass* (c. 1500)

GENRE: Mass, Kyrie   BASIS: Gregorian chant   SATB choral

CD 3 Tracks 8–10
3 minutes 15 seconds

0:00   8   0:00   Tenors enter singing "Kyrie eleison."

        0:03   Basses enter singing "Kyrie eleison" in imitation.

        0:12   Sopranos enter singing "Kyrie eleison" in imitation.

        0:20   Altos enter singing "Kyrie eleison" in imitation.

        0:24   Basses enter again followed by tenors and then sopranos.

0:50   9   0:00   Basses sing "Christe eleison." Altos soon follow.

        0:17   Tenors sing "Christe." Sopranos soon follow.

2:16   10   0:00   Sopranos sing "Kyrie eleison," but the melody differs from the first Kyrie. Altos, tenors, and basses follow.

        1:02   After an extended cadence, the Kyrie concludes.

SINGING ANGELS, from the *Cantoria,* or singers' pulpit, by the Renaissance sculptor Luca della Robbia.

The Kyrie has three sections based on the text, and each section contains several points of imitation.

More than any previous composer, Josquin was aware of a consistent organization of harmonies. Closely related to more-sophisticated harmony was the development of the bass line. Before Josquin, composers started adding melodies to chant; they placed the chant around middle C and put the additional melodies above it. But this did not provide a convincing sense of chord movement. Therefore, around the year 1450, composers began to add another line *below* the chant to give the music a more solid foundation. Even today this arrangement of voice parts remains the standard for a choral group containing men's and women's voices. At the time, the sections were called *superius, altus, tenor,* and *bassus;* today they are called soprano, alto, tenor, and bass.

The most esteemed composer of the late Renaissance was Giovanni Pierluigi da Palestrina. Historical circumstances encouraged him to be a conservative reformer, musically speaking. The Council of Trent was held intermittently between 1545 and 1563. The Church felt threatened by the Protestant Reformation, so the council met to respond to that situation and to acknowledge the need for some reform within the Church.

One aspect that was under attack was its music, which over the centuries had strayed far from the ideals of Gregorian chant. Complaints were voiced about the use of secular tunes, the complicated polyphony that made the words nearly impossible to understand, the use of noisy instruments, and the irreverence of the singers. The council directed that the music be purged of "barbarism, obscurities, contrarieties, and superfluities" so that "the House of God might rightly be called a house of prayer." To his credit, Palestrina achieved a return to the purity and reverence of earlier music without discarding the highly developed style of his predecessors.

THE RENAISSANCE MOTET

The Renaissance motet is very different from the medieval motet. The **Renaissance motet** is a unified piece with all voices singing the same Latin text. It borrows some phrases from chant, and it conveys the desired spirit of reverence. Above all, the Renaissance motet is serious, restrained, and designed for inclusion in the worship service.

LISTENING GUIDE

GIOVANNI PIERLUIGI DA PALESTRINA

"Sicut cervus," Part I (c. 1577)

GENRE: Motet   SATB choral

CD 1 Tracks 16–18
3 minutes 32 seconds

0:00 **16** 0:00   Tenors sing "Sicut cervus."

0:07   Altos follow with "Sicut cervus" five notes higher.

0:12   Sopranos sing "Sicut cervus" one octave higher than tenors sang the phrase.

0:19   Basses sing "Sicut cervus" on the same pitch on which the tenors started.

1.18 **17** 0:00   Basses sing "ita desiderat." Tenors, sopranos, and altos follow in imitation.

2:10 **18** 0:00   Sopranos sing "anima mea ad te Deus." Altos, tenors, and basses follow in imitation.

1:11   After the voice parts have sung "ad te Deus," Part I of the motet concludes.

Palestrina's "Sicut cervus"

Palestrina's works have a pure, celestial quality. His "Sicut cervus," included on the CD, is a good example of the Renaissance motet:

- The text is in ecclesiastical Latin. It is a portion of Psalm 42, with Part I using only the first two lines. In the Revised Standard Version it reads:

The word *hart* means a male red deer, a stag.

> *As a hart longs for flowing streams,*
> *So longs my soul for Thee, O God.*
> *My soul thirsts for God, for the living God.*
> *When shall I come and behold the face of God?*
> *My tears have been my food day and night,*
> *While men say to me continually, "Where is your God"*

- The music is polyphonic. All the lines are given equal attention, and each has distinct melodic character.

- Each voice usually enters in imitation of another when new text is introduced.

- The music does not have a strong feeling of chord progression.

- "Sicut cervus" does not have a strong meter or beat. Although it moves along steadily, it certainly is not toe-tapping music. Today's versions of the music have bar lines, but these have been added by modern editors so singers can more easily keep their place. The bar lines do not imply a metrical pattern.

- Motets today are almost always sung without accompaniment. During the Renaissance, however, the voices were sometimes doubled by a few instruments. But the

Giovanni Pierluigi da Palestrina

Palestrina (c. 1526–1594) was born in the small town of Palestrina outside Rome, which provided him with the name by which he is known today. He began his career as chorister at Santa Maria Maggiore in 1537 in Rome. He returned to his native town in 1544 as organist and choirmaster, where he married and had two sons.

In 1550 the bishop of Palestrina was elected pope, assuming the name Julius III. A year and a half later, he summoned Palestrina back to Rome to become choirmaster of the Cappella Giulia in the Vatican. Soon he was to publish his first book of Masses.

Pope Julius III died and was succeeded by Pope Paul IV, who was determined to reform what he considered the excesses in church music. In 1555 Palestrina was dismissed from his job because he was married. He was soon appointed choirmaster at the Church of Saint John Lateran in Rome, where he stayed for five years. He then returned to Santa Maria Maggiore and published his first book of motets. In 1571 he returned to Cappella Giulia, but misfortune struck when his two eldest sons and wife died of various diseases.

Palestrina married again and entered the fur business, and he proved to be a highly successful businessman. His more than adequate funds allowed him to publish about sixteen collections of music. He died in 1594, leaving a wealth of beautiful and finely crafted music and the distinction of creating the finest church music of his time.

© The Bridgeman Art Library

BEST-KNOWN WORKS

choral:
- *Pope Marcellus Mass*
- *Sicut cervus*

---

ideal was a purity of sound, which implies no accompaniment or, in musical terms, **a cappella.**

- A small group of singers is the authentic performance medium for Renaissance motets. Probably no more than three singers were originally assigned to each part. Boys, or men singing in falsetto, sang the high voice parts.

- The lines of melody are very singable. The range for any one voice part does not exceed an octave, except for the bass. Furthermore, the lines do not move far from one pitch to the next. The melodies are quite smooth and conjunct.

- The form of a motet is usually based on the structure of the text, which in this case is a psalm, so each verse has its own polyphonic setting.

- The music has a restrained quality. Bombast and showmanship were considered not in keeping with the attitude of reverence and awe that should prevail in worship.

- The melodic lines are woven together with great skill and beauty. That is the main reason Palestrina's music is so highly esteemed and still sung today.

The term *a cappella* literally means "for the chapel."

Women were not permitted by the Church to celebrate the Mass or to sing in choirs.

THE MADRIGAL

The Renaissance also had a distinctly worldly side, as was noted earlier. Many types of secular music were composed and performed, and some of this music contained features of the musical style of a particular country. The most significant type of secular music at this time was the madrigal.

Madrigals are both similar to and different from motets. They are similar in that they were written for a small group of singers. They also have some imitative entrances of new phrases of text, contain singable vocal lines, and are generally more polyphonic than homophonic. But there are some important differences.

- Madrigals are in vernacular languages, and their texts often deal with sentimental and sometimes erotic love.

There were also a few *madrigali spirituali*, which were nonliturgical songs on religious topics.

- They tend to have stronger and more regular rhythm, and most of them are composed to be performed at a faster tempo.
- Madrigals were sung at courtly social gatherings and meetings of learned and artistic societies, so they were not the popular or folk music of the day. They were very popular, however, among the aristocratic, educated class, and an enormous number of them were composed. In England madrigal singing—with its implied requirement of music reading—was expected of educated persons.
- They often contain **text painting,** or **word painting,** in which the music attempts to depict the words being sung.

Because madrigals were written for secular situations, they were not limited by religious traditions. They therefore contained more innovative musical ideas, such as word painting. This practice is especially evident in the madrigal "As Vesta Was from Latmos Hill Descending."

The madrigal was originally an Italian development associated with such composers as Cipriano de Rore and Luca Marenzio. By the mid-1500s madrigals had spread to other countries. Interest in madrigals reached England late in that century. English madrigals are especially enjoyable to listeners today for three reasons:

- Their texts are in English, so no translation is necessary for English-speaking people.
- English composers had a knack for making the lines of music tuneful and singable.
- The English had the delightful trait of not taking themselves too seriously. No matter how sad a song may be, the listener senses a detached quality.

Weelkes's "As Vesta Was from Latmos Hill Descending"

Thomas Weelkes was one of England's finest composers of madrigals. "As Vesta Was from Latmos Hill Descending" is from an anthology of madrigals, *The Triumphs of Oriana*. It was composed in honor of Queen Elizabeth I, who was often called "Oriana." This madrigal is written for six voice parts instead of the usual four. Vesta is the Roman goddess of the hearth and home, and Diana is the goddess of the hunt, chastity, and the moon. The text tells about Vesta coming down a hill with her attendants, who are referred to as "Diana's darlings." At the same time, Oriana, the "maiden queen," climbs the hill with her shepherd attendants. Vesta's attendants leave her and hurry down to join Oriana.

> **Notice the use of characters from Roman mythology.**
>
> **Queen Elizabeth never married and was often referred to as the "maiden" or "virgin" queen.**

Weelkes's madrigal makes much use of word painting. For example, the words *ascending* and *descending* are each set with scales that move in the direction implied by the words.

When the text tells about Vesta's attendants leaving her to run down the hill, Weelkes has the appropriate number of singers singing—two, then three, and then one. Later in the piece, the word *long* is the longest note in that portion of the madrigal.

THOMAS WEELKES

"As Vesta Was from Latmos Hill Descending" (1590)

GENRE: Madrigal   6-Part vocal

CD 1 Tracks 19–20
3 minutes 7 seconds

0.00	**19**	0:00	As Vesta was from Latmos hill descending,	*Descending scales*
		0:12	she spied a maiden queen the same ascending,	*Ascending scales*
		0:33	attended on by all the shepherds swain,	
		0:49	to whom Diana's darlings came running down amain.	*Rapid descending notes*
1:12	**20**	0:00	First two by two, then three by three together,	*Two voices, three voices, then all voices*
		0:09	leaving their goddess all alone, hasten thither,	*One voice*
		0:22	and mingling with the shepherd of her train	
		0:29	with mirthful tunes her presence entertain.	*Short, happy phrase in imitation*
		0:43	Then sang the shepherds and nymphs of Diana,	*Flowing melody*
		0:54	Long live fair Oriana!	*Long notes in the bass part*
		1:55	Madrigal concludes with sustained notes.	

The word *swain* in the text refers to male admirers.

Weelkes also fits the words and rhythm of the music together in a way that would be natural if they were spoken. Often the rhythmic setting of the words contributes to their expressiveness.

Thomas Weelkes

Thomas Weelkes (c. 1576–1623) was one of several excellent composers of choral music who flourished at the end of the sixteenth century and the early part of the seventeenth. His contemporaries included William Byrd (1543–1623), John Dowland (1562–1626), Thomas Morley (c. 1557–1603), Thomas Tallis (c. 1501–1585), and John Wilbye (1574–1638). Although madrigals were slow in coming to England, interest in them seemed to explode once they finally arrived.

Weelkes was organist first at Winchester College, but spent most of his career in Chichester. There he married the daughter of a wealthy merchant, and they had three children. His most musically productive years were the early ones in Chichester. As the years went by, he became more negligent in his church music duties and drank heavily. He was reported to the bishop as being "noted and famed for a common drunkard and notorious swearer and blasphemer." By 1617 he was fired from his job and apparently was employed only sporadically after that.

Whatever Weelkes's personal foibles, he composed some of the finest church music and madrigals during that period of English history. Typical of most of his contemporary composers, he wrote madrigals that were lighter and more experimental than his church music.

Lebrecht Music and Arts Library

RENAISSANCE INSTRUMENTAL MUSIC

Frets are metal strips placed across the fingerboard to help the player in accurate finger placement.

Composers during the Renaissance devoted almost all their efforts to vocal music. Instruments did often accompany the singing of secular music, especially a lute or harpsichord. Instrumentalists simplified the written parts by reducing the polyphony to chords. The lute was the most popular instrument of the Renaissance. As can be seen in the painting, it has a pear-shaped body, frets, and several strings. Its pegbox is slanted back sharply away from the body. It is played by plucking, and intricate music can be performed on it.

Instruments were used extensively for dance music. One of the most popular dances of the time was the *pavane* ("pa-*vahn*"), a solemn dance in two beats to the measure with the dancers moving in a formal way. The pavane was often paired with the *galliard*, which had three beats to the measure. These and other dances are made up of clearly identifiable sections that produced forms such *A A B B* and *A A B B C C*.

Courtesy and photo © Isabella Stewart Gardner Museum, Boston

A GIRL WITH A LUTE, an oil painting on wood by Bartolomeo Veneto. The lute reached its peak of popularity during this time, both as a solo instrument and as accompaniment to singing.

Features of Renaissance Music

Melodies	Flowing to adjacent notes within a somewhat limited range
Rhythm	Even, steady flow without a clear sense of beat
Texture	Mostly polyphonic
Dynamic levels	Restrained and rather soft
Performance media	Small, unaccompanied groups of singers, some with soprano, alto, tenor, and bass voice parts A small amount of lute and keyboard music
Forms	Phrase by phrase; a few pieces in sectional form
Genres	Mass Renaissance motet Madrigal Dance music

CODA

Renaissance music was not intended for the concert stage; its subtle qualities are lost in an auditorium. It is not massive and colorful. Instead, it has other virtues. The centuries since that time have seen the development of new forms and new genres. The world of music has grown much larger, which makes it more difficult to give each musical style the attention it deserves.

That's too bad, because Renaissance composers achieved a quality in their motets and madrigals that has never been surpassed. Different works in different styles have been written since then, but subsequent efforts have not diminished the quality of the music of the sixteenth century.

PART III

Baroque Music

	1600	1650
Historical Events	● First settlements in America	
	● King James version of Bible	
	Thirty Years' War	
		● Harvard founded
		Louis XIV reigns in France
Visual Arts	Poussin	
		▲ Bernini colonnades at St. Peter's (above, right)
		● Rubens, *Abraham and Melchizedek*
		● Rembrandt, *Descent from the Cross*
Literature and Theater	● Cervantes, *Don Quixote*	
Philosophy and Science	Grotius	
		Spinoza
	Galileo publishes on astronomy	
	Descartes	
		Locke
Music	● First operas	Monteverdi, late madrigals ● and operas
		Lully at French court
		Arcangelo Corelli

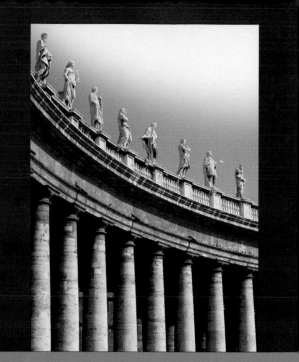

1700   **1750**

● Ottomans seize Vienna

● Salem witchcraft trials

Boucher

Gainsborough

Fragonard

Watteau

● Milton, *Paradise Lost*   ● Defoe, *Robinson Crusoe*

Swift, *Gulliver's Travels* ●   ● Fielding, *Tom Jones*

● Newton's laws of physics

Voltaire

Hume

● Purcell, *Dido and Aeneas*   ● Handel, *Messiah*

● Fugues   ● Vivaldi, *The Four Seasons*

◄ J. S. Bach (left) and ▲ Handel (above), instrumental and choral works

10 *The* Baroque Period

Even before 1600, the approximate beginning of the Baroque period, a new style had been emerging. The Renaissance ideals of restraint and balance began to fade. The change could be seen in the growing emotion displayed in the later works of Michelangelo, and it could be heard in Giovanni Gabrieli's massive works for instruments and two choruses. The initial reaction to the new style can be seen in the word *baroque* itself, which was probably derived from a Portuguese word meaning "irregularly shaped pearl."

Sometimes baroque means extravagant, grotesque, and in bad taste, which is perhaps a carryover from its original meaning. In discussions of music, however, **Baroque** refers only to the style that prevailed from about 1600 to 1750. And that style was certainly not grotesque or in bad taste.

STYLES IN MUSIC

What do we mean by a musical style? Simply that the elements in a particular style are generally treated in a similar way. In some styles, for example, there is little sense of meter, in other styles it is very pronounced, and in yet others the metrical patterns are often irregular. The same is true of melodies, size and nature of performing groups, texture, type of harmony, and so on. Many of these similarities can be partly described in words. But a clear understanding of the characteristics of a style can come only from hearing them.

When a large amount of music over a long span of time has used musical elements in a similar way, it has been grouped by scholars and given a name—Renaissance, Baroque, and others. These names are usually designated quite a few years *after* the years in which a style was dominant. No one got up on the morning of January 1, 1600, and thought, "Well, the Baroque period has finally arrived."

Why do writers and scholars designate periods in music and history? Just as it helps to divide a book into units and chapters, it helps to divide the thousands of years of human history into periods. The idea of style periods permits us to organize topics according to similarities and to talk, think about, and remember them more easily.

An understanding of styles in music also clues us in on what to listen for, as well as what not to expect. For instance, you don't encounter an accompanied solo singer in music written before 1600. So, when you hear such a work, you will know that it's not in Renaissance style. Being able to recognize the differences between styles from listening is an excellent indicator of how well you are connecting what you hear with what you know.

CHARACTERISTICS OF BAROQUE STYLE

It is difficult to summarize in a few paragraphs a period of 150 years in which major changes took place and contrasting forces were at work. Three general characteristics, however, mark the Baroque style: grandiose dimensions, love of drama, and religious intensity.

Grandiose Dimensions

The artists and musicians of the Baroque period were fond of the large and grandiose. In music this characteristic is evident in the prominent place given the pipe organ—the largest and most powerful instrument of the time. In architecture the love of grandeur can

> Some of the time a style is recognized "just because it sounds like it."

> People have always thought of themselves as modern and up to date, which, of course, at the time they were.

> What you hear in a piece of music and what you know about it reinforce each other.

be seen in Gian Lorenzo Bernini's monumental colonnades encompassing the vast piazza in front of Saint Peter's Basilica in Rome. The huge columns reach out before Saint Peter's like giant pincers seeking to draw everyone into the building. Four rows of columns run parallel to one another. But when standing in the center of the piazza, viewers can see only a single row of columns, because the other three rows are perfectly blocked out. The colonnade is made up of 284 different columns, and statues of 140 saints are placed on top of the columns.

Love of Drama

Baroque artists and musicians were fond of drama. Three major dramatic forms were developed in music: opera, oratorio, and cantata. Drama can also be seen in the twisted lines and struggling subjects in artworks. Both size and twisting motion are evident in the ceiling paintings and many other Baroque works of art.

Religious Intensity

The years of the Baroque period were a time of strong religious feelings—and conflicts. The Protestant churches established themselves generally in northern Europe and on the British Isles. Protestant worship was devout, plain, and deadly serious. John Milton's *Paradise Lost* and John Bunyan's *Pilgrim's Progress* were two monumental writings containing the Protestant viewpoint.

The Catholic faith was generally found in southern Europe. The Catholic Counter-Reformation developed in response to the Protestant Reformation and a sense that the Catholic Church was in need of reform. The times were marked by a series of tragic religious wars between Protestants and Catholics. A positive by-product of this religious intensity, however, was the creation of some outstanding art.

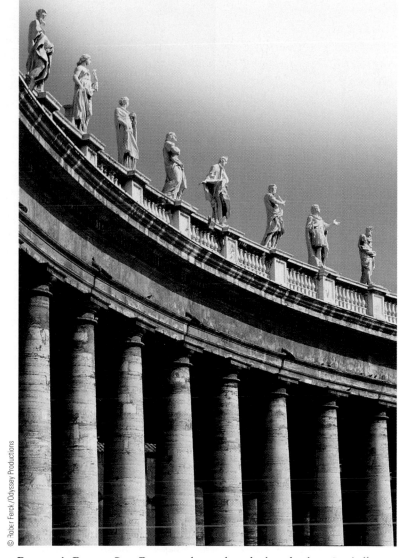

© Rober Ferck/Odyssey Productions

BERNINI'S PIAZZA SAN PIETRO is larger than the length of two football fields and took eleven years to complete.

BAROQUE ART

Baroque artworks are very different from those of the Renaissance. Consider Peter Paul Rubens's *The Meeting of Abraham and Melchizedek*, which was painted about 1625 (page 78). Originally designed for a tapestry, this work is the opposite of the calm, posed quality of Giotto's *Madonna and Child*. A similar change can be observed in Baroque music, with its development of opera and oratorio. The painting looks as though a movie director had shouted "Action!" to the figures; even the horse on the left side of the picture appears to have responded to the command. The bodies of the figures are often twisted to add to the dramatic effect. Abraham and Melchizedek lean actively toward each other. The men on each side are set in a tight design of profiles and frontal poses. Their bodies look natural and robust. The edges of the painting show a luxurious carpet piled up on a

THE MEETING OF ABRAHAM AND MELCHIZEDEK by Peter Paul Rubens. The painting is filled with the sense of drama that Baroque musicians and artists created in their works.

ledge, and the scene is anchored by the columns on the right and clamped into place by the servants in the foreground.

Rembrandt van Rijn's *Descent from the Cross* shows another side of Baroque painting. It features the dramatic treatment of light on the faces of people, much like a spotlight in a stage production centers attention on a particular character. The light focuses on two parts of the painting. One is the body of Jesus and the face of the man helping lower his body. The other, weaker spotlight is on the woman, presumably Mary, on the right-hand side. The light in this painting seems to be coming from the candle shielded by a man's hand, which gives the scene an eerie pall. To increase the spotlight effect, Rembrandt painted an almost black background.

Another Baroque characteristic of Rembrandt's painting is the twisted, almost corkscrew design. Notice that Jesus' body is turned, as are most of the other figures in the painting; none is facing straight ahead or sideways. And the cross is not in the center of the painting, as it would have been if this were a Renaissance work. As if the spotlighting and twisted figures were not enough, you can also see the tenderness and grief in the faces of the people. It's a very dramatic painting.

The Baroque love of size and grandeur is evident in the ceiling painting *Apotheosis of Saint Ignatius* by Andrea Pozzo, which adorns the San Ignazio (St. Ignatius) Church in Rome (page 80). The work is a fresco; that is, it was painted right into the ceiling plaster while it was still fresh. It is one of a number of ceiling paintings completed during the Baroque period, the most famous of which are Michelangelo's frescoes for the Sistine Chapel in the Vatican in Rome. It seems that Baroque artists (and/or their patrons) thought that bigger was better. Works of music became much longer and involved more performers, and artwork became larger, both in concept and in actual size. This fresco tries to exceed its physical limits by creating the illusion that the viewer is gazing into heaven. The scene depicts saints, angels, and sinners all overwhelmed by what they see.

BAROQUE INTELLECTUAL ACTIVITY

Although it was marked by religious fervor, the Baroque period was also a time of important advances in science.

- Sir Isaac Newton developed the theory of gravity.
- Johannes Kepler and Galileo Galilei developed Copernicus's theories about the movements of the planets.
- William Gilbert introduced the word *electricity* into the language.
- Robert Boyle helped develop chemistry into a science.
- Robert Hooke first described the cellular structure of plants.
- William Harvey described the circulation of blood in the human body.
- Gottfried Wilhelm von Leibniz with Newton developed infinitesimal calculus.
- René Descartes founded analytical geometry.

EARLY BAROQUE MUSIC

No musical style is ever fully uniform, and this is especially true of the Baroque. Some scholars have divided the period into three subperiods: early, middle, and mature. Music in the early years of the Baroque was more experimental; the style usually associated with this period developed during the middle and mature years.

The transition from the Renaissance to the Baroque style resulted in some powerful music by a number of composers. An important group worked in Venice, which was a major cultural center throughout the sixteenth and into the seventeenth century. Venice's musical activity centered around the Basilica of Saint Mark. The position of organist-choirmaster there was the most sought after in all of Italy. Over the years the distinguished musicians who held that post composed more and more for two choruses placed with the two organs on each side of the church. And not only were there singers and pipe organs; there were also trombones, cornets, and viols.

The result was a powerful and exciting stereophonic sound with one group of performers answering the other. This technique was known as *polychoral* or *antiphonal singing*. Giovanni Gabrieli (1555–1612) brought antiphonal music to a peak in the early years of the seventeenth century. He was also the first composer to specify particular instruments for a part and the first to indicate dynamics in music notation.

MUSIC IN THE BAROQUE

During the Baroque, Europe consisted of many small principalities and states. As expensive cars and designer clothing are today, music and art became status symbols among the nobility and wealthy merchants. Composers often worked under a patronage system

DESCENT FROM THE CROSS by Rembrandt van Rijn. The painting adds to the sense of drama by spotlighting the faces of the figures in the scene similar to the way that singers and actors are spotlighted on a stage.

René Descartes is also remembered for his "I think, therefore I am" philosophy.

Viols are string instruments that look something like those of today, but viols have frets, flatter and less curving bodies, and more strings.

There were three hundred principalities in what is present-day Germany.

© Art Resource

APOTHEOSIS OF ST. IGNATIUS by Andrea Pozzo. The pipe organ was the most powerful instrument during the Baroque, and the ceiling painting was the most massive type of painting.

In was not uncommon in Handel's day for a king or queen to be from another country. Royal blood was considered more important than nationality. A monarch from another country would be appointed when the previous ruler had no heir apparent or because there was political turmoil. King George I began England's rule by the House of Hanover, which still rules today.

The duke of Weimar had his court musician, J. S. Bach, jailed for a month because he refused to leave his job. (Bach could be quite stubborn.)

in which they composed music exclusively for their employer. George Frideric Handel (1685–1759), for example, was employed by the elector of Hanover in Germany (where his name was Händel) and was on leave for a second time in England when the elector was crowned King George I of England.

The patronage system had its good and bad points. It could provide a composer steady employment, but the position also demanded that he please his employer or he would need to find another job. And the job often involved teaching singers, rehearsing instrumentalists, and even quelling squabbles among the musicians, as well as writing music "on demand."

Being a musician was often a family tradition. For example, the Bach family tree contains about sixty outstanding musicians, including thirty-eight composers. Education beyond the elementary school level was limited to those who were rich or born into noble families. Learning to be a composer consisted of copying music when young and later studying as an apprentice with a master composer. A few musicians studied an instrument or voice at one of the newly emerging conservatories, but rarely was composition taught there during the Baroque.

There was no established body of music such as we have today. Almost all music was expected to be, and was, new. For this reason, many Baroque composers wrote huge amounts of music. Georg Phillip Telemann (1685–1767), for example, composed more than three thousand pieces, and many other Baroque composers produced prodigious amounts of music. How did they do it?

1. They must have worked very hard.

The system is called *figured bass*.

2. They used a shorthand system in which they did not have to write in every note in a chord.

3. They used some of their own themes (and once in a while a theme by another composer) in more than one of their works.

4. They had young boys (future musicians) copy a lot of the parts for the instrumentalists and singers.

5. They didn't fuss over details, often because they were going to perform a work themselves. They never dreamed (at least as far as anyone can determine) that people hundreds of years later would be performing and listening to their music! They thought of themselves as skilled craftsmen, not artists who were creating music that future generations would understand and appreciate.

PERFORMANCE OF BAROQUE MUSIC

There were no professional orchestras during the Baroque. The only orchestras were associated with courts and employed part-time performers. The orchestras were also small (about twenty players), and there was no need for a conductor. Usually the keyboard player would simply nod his head to indicate when the music was to begin. Public performances were rare; usually they were held in churches or palaces. Opera companies were a different matter. A number of cities in Italy had them. Performances took place in opera houses and were attended by the public.

The quality of playing on most orchestral instruments was probably not at all impressive compared to the quality of performers today. Most players held other jobs, often not associated with music, and the development of playing skills was limited. Many of the instruments were not fully developed. Some organists and harpsichord players were outstanding performers, however. It was different in the case of singers. Some of them were reputed to possess sensational ability.

Improvisation was an important feature in Baroque music. An organist was expected to be able to improvise intricate and complex music. During their lifetimes Bach, Handel, and several other Baroque composers were known as much for their ability to improvise as for their compositions. Singers and instrumentalists frequently added ornaments to a melody, so what is seen in the notation of Baroque music was sometimes only a skeleton of what was actually performed.

At one time in the seventeenth century, Venice, which had at the time a population of 125,000, supported six opera houses.

Woodwinds had few keys, and brasses had no valves with which to produce pitches not in their basic overtone series.

Handel continued to give organ concerts in which he improvised even after he became blind.

CHARACTERISTICS OF BAROQUE MUSIC

The differences between the Renaissance music of composers such as Josquin and Palestrina and the Baroque music of J. S. Bach, Handel, and Vivaldi are immense.

Homophony

From the monophonic texture of Gregorian chant, music moved to simple organum and then to highly polyphonic music of medieval times and the Renaissance. Polyphonic music can be beautiful and interesting, but it does have drawbacks. When several different voice parts are singing at the same time, the words tend to be obscured by other voice parts. It's somewhat like trying to listen to two or more different conversations at the same time. What's more, because they need to fit with other lines of music, it's difficult for the lines in polyphonic music to be expressive of the words.

Although there are moments in Renaissance music in which all the voice parts move together, these places are not truly homophonic in the sense that one melody predominates and the other parts are supportive of it. Near the beginning of the Baroque period, several composers in and around Florence, Italy, decided to have a singer sing one line and make that line of music expressive of the text being sung, while the other parts became just accompaniment. In this way, the music could be much freer and more dramatic, a characteristic of Baroque music. Homophony developed from these efforts, and over the years it was to become as important as polyphony.

The transition from the polyphony of the Renaissance to the homophony of the Baroque can be seen in the books of madrigals by Claudio Monteverdi (1567–1643).

The type of homophony consisting of a solo line with instrumental accompaniment that flourished in the early seventeenth century is often called *monody*.

Between 1587 and 1603, he published four books of polyphonic madrigals in Renaissance style. In 1605, however, he published a book of homophonic pieces, some of which have accompaniments. By the eighth book, in 1638, Monteverdi's music also contained works for small vocal and string ensembles.

Recitative

The early efforts to have one expressive line of melody were almost entirely in a singsong style called **recitative** ("*reh*-si-tah-*teev*"). During some early recitatives, singers went so far as to grimace, act, and imitate inflections of crying and gasping. Whatever the merits of such attempts at artistic expression, they did open up a new dimension in vocal music. The single melody could have a wider range, more movement by half steps, and more rhythmic freedom than a line in a traditional Renaissance motet.

Because the main objective of recitatives was to express the text, composers did not attempt to write memorable melodies for them. They would save such melodies for other pieces of music. And they seldom repeated words in recitatives because they wanted to cover the text in as direct and expressive a way as possible.

Metrical Rhythm

Renaissance music usually has a sense of even flow. It does not, however, provide a sense of metrical pattern. That was to change in Baroque music. Regular metrical patterns became the norm. In fact, Baroque music seemed to be subject to what was sometimes referred to as "the tyranny of the bar line." And bar lines began to appear in music notation during this time. Because of its regular beat, and because most Baroque orchestras and choral groups were small, musical works were performed without a conductor.

There is one exception to the strict metrical quality of Baroque rhythm: recitatives. Although the notation of recitatives contains bar lines, musicians understood then, and still understand today, that the music is to be performed very flexibly. The accompanying orchestra or keyboard player follows whatever changes singers make in the flow of the music.

Major/Minor Keys

Prior to the Baroque, musicians had used scale patterns called **modes**. The modes followed the pattern of whole and half steps beginning and ending on each of the white keys on the piano — C to C, D to D, and so on. Two of those patterns were retained in the Baroque: the one from C to C, which is major, and the one from A to A, which is minor. The other five patterns were almost never used again until the twentieth century, although they continued prominently in folk music.

Actually, the mode from B to B was rarely used. Try playing it on a keyboard instrument, and you will hear why.

Tonal Center

Tonality and cadences are discussed in Chapter 3.

The Baroque period saw the establishment of music with a **tonal center,** or **key center,** and the systematic use of harmony. Prior to that time, composers concentrated on fitting the lines of music together well. Now composers began to think much more about how the progression of chords affected the music. They based their use of chords around the "magnetic pull" of the tonal center.

Modulation

Music with no modulations is like a room with beige carpeting, beige draperies, beige walls and ceiling, and beige furniture.

Having established a key center, Baroque composers then devised ways of changing it during a recitative or other musical work. Today listeners are so used to hearing music modulate that they are not aware of how monotonous music would sound without it. Changes of key center, or **modulation;** make music more interesting.

Doctrine of Affections

The distinctive treatment of the words in recitatives and other vocal music illustrates the belief of Baroque composers in projecting the ideas of the text in the music. Called the **doctrine of affections** or **doctrine of affects,** this belief is often evident in Baroque music. Because the type of music associated with particular moods or ideas is often not known by listeners today, this doctrine is largely of historical interest; however, the concept of music expressing the text certainly is not. The doctrine of affections is also reflected in the consistent mood that is maintained throughout an entire section of a work.

As used in the doctrine of affections, the word *affections* refers to all feelings, not just love.

HANDEL'S "THE VOICE OF HIM THAT CRIETH IN THE WILDERNESS" FROM *MESSIAH*

The recitative "The Voice of Him That Crieth in the Wilderness" contains all the features of Baroque music discussed thus far, except metrical rhythm. It is for a tenor and appears early in Handel's oratorio *Messiah*, which is presented in the next chapter. It is typical for the following reasons:

The "voice in the wilderness" refers to John, the Baptist.

- It is very expressive of the text. Notice the treatment of the word *crieth* in the first phrase, the word *straight* in the third phrase, and the word *highway* in the fourth phrase. Listen to how the singer brings out these words.

- It features a single melodic line with accompaniment; it is clearly homophonic in texture. Almost all the musical interest is in the melodic line; the accompanying part is limited to a few chords.

- Its melody is not very distinctive. The more memorable melodies are found elsewhere in Baroque music.

- The singer sings the rhythm freely, even though it has bar lines and a meter signature.

- It begins with a tonal center, E major.

- It modulates and concludes with a different tonal center, A major, which is firmly established with a V-I cadence in the final two chords of the accompaniment.

- It demonstrates the doctrine of affections by the emphasis it places on words such as *crieth* and *highway*.

GEORGE FRIDERIC HANDEL

"The Voice of Him That Crieth in the Wilderness" from *Messiah* (1741)

GENRE: Recitative, oratorio   Tenor and orchestra

CD 1 Track 21
27 seconds

0:00 **21** 0:00 Accompanied by a few chords, the tenor sings:

The voice of him that crieth in the wilderness,
Prepare ye the way of the Lord,

0:15 *Make straight in the desert*
A highway for our God.

0:27 Recitative ends with simple V-1 cadence.

LISTENING GUIDE

FEATURES OF BAROQUE INSTRUMENTAL MUSIC

Tuning

A significant breakthrough was made during the Baroque in how instruments were tuned, a problem that had plagued musicians since the time of Pythagoras around 555 BC. Pythagoras's discovery of certain basic intervals did not solve the problem of precisely where the intervening notes should be placed. The situation was made much more difficult by a caprice of nature. Theoretically, if you play a series of intervals of a fifth, ascending or descending from a given note, the thirteenth note should duplicate the original pitch. But if the Pythagorean ratio for the fifth is used, and if the fifths are computed upward, the thirteenth note is noticeably higher than it should be!

This phenomenon is known as the *Pythagorean comma*.

This pitch problem did not bother singers or string players, because they could easily make slight pitch adjustments to account for it. But it was quite different for keyboard instruments, which have fixed pitches. To get perfect tuning in some keys, people who tuned keyboard instruments had to sacrifice the pitch accuracy in others. Keys with several sharps or flats were therefore usually avoided, because keys with few sharps or flats were normally favored in the tuning process. These tuning complications meant that the only modulations likely on keyboard instruments were those to nearly related keys.

Bach's two-volume (forty-eight-piece) work known as the *Well-Tempered Clavier* is a musical landmark.

The problem was resolved through a compromise: Make all the intervals slightly off so that the distance between all half steps is equal. The term for this tuning practice is **equal temperament,** and it is the system of tuning still used today. To promote better systems of tuning and to help develop a player's technique for playing in all keys, a few composers, including Bach, wrote a series of pieces in all twenty-four major and minor keys.

Terraced Dynamics

A gradual increase or decrease in dynamic levels was not common in Baroque music. Renaissance composers placed no dynamic markings in their music at all, and Baroque composers wrote very few. Often composers rehearsed and performed their own music, so extensive markings were not necessary. The few indications that are present, however, call for abrupt changes of dynamic level. A *forte,* or loud level, changed suddenly to a *piano,* or soft level, and vice versa. These abrupt changes are called **terraced dynamics.** They were probably made in this way because Baroque artists and musicians were interested in dramatic contrasts. Also, the keyboard instruments of the time could not make gradual changes. The organ and harpsichord could change dynamic levels only by coupling manuals, adding pedals, or pulling out stops.

Continuo

The harmonies in Baroque music became so well standardized that musicians devised a shorthand system called **figured bass** to notate chords. The composer provided a bass line that contained cues in the form of numbers and an occasional sharp, flat, or natural to indicate the parts between the highest and lowest notes. Keyboard players were expected to read these symbols while performing the music, a process called **realization.**

The highest and lowest parts became the two important lines, with the melody being the most important. The bass part provided a foundation to the music. Because it sounded nearly all the time, it came to be known as the **basso continuo** (continuous bass), which for convenience is usually shortened to **continuo.** A cello, gamba, or bassoon usually played the continuo line along with the keyboard player.

CODA

In many important ways Baroque music differs from Renaissance music. Homophonic texture was developed for the dramatic expression of the text (especially in recitatives), metrical rhythm became standard (except in recitatives), systematic harmony with its movable tonal center became the norm, major and minor keys and chords replaced modes, equal temperament was introduced, and the continuo part became a feature of instrumental music along with the use of terraced dynamics. Many of these features can be found in much of the music being composed today.

11 Oratorio *and* Cantata

Opera is presented in Chapter 12.

Three dramatic genres of music were developed during the Baroque period: oratorio, cantata, and opera. This chapter concentrates on the oratorio and the cantata.

ORATORIO

Because of the cost of hiring an orchestra, oratorios are usually performed with organ.

An **oratorio** is a lengthy musical work for voices and orchestra. Oratorios consist of many arias, recitatives, and choruses, plus a few sections for the accompanying orchestra. When oratorios first appeared on the musical scene early in the Baroque, they were more like operas on religious topics, complete with scenery, costumes, and actions. Long before the end of the Baroque, however, the stage elements had been discarded, but the idea of drama remained. Soloists still represented specific characters, the text related a story, and the music exploited the dramatic situation.

The Old Testament with its dramatic stories is an especially rich source for oratorio texts.

Although oratorios are on religious topics, they are not intended for use in worship services. They are too long and require too many performers. Instead, they were created for performance in concert halls or special occasions in churches.

Handel's *Messiah*

Nearly three hours are required to perform all the music in *Messiah*. Today conductors usually select which sections they wish to perform.

Probably the most famous oratorio of all time is *Messiah* by George Frideric Handel. It consists of fifty-three sections: nineteen choruses, sixteen arias, sixteen recitatives, and two sections for orchestra alone. It is typical in terms of its length and distribution of sections. It is not so typical, however, in that its text is taken entirely from the Bible. Although based on biblical stories, oratorios normally were not confined to scripture. *Messiah* also lacks a role for a narrator, usually a tenor, who relates the story. It is primarily a contemplation on Christian belief in three parts: the prophecy and Christ's birth, his suffering and death, and the Resurrection and Redemption.

Word of the new work spread before the premiere. Because only seven hundred people could be squeezed into the hall—even though they stood because the hall had no seats—advertisements requested that ladies avoid wearing dresses with hoops and men come without swords.

Messiah is also atypical in terms of its success with audiences over the more than 250 years since it was written, as well as its many translations into other languages and a multitude of recordings.

ARIA

In addition to recitative, a second type of music for one singer with accompaniment that developed during the Baroque was the **aria** ("*ar*-ee-ah"). Arias are very different from recitatives in a number of ways.

1. Arias are much longer than recitatives. For example, "Ev'ry Valley Shall Be Exalted" from Handel's *Messiah* is eight times as long as the recitative "The Voice of Him."
2. The accompanying orchestra has a much larger and more important role in the aria. The accompaniments usually have some musically interesting passages, which they often perform without the soloist. The orchestra may also reiterate a figure that the soloist has sung, or it may play musical material of its own.
3. In arias the soloists frequently sing rapidly moving notes or perform long phrases on one word or syllable, a feature that is prominent in "Ev'ry Valley Shall Be Exalted."

4. Although most arias are much longer than recitatives, often their texts are shorter. Arias are usually longer because they often repeat words and phrases, as well as contain passages for the accompanying instruments.

5. The texts of arias dwell on a single idea. Sometimes they are like sung soliloquies that offer reactions to situations. Usually, they do not advance the story by describing an event. The mood of "Ev'ry Valley Shall Be Exalted" is filled with a sense of anticipation.

6. Arias often have a formal pattern, and sections of them are generally repeated. "Ev'ry Valley Shall Be Exalted" follows a binary *A B A B* form.

7. Arias follow the strict metrical rhythm and steady beat found in most Baroque music. Except for unmetered recitatives, Baroque rhythm is very straightforward. Changes of tempo in arias and other works are permitted only near the ends of sections in a long work.

8. Composers intended arias to stand on their own musical merits to a much greater extent than recitatives, which often serve mainly to advance the story or to be a bridge between sections. For this reason, they gave arias more memorable melodic and vocal qualities.

"Ev'ry Valley Shall Be Exalted" from *Messiah*

The upbeat mood of "Ev'ry Valley" allowed Handel to write music that shows off the singer's vocal prowess through long series (called **runs** by musicians) of sixteenth notes on the word "exalted":

These runs are examples of the Baroque practice of *virtuoso singing*. A **virtuoso** is someone who has outstanding skill in performing.

Much attention was given to soloists in the Baroque. Vocalists competed with one another for the favor of audiences by adding flashy runs and ornaments to the music. This custom grew until the music became merely a framework for soloists to build on as they wished. Some astonishing singing skill was the result, but the quality of the music often suffered. Although the situation had been somewhat moderated by Handel's time, the virtuoso style was still very much alive, and audiences expected to hear some vocal displays.

In "Ev'ry Valley" the runs do more than show off the skill of the singer. Handel integrates them into the overall musical fabric so that they enhance the effect of the music and emphasize the message of the words.

The text of "Ev'ry Valley" says basically that things are going to be turned upside down when the Messiah comes. The valleys will be raised up—they will be exalted. By having the soloist sing long runs on "exalted," Handel emphasizes that thought.

Virtuoso passages in Baroque vocal music are sometimes baffling to people who are not familiar with it. At first glance it is difficult to understand why one syllable or word is stretched out over forty or more notes. "Exalted" could be sung with just three notes, of course. In everyday practical terms, it seems pointless to use forty notes to sing one syllable or word. But the music would not have nearly so much impact and interest. It is impressive to hear a skilled singer execute long runs and to hear them fit so well into the music.

The word *virtuoso* is not restricted to music. It can also describe performances by very skilled athletes, dancers, and others.

Handel follows the doctrine of affections in the aria as well as the chorus. The words "The crooked straight" are set to pitches that rock back and forth one step apart, except the word "straight," which is a steady long note. The word "mountain" is high, and the word "low" is low. The word "plain" is set in a sequence of smooth planes.

LISTENING GUIDE

GEORGE FRIDERIC HANDEL

"Ev'ry Valley Shall Be Exalted" from *Messiah* (1741)

GENRE: Aria, oratorio   Tenor and orchestra

CD 1 Tracks 22–23
3 minutes 40 seconds

Form: *A B A B*

0:00	**22**	0:00	The orchestra plays a *ritornello* (refrain).
		0:22	The tenor soloist sings "Ev'ry valley shall be exalted" (A).

Ev-'ry val - ley,   ev-'ry val - ley ——shall   be ex-alt - ed,

		0:35	First long run on "exalted."
		0:50	Second long run on "exalted."
		0:58	Aria continues "and ev'ry mountain and hill made low."
1:04	**23**	0:00	B portion begins with "the crooked straight" and continues with "and the rough places plain."
		0:42	A returns with some changes.
		1:24	B returns with some changes.
		1:54	Tempo slows, and some decorative notes are added.
		2:12	The orchestra repeats the ritornello.
		2:36	"Ev'ry Valley" concludes with a solid ending.

What is it about the arias from Handel's *Messiah* that motivates people to listen to them more than 250 years after they were written? They feature several exceptional qualities:

- They demonstrate the expressive impact when words and music are combined so skillfully. When a sensitive recitative or a tender aria is sung well, the music has much expressive power.

- They exhibit the virtuoso techniques of a good singer. Hearing a virtuoso singer executing the difficult or showy passages of an aria is similar to watching a champion figure skater flawlessly execute a difficult routine.

- They contain the qualities of Baroque music that help it "wear well" with listeners.

Handel established a standard for the oratorio in England and America, a standard that has lasted.

CHORUS

This is logical, albeit a bit confusing.

The word **chorus** has two meanings in music. One is a group that sings choral music. The other meaning refers to the choral sections of a large choral work such as an oratorio or opera. So a chorus sings a chorus.

George Frideric Handel

© Corbis-Bettmann

George Frideric Handel (1685–1759) was a German by birth, the son of a well-to-do barber-surgeon in the city of Halle in Saxony, who never wanted his son to pursue music as a career. Young George showed much talent in composing and playing the harpsichord and organ. His father's early death removed the obstacle to pursuing a career in music. After a year of college, he went to Hamburg, where he got a job playing in an orchestra.

Handel soon moved to Italy, which was the center for music at that time. He studied composition and cultivated friendships with music patrons. At the age of twenty-five, he returned to Germany as music director of the Electoral Court at Hanover. In two years he managed to take two leaves of absence to go to London, where his operas (in Italian) were very successful. He was in London when the elector of Hanover was proclaimed King George I of England.

Handel stayed in London for the remainder of his life. For eight years he held an important position as director of the Royal Academy of Music, which was founded to present Italian opera. The job was not an easy one. The musicians were temperamental and engaged in much infighting, and the situation was not helped by Handel's stubborn and overbearing personality.

One hair-pulling and shouting fight between singers took place at a performance when Princess Caroline (for whom North and South Carolina were named) was in the audience.

In time another type of musical theater became fashionable with English audiences. Called *beggar's opera*, it was more like a play with politically satirical songs inserted. Handel refused to abandon his Italian operas, however. After nine more years of writing and losing money in that endeavor, his health broke and he was heavily in debt. He went abroad to recover.

And recover he did. After a few more futile tries at reviving Italian opera, he turned to oratorios. Within a few years, he was again at the top of the English musical world. He wrote more than twenty-six oratorios, but none is heard as often today as *Messiah*. Handel composed this monumental work in 1741 in a little more than three weeks! He worked at it almost constantly and paid little attention to the meals servants left at his door. Its first performance was a benefit concert in Dublin, Ireland. It was a tremendous success, although later performances in London were received more coolly.

In 1759 Handel collapsed after conducting a performance of *Messiah*. He died eight days later and was interred with state honors in Westminster Abbey.

BEST-KNOWN WORKS

oratorios:
- *Messiah*
- *Israel in Egypt*
- *Samson*
- *Saul*

opera:
- *Acis and Galatea*
- *Giulio Cesare (Julius Caesar)*
- *Semele*
- *Hercules*

instrumental suites:
- *Water Music*
- *Fireworks Music*

Choruses can vary a lot in size. They can have as few as sixteen singers, although that is unusual, or they can have several hundred singers, but that also is unusual. More typical is that they contain approximately an equal number of men and women, unless they are specifically limited to men or women. The choruses that sang Handel's *Messiah* during his lifetime were definitely on the small side; only eighteen singers made up the chorus at its premiere performance.

The following are characteristics of choruses in Baroque choral works:

- They are somewhat lengthy and often repeat words.
- The rhythm is strictly adhered to, unlike what happens in recitatives.
- The accompanying part plays an important role.

A hundred years later at a festival honoring Handel, a chorus of four thousand and an orchestra of five hundred performed his music!

- The music for choruses normally requires more than average singing skill. In fact, some of them are quite challenging and contain virtuoso-like passages.
- They are often contrapuntal. The various sections often enter in imitation.

"Hallelujah Chorus" from *Messiah*

The "Hallelujah Chorus" is familiar to most people and is traditionally performed at Christmas. In fact, at the first performance of *Messiah* in London, King George II was so impressed when he heard "Hallelujah Chorus" that he stood up. In those days, when the king stood, everyone stood. King George's spontaneous action started a tradition that is still honored today.

As you listen to this chorus, notice how skillfully Handel has placed the words in terms of their rhythmic emphasis. The word *Hallelujah* is written as one would say it when really pleased. In phrases such as "and He shall reign forever and ever," the important words in the phrase land on the important beats and parts of the beats in the rhythm pattern. The important words in the phrase are *He, reign,* and *ev-* of *forever,* because it is the emphasized syllable in that word. It would be much more difficult to sing the phrase, "*and* he *shall* reign *for-ev-er,*" and it would sound awkward and unmusical.

Handel did a lot of things right in "Hallelujah Chorus" in addition to matching words and music so well. In the first part, he contrasts quick "Hallelujahs" with the steady, solid-sounding "For the Lord God Omnipotent reigneth." He uses text painting when he has the first four notes of that phrase ascend by step up to the word "God." In the middle section, the words "The Kingdom of the world" are sung softly at a low pitch level. Then they become much louder and higher as the words progress: "is become of the Kingdom of

> To realize how important the placement of emphasis in words is, try saying "Hallelujah" in different ways: "*HAL*-le-*lu*-jah," "Ha-*le*-lu-*JAH,*" and so on.

> Handel's success in matching words and music is especially interesting because he never learned to speak English well after emigrating from Germany in his late twenties.

LISTENING GUIDE

GEORGE FRIDERIC HANDEL

"Hallelujah Chorus" from *Messiah* (1741)

GENRE: Chorus, oratorio   Chorus and orchestra

CD 1 Tracks 24–26
3 minutes 37 seconds

0:00 **24** 0:00 Orchestra plays a short introduction.

0:07 Chorus sings "Hallelujah" five times, then five more times at a different pitch level.

0:24 Chorus sings "for the Lord God Omnipotent reigneth," followed by four "Hallelujahs."

0:35 Altos, tenors, and basses repeat "for the Lord God . . . ," followed by four "Hallelujahs."

0:46 Sopranos sing "for the Lord God . . . ," with chorus singing "Hallelujah" in counterpoint.

0:53 Tenors and basses sing "for the Lord God . . ." while sopranos and altos sing contrasting "Hallelujahs."

1:02 Altos and tenors sing "for the Lord God . . ." while sopranos and basses sing contrapuntal "Hallelujahs."

1:12 **25** 0:00 Chorus sings together "The kingdom of this world is become the Kingdom of our Lord and of His Christ."

1:30 **26** 0:00 Basses begin new melodic phrase and text, "and He shall reign forever and ever," followed in imitation by tenors, altos, and sopranos.

0:22	Sopranos and altos sing alternately "King of Kings" and "Lord of Lords" while basses and tenors sing "forever and ever, Hallelujah." Same pattern repeated four times, each time at a higher pitch level.
1:03	Basses begin "and He shall reign . . ." as other sections sing contrasting material.
1:14	Tenors sing "King of Kings" and "Lord of Lords" while other sections respond with "forever and ever" and "Hallelujah."
1:23	Chorus sings together, with basses singing "and He shall reign . . . ," followed by "King of Kings."
2:07	"Hallelujah Chorus" ends after four "Hallelujahs" and one long final "Hallelujah."

our Lord . . ." At one point in the third section, he builds on the words "King of Kings, and Lord of Lords" by repeating them several times in succession, each time at a higher level of pitch. Finally, the trumpets enter to bolster the dramatic impact of the music at that point. Especially important is the sense of power and grandeur that this chorus conveys.

CHORALE

The chorale was a product of early Protestant belief and practice in the sixteenth century, when Martin Luther's break from the Roman Catholic Church became final. Luther and some of his colleagues set about providing music suitable for worship in the newly developed services. They wanted the members of the congregation to be participants in the service, not just observers.

One way to involve them was to have them sing. But what should they sing? Chant was associated too strongly with the rejected Roman Catholic Church. Also, its style and subtleties are difficult for untrained singers to perform properly. The answer was to create a new body of religious music that had strong, simple melodies. So from German religious songs, from adaptations of chant and secular tunes, and from the pen of Luther himself and others came the **chorale,** which is basically a German Lutheran hymn.

Luther believed not only that worshipers should sing but also that their music should encourage the proper religious attitude. So one purpose of the chorale was to proclaim beliefs and contribute to the spirit of worship. The Protestant attitudes of that time are clearly expressed in "A Mighty Fortress Is Our God." Here is a translation of one verse:

> *Though devils all the world should fill,*
> *All eager to devour us;*
> *We tremble not, we fear no ill,*
> *They shall not overpower us.*

As his metaphor for God, Luther chose the German word *Burg*, a medieval stone fortress, a symbol of austere strength. The chorale reflects the serious religious outlook of the early Protestants. Each note in its melody stands like a block of stone in a fortress.

Musically, a chorale-hymn is very different from Gregorian chant:

- A hymn has a regular rhythm.
- It is in German or other vernacular language.
- It has several verses of words for the same melody.
- It can be accompanied by organ or other instrument.

On first hearing, a chorale, like Gregorian chant, may seem uninteresting. It's true; both lack novelty and flashiness. But religious music seeks to express what the faithful believe to be the ultimate and eternal. Theological beliefs and the music need to be congruent, with one reflecting the other. Furthermore, both the chorale and the chant provide devout worshipers with a sense of communion with believers who have gone before, as well as suggest the timeless nature of their beliefs.

It is very likely that Luther himself composed the words and music for "A Mighty Fortress Is Our God."

A chorale is presented as part of Bach's cantata later in this chapter.

JOHANN SEBASTIAN BACH

"Zion Hears the Watchmen" (Section 4) from Cantata No. 140 (1731)

GENRE: Cantata Tenor section and orchestra

CD 1 Tracks 27–28
4 minutes 15 seconds

0:00 **27** 0:00   Upper strings play a flowing melody above a steady bass:

0:43   Tenors sing the first three phrases of the chorale in unison:

Zion hört die Wächter singen,	*Zion hears the watchmen calling,*
das Herz thut ihr vor Freuden springen,	*her heart within her leaps for gladness,*
sie wachet, und steht eilend auf,	*she wakes and stands to hasten forth,*

1:11   The flowing melody is repeated by upper strings.

1:52   The first three phrases of the chorale are repeated, but with different words:

Ihr Freund kommt vom Himmel prächtig,	*Her friend comes from Heaven in splendor,*
Von Gnaden stark, von Wahrheit mächtig,	*In mercy strong, in truth almighty,*
Ihr Licht wird hell, ihr Stern geht auf.	*Her light grows bright, her star appears.*

2:22   The flowing melody is repeated by upper strings.

2:47 **28** 0:00   The fourth, fifth, and sixth phrases of the chorale are sung:

Nun komm, du werthe Kron',	*Now come, thou precious crown,*
Herr Jesu, Gottes Sohn,	*Lord Jesus, God's Son,*
Hosianna!	*Hosanna!*

0:23   The flowing melody continues, but in minor.

0:41   The seventh and eighth phrases of the chorale are sung.

Wir folgen all' zum Freudensaal,	*We follow all to the festive hall,*
und halten mit das Abendmahl.	*and share in our Lord's Supper there.*

1:28   The section of the cantata concludes with upper strings playing the flowing melody.

renewed interest in other music by Bach. Like the cantatas, the *St. Matthew Passion* gives a prominent place to a chorale, "O Sacred Head Now Wounded."

There is also a Baroque motet. It is an unaccompanied, religious, and polyphonic work. In the Baroque, however, the music had a strong sense of metrical rhythm and systematic harmony. It was also written in a vernacular language.

CODA

Baroque music is rarely flashy or overwhelming. Instead, it is quite predictable as it moves along through its somewhat standardized style. Yet there is something about it that is so logical, so satisfying, so comfortable, so moving, so right!

Opera *in the* Baroque

12

Drama was one of the main features of Baroque style. The carefully planned figures in Renaissance paintings were replaced with twisting lines and energetic poses, and restrained polyphonic motets and madrigals gave way to recitatives and arias that projected emotion and feelings. The goals of artists and composers had changed—dramatically.

Opera was one result of the desire to make music more expressive. It was founded as an attempt to re-create the dramas of ancient Greece. Around 1600 a group of noblemen in Florence, Italy, believed that a single line of melody with simple accompaniment would be much more expressive of the words. The result was the development of recitative. In fact, the earliest operas consisted almost entirely of recitatives.

One of the group of noblemen was Vincenzio Galilei, father of the famous astronomer Galileo Galilei.

But do audiences enjoy listening to a couple of hours of nothing but one recitative after another? Soon composers began to realize that the answer to that question was no. Something more was needed. By the time the first opera house opened in Venice in 1637, the artistic goal of a musical version of ancient Greek drama had been largely forgotten. The stories became burdened by the addition of irrelevant incidents, spectacular scenes, and incongruous comedy episodes. But other changes were more constructive. Arias, duets, and ensembles evolved, and the accompanying orchestra took on more importance.

As opera spread throughout Europe, its dramatic elements were largely absent. The singers reigned supreme. In their desire to hold the attention of the audience, soloists added all sorts of embellishments to a melody to show off their singing prowess. In fact, the musical notation of an opera was often only a framework around which singers created elaborate vocal structures.

Although opera was a child of the Baroque, the operas of that period are not often performed today in opera houses in Europe or America. The reason is not that the Baroque operas lack musical merit but that opera companies can produce only a limited number of operas, and subsequent operas have found greater favor with audiences. Nevertheless, the operas of a few Baroque composers stand out, especially those of Claudio Monteverdi and Henry Purcell, which are presented later in this chapter.

THE ELEMENTS OF OPERA

Each element in the amalgam that is opera makes a particular contribution, and each merits further discussion, beginning with singers and their voice ranges and types.

Voices and Roles

Opera has acquired a number of traditions regarding the types of voices and characters portrayed. The heroine is almost always a soprano. In most operas she is young and beautiful, so a high, lighter voice is appropriate. Often the heroine's part calls for virtuoso singing. Some female parts are written for lower or heavier voices such as mezzo-soprano or contralto. These roles often portray older women, servants, rivals, or villainesses.

The leading male role is often for a tenor. He is young and frequently sings duets with the leading soprano, often doubling her pitches one octave lower. This puts his notes near the top of the male voice range and gives the singing more intensity. Other male parts may be sung by a baritone, a voice that is lower and heavier than the tenor. The

In Western civilization there seems to be an association in people's minds between age and the pitch level of the voice: the older a person is, the lower the voice.

SINGERS PERFORM IN *THE CORONATION OF POPPEA*
Nigel Robson and Marie Angel perform in an Opera Factory production of *The Coronation of Poppea*.

bass, which is the lowest and heaviest male voice, is often used to portray villains, older men, or authority figures such as kings.

The vocal and dramatic demands for singing operatic roles are great. Almost all roles require extensive training in the use of the voice to achieve the necessary breath control, endurance, wide pitch range, richness of tone quality, control of dynamic levels, and technical know-how, not to mention the ability to project the singing over an orchestra all the way to the last row of the balcony. Not only do opera singers sing but they must also be actors in a drama. They must make their efforts sound and look convincing.

Operas are usually sung without amplification.

Ensembles

Most operas have parts for small ensembles and choruses. **Ensembles** frequently consist of several characters singing different words and music expressing their particular feelings, creating a kind of musical and emotional counterpoint.

Operatic choruses usually appear in scenes with many people — a wedding, a coronation, a crowded tavern. To a degree, the chorus participates in the stage action, but usually from behind the soloists. Often the words the chorus sings are a commentary on the situation.

The Orchestra

The orchestra is placed largely out of sight in a pit in front of the stage. Although unseen, it has an important role in opera. Not only does the orchestra accompany the singers, it also sets moods, enhances the actions onstage, and performs overtures and preludes while the curtain is closed. The orchestral music written for operas by some nineteenth-century composers is so complete that today portions of it are frequently performed as concert works without any singing at all.

The Libretto

Libretto means "little book" in Italian.

The script or text of an opera is called the **libretto.** The composer of the music usually does not write the libretto for the opera. Instead, a librettist generally creates a version of a play, historical event, or story. Often the libretto is set in poetic form, especially the portions that are likely places for arias or choruses. Once the libretto has been written, the composer takes over and sets the words to music.

Staging

Visual elements are an integral part of opera. The quality of acting, costumes, scenic design, lighting, and dancing makes a great difference in the success of an opera. The lighting and stage effects that can be achieved in a first-rate opera house are truly amazing and at times dazzling. For example, if a character is to be demolished in smoke and fire, this can be done in quite a convincing and dramatic way.

Smoke and fire finish off Don Giovanni in Mozart's opera.

The need for set designers, costumers, electricians, and stagehands in addition to singers, orchestral musicians, and sometimes dancers is one of opera's greatest obstacles: It is a very expensive art form. A large opera can require the services of several hundred highly skilled technicians and musicians, and this need is usually reflected in the high ticket prices and the chronic financial problems of opera companies. A lack of funds also discourages touring by opera companies and presentations of new operas. The fact that opera is still active and vital in American musical life, in spite of its high costs and lack of familiarity to much of the population, is eloquent testimony to its musical and dramatic value.

The technicians and stagehands often are paid more than the dancers or members of the chorus.

OPERATIC CONVENTIONS

All forms of theater have conventions and customs that audiences accept. For example, in films an orchestra is heard in the background, adding to the suspense as an actor is about to be attacked in a dark, deserted house. What's an orchestra doing there? No one wonders about that, because viewers are accustomed to the convention of background music. Nor is anyone bothered when a scene changes in a few seconds to one that supposedly occurs hours or even years later, or that the stage in a theater is like a room with one wall removed so that the audience can see what's going on.

Music for films is discussed in Chapter 39.

The reason people are not bothered by these conventions is simple: They are used to them. On the other hand, most people are not familiar with operatic customs, and so such customs often hinder their enjoyment.

What are the more obvious conventions associated with opera? One is the replacement of speaking with singing. In everyday life a phrase such as "Robert will be here at three o'clock" is spoken. Furthermore, sometimes rather robust singing takes place when logically it does not make a lot of sense—such as when a character is dying or very sick.

Not only are all the words sung, but they are sung in a highly trained style, which is another operatic convention. Most operas have a "bigger than life" quality about them, and that is one of their attractive features. The style of singing, therefore, needs to be bigger than life. It must have enough power to be heard over an orchestra in a large hall, and it should have a quality that moves listeners emotionally. Folk singers can sing their ballads in a simple, unaffected style because they usually perform in a small room accompanied by a guitar, and even then their singing is often amplified.

Neither singing style is more musical than the other because each is appropriate for a particular type of music and setting.

Another convention concerns the words. Even when sung in English, they are not easily understood. The problem is increased by the large number of operas in foreign languages. These operas can be translated and sung in English, but should they be? Although translations are not easy, involving correct numbers of syllables, natural accents, shades of meaning, and rhyme schemes, the answer is probably yes, at least for people who are not familiar with opera. When operas are sung in languages other than English, listeners need to follow a translation or a good synopsis of the opera.

It is almost impossible to translate the lines of an opera without losing some of their original meaning.

A fourth convention involves the element of time. In addition to the usual flexibility in the treatment of time in films and dramas, operas have to deal with the impact of singing on the amount of time available. If the words "Robert will be here at three o'clock" are spoken, they don't require much time. If those words were set to a nice melody, however, they would take much more time. The difference would be some pleasant music, but an interruption of the story. If the words were to be sung in about the same

The increased impact of music on words can be demonstrated by reading the words of an aria or a chorus aloud and then hearing those same words as they have been set to music by a great composer.

amount of time as when spoken, they would not be of much musical interest. Opera-goers accept the distortions of time caused by the addition of the music, because of the heightened overall musical and dramatic impact.

ENJOYING OPERA

When the conventions of opera are accepted, most people find that they enjoy attending an opera. This is true for several reasons:

- The music is often stunning and beautiful. Operas offer listeners a rich source of flowing melodies, impressive tonal effects, and sensuous harmonies. And, of course, there is a great deal of outstanding singing.

- The combined expressiveness of words and music is a pleasure to hear. Opera sets up situations in which the combination of the two can have even greater emotional impact than music apart from the dramatic situation. While the singing of the text may slow down the action on stage, it adds much to the overall drama. Some operatic I-love-yous, for example, can cause chills to run up one's spine.

- Opera appeals to both the ears and the eyes. Looking at an opera without hearing the music is an incomplete experience, just as it would be when listening to the music without seeing what takes place onstage.

Soap operas were given that name because originally they were often sponsored by soap companies, and also because the character's lives are much more crisis-ridden than those of ordinary people.

- Opera lets people see and hear experiences that are beyond ordinary life. For some rather deep-seated psychological reasons, people enjoy stories, films, television shows, and the like that take them temporarily out of their own everyday existence. In soap operas, for example, the actors undergo traumatic experiences with a frequency and an intensity that (fortunately) far exceed what most people encounter in their lives. Good opera is good theater.

Claudio Monteverdi

BEST-KNOWN WORKS

opera:
- *Combattimento di Tancredi et Clorinda*
- *L'incoronazione di Poppea*
- *L'Orfeo*

The most influential composer of the early Baroque was **Claudio Monteverdi** (1567–1643). He was born in Cremona, Italy, which was famous for its violin makers, and his early musical training included learning to play the violin. His father was a chemist/physician who wanted his son to have a good education in music. Monteverdi was first employed as a court musician at Mantova and later was appointed to be in charge of the music there. He left when the duke failed to pay him some of the wages due him. At the age of forty-five, he was awarded the coveted position as music master at Saint Mark's in Venice.

Monteverdi began writing madrigals in the Renaissance, but slowly his madrigals began to change. Instrumental parts were added, and they became more homophonic in texture. In a real sense, he bridged the Renaissance and Baroque periods and helped bring about a major change in music.

Although his position in Venice was to produce music for the church, he never stopped composing operas. *L'Orfeo* (*Orpheus*), written in 1607, was his first successful opera and one of the most important in the development of Western music. *L'incoronazione di Poppea* (*The Coronation of Poppea*), composed in 1642, was his last. He was very effective in injecting emotional qualities into his music. He was also probably the first composer to ask the violinists for effects such as *tremolo* (rapidly moving the bow back and forth on the string) and vibrato to add warmth to the tone quality.

MONTEVERDI'S *CORONATION OF POPPEA*

Monteverdi was the most important composer of the early Baroque, and especially of opera. His last opera was *The Coronation of Poppea*. The story is based very loosely on the Roman emperor Nero, who reigned from AD 54 to 68 and who is remembered throughout history for fiddling while Rome burned. He was a weak, vain man who pursued many women. Poppea knew how to play up to Nero's passions, and by careful scheming she was able to dispose of his wife so that Nero would marry her and make her empress.

The plot of Monteverdi's opera is characterized by much intrigue among the characters. Poppea is spared from an assassin by the intervention of the god Cupid, and she achieves her goal of becoming empress of the Roman Empire.

Many characteristics of recitative can be heard in a portion of Monteverdi's *Coronation of Poppea*. In the excerpt presented here, dawn has just broken, and the scheming Poppea, having enticed Nero to spend the night with her, tries to delay his departure as long as possible and make him promise to return. Several times she sings the word "Tornerai?" ("Won't you return?") in a seductive way. Notice how the singers' lines follow the natural rise and fall and changes of speed and inflection as the words would if spoken. The recitative style is broken only by a short solo in which Nero sings passionately that he cannot live without her.

Actually, he did not fiddle. Instead, he probably played a lyrelike instrument and sang. He thought of himself as a great singer. Before he committed suicide, he is reported to have said, "What an artist the world is losing in me!"

Poppea's success was short lived. She was murdered, possibly by Nero himself, after only a few years as empress.

Is Poppea able to work her charms on Nero? Check out the Listening Guide.

CLAUDIO MONTEVERDI

Recitative from *The Coronation of Poppea*, Act I, Scene 1 (1642)

GENRE: Recitative duet, opera   Soprano, tenor, and orchestra

CD 3 Track 12
2 minutes 41 seconds

0.00	12	0:00	POPPEA: Tornerai?	Won't you return?
			NERO: Se ben io vò	I leave you only
			Pur teco io stò, pur teco stò . . .	to be with you all the more . . .
			POPPEA: Tornerai?	Won't you return?
			NERO: Il cor dalle tue stella	My heart can never be torn away
			Mai mai non se divelle . . .	from your beautiful eyes . . .
			POPPEA: Tornerai?	Won't you return?

| | | 0:33 | NERO: Io non posso da te, non posso da te da te viver disgiunto | I can never really live away from you |
| | | | Se non si smembra la unità del punto . . . | no more than a soul can be severed from itself . . . |

(Line repeated)

		1:04	POPPEA: Tornerai?	Won't you return?
			NERO: Tornerò.	I will return.
			POPPEA: Quando?	When?
			NERO: Ben tosto.	Very soon.
			POPPEA: Ben tosto, me'l prometti?	Very soon, you promise?
			NERO: Te'l giuro.	I swear it.

| | | 1:17 | POPPEA: E me l'osserverai? | And you will keep your promise? |
| | | | NERO: E s'a te no verrò, tu a me verrai! | If I do not come, you'll come to me! |

(Two lines repeated)

			POPPEA: Addio . . .	Good-bye . . .
			NERO: Addio . . .	Good-bye . . .
			POPPEA: . . . Nerone, Nerone, addio . . .	. . . Nero, Nero, good-bye . . .
			NERO: . . . Poppea, Poppea, addio . . .	. . . Poppea, Poppea, good-bye . . .
			POPPEA: Addio, Nerone, addio!	Good-bye, Nero, good-bye!
			NERO: Addio, Poppea, addio!	Good-bye, Poppea, good-bye!

| | | 2:37 | Scene 1 closes. | |

PURCELL'S *DIDO AND AENEAS*

The story of Dido and Aeneas comes from Virgil's *Aeneid*, one of the masterpieces of classical Latin literature.

Dido and Aeneas was written for a private girls' school in Chelsea outside London. Aeneas, the hero of Troy, is fleeing from his conquered homeland. He sets sail to found the city of Rome but is blown off course onto the shores of Carthage, where Dido is the widowed queen. They meet and fall in love, but soon the gods order Aeneas to continue on to found Rome. Feeling very alone and betrayed, Dido expresses her feelings in the tender and beautiful aria "When I am laid in earth," which is often called "Dido's Lament." Dido and her servant, Belinda, are alone onstage, and only Dido sings. The ostinato is a distinctive feature of this aria.

The term **ostinato** comes from the Italian word for stubborn, and indeed ostinatos are persistently repeated musical phrases. Dido sings her moving melody over the ostinato, and the combination gives the aria the qualities of both unity and variety.

Notice that Dido's phrases are incomplete, as though she were consumed in her thoughts. The exclamation "ah" is sung four times in the aria on a major chord but is followed by a minor chord, as if it cannot shake the shadow of death. Six times she asks to be remembered. She dies as the orchestra plays its closing appearances of the ground bass.

LISTENING GUIDE

HENRY PURCELL

"Dido's Lament" from *Dido and Aeneas* (1689)

GENRE: Recitative and aria, opera   Soprano and orchestra

CD 3 Tracks 13–14
4 minutes 30 seconds

0:00	**13**	0:00	Music opens with a short recitative accompanied by lute and low strings. Dido sings "Thy hand, Belinda! Darkness shades me; on thy bosom let me rest. More I would—but Death invades me: Death is now a welcome guest."
0:47	**14**	0:00	Lute plays the basso ostinato (ground bass).
		0:14	Strings join ground bass. Dido sings "When I am laid in earth, may my wrongs create no trouble in thy breast. Remember me, but ah! forget my fate."

0:34   Ground bass appears seven more times as words of aria are sung.

2:58   Instruments play final two appearances of ground bass.

3:43   Aria concludes quietly.

Henry Purcell

Stapleton Collection / The Bridgeman Art Library

Henry Purcell (c. 1659–1695) was born and lived in England. Despite his short life, he composed an enormous amount of excellent music. Trained as a choirboy, he began composing when he was eight. His voice changed early, so he worked as an assistant in caring for the king's keyboard and wind instruments. He was later appointed organist at Westminster Abbey and composed much music. He probably died of pneumonia. Purcell was buried in Westminster Abbey in recognition of his great contributions to English music.

Purcell was especially adept at writing music for the stage. Although *Dido and Aeneas* was his only true opera, he composed a number of works that combined spoken words with music, as well as music for royal occasions, including the funeral of Queen Mary the year before he died.

BEST-KNOWN WORKS

opera and stage works:
* *Dido and Aeneas*
* *The Fairy Queen*

CODA

Monteverdi's and Purcell's music demonstrates the imaginative quality of Baroque operas. The example by Monteverdi makes effective use of recitative in a duet, whereas Purcell employs an ostinato–ground bass to write a touching, sensitive aria. Opera had been given a good start.

13

Baroque Instrumental Music: Suite *and* Sonata

Some important differences existed between instrumental and vocal music during the Baroque period. That fact alone makes the Baroque different from earlier periods. Until the Baroque, a piece of music was not composed specifically for a particular instrument, with the exception of works for lute or keyboard instruments. In fact, many works could be performed by instruments or voices or both.

The eventual distinction between vocal and instrumental styles was probably inevitable. Instruments and voices do not produce music in the same ways; certain types of music are more suitable for the voice, and others lend themselves better to instruments. For example, a violin or flute can easily produce sounds that are higher than the upper limits of the human voice. Performers on most instruments can also play notes with a speed and clarity that is impossible for a singer to achieve.

In general, Baroque instrumental music tended to be more contrapuntal than homophonic, but the opposite tended to be true for vocal music. There is a logical explanation for this. In vocal music composers tried to project a message; recitatives and arias were developed as a means of giving expression to the ideas contained in the text. Instrumental music was, of course, not affected by a text.

> The human voice has an expressive capability that cannot be achieved on an instrument.

BAROQUE INSTRUMENTS

Two keyboard instruments were important in the Baroque period: the organ and the harpsichord (described in Chapter 6). The organ had existed in a rudimentary form for fifteen hundred years, but it reached its height of development during the Baroque. In fact, some organs built today attempt to replicate those of the eighteenth century. During the late nineteenth and early twentieth centuries, several ranks of pipes were added to organs, especially those built for use in theaters, to imitate the sound of trombones and other instruments. But these synthesized sounds were seldom musically satisfying.

The harpsichord was frequently played during the Renaissance, and it became even more important in the Baroque. When the Baroque period ended, the harpsichord receded insignificance, and it was not heard from much until the twentieth century. There has been a revival of interest in the harpsichord, and new ones are being constructed.

Several orchestral instruments are featured prominently in Baroque music. One is the "whistle" flute, or *recorder*, which is played straight forward from the player's mouth, rather than sideways as flutes are today. This flute was made of wood and had a lighter, less brilliant tone quality.

The trumpet, too, was given important roles during that period. It had no valves, so pitches had

THE ORGAN AND CHOIR LOFT of St. Thomas Church in Leipzig, Germany, where J. S. Bach served for many years.

to be controlled entirely by the player's lips. Many Baroque trumpets were smaller and had narrower bores, which made it easier for players to reach the high notes found in some Baroque compositions.

The violin also played a major role in the Baroque. It looked a little different from the violins of today. The fingerboard was shorter because the players did not play very high notes. The bow curved slightly away from the hair, with a shape somewhat resembling an archer's bow, from which it got its name. The tension on the bow hair was looser, too, and the strings of the instrument were set on a flatter plane, making it easier for violinists to play more than one string at a time. Gut strings were used instead of the metal strings generally in use today.

> Gut strings are really made from dried and treated animal intestines.

PACHELBEL'S CANON IN D

Pachelbel's Canon in D is an unusual work. To begin with, although it was composed around 1680, it was largely forgotten until the latter half of the twentieth century. Suddenly, it seemed to have been "found" by many musicians and has enjoyed enormous popularity since, at least in terms of concert music. More than two hundred versions of it have been recorded, including a few in rock style, and it has found its way into many television commercials and several motion pictures.

> It has served as background music for commercials ranging from GE lightbulbs to Taster's Choice coffee, and in the Academy Award–winning film *Ordinary People* as well as *Father of the Bride*. It was also played at Princess Diana's funeral.

LISTENING GUIDE

JOHANN PACHELBEL
Canon in D (c. 1680)

GENRE: Canon   String orchestra and continuo

CD 3 Tracks 15–17
3 minutes 54 seconds

0:00   **15**   0:00   Continuo part sounds alone.

		0:09	First violin plays one note to the beat. Second violin follows eight beats later, and third violin eight beats later than the second.
		0:26	First violin plays two notes to the beat. Then it plays:
		0:43	—four notes to the beat
		1:00	— one and two notes to the beat in higher range
1:16	**16**	0:00	—part with many notes at the speed of eight to the beat
		0:16	— one short note on the beat, and then off the beat
		0:32	—four notes to the beat that alternate between higher and lower pitch levels
		0:47	—four repeated notes on many beats
2:19	**17**	0:00	—line with two fast notes in each beat
		0:15	—long notes
		0:30	—a contrasting melody
		0:47	—long notes, some starting in the middle of the beat
		1:04	—notes that move one octave to another
		1:35	Canon concludes.

Johann Pachelbel

Adam Woolfitt/Corbis

Johann Pachelbel (1653–1706) was born and died in Nuremberg, Germany. He was a church organist and teacher, counting among his pupils J. S. Bach's teacher. He held several positions as organist and choir director, including one in Stuttgart from which he had to flee because of the French invasion. His longest position was in his native Nuremberg. He composed a great deal of religious choral music and works for organ, which were much admired by J. S. Bach. It's ironic that today he is remembered mostly for just one work, Canon in D.

BEST-KNOWN WORKS

organ:
• Fugues on the *Magnificat*

Purcell also used a ground bass in "Dido's Lament," which was presented in Chapter 12.

Canon in D is unusual in that it combines two different approaches to composition. It is built on a ground bass of eight notes, all of equal length, with every other note a fourth apart. In addition, melodic variations are played over the ground bass twenty-seven times. They appear in three instrumental parts, one following the other eight beats apart in strict imitation—thus the name *canon*.

Originally for three violins and continuo, today it is usually played by a string orchestra and continuo.

National Gallery, Prague, Czech Republic/Giraudon/Art Resource, NY

View of the Thames River and London with St. Paul's Cathedral by Canaletto (1697–1768). The barges are much more elegant than what we think of as barges today.

THE SUITE

The word **suite** ("sweet") as used in music is a series or set of musical works that belong together. During the Baroque, a suite referred to a collection of dances that were intended for performance as a group. Suites were usually written for keyboard instruments.

The dances included in the suites of Handel and other composers of the time were *stylized*; that is, they were "dressed up" to make them interesting pieces for listening. Composers wrote their own music for them, but the meter, tempo, and other characteristics were derived from various types of dances that had previously been in fashion.

A contemporary composer might do the same thing by taking a popular dance of a generation or more ago and writing similar music with more-interesting harmonies while retaining the essential rhythm and style of the original.

Handel's "Hornpipe" from Water Music Suite

Typically, stylized dances are charming, enjoyable short works. Not all suites were written for keyboard instruments. Handel and others composed collections of stylized dance music for wind and string groups as well. Handel's *Water Music*, HWV 348–350, consists of an overture and about twenty dances. It was written in 1717 for an excursion by King George I as he and his large party floated down the River Thames on barges. The king reportedly liked it so much that he had it played three times. It was performed on a total of fifty instruments of different types.

A hornpipe is an energetic, jaunty dance in three beats to the measure. It is in binary form, and the theme is repeated by different groups of instruments.

GEORGE FRIDERIC HANDEL
"Hornpipe" from *Water Music* (1717)

GENRE: Suite   Orchestra

CD 3 Tracks 18–19
2 minutes 23 seconds

Form: Binary

0:00   **18**   0:00   Strings play A theme and then repeat it.

0:24   **19**   0:00   Strings play B theme and then repeat it.

0:23   Woodwinds play A theme and then repeat it.

0:47   Woodwinds play B theme and then repeat it.

1:10   Strings play A theme and then repeat it.

1:34   Strings play B theme and then repeat it.

2:08   The hornpipe ends quietly.

LISTENING GUIDE

THE SONATA

The word **sonata** is used often in music. It first appeared in the Baroque period, and it simply referred to an instrumental work for one or a few instruments. At that time there were two types of sonatas — one was the church sonata (*sonata da chiesa*); and the other, the chamber sonata (*sonata da camera*). The former was more serious and included some thoughtful music and quite a bit of imitation among the melodic lines. The chamber sonata consisted largely of stylized dance music and was lighter in character.

Probably the most prominent type of sonata during the middle of the Baroque was the *trio sonata*. Actually, the designation is not accurate, because it includes two violins and one lower instrument (gamba or cello) plus the continuo, which was usually played by a keyboard instrument.

Almost all sonatas were divided into *movements*, a term introduced in Chapter 2. Four movements were typical, and they were often arranged so that their tempos contrasted with one another.

Corelli's Trio Sonata

Numbers are rarely used for works of vocal music, because they can be identified by the words in their texts.

The Trio Sonata in F, Op. 3, No. 1, is one of the twelve sonatas published together as "Op. 1." The abbreviation *Op.* is from the Latin word *opus*, meaning "work," and is used to identify individual instrumental works. Generally, the numbers indicate the order in which a composer wrote his or her music, but opus numbers were not employed consistently until early in the nineteenth century. Sometimes publishers attached opus numbers to works composed before then. In some instances, scholars have cataloged the works of composers such as Bach, Schubert, and Mozart, in which cases the name or initials of the cataloger appear along with a catalog number.

Corelli's trio sonata has four movements; the second and third are presented here. The first movement of this church sonata is typically a slow, solemn movement marked *Grave*. The cello sounds a steady stream of low notes while the two violins play higher notes for the first half of the movement.

When used in conjunction with music, the word *grave* is pronounced *"grah-vay."*

The second movement has a fast tempo and contains much imitation among the three instruments. After each instrument enters in imitation, it continues with free contrapuntal material. The opening theme appears four more times in the movement, including a shortened version near the end of the movement.

ARCANGELO CORELLI

Trio Sonata in F, Op. 3, No. 1, Second Movement (1681)

GENRE: Trio sonata   Allegro   Violins, cello, and continuo

CD 3 Track 20
1 minute 18 seconds

0:00   **20**   0:00   First violin enters, second violin follows, and then cello.

0:17   Free counterpoint follows.

0:44   Opening theme appears twice as rapidly moving notes are played.

1:05   Opening theme played one more time before movement concludes.

Arcangelo Corelli

Arcangelo Corelli (1653–1713) lived at a time when the violin was replacing the viol. He was one of the first great violinists, teachers, and composers, and he promoted the technical and tonal capabilities of the violin. He spent most of his life in Rome in the service of Cardinal Ottoboni, whose concerts he directed. His "Christmas" concerto was completed shortly before he died. Unlike many composers, he died having amassed a large fortune. In return, he left the world a fortune in string music.

Museo di Strumenti del Conservatorio, Naples, Italy/
The Bridgeman Art Library

BEST-KNOWN WORKS

- Violin Sonatas (12)
- Concerti Grossi (12)

The third movement has a waltzlike character with its three rapid beats in each measure. Several times Corelli presents a melody consisting of two phrases each four measures long, and then repeats it accompanied by decorative notes played by the violins. Some of the time he has the two violins playing the same music in imitative lines that almost sound entangled with each other. The two parts can be heard clearly in a live performance where the performers are several feet apart, but the parts are more difficult to hear in a recording when the sounds are coming from loudspeakers.

The fourth movement is similar to the second. It has a rather fast tempo and contains much imitation.

ARCANGELO CORELLI

Trio Sonata in F, Op. 3, No. 1, Third Movement (1681)

GENRE: **Trio sonata** **Vivace** **Violins, cello, and continuo**

CD 3 Track 21
2 minutes 30 seconds

0:00	**21**	0:00	A section played, then repeated with decorative notes.
		0:19	A theme continues, ending with echolike phrase.
		0:34	A section repeated, ending with echolike phrase.
		1:03	B section contains changes of key.
		1:52	B section repeated, leading to quiet ending.

LISTENING GUIDE

OTHER BAROQUE COMPOSERS

GIOVANNI GABRIELI (1557–1612) studied music with his uncle Andrea in Venice; later he probably studied with Orlando di Lasso in Munich. In 1585 he succeeded his uncle as organist at Saint Mark's, a position that he held until his death twenty-seven years later. Until about 1600, his compositions were in the Renaissance style. His later compositions were in the new Baroque style. Although an organist and master at writing choral music, he is remembered more today for his use of instruments, especially brasses. They included trombones (which were puny instruments compared with the modern versions) and cornetto. His *Sonata pian'e forte* is recognized as probably the first work to specify dynamic levels.

The *cornetto* was a wooden instrument that bears little resemblance to the present-day cornet.

JEAN-BAPTISTE LULLY Though Italian by birth, Jean-Baptiste Lully (1632–1687) made his way into the court of French kings by wit and luck. He changed his name from the Italian *Lulli* to the French version by which he has been known throughout history. Lully was a supreme entertainer in what was the most sumptuous court in Europe. There he staged dance spectaculars and other performances. He developed the *French overture*. It had a slow introduction with many dotted rhythms, a fast middle section with imitation of a short melody, and usually a third section in a slow tempo like the first.

The story of Lully's death is probably true. To keep the performers together, he would mark the beat by pounding a stick on the floor. One day he hit his toe, which later became infected. He died from the infection.

GEORG PHILLIP TELEMANN One of the best-known composers of the first half of the eighteenth century, Georg Phillip Telemann (1685–1767) spent most of his life near Hamburg, Germany. He left a huge amount of music—forty operas, forty-four passions, twelve Lutheran services, and more than three thousand works of other types! He was adept at composing instrumental music, especially for the flute.

CODA

ThomsonNOW
Begin reviewing characteristics of Baroque music in *ThomsonNOW*'s "Connecting the Dots" lecture, Chapter 13.

The suite and sonata demonstrate several features of Baroque instrumental music:

- Metrical rhythm
- Many examples of imitation and counterpoint
- A continuo part
- Many examples of ostinato, including some built over a ground bass
- Tonal harmony and the use of modulations

Baroque Instrumental Music: Concerto *and* Fugue

14

In a sense, the concerto grosso, the solo concerto, and the fugue represent the more mature instrumental works composed during the Baroque. They were generally written in the eighteenth century by composers whose music is performed frequently today. The examples of concerto grosso and fugue represent a high point for their particular type of music, and some of the solo concertos of that time are still staples of concert music today.

THE CONCERTO GROSSO

A favorite musical effect during the Baroque was the contrast between groups of instruments, or what is called **concerted style.** There are two types of **concerto grosso.** One featured the contrast between different types of instruments, such as woodwinds and strings. The other, more common, type presented contrast between a few instruments and the orchestra. The contrast between groups is more than just a case of taking turns in answering each other, especially in the later concerto grossi. They are more subtle and complex than that, but the basic idea of contrast is present. The idea of contrast also carried over to the movements of the concertos. Typically, they consisted of three movements: fast-slow-fast.

> The word *grosso* means "grand," not "ugly" or "disgusting."

There is little difference in the difficulty of the music that the small group and the larger group (called the *tutti*) perform. No attempt was made to have one group show off, as is true in later concertos. The small group remains seated and often plays along in unison with the *tutti*. Usually, concerti grossi are composed for strings, with a harpsichord filling in the harmonies. A few wind instruments are sometimes included in the small group.

> Players in the small group were generally the first-chair players in their respective sections.

The fact that the same or similar instruments play the same music sometimes makes it difficult to distinguish which group is playing at a particular moment. Orchestras during the Baroque were small, so the larger group really wasn't large by today's standards. Also, three or four good string players can produce a quite vigorous sound. Recordings tend to make the groups less distinguishable by taking away most of the physical distance of live performances.

The most common form of the movements in a concerto grosso is **ritornello form.** It presents a pattern in which the main theme alternates with a contrasting section, with modifications as the movement progresses.

Bach's Brandenburg Concerto No. 5

The margrave of Brandenburg was one of the more important rulers in what is Germany today. In 1717 Bach was court composer at Cöthen and had a chance to perform for the margrave, who was visiting there. The margrave was so impressed that he asked Bach to write some music for his orchestra. In 1721 Bach sent him six concertos, complete with dedication to "His Highness," that contrasted a variety of small instrumental groups with the orchestra. Later they became known as the Brandenburg Concertos.

Whether the margrave ever responded to Bach's gift is not known. In fact, the concertos were placed in the margrave's library and were never performed by the musicians

> Bach may have hoped that his gift of six concertos with a glowing dedication would lead to a job offer from the margrave. None ever came.

109

ANTONIO VIVALDI

"Spring" from *The Four Seasons,* First Movement (1725)

GENRE: Solo concerto   Solo violin and orchestra

CD 1 Tracks 29–33
3 minutes 35 seconds

0:00 **29** 0:00 Entire string orchestra plays the main theme (ritornello) and then repeats it softly. The words in the score can be translated "Spring with all its happiness is here."

0:16 Orchestra plays second half of ritornello theme and then repeats it.

0:33 **30** 0:00 Solo violin plays chirping, birdlike sounds: "And the birds welcome it with happy songs." Orchestra repeats second half of ritornello.

1:18 **31** 0:00 Orchestra plays short, flowing, rapidly moving notes: "And the brooks, touched by the breezes, flow with sweet murmurings."

0:25 Second half of ritornello is repeated.

1:52 **32** 0:00 Music changes to minor. Orchestra plays rustling, nervous sounds (tremolos), and violins zip up notes of the scale: "Dark clouds fill the sky announced by lightning and thunder."

0:28 Orchestra plays second part of ritornello again but in minor.

2:28 **33** 0:00 Solo violin plays birdlike sounds: "But when everything is quiet, the birds begin to sing again their enchanting song."

0:17 Orchestra plays first part of ritornello in major, and then solo violin enters.

0:43 Orchestra again plays second part of ritornello and then repeats it softly.

1:08 "Spring" concludes.

thing in common: They are contrapuntal, with the lines of music often imitating one another.

What makes fugues interesting to listen to? At least three things:

- Fugues are built around one main theme, which helps give the work a strong sense of unity. This theme is featured alone at the beginning and then repeated often during the work.

- Contrasting lines of counterpoint give the work variety and make it more interesting. These lines fit together with the theme and with one another.

- The entire work is crafted so that it evolves in a wonderfully logical manner. The musical process of a fugue is somewhat like a complicated mathematical formula working itself out to a beautifully correct conclusion.

Fugues have their own vocabulary. The various lines are called **voices,** even though they are actually played on an instrument, not sung. The main theme is called the **subject,** and the contrasting theme is called the **countersubject.** The opening section that presents the subject in each voice is termed the **exposition;** the remainder of the fugue is known as the **development.** Sections of the fugue following the exposition in which the subject does not appear are called **episodes.**

The pattern of a typical four-voice fugue is shown in the following diagram:

This fugue has four voices, which is the usual number, but it could have had two, three, or five. The order in which the voices enter is a matter of choice for the composer. Each fugue is structured somewhat differently.

Bach's Toccata and Fugue in D Minor

Toccata and Fugue in D Minor by Bach presents a fugue surrounded by a **toccata,** which is a free-sounding virtuoso work, usually for keyboard. Both the fugue and the toccata offer the organist plenty of chances to show off the tremendous tonal possibilities of the instrument, as well as virtuoso skill as a performer. The third and concluding section of this work is another toccata that Bach labels *recitativo*. The word refers to the free and expressive style of singing described in Chapter 10. It is a work filled with drama.

Three features of Baroque instrumental music are prominent in this fugue. One is the use of **sequence.** A sequence is a pattern of notes repeated several times in succession, but each time at a different pitch level. Sequences are a staple of Baroque music, and Toccata and Fugue in D Minor contains many of them.

Second is the use of repeated notes in a theme. The subject of the fugue contains a lot of notes, which gives the music more energy. But only half of the notes form the basis of the subject. The circled notes in the music example change; the others do not.

For this reason, you should focus on the notes that change as you listen to the subject of this fugue.

The third feature is a bit more complicated. Composers, especially in the Baroque period, created a pattern of tension and release by holding a consonant note from one chord over into the next chord, where it was dissonant, and then resolving that note to a consonant note in the new chord—suspension. Suspensions are more frequent in cadences near the conclusion of phrases. At the end of the entire Toccata and Fugue it may sound as if Bach is simply holding a long chord. But listen carefully as notes in the middle of the chords change and finally resolve. The interplay of consonance and dissonance makes for some very interesting and challenging listening.

OTHER KEYBOARD FORMS

The fugue was not the only musical form composed for keyboard instruments during the Baroque. Two forms based on the chorale are chorale variations and chorale prelude. In *chorale variations* a chorale melody is repeated several times in succession but with

ThomsonNOW™

"Hear It Now: Features of Bach's Fugue," in *ThomsonNOW*, Chapter 14.

ThomsonNOW™

"Hear It Now: Suspensions," in *ThomsonNOW*, Chapter 14.

PART IV

Classical Music

	1750	1775
Historical Events	● Factory system begins	American Revolutio
		● Watts develops steam engine
Visual Arts	Boucher	
	Fragonard	
Literature and Theater		● Voltaire, *Candide*
		Wordsworth
		Robert Burns
		Coleridge
		Schiller
Philosophy and Science	Kant	
		● Rousseau, *Social Contract*
Music	C. P. E. Bach	
		Haydn composer for Esterházys
	J. C. Bach	
	Mannheim Orchestra thrives	

1800   1820

French Revolution   ● Louisiana Purchase   ● Napoleon defeated

● David, *Death of Socrates*   ● Goya, *The Third of May*

                                        ● Goethe, *Faust*   ● Scott, *Ivanhoe*

● Jenner, smallpox vaccine

▲ Mozart symphonies and operas (above)

► Beethoven symphonies (right)

Schubert songs

15 Classicism *and* Classical Music

When most people use the word *classic* to describe something, they mean that it has an enduring quality of excellence. *The Wizard of Oz* is a classic motion picture and *Moby Dick* is a classic novel, to give two examples. That use of the word is close to the original Latin *classicus*, meaning "something of highest quality."

When most people use *classical* with regard to music, they mean concert or art music, music that is not popular or folk. On the other hand, when musicians use the word *Classical* (written with a capital C), they are talking about the musical style that prevailed from about 1750 to around 1820.

CULTURAL SETTING

Although the approximate dates of the **Classical period** give it a life span of only about seventy years, it produced much wonderful and enjoyable music. Instrumental music developed and equaled or exceeded vocal music in importance. The symphony, solo concerto, and chamber music and musical forms associated with them were developed. Opera also continued to flourish.

The center of music moved from the cities of Italy to Vienna, the capital of the Austrian Empire. Four master composers lived there—Mozart and Haydn during the Classical period and then Beethoven and Schubert, whose music bridged into the nineteenth-century style.

During the eighteenth century, there was a widespread interest among the educated population in intellectual accomplishments in the philosophy, science, and arts of the ancient Greeks. Therefore, these years are often referred to as the Age of Enlightenment or the Age of Reason. This interest can be seen in the publication of Denis Diderot's *Encylopédie* in France and the *Encyclopœdia Britannica* in England. These books sought to break away from the religious restrictions of the past and promote reason and scientific thinking.

Four Leaders

Four persons are especially representative of the spirit of the time. One was Frenchman François Marie Arouet (1694–1778), who called himself Voltaire. His writings spoke out for justice and challenged the government and religion of France at that time, even to the point where he spent a year in prison for his beliefs. But he had his weak and inconsistent side too. He was shrewd at business and lived comfortably, and some of his writings were published anonymously. Later when questioned about them, he continued to deny having written them. But in the end, his influence toward an enlightened outlook was enormous.

The Swiss-French Jean-Jacques Rousseau (1712–1778), like Voltaire, sought to reform the moral climate and governmental policies. In his writings he strongly urged a less dogmatic, formal system of government. He believed that people were naturally good and that they had been corrupted by civilization, education, and governments. Rousseau was a skilled musician who advocated a new system of music notation. He composed music and wrote comedies. His music was simple and folklike in comparison to the highly decorated style of the other French composers of the time.

A third person representative of the spirit of the Age of Enlightenment was the American Benjamin Franklin (1706–1790). In spite of his rather unkempt appearance,

---

Haydn, Mozart, Beethoven, and Schubert are often referred to as the "Viennese Classicists."

The word *encyclopædia* (the traditional English spelling) is from two Greek words meaning "general education." The ligature œ also reveals the word's Greek heritage.

This was the time of the House of Bourbon, and its kings were very repressive and self-indulgent.

Elements of Rousseau's beliefs are still very much alive in the United States today.

The glass *armonica*, as Franklin called it, was a rank of glasses set perpendicular to the player like a series of grindstones. The player used a pedal to spin the glasses as his or her wetted fingers rubbed the rims of the glasses, causing eerie, ethereal sounds.

he was a brilliant and well-read man who published books and magazines, promoted education, was pivotal in bringing about the Constitution of the United States, contributed much to the understanding of electricity, invented the Franklin stove and bifocal glasses, and developed a musical instrument called the "glass harmonica."

Thomas Jefferson (1743–1826), the fourth representative of the outlook of the period, was not only author of the Declaration of Independence and third president of the United States but was also an outstanding scholar and architect. His ideas can be seen in his home (which he named Monticello) at Charlottesville, Virginia; the University of Virginia (which he founded); and the Library of Congress (which he also founded—his books served as the nucleus of its original holdings). He was also a competent violinist and singer. The music stand he used for string quartet playing is on display today at Monticello.

SUPREME COURT BUILDING

Architecture

Admiration for the ancient Greeks and Romans can also be seen in architecture and art. Greek pillars and symmetrical, balanced designs are found in many public and private buildings in America today. The front of the U.S. Supreme Court Building in Washington, D.C., is very much in the Greek tradition. Note the sensible proportions of the triangle above the pillars; it is neither too tall nor too low from the baseline to the peak. Notice also the symmetry of the columns to each side of the center of the roof.

Philosophy

The philosophical approach of eighteenth-century thinkers was founded on three basic propositions:

1. Reason and logic are the way to truth. Emotions are false and misleading.
2. The universe is governed by permanent laws that people cannot alter. What is true is true throughout the world and for all time. It is universal and eternal.
3. Therefore, the intellect should control people's activities, including art and music.

These philosophical ideas began with Socrates and Plato in ancient Athens, but they were refined and applied to many areas of culture and scholarship by thinkers in the eighteenth century. One of the many areas affected by the Classical outlook was music, which is explored later in this chapter.

TOWARD CLASSICISM: THE ROCOCO STYLE

A forerunner of sorts of the more typical Classical style in the arts was the **Rococo** or **galant style,** which was popular mainly in France during the first half of the eighteenth century. Coming from the French word *rocaille,* meaning "shellwork," the Rococo style marked the acme of the highly decorative, almost frivolous French style of the Court of Versailles. It can be seen in the paintings of François Boucher (1703–1770), Antonie Watteau (1684–1721), and Jean Honoré Fragonard (1732–1806).

Two Rococo composers who merit mention are François Couperin (1688–1733) and Jean-Philippe Rameau (1683–1764). The happy tunes and almost frilly quality in Rameau's music seem perfectly suited for the powder-and-wig world of the Court of

As used in this sense, *galant* is much closer in meaning to *elegant* than to *gallant.* It is pronounced "gah-*lahnt.*"

Much of Rameau's and Couperin's music is for a French version of the harpsichord called the *clavecin.*

THE DEATH OF SOCRATES, by Jacques-Louis David. This painting shows the formal properties of balance and restraint that are found in much of the music of Mozart and Haydn.

Versailles at the time of Louis XIV. Rameau is also important in music history for a book he wrote on harmony. In it he outlined principles of chord structure and progressions that prevailed for hundreds of years.

CLASSICAL ART

The Death of Socrates by Jacques-Louis David depicts the great philosopher of ancient Greece just about to drink the poisonous cup of hemlock. His students grieve while he remains composed and upright. In spite of the anguish of the scene, the figures seem almost frozen or posed. There is a detached quality about the picture. The admiration of the culture of ancient Greece and Rome can be seen in its symmetrical, balanced design. Groups of men are placed on each side of Socrates, who is the focus of attention. The colors are somewhat muted in keeping with the overall nature of the scene. The arches of the building add a linear perspective to the painting.

Boucher's *Venus and Cupid* is a good example of Rococo art, which was strongly associated with the court of the French kings at Versailles. Boucher was trained as a decorator by his father, who designed embroideries. That influence can be seen in the exquisite lightness and decorative qualities of his paintings. The aristocracy of the time demanded a type of art and music that was pretty and decorative, even if it was superficial. A wide range of colors was used. Often the subjects of Rococo art were mythological or allegorical. The protagonist almost always appears as a young, elegant, and sensually abandoned woman. Cupids, nymphs, and doves are found in many paintings, which are frequently set in beautiful gardens or forests.

CHARACTERISTICS OF CLASSICAL MUSIC

The overall impression of Classical music is that it is light, airy, elegant, and well thought out. It is music in which reason prevails over feelings. Composers thought more about creating beautiful and interesting works of music than pouring out their personal feelings in their music.

VENUS AND CUPID, by François Boucher. The Rococo subperiod favored decorative works of art and music, including melodies with many ornaments.

Much music of the time was written under a patronage arrangement. The patronage system during the Classical period, therefore, produced a quite homogeneous style of music. For example, although there are subtle differences between the music of Haydn and Mozart, their works tend to sound quite similar. In fact, using themes of other composers was an accepted practice at the time. The original composer of the theme considered its appropriation by another composer a compliment, not a case of plagiarism. One theme called the "Mannheim rocket," for example, was used by Mozart, Beethoven, and many other composers.

People in the Classical period, including composers, seemed to attribute little mystery to the act of creating music, an attitude that would change radically in the nineteenth century. For example, Mozart prepared a booklet with which anyone with a pair of dice could "compose" a piece of music. The booklet contained a short work for two violins, flute, and bass with each measure numbered. A chart indicated which measure of the work should be used for each of the eleven numbers that could appear on the dice. Whatever one's luck with the dice, a pleasant piece of music was certain. The style of Classical music could be systematized to that extent.

The "rocket" is discussed further in Chapter 21.

Mozart's booklet went through six or seven editions. It was published in London under the title *Mozart's Musical Game,* **fitted in an elegant box, showing by an** *Easy System how to compose an unlimited number of Waltzes, Rondos, Hornpipes, and Reels.*

FEATURES TO LISTEN FOR IN CLASSICAL MUSIC

Melody

For the most part, the themes are pleasant and tuneful. Most of them can be sung, if put in the right range. These melodies are made up of short phrases of two and four measures in length. And the phrases often are arranged in a statement–answer pattern. They form a musical equivalent of "How do you do?" and "Very well, thank you." Such paired patterns are balanced and symmetrical, and they contribute to the clear, logical quality of the music.

Homophony

The music of the Classical period was usually homophonic—melody plus accompaniment. There is some counterpoint in Classical music, but it is more the exception than the rule.

Harmony

Classical composers used essentially the same system of harmony as Baroque composers, but they made two important changes: (1) They abandoned the continuo part and the filling in of chords from figured bass, and (2) they changed chords less frequently. Sometimes Classical composers would keep the same chord for a measure or two before making a change, and then they might change chords several times in a rather short span of time. Classical harmony has the role of providing a backdrop for the melodies and does not draw attention to itself.

Rhythm

Classical music follows regular metrical patterns with few fluctuations in steadiness of the beat, except for recitatives in operas and oratorios. But it lacks the persistent quality of the rhythm of many Baroque works. Part of the reason for this difference is the result of abandoning the continuo and its steady stream of notes.

Dynamic Levels

The gradual **crescendo** and **decrescendo** developed during the Classical period. These gradual changes in dynamic level were considered quite dramatic at the time. They were an important contribution of that period to the development of music.

Performance

There were no permanent orchestras in the Classical period.

The orchestras of the Classical period grew somewhat but did not reach the size of the symphony orchestras of today. When orchestras today perform a symphony by Haydn or Mozart, they often reduce the size of the string section by about one-fourth. Orchestras during the Classical period used only pairs of woodwinds and brasses. No trombones or tubas were included, and the percussion section usually consisted of the timpani player.

Orchestra players were part-time musicians who also held other jobs, so the level of performance was probably not high by today's standards.

Public concerts began during this time in the sense that performances were not always closed to all except invited guests in a palace. Public concerts were available in a few large cities such as Paris, London, and Leipzig, and they were within the financial means of the prosperous merchant class.

Forms

Absolute music has no association with any object, idea, or event outside itself. It is the opposite of *program music,* which is presented in Part V.

An important feature of Classical music is the development and refinement of various forms of instrumental music. Such music is referred to as **absolute music.** The rational outlook of the time encouraged the creation of music that was well ordered and planned, as well as in good taste. Writing music (especially instrumental music with its lack of a story and text) that spans more than a few minutes generally requires some means of organization, some plan. Classical composers continued to use the sectional forms of the Baroque, but they also developed and expanded sonata, rondo, and theme-and-variation forms. These forms contributed to the creation of symphonies, concertos, and chamber works.

CODA

It is easy to understand why the rational, intellectual outlook of the Enlightenment and its goal of beauty and good taste encouraged the kind of music that was composed during the Classical period. Loud, crass music would have been as out of place as wearing a clown suit and red rubber nose to a formal banquet.

16

Sonata Form

The most important form developed during the Classical period was **sonata form**, which is also called *first movement form* or *sonata–allegro form*. It became the expected form for the first movements of symphonies, concertos, and chamber music works in the last part of the eighteenth century and, with modifications, in the nineteenth century as well. And it is still used in compositions today. Sonata form was also found in other movements of multimovement works. Although the same word is used, *sonata form* and a *sonata* are different. One is a form, but a sonata is a genre of instrumental music.

DEVELOPMENT IN MUSICAL WORKS

Sonata form is more than just a plan or schema, however. It features a fundamental idea in concert music: *the development of themes*. True, sonata form contains themes, which are of interest, but what a composer does with the themes makes the music even more interesting and enjoyable to listen to. The themes are at best only half of what music in sonata form has to offer. The other half is the way the themes are developed.

As the word is used in music, *development* does not mean "building up" or "finishing," but rather "working with."

Several years ago people in a small town in Ohio realized that zucchini grew abundantly in their gardens and farms. In fact, the conditions one summer were so good that they could never use all of it, and a lot of zucchini would rot unused on the vine. What to do? They decided to hold a "Zucchini Festival," complete with crafts, dancing, music, and, of course, zucchini. Sure enough, it was chopped, sliced, and ground up and incorporated in all sorts of vegetable dishes, made into preserves and pickles, and blended in bread and muffins. Even the arts were included, as many fine pieces of zucchini sculpture were carved.

It's a bit like that with the development of themes in sonata form. Composers take a theme and work with it in all sorts of ways. The themes — or at least parts of them — are still there, but they have been given a variety of treatments.

MOZART'S SYMPHONY NO. 40, K. 550

As the biographical sketch on the next page points out, Mozart was perhaps the greatest musical genius of all time. He wrote a huge amount of music, much of which is still performed today. His Fortieth Symphony was composed in 1788. Why he composed it and two other symphonies that year is not known. It is unlikely that he ever heard them performed.

The score calls for the typical orchestra of the time: violins, violas, cellos (doubled by string basses in performance), a flute, two oboes, two bassoons, and two French horns. Later Mozart revised the score to include two clarinets.

Actually, it is not Mozart's fortieth symphony. That number is the order of its publication among his symphonies. He wrote about fifty symphonies in all.

The *K.* by the title comes from the name of a person — Ludwig Köchel — who catalogued Mozart's music.

Chromatic movement is movement by half steps. Usually it can be seen in the added sharps and flats.

- It contains few skips up or down to other notes.
- It is more difficult to remember than the first because of its chromatic movement.
- It is in a different key from the first theme, which is true of the themes in the exposition. If a movement begins in a minor key, the second theme is generally in the relative major key. If the movement is in major, the second theme often is in the major key five notes higher.

Following the second theme, another transition appears. Fragments of the first theme are interspersed in it. At this point in sonata form, composers have some options. They can introduce a third theme (sometimes called the *closing theme*), they may write an extended transition, or they may borrow a fragment from one of the themes, which is what Mozart did here.

The transition concludes with a *codetta,* which is a short concluding section. Sometimes codettas have a brief melody of their own.

So far, only the first of the three sections that sonata form comprises has been presented. The exposition can be depicted:

Exposition

First theme	Transition	Second theme	Transition	Codetta
In tonic key		*In dominant key or relative major*		

Classical composers usually indicated that the entire exposition was to be repeated. In performances today the repeat sign is sometimes ignored, and the music moves directly into the next section.

Development

Logically, the **development** section is where much of the development of themes described earlier in this chapter takes place. What does Mozart do in the development section of the first movement of Symphony No. 40? Essentially, he treats the first theme in three ways:

1. The first half of the first theme is played three times, each time in a different key.
2. Counterpoint is introduced. While the lower strings play the first theme in a different key, the violins begin a countermelody of rapidly moving notes:

When the lower strings finish the first half of the first theme, they take up the countermelody while the violins play the theme. A similar exchange occurs two more times, each time one note lower than its preceding phrase.

3. The first theme is fragmented even further. The first few notes are tossed back and forth among the flute, clarinet, and violins. The music modulates often, but this section is quiet compared with the busy, vigorous exchanges between low and high strings that preceded it. Soon the answer in the woodwinds is shortened again to include only its first three notes. Several times the melodic figure is inverted, so it ascends in pitch rather than descends:

Fragments of the first theme appear in *all but the first two measures* of the development section. Fragments of the theme also appear in the transition leading from the development into the next main section of sonata form.

WOLFGANG AMADEUS MOZART
Symphony No. 40, First Movement (1788)

GENRE: **Symphony** **Allegro molto (fast tempo)** **Symphony orchestra**

CD 1 Tracks 38–42
8 minutes 10 seconds

Form: Sonata

Exposition

0:00 **38** 0:00 First theme begins in violins and is repeated. (Repeats at 1:10)

0:33 Transition containing short motive and many scalewise notes. (Repeats at 1:43)

0:51 **39** 0:00 Violins and woodwinds play second theme. (Repeats at 2:02)

0:11 Woodwinds and violins repeat second theme; then transition begins. (Repeats at 2:12)

0:56 Codetta begins with fast notes by violins. (Repeats at 2:48)

1:09 Codetta concludes with a solid chord. (Repeats at 3:10)

Development

4:02 **40** 0:00 Development section begins with two short chords and notes by woodwinds.

0:05 First theme appears three times in sequence, each time one note lower.

0:18 Upper and lower strings alternate portion of first theme and rapidly moving notes.

0:46 Motive from first theme alternates between violins and flute.

Recapitulation

5:22 **41** 0:00 First theme returns played by violins in the tonic key and is repeated.

0:33 Transition begins but is longer and more complex than in the exposition.

1:15 Woodwinds and strings play second theme.

1:26 Second theme repeated; then transition begins.

1:58 Clarinet and bassoon exchange the motive from the first theme.

7:38 **42** 0:00 Coda begins with fast scalewise passages.

0:11 Strings and woodwinds play motive from first theme several times.

0:32 Movement closes with three solid chords.

In this particular development, Mozart works with only the first theme. He breaks it apart, modulates frequently, adds countermelodies, and inverts it. Such treatments of the theme are typical of development sections in sonata form. He could have done other things as well. He could have developed the second theme, or he could have introduced a new theme. He might have altered the rhythm, written different chords for it, or combined two themes in a contrapuntal manner. The means of development are endless.

Recapitulation

The word *recapitulation* literally means "return to the top."

The term for the third section of sonata form is **recapitulation**. The first five letters of the word *recapitulation* form the word *recap*. And, sure enough, Mozart comes back to the first theme. It is played by the same instruments and with the same accompanying music. This literal repetition doesn't last long, however. Changes are introduced gradually as the bassoon adds a few notes in contrast.

More changes occur as the music moves into the transition heading toward the second theme. The transition is longer than it was in the exposition. In fact, for a short time it sounds almost as if another development section has begun. While the second violins play rapidly moving notes, the short fragment heard just briefly in the exposition is exchanged between the first violins and the low strings:

There is another difference. The second theme is not in a new key; it stays in the tonic. If the second theme were in a different key, the composer would have to have the music modulate quickly back to the tonic before the movement ends and sound convincing about it. That is not an easy thing to do. Following the second theme, the transition uses music similar to what was played at the comparable place in the exposition.

Coda means "tail" in Italian.

The movement ends with a *coda*. The coda is like the codetta, except that it is longer so that it can provide a convincing conclusion to the entire movement. In this coda Mozart again uses a fragment from the first theme. Dominant (V_7) and tonic (I) chords alternate in typical Classical style to give the movement a solid ending.

No two movements in sonata form are exactly alike; each is unique. In general, however, sonata form can be diagrammed as shown here.

A simplified line score of the first movement of Mozart's Symphony No. 40 is included in the *Study Guide* that is ancillary to this book.

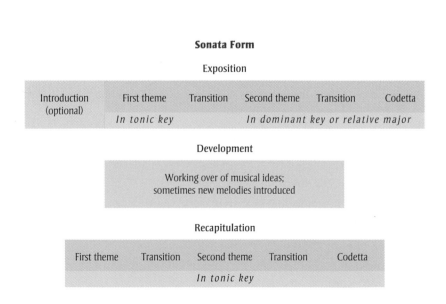

Sonata Form

Exposition

Introduction (optional)	First theme	Transition	Second theme	Transition	Codetta
	In tonic key		*In dominant key or relative major*		

Development

Working over of musical ideas; sometimes new melodies introduced

Recapitulation

First theme	Transition	Second theme	Transition	Codetta
		In tonic key		

OTHER ASPECTS OF SONATA FORM

The key of the music was important in the Classical period. The key is usually provided along with the title of the work: Symphony No. 40 in G Minor by Mozart. Sometimes a work is referred to by its key, for example, Mozart's G Minor Symphony. Today, however, the key of a work is not particularly important to listeners. Music of the nineteenth century modulated so often and so far from the tonic that the impact of key change has been greatly reduced. And music in the twentieth century continued this trend, even to the point where some music has no key center at all.

You need to keep in mind that *everything* in a movement matters. It is not that the themes are the really good stuff and the transitions are just filler around them. As in doing a puzzle, every piece of it is needed for the complete picture.

Many movements in sonata form have introductions, although Mozart's Symphony No. 40 does not. They are usually in a slow tempo and seldom have much musical relationship with the rest of the movement in terms of their themes.

CODA

What makes sonata form and the first movement of Mozart's Symphony No. 40 musically satisfying and enjoyable to listen to?

- Sonata form is a plan that, when fulfilled by a composer of Mozart's capabilities, results in a balanced, symmetrical, and beautifully logical piece of music.

- The themes demonstrate the composer's skill in developing musical ideas. Development answers the question: When is a theme more than a theme? The answer: When it is developed by a talented composer.

- The music of the Classical period has a bright, sunny quality to it.

- The music demonstrates the craftsmanship and imagination. Listening to Mozart's music is like admiring the delicate beauty of a fine piece of china or the subtle perfection of a prize rose. His music is so—musical!

ThomsonNOW™
Begin reviewing characteristics of Classical music in *ThomsonNOW*'s "Connecting the Dots" lecture, Chapter 16.

17

The Concerto

Neil Simon, the highly successful playwright, has written two plays consisting of three short plays that take place in the same location. But each play has characters and stories not found in the other plays. The location of *Plaza Suite* is New York's Plaza Hotel; *California Suite* utilizes a hotel setting in California. The only connection among the acts of each play is the suite of rooms.

It is somewhat like that with the multimovement works composed during the Classical period. Instead of a single location, however, Classical composers related the movements only in terms of tempos and keys. They planned for contrast among the movements in terms of forms, melodic character, amount of development, tempo, and so on. In this chapter we look at how composers during the Classical period achieved contrast among movements in the solo concerto.

THE SOLO CONCERTO

The word *concerto* is not a new one to you. First it appeared in Rodrigo's *Concierto de Aranjuez* for guitar and orchestra in Chapter 4. Then it appeared in Chapter 14 in Vivaldi's *Four Seasons* and Bach's *Brandenburg Concerto No. 5*, which pitted a solo part or a part for a small group against a larger group. The difference between these two types of concertos does not involve only the size of the group contrasted with the orchestra. In the solo concerto the solo part is more showy than the orchestra part.

The concerto grosso of the Baroque period with its continuo part and contrast in size of groups went out of fashion in the Classical period and was replaced by the solo concerto. Since that time, the word *concerto* refers only to a solo concerto.

The advent of the solo concerto also parallels to some degree the beginning of public concerts, for which the composer organized and managed most of the administrative details. Audiences were then, as today, attracted by the opportunity to hear an outstanding performer. The small group was not the best means of presenting the talents of virtuoso performers; it is difficult to write music that really shows off two or more performers.

Mozart and Haydn composed many concertos and brought the solo concerto to a new level of musical sophistication. It is through their works that the solo concerto of the Classical period is examined here.

Most concertos are for the piano or violin, which are the most frequently featured instruments in concertos. Both Haydn and Mozart also composed concertos for less typical instruments such as clarinet, trumpet, bassoon, and French horn. These works are of such high quality that they are performed often today.

In the nineteenth century, Johannes Brahms composed a double concerto for violin and cello, and Beethoven a triple concerto, but such works are rare.

The concertos for these instruments are amazing in terms of overcoming or working around the technical limitations of wind instruments at the time.

MOZART'S VIOLIN CONCERTO NO. 5, K. 219

Mozart must have liked, or thought his listeners would like, solo concertos, because he certainly wrote a lot of them: about twenty-seven for piano, seven for violin, four for French horn, two for flute, and one each for bassoon, clarinet, and oboe. In addition, he composed a number of concertos for two violins and other combinations of instruments.

Mozart composed his Violin Concerto No. 5 when he was nineteen years old. He probably composed it for himself to play as first violinist of the orchestra at Salzburg. In any case, its first movement serves as the exemplar here for the initial movements of almost all concertos of that time.

Mozart's principal instrument, however, was the piano.

WOLFGANG AMADEUS MOZART
Violin Concerto No. 5, First Movement (1775)

GENRE: Concerto   Allegro aperto (rather fast)   Violin and orchestra

CD 3 Tracks 25–30
9 minutes 43 seconds

Form: Sonata

Exposition 1

0:00   **25**   0:00   Strings play first theme, which is built around a major chord.

0:35   Strings play contrasting second theme.

1:02   Orchestra plays codetta.

1:18   **26**   0:00   Solo violin enters playing a calm interlude.

Exposition 2

2:17   **27**   0:00   Second exposition begins. Orchestra plays first theme while solo violin plays a countermelody above it.

0:28   Soloist and orchestra play a transition.

1:10   Soloist plays second theme.

2:13   Orchestra plays codetta.

Development

4:41   **28**   0:00   Soloist and orchestra exchange themes as music modulates several times.

Recapitulation

5:32   **29**   0:00   Soloist plays the return of first theme.

0:20   Orchestra and soloist play transition.

1:19   Soloist and orchestra play second theme.

8:06   **30**   0:00   Soloist plays cadenza.

1:20   Orchestra begins coda.

1:36   Movement concludes quietly and quickly.

Three features characterize the first movements of Classical concertos.

DOUBLE EXPOSITION Although the movement is in sonata form, a second or **double exposition** is incorporated in the form. The first exposition is played by the orchestra; the second by the orchestra and the soloist. Because the second exposition usually includes music that shows off the soloist's prowess on the instrument, it tends to be longer than the first exposition.

CADENZA The movement usually specifies a cadenza just before the coda. The difference between the cadenza in Classical concertos and the cadenza in Rodrigo's *Concierto de Aranjuez* is that Rodrigo wrote out every note for the performer to play. In the Classical period, composers just wrote the word *cadenza* or its abbreviation *Cad.* at the appropriate place in the music. The performer was expected to make up a technically impressive paraphrase of the themes in the movement.

> At some of his performances, Mozart would accept themes handed to him by members of the audience and make up music based on them.

Whether soloists actually did so onstage is open to question. Improvisation was a far more common practice during the Baroque and Classical periods than it is today. Performers at that time probably worked at being good improvisers, but one wonders about doing so before an audience without prior preparation. For this reason concerto programs today will sometimes indicate who wrote the cadenza for a particular Classical concerto, and the cadenzas will differ depending on the preferences of the soloist.

LENGTH Movements written in sonata form tend to be longer than the movements in the typical concerto grosso. Not only does it take more time to perform the various parts of the sonata form, but more time is also needed to show off the soloist's abilities.

No two movements in sonata form are exactly alike. And Mozart adds a few unique features to the first movement of his Violin Concerto No. 5. The orchestra plays the usual two themes in its exposition.

- When the soloist enters, an expressive interlude is inserted before the soloist and orchestra take up the first theme together.
- When the first theme does appear in the second exposition, the solo violin plays a brilliant countermelody above the theme in the orchestra.
- The development section is not particularly complex. The attention in this work is on melodies and the soloist's playing abilities; it is not on the development of themes.

THE SECOND MOVEMENT OF CONCERTOS

The second movement of almost all concertos composed in the Classical period features beautiful melodies and a slow tempo. This practice has continued into the nineteenth and twentieth centuries. As you will recall, the second movement of Rodrigo's *Concierto de Aranjuez* has these qualities, so in that regard it can be an exemplar for the second movement of most concertos, even those composed two centuries earlier.

RONDO FORM

> The word *rondo* comes from the French *rondeau,* meaning "to come around again."

Most third movements of concertos are written in rondo form. The basic idea of a **rondo** is the return of the same themes several times after other themes have been interjected among its various appearances. A rondo can be represented A B A C A D A and so on. Theoretically, there is no limit to the number of sections possible in a rondo, but five is the minimum number of sections. The pattern does not need to alternate as indicated by the foregoing example. They can be juggled A B A C A B A, or A B A C D A, or the shorter A B A C A, and so on, so long as the principle of the return of the A theme is followed.

The themes used in rondos tend to be shorter, less complicated, and happier than those in the first or second movements. Because the sections of a rondo are not usually long, composers do not have much room in which to develop themes or complex musical ideas.

Movements in rondo form seem especially suited to the final movements of concertos and symphonies because they leave the listeners in an upbeat mood. The principle of the rondo is found in the final movement of most multimovement works composed during the Classical period and many such works since then.

HAYDN'S TRUMPET CONCERTO

Haydn composed his Trumpet Concerto in E-flat in 1796 for a keyed (not a valve) trumpet. Keys were added to the sides of the instrument somewhat like keys on a clarinet or saxophone. The work was written for the trumpet virtuoso of the time, Anton Weidinger.

Valves, which are clearly superior, replaced keys on the trumpet about 1813.

FRANZ JOSEPH HAYDN

Concerto for Trumpet in E-flat, Third Movement (1796)

GENRE: Concerto   Allegro (lively)   Trumpet and orchestra

LISTENING GUIDE

CD 1 Tracks 43–45
4 minutes 7 seconds

Form: Rondo

0:00   **43**   0:00   Violins play main theme (A) softly and rather fast.

0:21   **44**   0:00   Violins play first contrasting theme (B).

0:15   Solo trumpet enters playing A theme.

0:44   Trumpet and violins alternate playing B theme in a new key.

1:23   **45**   0:00   Violins and trumpet play second contrasting theme (C) in minor.

0:22   Trumpet plays A theme.

0:31   Trumpet and orchestra play short development of A theme as music changes key several times.

1:08   Trumpet plays a repeat of A theme.

1:23   Trumpet and violins play B theme.

1:54   Trumpet plays first portion of A theme.

2:03   Violins and trumpet play part of C theme.

2:30   Coda begins as trumpet plays part of A theme softly.

2:46   Rondo closes with a crescendo and a full-sounding chord.

He must have been quite a performer, because Haydn did not hesitate to write difficult passages for him to play.

What makes Haydn's Trumpet Concerto exciting to listen to?

The University of Michigan School of Music, Stearns Collection

THE KEYED TRUMPET

- The trumpet has a brilliant, full sound.

- The music has a truly happy quality to it, with its bubbling personality.

- Rondo form gives listeners the expectation that the main theme will return. When it does, they have the satisfied feeling of being right.

Franz Joseph Haydn

© Archivo Iconografico, S.A./CORBIS

BEST-KNOWN WORKS

chamber music:
- String Quartets (6) Op. 76
- Piano Trios Nos. 27, 28, and 29

concertos:
- Concerto No. 1 for Cello
- Concerto for Trumpet

choral:
- *The Creation*
- *Lord Nelson Mass*
- *The Seasons*

orchestra:
- Symphony Nos. 92 ("Oxford"), 94 ("Surprise"), 100 ("Military"), 101 ("Clock"), and 104 ("London")

Franz Joseph Haydn (1732–1809) was born the same year as George Washington, in eastern Austria. An uncle with whom Haydn went to live at the age of six gave him his first instruction in music. At eight, he became a choirboy at the Cathedral of Saint Stephen in Vienna. When his voice changed, he was dismissed. For the next few years, he managed to exist doing odd jobs and teaching, as well as studying music theory. At the age of twenty-nine, he was taken into the service of Prince Paul Anton Esterházy, head of one of the richest and most powerful noble families in Hungary.

The next year Nicholas Esterházy succeeded his brother Paul. Nicholas was a connoisseur of music. Most of the time, the Esterházys lived at a country estate that rivaled the French court at Versailles. On the estate were two concert halls and two theaters, one for opera and one for marionette plays. Prince Nicholas was also an amateur performer on a string instrument called a baryton that looks something like a cello.

As was typical of the time, Haydn not only composed but also conducted the performances, trained the musicians, and kept the instruments in repair. Fortunately, he had twenty-five good instrumentalists and a dozen or so fine singers. His contract was typical in that it required him "to produce at once any composition called for" and to smooth out all difficulties among the musicians. He was expected to present himself twice daily to await orders.

For the most part, Haydn's experience with the Esterházy family represented the patronage system at its best.

After Haydn had been with the Esterházys for thirty years, Prince Nicholas died. Haydn subsequently made two visits to London in the 1790s. For each trip he composed six symphonies. After the London visits, he returned to work for a while for Nicholas Esterházy II, who was not as interested in music as his father had been. He gradually retired from composing and died in 1809, the same year Abraham Lincoln was born.

Haydn is sometimes referred to as the "father" of the symphony, the string quartet, the modern orchestra, and instrumental music in general. Although such claims are exaggerated, they give an indication of his importance. What Haydn actually did was work out a better balance for the new forms. For example, he developed the finale of the symphony. Before him, the fourth movement had been no more than a light little section.

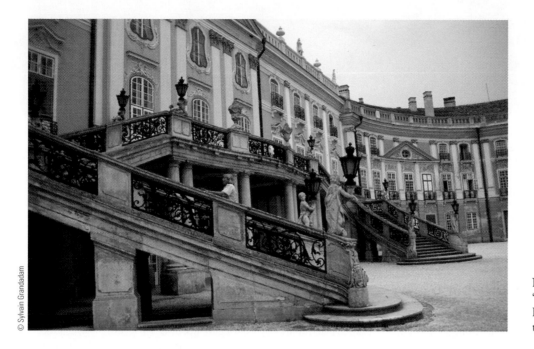

© Sylvain Grandadam

ESTERHÁZY PALACE, the "Hungarian Versailles," where Haydn was court musician for thirty years

- Rondo form contains both something old and something new. The main theme appears a number of times with new material interspersed.

Often the contrasting sections in a rondo do not have memorable themes. Also, occasionally the composer works the material into a short development section, as Haydn does in this concerto. The movement concludes with a coda that contains two brief statements of the main theme.

ThomsonNOW
Continue reviewing characteristics of Classical music in *ThomsonNOW*'s "Connecting the Dots" lecture, Chapter 17.

CODA

The music of the Classical period seems so—civilized. It presents neatly organized themes in balanced, sensible formal plans. Those forms are applied to works for instruments and orchestras in interesting and musically satisfying ways.

18

Classical Opera

A span of about 185 years passed between the first Baroque operas and Mozart's highly successful operas. In some ways, the genre had changed somewhat during that time, but in other ways it was similar. It was still the great amalgamation of the arts that brought together vocal and instrumental music, theater, and sometimes dance. And the music still consisted of accompanied recitatives, arias, and choruses that are clearly distinguishable from one another.

THE DEVELOPMENT OF OPERA

But changes had taken place. Although operas began around 1600 consisting largely of dramatic singing in recitative style, that soon became much less important than arias displaying virtuoso singing. The combination of music and drama had grown so out of balance that near the end of the Baroque, the composer Christoph Willibald Gluck (1714–1787) felt compelled to lead a reform movement. Gluck had composed many operas himself, so he knew the genre well. He tried to bring back its dramatic integrity by making the music serve the text. Everything in opera, including ballet, was to be an integral part of the drama. Gluck composed several operas that demonstrated his reforms.

"The War of the Buffoons" occurred about the middle of the eighteenth century in Paris between those who favored opera buffa and those who favored the more serious court opera. The word *buffoon* is derived from *buffa*.

In the decades following the opening of the first opera house in Venice, opera divided into two rather distinct styles. **Opera seria** had a serious nature and was closer to the original dramatic intent of the first operas. **Opera buffa** ("*boo*-fah") was a light style that was often comic.

MOZART'S OPERAS

Mozart's operas differed from Baroque operas in several ways. For one thing, his more successful ones were not based on historical or mythological characters such as those in Purcell's *Dido and Aeneas* (mythological) or Monteverdi's *Coronation of Poppea* (historical). In short, they were much more human. They were often about the nobility, who sometimes came off looking less than noble.

The play on which Mozart's *The Marriage of Figaro* is based has a servant outwitting a count. The play was forbidden in Vienna. The libretto was made less offensive and was acceptable because it was sung, not spoken.

Another difference was that Mozart composed in both the seria and buffa types. His biggest successes were of the buffa type, which were in German, his native language. His seria operas were in Italian, a language that Mozart knew quite well because of his visits to Italy. Opera audiences in Vienna at the time were used to hearing operas in Italian and were fond of that style.

Mozart's operas also differed from Baroque operas because he was such a gifted composer. His arias are usually of exceptional musical quality, so much so that many of them are often sung at performances apart from the opera. Several of the orchestral overtures to his operas enjoy similar status.

MOZART'S *DON GIOVANNI*

Don Giovanni (*Don Juan*) is a legendary Spanish nobleman whose appetite for women attracted many composers and playwrights before Mozart. Don Juan's exploits seemed to provide a source for artistic ideas. Mozart received a commission for the opera from an opera company in Prague, largely because of the huge success a year earlier of his opera *The Marriage of Figaro*. The libretto for both operas was written by the Italian Lorenzo da Ponte, the most recognized librettist of his day. *Don Giovanni* was warmly received in Prague but was less successful in Vienna. Apparently, the Viennese did not take to what seemed to them the opera's heavier qualities.

For the most part, *Don Giovanni* is opera seria. It contains some humorous moments, but its outlook is serious. Because of the opera's length, the discussion here is limited mainly to the last portion. The plot is intricate, so the opera should be listened to with the aid of an English translation of the libretto.

Don Giovanni opens with a typical overture. The stage action starts as Don Giovanni begins his adventures with Ottavio's fiancée, Donna Anna. She refuses his advances, and her father, the Commendatore (the Commandant), is killed by Don Giovanni in a duel while defending his daughter's virginity. At an engagement party, Don Giovanni attempts to seduce Zerlina, the bride of the peasant Masetto.

Later Don Giovanni plays a cruel trick on Donna Elvira, whom he had seduced long ago and then deserted, and pursues other sexual adventures and pleasures. During one of his escapades, he takes refuge in a cemetery, where he discovers the statue of the Commandant and mockingly invites it to dinner. The statue nods its head to accept the invitation.

The final scene is set in the banquet hall in Don Giovanni's palace. The light, bouncy music lets the audience know immediately that the Don isn't worried. In fact, he seems to have forgotten all about the graveyard and the statue. He commands his private orchestra to play some dinner music. A wind ensemble plays a song from a popular opera of the day:

Leporello serves the table and looks hungrily at the food. "What a greedy appetite," he complains as he watches Don Giovanni down one mouthful after another.

A second piece is heard from the wind ensemble:

Leporello pours the Don some wine and, thinking that he won't be seen, stuffs some food in his mouth. As the third number begins—"Non più andrai" from Mozart's own *Marriage of Figaro*—Leporello helps himself to more food.

The Don, realizing that Leporello's mouth is full, asks him to whistle along with the music from *Figaro*. Poor Leporello is forced to admit that he has been snitching. The whole scene bubbles along like champagne.

Donna Elvira breaks the mood as she rushes in and throws herself at Don Giovanni's feet. She begs her former lover to give up his immoral ways. Leporello is moved, but not Don Giovanni. He mocks Donna Elvira by proposing a toast to her ("Long live women and good wine!"). Angered and humiliated, she turns and runs out the door. As she is leaving, she screams as she sees the statue of the Commandant.

The music reflects the lines of the characters—the sternness of the Commandant, the cowardice of Leporello, and the cockiness of Don Giovanni. At several points in the music, Mozart has the singers repeat words or phrases. In this book those repetitions appear only the first time they are sung, which makes the libretto less cluttered.

The fascination with Don Juan continued well into the nineteenth century with Richard Strauss's orchestral tone poem *Don Juan*.

It is claimed that Mozart composed the overture only one day before its performance.

Notice how the story and music build to a climactic movement.

WOLFGANG AMADEUS MOZART
Don Giovanni, excerpt from Act II, Scene 5 (1778)

GENRE: Opera   Soloists, chorus, and orchestra

CD 1 Tracks 46–49
8 minutes 52 seconds

Donna Elvira screams.

0:00 **46** 0:00   **DON GIOVANNI:** Che grido è questo mai? | **DON GIOVANNI:** What's that scream about?

LEPORELLO: Che grido è questo mai? | **LEPORELLO:** What's that scream about?

DON GIOVANNI: Va a veder che cosa è stato. | **DON GIOVANNI:** *(to Leporello)* Go and see what's happened.

Leporello goes to the first door, looks out, screams, and returns.

LEPORELLO: Ah! | **LEPORELLO:** *(screaming)* Ah!

DON GIOVANNI: Che grido indiavolato! Leporello, che cos'è? | **DON GIOVANNI:** What a devilish scream! Leporello, what is it?

LEPORELLO: Ah! Signor! per carità! non andate fuor di quà! l'uom di sasso, l'uomo bianco, ah! padrone! io gelo, io manco. Se vedeste che figura, se sentiste come fa ta, ta, ta, ta! | **LEPORELLO:** Ah! Sir, for pete's sake don't go out there! The man of stone, the white man. Ah! Master! I'm cold; I'm shaking. If you had seen that form; if you had heard how it goes—ta, ta, ta, ta!

DON GIOVANNI: Non capisco niente affatto. | **DON GIOVANNI:** I don't understand this.

LEPORELLO: Ta, ta, ta, ta! | **LEPORELLO:** *(imitating the statue)* Ta, ta, ta, ta!

DON GIOVANNI: Tu sei matto in verità, in verità, in verità! | **DON GIOVANNI:** Really, you're crazy!

A knock is heard.

LEPORELLO: Ah! sentite! | **LEPORELLO:** Ah! Do you hear!

DON GIOVANNI: Qualcun batte! Apri! | **DON GIOVANNI:** *(impatiently)* Someone's knocking! Open it!

LEPORELLO: Io tremo! | **LEPORELLO:** I'm trembling!

DON GIOVANNI: Apri, dico! | **DON GIOVANNI:** Open it, I say!

LEPORELLO: Ah! | **LEPORELLO:** *(pleading and terrified)* Ah!

DON GIOVANNI: Apri! | **DON GIOVANNI:** Open it!

LEPORELLO: Ah! | **LEPORELLO:** Ah!

DON GIOVANNI: Matto! Per togliermi d'intrico ad aprir io stesso andrò. | **DON GIOVANNI:** Madman! In order to clear this up, I'll open the door myself!

Don Giovanni takes one of the candle stands from the table and goes to the door.
Leporello crawls underneath the table.

LEPORELLO: Non vo' più veder l'amico, plan, pianin, m'asconderò! | **LEPORELLO:** I don't want to see my friend again. Quietly, very quietly, I'll hide!

With a rumbling of timpani, the marble statue
of the Commandant enters the room.

1:30 **47** 0:00   **STATUE:** Don Giovanni! a cenar teco m'invitasti! e son venuto! | **STATUE:** Don Giovanni! You invited me to dine with you! And I have arrived!

Don Giovanni is somewhat startled but conceals his surprise under an air of cockiness.

DON GIOVANNI: No l'avrei giammai creduto; ma farò quel che potrò. Leporello! un'altra centa! fa che subito si porti!

DON GIOVANNI: I can hardly believe this. But I'll do what I can. Leporello, another dinner! Bring it immediately!

Leporello peers out from under the table with a bewildered look on his face.

LEPORELLO: Ah, padron! slam tutti morti!

LEPORELLO: Ah, master! We're as good as dead!

DON GIOVANNI: Vanne, dico!

DON GIOVANNI: Get to it, I say!

Leporello begins to crawl out.

STATUE: Ferma un po'! non si pasce di cibo mortale, chi si pasce di cibo seleste! Altre cure più gravi di queste, altra brama quaggiù mi guidò.

STATUE: Wait a minute! One who partakes of heavenly food does not partake of mortal food. Things more serious than these brought me down here.

Leporello crawls back under the table.

LEPORELLO: La terzana d'avere mi sembra, e le membra fermar più non sò.

LEPORELLO: I have the chills and I can't stop shaking.

DON GIOVANNI: Parla dunque! che chiedi? che vuoi?

DON GIOVANNI: *(to the Statue)* Speak, then! What do you want?

STATUE: Parlo: ascolta! più tempo non ho.

STATUE: I speak—listen! I don't have much time.

DON GIOVANNI: Parla, ascoltando ti sto.

DON GIOVANNI: Speak! I am listening.

LEPORELLO: Ah le membra fermar più non sò. la terzana d'avere mi sembra, le membra fermar più non sò!

LEPORELLO: Ah! I can't stop shaking. I have the chills.

STATUE: Parlo: ascolta! più tempo non ho.

STATUE: I speak—listen! I don't have much time!

Don Giovanni becomes more defiant.

DON GIOVANNI: Parla, ascoltando ti sto.

DON GIOVANNI: Speak! I am listening!

STATUE: Tu m'invitasti a cena, il tuo dover or sai, rispondimi, verrai tu a cenar meco?

STATUE: You invited me to dinner. Do you know your obligation? Answer me! Will you come to dine with me?

Leporello shakes with fear beneath the table.

LEPORELLO: Oibò, tempo no ha, scusate.

LEPORELLO: Oh! He doesn't have time, sorry.

DON GIOVANNI: A torto di viltate tacciato mai sarò.

DON GIOVANNI: *(coolly)* I will never be accused of being a coward.

STATUE: Risolvi!

STATUE: Decide!

DON GIOVANNI: Ho già risolto!

DON GIOVANNI: I have already decided!

STATUE: Verrai?

STATUE: You will come?

LEPORELLO: Dite di no! dite di no!

LEPORELLO: Say no. Just say no!

DON GIOVANNI: Ho fermo il core in petto, non ho timor, verrò!

DON GIOVANNI: My heartbeat is steady. I am not afraid! I will come!

The statue extends a hand toward Don Giovanni.

6:10 **48** 0:00 **STATUE:** Dammi la mano in pegno!

STATUE: Give me your hand as a pledge!

Still defiant, Don Giovanni gives the statue his hand.

DON GIOVANNI: Eccola! Ohime!

DON GIOVANNI: Here it is! Ah!

STATUE: Cos'hai!

STATUE: What's the matter?

DON GIOVANNI: Che gelo è questo mai?

DON GIOVANNI: It's freezing cold!

STATUE: Pentiti, cangia vita, è l'ultimo momento!

STATUE: Repent! Change your life! It's your last chance!

(continued)

Don Giovanni tries to withdraw his hand.

DON GIOVANNI: No, no, ch'io non mi
pento, vanne lontan da me!

DON GIOVANNI: No, no. I will not repent! Get
away from me!

STATUE: Pentiti, scellerato!

STATUE: Repent, villain!

DON GIOVANNI: No, vecchio infatuato!

DON GIOVANNI: No, you stupid old man!

STATUE: Pentiti!

STATUE: Repent!

DON GIOVANNI: No!

DON GIOVANNI: No!

STATUE: Pentiti!

STATUE: Repent!

DON GIOVANNI: No!

DON GIOVANNI: No!

STATUE: Sì!

STATUE: Yes!

DON GIOVANNI: No!

DON GIOVANNI: No!

STATUE: Sì!

STATUE: Yes!

DON GIOVANNI: No!

DON GIOVANNI: No!

With a desperate effort, he wrests his hand away from the statue.

STATUE: Sì! Sì!

STATUE: Yes! Yes!

DON GIOVANNI: No! No!

DON GIOVANNI: No! No!

The Commandant's statue begins to move toward the door.
Roaring flames begin to surround Don Giovanni.

STATUE: Ah! tempo più non v'è!

STATUE: Ah! There is no more time!

DON GIOVANNI: Da qual tremore insolito
sentoassalir gli spiriti! dond'escono
quei vortici di foco pien d'orror?

DON GIOVANNI: I feel my strength afflicted by
really unusual trembling! Where are those
horrible whirlpools of fire coming from?

A chorus of ghostly demon voices sounds from below.

7:42 **49** 0:00 DEMON VOICES: Tutto a tue colpe è
poco! vieni! c'è un ma! peggior!

DEMON VOICES: This is nothing compared to your
crimes! Worse things await you!

DON GIOVANNI: Chi l'anima mi lacera?
Chi m'agita le viscere? Che strazio,
ohimè, che smania! Che inferno, che
terror!

DON GIOVANNI: Who rips my spirit? Who shakes
my innards? What twisting, alas, what frenzy!
What hell! What terror!

LEPORELLO: Che ceffo disperato! Che
gesti da dannato! che gridi! che
lamenti! come mi fa terror!

LEPORELLO: What a terrible look on his face!
What gestures of a damned soul! What shouts!
What wailing! It terrifies me!

DEMON VOICES: Tutto a tue colpe
è poco!

DEMON VOICES: All this is nothing compared to
your crimes!

DON GIOVANNI: Chi l'anima mi lacera?

DON GIOVANNI: Who rips my spirit?

LEPORELLO: Che ceffo disperato!

LEPORELLO: What a terrible look on his face!

DEMON VOICES: Vieni! c'è un mal
peggior!

DEMON VOICES: Come! Worse things await you!

DON GIOVANNI: Chi m'agita le viscere?
che strazio, ohimè, che smania!
Ah! che inferno! che terror!

DON GIOVANNI: Who shakes my innards?
What twisting, alas, what frenzy!
Ah! What hell! What terror!

LEPORELLO: Che gesti da dannato! che
gridi! che lamenti! Come mi fa terror!

LEPORELLO: What gestures of a damned soul!
What shouts! What wailing! It terrifies me!

DEMON VOICES: Vieni! vieni! vieni!
c'è un mal peggior!

DEMON VOICES: Come! Worse things await you!

DON GIOVANNI: Ah!

DON GIOVANNI: (*screaming*) Ah!

Don Giovanni utters his final sound, is enveloped by flames, and sinks to hell.
Leporello echoes the Don's shout.

LEPORELLO: Ah!

LEPORELLO: Ah!

1:12 Recording fades.

Don Giovanni on Stage in London Gerald Finley (as Don Giovanni) and Robert LLoyd (as Commendante) in the production "Don Giovanni" at the Royal Opera House in Covent Garden.

Following the immolation of Don Giovanni, the mood suddenly changes to something more lighthearted. Donna Anna, Donna Elvira, and Zerlina rush in, followed by Ottavio and Masetto. They find Leporello crawling about on the floor and demand to know what has happened. Leporello stammers out the story of what he just witnessed.

The music is again filled with wit and sparkle. Don Giovanni is already just a memory. In a brief duet, Donna Anna and Ottavio tell of their plans to marry after her year of mourning for her father is over. Donna Elvira pledges to end her days in a cloister. Zerlina and Masetto are anxious to be off so they can have dinner. And Leporello sets about finding himself a new master. As the six singers face the audience, they deliver the moral of the opera. The whole scene is so mischievous that one wonders whether Mozart was not really attempting to have the last laugh with the moralizing. The sextet sings:

> *Such is the end*
> *Of those who do evil.*
> *The death of the wicked*
> *Always matches their life.*

This last scene containing moralizing by the sextet has often been omitted from the opera. In the nineteenth century, it was thought out of place after the damnation of Don Giovanni. Mozart himself approved the deletion the second time it was staged.

CODA

The music of Mozart's opera represents its eighteenth-century outlook in its good taste and controlled emotions. True, the librettos of his comic operas are sometimes spiced with double entendres, and the singers' emotions are exaggerated for comic effect, but the situations in his serious operas often contain strong emotions and drama. And the music is always handled with a restraint that contrasts nicely with any incongruities of text or action. Even in serious moments, he does not allow the music to become too overbearing or sentimental. There is about his operatic writing a light touch, an awareness that music can be of high quality even when conceived of as entertainment.

© Robbie Jack/Corbis

LISTENING GUIDE

LUDWIG VAN BEETHOVEN

Piano Sonata No. 21, Op. 53, "Waldstein," First Movement (1804)

GENRE: Sonata   Piano

CD 4 Tracks 1–5
11 minutes 11 seconds

Form: Sonata

Exposition

0:00	**1**	0:00	First theme in major, with many repeated notes and two motives. (Repeats at 1:28)

	0:22	First theme repeated with a different accompaniment. (Repeats at 1:50)
0:56	**2** 0:00	Second theme in a different major key, then repeated with some changes. (Repeats at 2:24)

	0:28	Transition begins with triplet figures. Then sixteenth notes take over. (Repeats at 2:52)
	1:05	Codetta with its own theme. (Repeats at 3:28)

Development

4:55	**3**	0:00	Motives from first theme modulate.
		0:38	More triplet figures.
		1:27	Music becomes quiet, then slowly builds.

Recapitulation

6:45	**4**	0:00	First theme returns.
		0:23	Short, quiet interlude.
		0:34	First theme repeated with a different accompaniment.
		1:10	Second theme returns.
		1:18	Second theme repeated in minor and then in major.
		1:38	Transition begins with triplet figures.

Coda

9:00	**5**	0:00	Coda theme in minor but soon repeated in major.
		0:29	Motives from first theme, with frequent changes of key.
		1:19	Long chords followed by pauses.
		1:26	Second theme returns quietly, followed by pauses.
		1:59	First theme returns vigorously.
		2:11	Movement ends with short, abrupt chords.

Ludwig van Beethoven

Ludwig van Beethoven ("*Bay*-toe-ven," 1770–1827) was born in Bonn, Germany. His father was an alcoholic musician who hoped that young Ludwig would be a prodigy like Mozart and bring in lots of money. Although talented, young Beethoven never became the prodigy his father hoped for. At the age of twenty-two, he set off for Vienna, which was to be his home for the remainder of his life.

Beethoven had little formal schooling. He studied composition with several teachers, including a few lessons with Haydn, and made a name for himself as a pianist. He was able to win the support and admiration of the aristocracy and in ten years established himself as a composer and performer. Although he was trained in the formal style of the Classical period, other events left a lasting impression on Beethoven. One was the revolutionary spirit that was awakening in Europe, which erupted in the French Revolution in 1789.

Then there was Beethoven's own personality. Were he alive today, he would probably identify himself with humanitarian causes and social protest groups. For example, as early as 1792 he had thought of setting German dramatist-poet Friedrich von Schiller's "Ode to Joy" to music. The ethical ideals of the universal human race and its basis in the love of a heavenly Father expressed in the poem appealed to Beethoven, and he used it as the text for the last movement of his Ninth Symphony. He was probably the first composer in history to be considered a "personality." His mature works sound like no one else's music.

Beethoven's high ideals did not carry over to his dealings with publishers. He was sometimes unscrupulous with them.

Beethoven's personality was also affected by a gradual loss of hearing that eventually led to complete deafness. The condition was evident by the time he was twenty-eight, and it caused him to lose contact with others and to withdraw into himself. His final compositions were products of this time in his life, and they tend to be more personal, meditative, and abstract.

How was it possible for Beethoven to write entire symphonies when he was deaf? The process can be understood if you think about your own experience. You can recall melodies and the sounds of people's voices in your memory, even though you aren't actually hearing them. Trained musicians can think out a large amount of music in their minds. And Beethoven was clearly a well-trained musician with outstanding abilities!

There is a second reason for his ability to compose while deaf. It was his custom to write down themes in a sketchbook. Then he would work over these themes, revising and rewriting them, and trying them out to determine their suitability for the piece he had in mind. This process went on over a period of years, so the themes for many of his later compositions had actually been worked out when he was still able to hear fairly well.

Beethoven was not a "natural" composer as Mozart was. He poured much effort into each measure he wrote, as is evident from the manuscript on page 166. As someone once said, his manuscripts look "like a bloody record of a tremendous inner battle."

Beethoven was more successful in writing instrumental music than vocal music. He composed much excellent chamber music, with his string quartets representing a high point for that ensemble. His five piano concertos and one violin concerto are staples in the music performed in concert halls today. His overtures to dramas and his opera are also performed often. He was not as at ease with music for singers. He composed only one opera, *Fidelio,* and compared its writing to the process of childbirth. He

BEST-KNOWN WORKS

chamber music:
- String Quartets Nos. 7 and 14

choral:
- *Missa solemnis*

orchestra:
- Piano Concertos Nos. 3, 4, and 5 ("Emperor")
- Violin Concerto
- *Egmont Overture*
- *Overture to Leonore No. 3*
- Symphonies Nos. 3 ("Eroica"), 5, 6 ("Pastoral"), 7, 8, and 9 ("Choral")

opera:
- *Fidelio*

piano:
- Sonatas Nos. 8 ("Pathétique"), 14 ("Moonlight"), 21 ("Waldstein"), and 23 ("Appassionata")

(continued)

(continued)

Courtesy Gesellschaft der Musikfreunde in Wien

ONE OF BEETHOVEN'S EAR TRUMPETS, an early type of hearing aid. The mechanist J. N. Mälzel, inventor of the metronome, made a variety of ear trumpets for the increasingly deaf composer.

did compose two major religious works, however, and his Ninth Symphony features a chorus and soloists in the fourth movement.

Beethoven's death from jaundice and cholera occurred during a thunderstorm, a coincidence that seems appropriate to the man and his life.

In a work such as this sonata, the pianist plays an enormous number of notes.

Following the second theme, the *triplets* (three notes to the beat) take over and become the main thought leading to the codetta:

The coda is greatly expanded. Instead of stopping after the closing theme, the first theme starts up again. Soon its two motives are treated to another development. This second development is much like the first, with the addition of rapidly moving scale passages.

Second Movement

There is an unconfirmed story that Beethoven wrote a lengthy second movement but was persuaded by a friend to exchange it for the present short version.

The second movement is hardly a movement at all. Instead, it is a short section that Beethoven labeled "Introduzione." It sounds like an introspective introduction to the third movement.

Third Movement

The third movement is a rondo—but what a rondo! Unlike the rondo in Haydn's Concerto for Trumpet in E-flat, with its short, happy melodies and four-minute length, this rondo has those monumental qualities that we will observe in Beethoven's Fifth

Symphony. As a result it is more than twice as long as Haydn's rondo. Its theme is presented several times, as happens in rondos, but several times it is treated like a theme in a symphony as it appears three times in a row, each time more magnificent than before.

CODA

It is difficult for us today, who have radios and CDs so readily available, to realize the important role that the piano played in making music available a hundred or more years ago. Very few people ever heard works for large ensembles until the twentieth century. For more than 150 years, the piano was the main means of presenting music. What Mozart, Haydn, and Beethoven began with their piano sonatas would be expanded by composers in the nineteenth century. But the groundwork had been laid in the Classical period.

The Symphony *and* Beethoven

Our discussion of the symphony is presented in conjunction with one of the biggest names in concert music: Ludwig van Beethoven. He did not develop the genre, but he certainly changed it in a massive way.

With Beethoven the symphony became the most important and largest musical genre during his lifetime and for nearly a hundred years afterward. Beethoven composed just nine symphonies, and most of them take about forty minutes or more to perform. Haydn wrote more than a hundred symphonies and Mozart about fifty, some as short as fifteen minutes. But number and length were not the only differences.

THE SYMPHONY

A **symphony** is a large work composed for an orchestra that is divided into movements, usually four. The four movements present a contrast of tempo and mood.

BEETHOVEN'S SYMPHONY NO. 5

Beethoven composed his Symphony No. 5 in C Minor, Op. 67, between 1804 and 1808, when it received its premiere performance. Less than twenty years passed between when Mozart composed his Symphony No. 40 and Beethoven composed his Symphony No. 5. But what huge changes Beethoven wrought in his symphony!

The difference might best be described by the word *more*. Mozart and Haydn developed themes and had some contrast in their music, but Beethoven presents much more development and more contrast of mood and character. In some of Beethoven's music, including his Fifth Symphony, he seems to want to burst the limits of musical sound. Musical ideas are worked and reworked and reworked again. Some chords are almost hammered into the listeners' ears, and at other times a quiet interlude is suddenly interrupted with a burst of sound.

The result of the sudden contrasts, the many repeated notes, and the extensive development of themes is music infused with more emotion. "The whole is greater than the sum of its parts" applies to all music, but especially to Beethoven's music. He achieved in it an emotional quality that had never existed before. His music often has more—much more—emotional content than the typical symphony or sonata of composers just one generation before him.

Beethoven was fortunate—and so is anyone who listens to it—that his music tends to be a bridge from the Classical style to the approaching Romantic style; it contains the best of both worlds. His training was in the style of Mozart and Haydn, as reflected in his early works. But then he added that "more" quality to his music, expanded it, and gave it greater emotional impact. His Fifth Symphony demonstrates these qualities well. From the "Fate knocking at the door" motive in the first movement, to the beautiful and dramatic second movement, to the lively and playful third movement, to the dramatic bridge leading to the monumental fourth movement, this

Beethoven also increased the size of the orchestra, including the addition of trombones and the piccolo.

ThomsonNOW™

"Hear It Now: Development in Music," in *ThomsonNOW,* Chapter 21.

symphony can appropriately be thought of as an emotional musical journey of epic proportions.

First Movement

This movement is a prime example of how Beethoven took what appears to be an ordinary theme and built something monumental out of it. It begins with a four-note motive. These four notes are repeated again and again, and they become the basis for the main theme:

And what happens to that theme? It is treated as a germinal idea. For example, right after the first theme is presented, it is developed somewhat in the transition leading to the second theme:

Most of the development section is an outgrowth of the original theme. Beethoven does such things as fill in the interval of the original motive:

Sometimes to the filled-in interval he adds the inversion—the upside-down version—of the motive:

He reiterates a few simple musical ideas based on the theme:

He also fragments themes. The notes circled in the second example in the Listening Guide are the two middle pitches from the transition played by the French horn. The

There have been several attempts to explain the origin of this motive. One is that it is Fate knocking at the door; another claims that the three dots and a dash stand for the letter *V* in Morse code. Neither of these theories has been substantiated. The latter is especially doubtful because Morse code was developed years after the writing of the symphony!

Notice the extensive use of sequence in this example.

two pitches are echoed between the woodwinds and the strings, and then the segment is fragmented further until just one note is echoed:

The first two-note fragments have boxes around them in the example.

There are also long, gradual crescendos and abrupt changes from loud to soft.

The recapitulation is followed by an extended coda. In fact, the coda in Beethoven's symphonies is almost as important as the other three sections of sonata form. He seemed to regard it as a second development section. A synthesis of the themes of the coda can be seen in this example:

The first theme is circled here.

The pitches of the first theme and the rhythm pattern of the transition are combined. The two-pitch fragment emphasized in the development appears again, this time in a downward sequence.

LISTENING GUIDE

LUDWIG VAN BEETHOVEN

Symphony No. 5 in C Minor, First Movement (1808)

GENRE: Symphony   **Allegro con brio (fast, with energy)**   **Symphony orchestra**

CD 2 Tracks 1–5
7 minutes 32 seconds

Form: Sonata

Exposition

0:00   **1**   0:00   Orchestra vigorously plays the four-motive from the first theme in minor. (Repeated at 0:41)

0:07   First theme followed by motive in sequence. (Repeated at 0:48)

0:22   Transition built around repeated fragments of first theme. (Repeated at 1:03)

0:44   French horn expands on four-note motive and creates two-note motive. (Repeated at 1:25)

0:46 **2** 0:00 Strings and woodwinds softly play second theme in a major key. Inverted version of four-note motive is soon heard on low strings. (Repeated at 1:28)

p sweetly

0:21 Codetta based on four-note motive. (Repeated at 1:49)

Development

2:54 **3** 0:00 French horns, then strings play first theme. Four-note motive, sometimes inverted, is passed sequentially among sections.

0:28 Winds and strings play full-sounding chords followed by silences.

0:36 Strings play first theme.

0:46 Winds and strings alternate playing the two-note motive derived from first theme. Soon reduced to one note.

1:09 Orchestra plays portion of first theme loudly, followed by soft notes in the woodwinds.

1:17 Motive repeated five times leading to . . .

Recapitulation

4:17 **4** 0:00 First theme.

0:20 Short oboe cadenza.

0:34 Transition.

0:55 French horn plays expanded motive.

0:58 Violins and woodwinds play second theme, again in major, followed by transition.

1:24 Violins outline chords based on first theme.

Coda

5:59 **5** 0:00 Strings vigorously play many repeated notes.

0:16 Expanded and extended treatment of four-note motive.

0:42 Woodwinds and strings alternate four-note motive. It is then fragmented to two notes.

1:08 Orchestra forcefully repeats first theme.

1:32 The movement closes with brusque chords.

Second Movement

The second movements of almost all symphonies created in the eighteenth and nineteenth centuries are slow and melodic in character. In addition to the contrast in character, second movements also differ in their home key. If the symphony is in a major key, the tonic of the second movement is usually in the major key four notes higher. For example, a symphony in G major would have a second movement in C major, a key that has one less sharp than G. If the key is in minor, the second movement is in the major key three steps higher. In the case of Beethoven's Symphony No. 5 in C Minor, the second movement is in E-flat major. Its signature is the same as the signature of C minor. The main point to remember is that the second movement is in a *different* key from the rest of the symphony.

Several forms can be found in second movements of symphonies. The most common is the large three-part form, *A B A*. Theme and variations are also encountered some of the time, and even sonata form with a shortened development section is used.

The second movement of Beethoven's Fifth Symphony reveals his ability to write beautiful melodies. He is so often thought of in terms of the brusque, forceful qualities

Keys are considered closely related if their key signatures are no more than one sharp or flat different.

The eighth note (♪) receives the beat in 3/8 meter. Therefore, the music moves much more slowly than it looks like it should.

LUDWIG VAN BEETHOVEN

Symphony No. 5 in C Minor, Second Movement (1808)

GENRE: Symphony   Andante con moto (walking)   Symphony orchestra

CD 4 Tracks 6–10
10 minutes 1 second

Form: Theme and variations

Themes

0:00   **6**   0:00   Theme 1: major, in three-beat meter with three parts. **Part 1:** violas and cellos.

0:24   Part 2 of first theme: woodwinds.

0:36   Part 3 of first theme: violins.

0:53   Theme 2: violins and woodwinds.

1:14   Brasses play second theme in an expansive style.

1:30   Music becomes quiet and mysterious.

Variation 1

1:58   **7**   0:00   On theme 1: Strings play steadily moving notes.

0:33   On theme 1: Strings play third part.

0:51   On theme 2: Woodwinds and violins are featured.

1:12   On theme 2: Brasses play in an expansive manner.

1:29   Music becomes quiet and mysterious.

Variation 2

3:52   **8**   0:00   On theme 1: Lower, then upper strings play rapidly moving notes.

0:36   On theme 1: Lower strings play rapidly moving notes.

1:12   On theme 1: Woodwinds quietly play fragments.

1:58   On theme 2: Orchestra plays in a majestic style.

2:44   On theme 1: Woodwinds play short notes in minor.

Variation 3

7:18   **9**   0:00   On theme 1: Violins play first part.

0:25   On theme 1: Woodwinds play second part.

0:35   On theme 1: Strings play third part.

Coda

8:09	🔟 0:00	Tempo increases as bassoons play beginning of first theme.
	0:14	Violins play fragments of second theme.
	0:29	Woodwinds and strings alternate parts of first theme.
	1:18	Low strings begin a crescendo using fragments of first theme.
	1:48	Movement concludes with abrupt chords.

in some of his music that it is easy to forget he could write lovely lyric melodies as well.

This movement of the Fifth Symphony is a theme and variations built on two melodic ideas. The first one contains three shorter melodic sections. During the course of the second movement, these ideas are varied by changing the melody and ornamenting it, and by altering the harmony, rhythm, dynamics, tempo, and type of accompaniment.

Third Movement

The third movement of the symphonies of Haydn and Mozart was a stylized dance—the minuet. With its graceful 3/4 meter, it provided a nice contrast to the lyric, melodious second movement. Even the three-part form of the minuet was followed, with the middle section being called the *trio*. This movement was in the home key of the symphony.

Beethoven made two important changes in the minuet of his predecessors:

- He called for a faster tempo, which gave the movement a more lively, energetic, jovial character. No longer was 3/4 felt in three beats per measure; rather, the music is felt in one strong beat per measure.

- He named the movement "Scherzo," a word that means "joke" in Italian. Accordingly, the movement did not just fulfill a formal pattern; it could—and often did—contain surprises for its listeners.

This was not the first time Beethoven had composed a scherzo for a symphony. The first one appears in his Third Symphony.

The main theme of the third movement is one that several other composers of the time had also used. In fact, the theme had acquired a name—the "Mannheim rocket." The *Mannheim* part of the name comes from the southern German city that figured prominently in the development of the symphony, and the *rocket* probably came from the fact that it is the ascending notes of a chord.

The trio of the movement is interesting in that it starts out sounding like a lively fugue, but Beethoven does not follow through with a full-blown fugue. In musical terms, he wrote a *fugato*—a fugue like passage.

Another feature of the movement is its attachment to the fourth movement. A movement normally comes to an end, and a few moments of silence are observed before the next movement begins. Beethoven and composers who followed him sometimes connected two movements.

Fourth Movement

The fourth movements of Classical symphonies are lively and filled with happy melodies. Apparently, the hope was to have the listeners leave feeling good. Often fourth movements are rondos. They were almost always in the home key of the symphony.

But Beethoven seems to have been more interested in leaving a serious but positive impression on his audiences. His optimism had deeper roots than just pleasant, cheery music.

LISTENING GUIDE

Symphony No. 5 in C Minor, Third Movement (1808)

GENRE: Symphony   Allegro (fast)   Symphony orchestra

CD 4 Tracks 11–14
5 minutes 28 seconds

Form: Scherzo and trio

Scherzo

0:00 **11** 0:00   Low strings play "rocket" theme softly in minor; music has an "eerie" character.

0:19   French horns forcefully play second theme in major.

0:40   Low strings softly play the "rocket" theme.

1:03   Orchestra plays second theme loudly.

1:24   Strings softly play opening theme.

Trio

1:58 **12** 0:00   Cellos and basses play a dancelike theme in a major key. Other instruments soon follow in imitation.

0:16   Imitative section is repeated.

0:59   Low strings play a short link to opening theme.

Scherzo

3:28 **13** 0:00   Low strings quietly play opening theme. More strings enter playing pizzicato (plucking).

0:21   Woodwinds play second theme softly.

Bridge to Fourth Movement

4:46 **14** 0:00   Strings quietly sustain a long note as timpani quietly play a slow, steady stream of notes.

0:13   Three-note pattern begins in violins and is repeated many times as music grows louder, key changes to major, and music leads without a break to fourth movement.

　　　The fourth movement of Beethoven's Fifth Symphony is in sonata form. A rondo would not have accommodated the monumental concept of this movement. The themes, especially the first one, contribute to it.

　　　An unusual feature of this fourth movement is the brief appearance of a theme from the third movement. The appearances of themes from other movements would become more common later in the nineteenth century, but it was very rare at the time the Fifth Symphony was composed.

LISTENING GUIDE

LUDWIG VAN BEETHOVEN
Symphony No. 5 in C Minor, Fourth Movement (1808)

GENRE: **Symphony** **Allegro (fast)** **Symphony orchestra**

CD 4 Tracks 15–18
8 minutes 32 seconds

Form: Sonata

Exposition

0.00 **15** 0:00 Orchestra, especially brasses, plays first theme.

0:33 French horns begin transitional theme.

0:59 Strings play second theme.

1:25 Codetta; same phrase appears three times.

Development

2:00 **16** 0:00 Violins play a portion of second theme.

0:08 Fragment from second theme becomes more prominent as music progresses through different keys.

0:23 Low strings play four-note motive as fragments of second theme continue.

0:59 Climax reached as orchestra loudly plays four-note motive followed by a pause.

1:34 Portion of scherzo theme played softly by violins and woodwinds.

Recapitulation

4:09 **17** 0:00 First theme played vigorously by orchestra.

0:33 Transition featuring French horns.

1:04 Second theme played by violins.

1:30 Woodwinds play theme for the codetta.

Coda

6:09 **18** 0:00 Second theme in violins over four-note motive from development in low strings.

0:31 Transition features woodwinds and French horns.

1:14 Tempo suddenly becomes very fast.

1:38 First theme played twice as fast (diminution) by brasses.

2:19 Movement concludes with several V-I cadences and successive soundings of final chord.

© AKG London

PAGES OF BEETHOVEN'S AUTOGRAPH MANUSCRIPT reveal his creative turmoil.

APPRECIATING BEETHOVEN'S MUSIC

The "Waldstein" sonata and the Fifth Symphony have provided a good idea of what Beethoven's music is like. What is it about his music that causes people to continue to listen to it today? What about it has contributed to continuing interest in the man himself? Among the many potential reasons, four stand out:

- *Contrast.* Beethoven's music is filled with dramatic contrasts. His themes often seem to be paired by opposites that can be thought of as male/female, rough/smooth, loud/soft, brusque/tender, and so on. A placid passage can be suddenly broken as a *sforzando* chord is sounded, or a raging section can abruptly cease and change to a gentle melody.

- *Motive development.* Beethoven's music is a showcase of developing musical ideas, especially short, simple ones. A theme becomes a seed that grows and takes many shapes, and it is fascinating to follow that musical process.

Features of Classical Music

Melodies	Often consist of short, tuneful phrases strung together; usually have a light, elegant quality; statement–answer pattern
Rhythm	Metrical with a steady beat, except in recitatives
Texture	Mostly homophonic
Harmony	Tonal with modulations mostly to nearly related keys; continuo part no longer present
Dynamic levels	Gradual crescendo and decrescendo developed
Performance media	Orchestra; chamber music groups; piano replaces harpsichord; vocal music
Forms	Sonata, theme and variations, rondo, and minuet and trio; forms often contain balanced and symmetrical phrases
Genres	Symphony, solo concerto, sonata, chamber music, opera

- *Sense of drive.* Beethoven's music contains a wonderful drive or what has been described as "inevitability." This quality is difficult to put into words, but his music seems always to be heading toward its final destination. Even though it has many changes and stops, the sense of inevitability is still there. Listeners sense that though the music is quiet at a particular moment, that situation will not last. The musical journey will resume and continue on to its inevitable conclusion.

- *Personality.* Beethoven's music has a personality all its own. His mature works don't sound like those of Mozart, Haydn, or any other composer. A person does not need to be familiar with a lot of concert music to sense that there is something unique about Beethoven's music. It presents listeners with dramatic contrasts, a fiery spirit, huge amounts of thematic development, and an inner sense of musical logic.

CODA

Concert music and the symphony were never the same after Beethoven. Now they had become something to be taken seriously. No longer was music just pleasing to hear and something to be enjoyed. Music had moved to a deeper and more profound level.

PART V

Romantic Music

	1820	1850
Historical Events	● Monroe Doctrine	California gold rush ● Revolutions in Europe ●
Visual Arts	● Delacroix, *The Bark of Dante*	

Literature and Theater	Keats
	  Byron
	    Poe
	    Dickens's work
	    Hugo's work
		Hawthorne
		Tennyson's work
		Dumas
		Longfellow's work

Philosophy and Science	Schopenhauer ● Morse telegraph Daguerre photography ●	Kierkegaard's work

Music	Schubert
	  Liszt
	    Mendelssohn's work
	    Chopin's work
	    Berlioz's work
		R. C. Schumann's work
		Verdi's work (right) ►

1875   **1900**

● Franco-Prussian War   ● First automobiles

American Civil War   ● Spanish-American War

                                                        Boer War in South Africa ●

Renoir's work   ● Munch, *The Scream*

● Corot, *Villa d' Avray*   Cezanne's work

Degas's work   ◄ Monet, *Rouen Cathedral* (left)

Dostoevsky's work   Wilde's work

                                                        Kipling's work

Twain's work

Tolstoy's work

T. H. Huxley's work   ● Mill's death   Bergson's work

● Darwin, *Origin of Species*   ● Bell telephone   Marconi radio ●

                    Nietzsche's work   ● Edison light bulb and phonograph

Smetana's work   Debussy's work

                                                        Puccini's operas

                            ● Wagner,   Dvořák's work
                              Bayreuth

Brahms's work

Mussorgsky's work

                                                        ▲ Tchaikovsky, *The Nutcracker* (top)

22 Romance and Romanticism

To most people, the word *romantic* refers to the emotion of love. To scholars, however, it means much more. It comes from *romance,* which originally referred to a medieval poem written in one of the Romance languages (those that developed from Latin) and dealing with a heroic person or event. Later the word took on the connotation of something far away and strange or something imaginative and full of wonder. Yes, it also includes the idea of love—romantic love.

Romanticism came of age during the nineteenth century. It began in some of the music of Beethoven and Schubert, and it continued into the early years of the twentieth century, roughly from 1820 to 1900. In fact, elements of romanticism are still encountered in some music being written today. The Romantic outlook affected every type of music, and it brought several kinds of music to their high point of development.

CHARACTERISTICS OF ROMANTICISM

Romanticism was an artistic viewpoint that also predominated in dance, theater, the visual arts, and music throughout the nineteenth century. What were the features of this outlook?

The love of mystery and the unknown is evident in the song "The Erl King," discussed in Chapter 23.

- Romanticists were fascinated by the unknown and stood in awe of the world. They were impressed by the mystery, not the clarity, of the world and its inhabitants. At times, they were almost mystic. They seemed especially fascinated by the mystery and power of evil.

- Romanticists also tended to rely on emotion and imagination rather than rational intellect, which had been central to the Classical outlook. Feelings replaced reason. Truth became what a person *felt* to be true, so it was wrong to deny one's feelings. Poet John Keats wrote in one of his letters: "I am certain of nothing but the holiness of the heart's affections, and the truth of the imagination. What the imagination seizes as beauty must be truth." Inevitably, Romanticism grew to distrust reason and science. To quote Keats again, this time from his poem "Lamia":

During Keats's lifetime the word *philosophy* was a synonym for *science.*

> *Do not all charms fly*
> *At the mere touch of cold philosophy?*

- Romanticists were fascinated by the long ago and far away. During the Classical era, intellectuals had thought of medieval times as the "Dark Ages"; the Romanticists considered them heroic. Literature is filled with examples of this attitude, including Alfred, Lord Tennyson's *Idylls of the King,* John Keats's "Eve of St. Agnes," Samuel Taylor Coleridge's "Christabel," and Sir Walter Scott's *Ivanhoe.*

- Not only were the Romanticists impressed by the unknown forces of the world; but they also reveled in the struggle against those forces. In Coleridge's poem *The Rime of the Ancient Mariner,* the sailor is "alone on a wide, wide sea."

- Romanticists were enthralled by nature. They had a rural outlook instead of the urban outlook of the Classical period. In Mozart's day the cities—London, Paris, Vienna—were the centers of artistic activity, so they attracted people with creative and artistic interests. To Romanticists, however, nature had more appeal because it

© Museum of Fine Arts, Boston

THE VIRTUES OF RURAL LIFE were celebrated by artists of the Romantic period, as shown in *Potato Planters* by Jean François Millet.

represented a world untainted by humans. Sometimes nature was extolled to the point of pantheism—the belief that God and nature are one. The rural interest of the time led to landscape painting, poems on natural phenomena, and works such as Beethoven's Symphony No. 6 ("Pastoral").

- Many Romanticists resented rules and restraints. They regarded the Classical period as cold and formal and were unimpressed by its rational deductions and universal laws. They felt perfectly capable of making their own rules—and proceeded to do so in their artworks. They cherished freedom, limitless expression, passion, and the pursuit of the unattainable. After all, what more glorious struggle could there be than seeking the impossible? This search is perhaps best represented in the legend of the Holy Grail.

- Beginning with Jean-Jacques Rousseau and the Earl of Shaftesbury (A. A. Cooper) and continuing through the American Henry David Thoreau in the nineteenth century to the present time, a group of philosophers have expounded the idea of natural goodness. The "artificialities" of civilization are rejected because they corrupt people. William Wordsworth summed up the Romanticists' thinking on nature when he wrote in his poem "The Tables Turned":

  > One impulse from vernal wood
  > May teach you more of man,
  > Of moral evil and of good,
  > Than all the sages can.

- Because Romanticists were highly subjective and individualistic, it is not surprising that they tended to be self-centered. Works of art were no longer objective examples of a person's skill. Instead, they were considered a projection of the person who created them. Romantic artists felt that a bit of their psyche had been given to the world

Beethoven intended the music of Symphony No. 6 to convey the moods evoked during his visits to the countryside around Vienna.

The Holy Grail was the cup that Jesus used at the Last Supper. It was believed to have special powers.

Vernal means springtime, and *sages* refers to wise men.

THE BARK OF DANTE, by Eugène Delacroix. Two features of Romantic art and music are evident in this work: love of drama and admiration of the Middle Ages.

VILLA D'AVRAY, by Jean-Baptiste-Camille Corot. Another characteristic of Romanticism was love of nature, which is evident in Beethoven's Symphony No. 6 and many other musical works of the nineteenth century.

in their poems and preludes. Their works were now created for posterity, for an audience that someday, somewhere, would appreciate their true value.

- Some Romanticists were nonsocial, if not antisocial. They withdrew into a world of their own, surrounded by a close circle of friends and admirers. Yet the Romantic era saw the establishment of the concert hall with its large audiences, and some Romantic musicians thoroughly enjoyed the adulation of the public.

- Romantic musicians were often concerned with the other fine arts as well as with philosophy. They were familiar with the writings of Johann Wolfgang von Goethe and Alphonse Lamartine, and many times they knew the writers personally. Franz Liszt wrote a number of literary works, including a book on gypsy music and another entitled *Life of Chopin*. Robert Schumann's literary interests led him to edit a music magazine. Richard Wagner wrote lengthy treatises on music, art, and philosophy. Romantic composers believed strongly in a unity of the arts. This attitude is epitomized in the music dramas of Wagner.

Unfortunately, Liszt's book contains many inaccuracies.

Wagner's music dramas are presented in Chapter 26.

ROMANTIC ART

Eugène Delacroix's *The Bark of Dante* depicts the struggling souls of the wicked people of Florence, Italy, trying to escape from Hell by climbing into the boat with the ancient Roman poet Virgil and the fourteenth-century poet Dante Alighieri, whose best-known work was *The Inferno*. It demonstrates the interest of Romantic artists in subjects from the past and their fascination with evil and its consequences. In the painting the sea and clouds swirl around ominously. The twisted and pained bodies of the Florentines are very much involved in the scene as they struggle hopelessly. There is little symmetry; Dante (in the green cloak) stands about a third of the way from the left. Straight angles are absent, too, as the bodies of the sinners writhe throughout the picture.

The Romanticists' love of nature can be seen in Jean-Baptiste-Camille Corot's *Villa d'Avray*. The painting is of a peaceful rural scene filled with flowers, beautiful trees, and a lake. The two figures in the foreground blend in with the scene. The lake is calm and reflects the villa on the other side. The message of the picture could easily be *Nature is good and beautiful*.

A *Traveler Looking over a Sea of Fog* by Caspar David Friedrich shows another aspect of Romanticism: the-individual-against-all-the-elements attitude, its self-absorbed outlook. Friedrich's belief was that the artist's feeling is his law. The erect, determined posture of the man viewing the fog and mountains is expressed well in the famous nineteenth-century poem "Invictus" by William Ernest Henley, which begins, "I am the master of my fate, the captain of my soul."

© The Bridgeman Art Library (Kunsthalle, Hamburg)

A Traveler Looking over a Sea of Fog, by Caspar David Friedrich. The heroic character was a part of Romantic art and music, culminating in Richard Strauss's tone poem *Ein Heldenleben (A Hero's Life)*.

THE SPLIT PERSONALITY OF ROMANTICISM

Every era in history seems to carry its contradictions. In the case of the **Romantic period,** those contradictions are massive. On the one hand, it produced much extremely beautiful and tender music and works of art. On the other hand, it showed a fascination with evil and misery. Song after song and opera after opera end unhappily, often with

THE DEATH OF SIEGFRIED, BY HENRI DE GROUX The Death of Siegfried is a scene from the Nibelungenlied, the epic poem made famous by Wagner's "Ring Cycle" operas.

the hero or heroine (or both) dying. For example, in Schubert's "Der Erlkönig" ("The Erl King") the son dies in his father's arms; in Wagner's *Götterdämmerung*, after Brünnhilde rides her horse into the funeral pyre of her beloved Siegfried, flames and then a flood engulf the home of the gods, Valhalla.

The fascination with evil led to the inclusion of the Dies irae chant in several musical works, and compositions such as *Mephisto Waltz* (Mephisto being another name for the devil), *Danse Macabre*, and *Totentanz* (*Dance of Death*). The disasters of the nineteenth century certainly did not reach the heights of mayhem that can be seen in films or described in books over the past few decades. They did, however, reveal a side of Romanticism that seemed to enjoy being miserable.

Romanticists also had their optimistic and happy side that loved beauty. The music of Brahms, Mendelssohn, Tchaikovsky, Grieg, Schumann, and many others contains rich harmonies and luscious melodies. Such music is difficult to top in terms of sheer beauty. Many paintings also reveal a love of beauty; Corot's *Villa d'Avray* is one example. Beauty of motion and movement was (and still is) one of the main goals of ballet. Often its stories are pure and lovely fantasy and present beauty that seems to exceed anything in ordinary life. The scene of the Snow Maidens dancing gracefully in *The Nutcracker* to Tchaikovsky's beautiful music as snow falls gently around them seems to be as total an experience of loveliness and beauty as can be conceived.

THE SNOW MAIDENS of Tchaikovsky's *The Nutcracker.*

CODA

In the arts one style tends to replace another over time. But that does not mean that the new style is *better*. Instead, it means only that the new style is *different* and that the new style is currently in vogue. Perhaps Mozart and Haydn had done all that could be done at the time with the Classical outlook. The Romantic style offered composers and artists venues that had never before been explored.

23 Early Romantic Music

The Romantic attitude and outlook had a massive impact on music. Changes happened not so much in new forms or techniques of composing, although some changes occurred in those areas, but more in what composers tried to accomplish in their works. Their music tended to be much more personal and expressive. They reveled in the qualities of mystery, emotional release, love of nature, and inner feelings that were fashionable during the nineteenth century.

WHAT TO LISTEN FOR IN ROMANTIC MUSIC

What makes music in the Romantic style of the nineteenth century different from the Classical style of Mozart and Haydn? Several things:

Some Romantic melodies might be compared to eating a piece of a rich chocolate cake with whipped cream on top.

- The melodies are more flowing and passionate. Whereas the melodies of Classical composers many times consisted of short fragments strung together, melodies in Romantic style are often sweeping and expansive.
- The harmonies are much richer. Chords contain more notes. Also, many more chromatic notes are used. Changes of key occur more often and to keys that are harmonically more distant. Harmony became much more than the functional accompaniment encountered in many works of the Classical period.
- Rhythm is treated more freely, especially in speeding up and slowing down the tempo. A rather steady beat and metrical rhythm are not abandoned, but they are less structured.
- Changes in dynamic levels are more frequent, with many of the soft places softer and the loud places louder. Often the dynamic levels have an almost undulating quality.
- The tonal qualities are richer. The size of the orchestra is increased significantly, and several new instruments, such as the piccolo and English horn, are added.
- The works, especially those for large ensembles, are often quite a bit longer. Many Romantic composers admired and desired long works.
- The element of contrast in music begun by Beethoven is a feature of nineteenth-century music. Tender portions are often contrasted with stormy sections, for example.
- These features of Romantic music often coalesce to produce music of outstanding beauty. Many works remind one of eating an especially rich-tasting dessert.

THE ART SONG

Lied ("leed") is the German word for "song"; *Lieder* is its plural.

The songs Schubert wrote are called art songs. An **art song,** or **Lied,** is a musical setting of a poem. The order is important here. Composers of art songs first select a suitable poem and *then* compose music that will best project the mood and thought of the text. The idea of preserving and building on the message of the words is fundamental to the art song.

Because the setting of the words was so vital, composers were not primarily concerned with writing a lovely melody. They wanted a good melody, of course, but more than that, they wanted the melody to express the words. The idea of expression also carried over to

THE ART SONG COMBINES poetry, melody, the expressiveness of the human voice, and the tonal power of the piano.

the piano part, which evokes a mood, paints a picture, or enriches ideas beyond what a singer can achieve. For example, through rapidly moving notes and changes of dynamic level, the piano can suggest wind blowing through the trees.

Singers of art songs must project the idea of the song. Sometimes they are called on to convey different roles in the same song. Any mood can prevail in an art song—anger, sadness, anxiety, joy, pity, contentment.

The demands on singers of art songs are, therefore, somewhat different from those required of opera singers. In fact, singers tend to specialize in one type of vocal music or another. The art song is less demanding in a technical sense; the vocal range is narrower and there are few virtuoso passages. But singers of art songs must be versatile and able to project the essence of a character or situation. Because art songs are sung in small recital halls, singers must establish a rapport with the audience while maintaining a balance between good taste and expressiveness. In some ways, art songs and chamber music have several musical similarities. Both are intended to produce a sense of intimacy, refinement, and listener involvement.

A sense of involvement is not achieved if the listener does not understand the words. Most art songs are in languages other than English. As was pointed out in Chapter 12, word placement in vocal music is crucial, so translations are difficult. In fact, strictly speaking, something is lost in translation, no matter how carefully it is done. Many words have shades of meaning that cannot be translated. For these reasons, art songs are usually sung in their original languages.

Translation difficulties are only part of the language problem. Many of the poems that Schubert and other composers set to music are not of high literary merit. Some of them seem overly sentimental to people today who have grown up with down-to-earth (if not downright earthy) popular songs.

Art songs are a type of music well worth knowing, however.

- They reveal much sensitivity and skill in combining words and music.
- They are very expressive of their texts. For example, when the singer of "Der Erlkönig" sings "My father, my father, can't you see . . . ," listeners can really sense the child's frustration and fear.
- The human voice can be a very expressive and beautiful musical instrument. When coupled with the tonal power of the piano in the infinite variety of the art song, the result can be very moving.

The different roles for the singer are crucial in "The Erl King."

SCHUBERT'S "DER ERLKÖNIG"

Schubert wrote "Der Erlkönig" ("The Erl King") when he was only eighteen. He chose a text from the great German writer Goethe. The overall mood of the song is one of fear and suspense because of the mythical king of the elves. According to legend, whoever is touched by him must die. The singer is required to represent the narrator, the father, the son, and the Erl King—quite an assignment. The piano sets the mood and helps delineate the characters in the song, as well as plays the role of the horse.

Before listening to the song, read over the text to determine which of the four roles the singer is presenting. As you listen, notice how Schubert, the singer, and the pianist treat the different roles. For example, be aware of how "My son, it's only a misty cloud" differs from "You lovely child, come . . ." and how "My father, my father, now don't you hear . . ." differs from "My son, my son, all I can see . . ." Notice not only the difference in the tone quality of the singer's voice for each role but also how the entire mood changes when the Erl King speaks.

None of the music is repeated in "Der Erlkönig." New lines of melody follow one another until the song ends. The term for this type of song is **through-composed,** meaning that no line repeats. The accompaniment adds to the mood with an agitated triplet figure and a foreboding bass pattern, which depicts the urgency of the scene.

Franz Schubert

Austrian National Tourist Office

BEST-KNOWN WORKS

chamber music:
- Piano Quintet ("Trout")
- *Arpeggione* Sonata

orchestra:
- *Rosamunde* (incidental music)
- Symphonies Nos. 8 ("Unfinished") and 9 ("The Great")

songs (more than 600) including:
- "Der Erlkönig"
- "Gretchen am Spinnrade"

song cycles:
- *Die schöne Müllerin*
- *Winterreise*

Franz Schubert (1797–1828) is often considered, along with Beethoven, to be a composer who marked the beginning of the Romantic style in music. And there is much about his life to justify his reputation as the prototype of the Romantic artist. Born into the family of a schoolteacher in a Vienna suburb, the young Schubert displayed creative talent while he was still a boy. After completing school, he tried to follow in his father's footsteps, but he could not accept the routine involved in teaching. He preferred to spend his time composing music.

Schubert did not adjust well to adult life. He never held a real job and made only halfhearted attempts to find one. He had a small circle of friends, who appreciated his talents. They housed and fed him when he was in need, which he often was. He was not good at dealing with publishers, who made hefty profits from his music.

As the years passed, Schubert became lonelier and more discouraged. He was even unlucky in love and once contracted venereal disease. He was not in good health the last five years of his short life, but his compositions kept on coming. He died from typhus at the age of thirty-one, leaving almost no worldly goods—except a vast store of beautiful music.

———•———

Schubert's Symphony No. 8 ("Unfinished") was not left incomplete because he was heartbroken over a failed romance, as is sometimes claimed. He simply never got around to finishing it.

———•———

Schubert was a versatile composer. He wrote piano works, chamber music, and symphonies. But it is his vocal music, especially his six hundred songs, that ensured his place in the world of music.

FRANZ SCHUBERT
"Der Erlkönig" (1815)

GENRE: Art song (Lied)   Fast tempo   Soloist and piano

CD 2 Tracks 6–8
4 minutes 5 seconds

Form: Through-composed

0:00	**6** 0:00	Piano sets an agitated mood.	

0:23	**NARRATOR:** Wer reitet so spät durch Nacht und Wind? Es ist der Vater mit seinem Kind; Er hat den Knaben wohl in dem Arm, Er fasst ihn sicher, er hält ihn warm.	Who rides so late through the night wind? It is a father with his child. He holds the boy within his arm, He clasps him tightly, he keeps him warm.
	FATHER: "Mein Sohn, was birgst du so bang dein Gesicht?"	"My son, why do you hide your face in fear?"
	SON: "Siehst, Vater, du den Erlkönig nicht? Den Erlenkönig mit Kron' und Schweif?"	"See, father, isn't the Erl King near? The Erl King with crown and shroud?"
	FATHER: "Mein Sohn, es ist ein Nebelstreif."	"My son, it's only a misty cloud."

1:29	**7** 0:00	**ERL KING:** "Du liebes Kind, komm, geh' mit mir! Gar schöne Spiele spiel' ich mit dir; Manch' bunte Blumen sind an dem Strand, Meine Mutter hat manch' gülden Gewand."	"You lovely child, come, go with me! Such pleasant games I'll play with thee! The fields have flowers bright to behold, My mother has many a robe of gold."
		SON: "Mein Vater, mein Vater, und hörest du nicht, Was Erlenkönig mir leise verspricht?"	"My father, my father, now don't you hear What the Erl King whispers in my ear?"
		FATHER: "Sei ruhig, bleibe ruhig, mein Kind; In dürren Blättern säuselt der Wind."	"Be calm, be calm and still, my child; The dry leaves rustle when wind blows wild."
		ERL KING: "Willst, feiner Knabe, du mit mir geh'n? Meine Töchter sollen dich warten schön; Meine Töchter führen den nächtlichen Reih'n Und wiegen und tanzen und singen dich ein."	"My lovely boy, won't you go with me? My daughters all shall wait on thee, My daughters nightly revels keep, They'll sing and dance and rock thee to sleep."
		SON: "Mein Vater, mein Vater, und siehst du nicht dort Erlkönigs Töchter am düstern Ort?"	"My father, my father, can't you see the face Of Erl King's daughters in that dark place?"
		FATHER: "Mein Sohn, mein Sohn, ich seh' es genau, Es scheinen die alten Weiden so grau."	"My son, my son, all I can see Is just the old gray willow tree."
		ERL KING: "Ich liebe dich, mich reizt deine schöne Gestalt, Und bist du nicht willig, so brauch' ich Gewalt."	"I love thee, thy form enflames my sense; Since thou art not willing, I'll take thee hence!"

3:15	**8** 0:00	**SON:** "Mein Vater, mein Vater, jetzt fasst er mich an! Erlkönig hat mir ein Leid's gethan!"	"My father, my father, he's grabbing my arm, The Erl King wants to do me harm!"
		NARRATOR: Dem Vater grauset's, er reitet geschwind, Er hält in Armen das ächzende Kind, Erreicht den Hof mit Müh' und Noth: In seinen Armen das Kind war tot!	The father shudders, he speeds through the cold His arms the moaning child enfold, He reaches home with pain and dread: In his arms the child was dead!
		The song ends with two solid-sounding chords.	

Dissonance is heard as the child expresses fear, and the father's music has a reassuring quality. Notice how effectively Schubert ends the song. The piano stops, and the singer declaims, "In his arms, the child"—a pause to allow anticipation to build up—"was dead."

Art songs provide a kind of music that is not duplicated in arias or folk songs; those forms of vocal music have other qualities and functions.

MENDELSSOHN'S SYMPHONY NO. 4, FOURTH MOVEMENT

As mentioned in his biographical sketch, Felix Mendelssohn grew up in a wealthy family. One of the benefits of this was the chance to travel extensively. In 1830 he spent several months in Italy, where he was introduced to its music. Two years later when he was commissioned by the London Philharmonic Society to compose a symphony, the memories of Italy were still fresh in his mind. The result is a happy work that seems as bright as sunlight.

The first movement is in the usual sonata form. The second movement features a choralelike melody over steady notes sounded by the low strings. The third movement is marked *Con moto moderato* (with moderate motion) and replaces the minuet and trio of the Classical period, but largely in name. The meter is the usual 3/4 of the minuet, and the three-part form is retained, with a trio in the middle.

Mendelssohn called the fourth movement a *saltarello*, which was an Italian folk dance with hopping movements. He marked the tempo *Presto* (very fast). One can sense the meter as four very fast beats or as two moderately fast beats. The attraction of the movement lies as much in its vibrant rhythm as it does in its themes. Although the symphony is in A major, its final movement is in A minor.

FELIX MENDELSSOHN

Symphony No. 4 in A Major, Op. 90 ("Italian"), Fourth Movement (1833)

GENRE: Symphony   Orchestra

CD 4 Tracks 19–22
5 minutes 18 seconds

Form: One main theme with subthemes

0:00	**19**	0:00	Main theme played by flutes and clarinets, followed by violins.
		0:40	Transition leading to second theme.
1:02	**20**	0:00	Second theme sounds like variant of the first.
		0:28	Woodwinds play steady notes as strings continue saltarello rhythm.
		1:03	Woodwinds exchange fragments of theme.
2:25	**21**	0:00	Violins and violas begin smooth, running notes.
		0:31	Woodwinds take up running notes.
3:06	**22**	0:00	Saltarello rhythm returns.
		0:49	Rapidly moving scalewise passages return.
		1:33	Coda containing fragments of theme begins.
		2:12	Movement concludes.

LISTENING GUIDE

The main theme is:

Felix Mendelssohn & Fanny Mendelssohn Hensel

FELIX MENDELSSOHN

FANNY MENDELSSOHN HENSEL

It is appropriate to couple **Felix Mendelssohn** (1809–1847) and his older sister, **Fanny** (1805–1847), in the same biographical sketch. The two were very close during their childhood and remained so throughout their lives. They took music lessons and read Shakespeare's plays together, and their young lives were certainly idyllic ones. Their father was a wealthy banker who hired musicians to come to the Mendelssohn home in Berlin to give concerts and later to play music that one of his children had composed.

In his adult life, Felix became a very successful pianist, composer, conductor, and organizer of concerts. He was one of the first conductors to stand in front of the orchestra, and he was very influential in stimulating an interest in the music of Bach with his performance of the *St. Matthew Passion.* He made ten journeys to England to conduct and perform and was warmly received by Queen Victoria at Buckingham Palace.

And what about Fanny's musical career? She, too, was a gifted composer and pianist, but her father insisted that a lady

of her social standing should not become a professional musician.

◆

As caring a brother as Felix was, that did not keep him from discouraging Fanny's efforts at composing.

◆

Eventually, she married the painter Wilhelm Hensel. She did not completely give up her interest in music, but she refrained from pursuing it as a career. She performed occasionally as a piano soloist and composed more than two hundred works, mostly songs, chamber music, and short piano pieces. Only a few of her compositions have been published.

In May 1847 Fanny died of a stroke during a rehearsal for one of the family concerts. Felix was crushed. Although his own health was failing, he composed a string quartet in her memory. He also journeyed to visit her grave, which was especially hard on him and hastened his death about six months later. He was buried near his sister.

BEST-KNOWN WORKS OF MENDELSSOHN

orchestra:
- Incidental Music for *A Midsummer Night's Dream*
- Symphonies Nos. 3 ("Italian") and 4 ("Scottish")
- Violin Concerto

oratorio:
- *Elijah*

BEST-KNOWN WORKS OF HENSEL

choral:
- *Gartenlieder*

songs:
- Op. 7

It follows the pattern based on three rapid notes (with an occasional rest) for each fast beat. A second theme is almost a smoother variant of the main theme.

A third portion of the movement features rapidly moving notes played by the first violins, then the second violins, and then the violas. The lines rarely appear contrapuntally; rather, it's more like taking turns. The music then works back to the saltarello theme. It appears to fade away in the coda but is revived for the final moments of the movement.

Where Are the Women Composers?

You have probably noticed by now a distinct absence of women's names among composers. Shouldn't there be a nearly equal number of men and women? Why such a preponderance of males? Granted, a few women have been successful composers: Hildegard of Bingen and Péronne d'Armentières in early music, Fanny Mendelssohn Hensel and Clara Schumann in the nineteenth century, and others. But the number of women composers and their compositions is small.

As is true of most things in life, there is no single, simple explanation for the paucity of women composers. Several factors very likely contribute to the situation. A major one was the fact that it was a "man's world" until only the past couple of decades. Women usually could not own property, vote in the few democratic countries that had elections, engage in enterprises outside the home, or travel overnight without an escort. They were generally treated as the property of their husbands. They were often discouraged from composing by their fathers or husbands, which happened in the case of Fanny Mendelssohn. Such circumstances hardly encouraged women to have the fortitude to compose music and hope to have it published.

An additional impediment to women composers is that it has seldom been easy for *anyone* to have compositions published. Until a composer had achieved a certain degree of name recognition, which made a publisher more confident of sufficient sales, getting a work published was no easy matter, a situation that is still true today. There are a number of works now well regarded for which composers had difficulty finding a publisher. And yet a publisher's cautious approach is understandable. After all, how many sales of a symphony could be anticipated at a time when there were few permanent orchestras and no residuals from the sale of recordings?

Another reason for the lack of women composers was the prejudice they faced in pursuing instruction in harmony, counterpoint, orchestration, and similar subjects. For example, the Paris Conservatory did not permit women in advanced theory classes until the late 1800s.

A few women authors, such as George Sand and George Eliot, were able to break the male dominance by writing under a male pseudonym. An undetermined number of Fanny Mendelssohn Hensel's songs were published under Felix's name! Are there other works by women published under a man's name? We don't know, but if it happened once with Fanny Mendelssohn, it probably happened with other women, too.

Has the situation changed for women in the world of musical composition? Fortunately, in at least two important ways it has. Much research has recently been conducted on locating compositions by women, and a considerable body of music has been uncovered. The other change is in the acceptance of women composers. Whether the playing field is level between men and women today in terms of recognition for their compositions is difficult to determine. However, Ellen Taafe Zwilich, Joan Tower, Libby Larsen, and others are rightfully being recognized for their works. Perhaps in another hundred years the question about the lack of women composers will no longer be a logical one to raise.

SOLO AND CHAMBER MUSIC

This type of piece is often called a "character piece." It is discussed in Chapter 24.

Although the Romantic era is noted for large compositions, its composers continued to produce many excellent works for small groups and solo works other than concertos. Schubert composed an enormous amount of chamber music, as did Mendelssohn. Two other early Romantic composers merit mentioning: Carl Maria von Weber (1786–1826) and Robert Schumann. Weber is known for his operas. Schumann is an important name in the world of music and is presented in the next chapter.

CODA

The Romantic period began geographically close to where the Classical period had ended: Vienna. In fact, Vienna and the Germanic style were to dominate the musical scene for the remainder of the nineteenth century. It was not that other kinds of music were lacking. Rather, German Romanticism was the pacesetter.

24 Romantic Piano Music

The Romantic period tended to exhibit two different viewpoints regarding piano music. One outlook exploited the power and brilliance of the instrument; the other treated the piano in a more intimate, sensitive way. These two approaches were by no means mutually exclusive, but they were distinctive enough to be noticeable. For example, Liszt composed piano music that dazzled his audiences with technical display and forceful sounds. Chopin, on the other hand, usually wrote piano pieces that sought to enchant listeners with their beauty.

> One type of piano music might be thought of as extroverted and the other as introverted.

The Romantic period featured piano music. An enormous amount of music was written for the instrument, not only at concert level but for amateur players as well. The piano was the most popular instrument in the home during the nineteenth century.

Piano recitals became important during this time. Many composers were also pianists themselves and introduced their own works to the public; Liszt, Beethoven, and Frédéric Chopin are among the composers who did this. But gradually a class of virtuoso performers emerged who were known for their interpretative abilities as well as their stunning technical virtuosity.

CHARACTER PIECES

Romantic composers did not want to be confined to the carefully balanced forms that Mozart and Haydn had used so well. To replace the rondo, sonata, and other forms, composers in the nineteenth century created many free, short forms that are often referred to as **character pieces,** such as the ballade, berceuse, étude, prelude, impromptu, fantasia, scherzo, and nocturne.

> *Étude* comes from the French word for "study."

The **ballade** ("bah-*lahd*") and **berceuse** ("bair-*soos*") are songlike pieces. The ballade is the longer and more complex of the two and is supposed to hark back to the ballad poems of the Middle Ages. An **étude** ("*ay*-tood") is an instrumental piece that develops a particular technique. Études were written for all instruments but were especially popular for the piano. In the hands of Chopin, Liszt, or similarly gifted composers, an étude is transformed into an exciting concert work. A **prelude** is a short work for piano.

> The word *nocturne* refers to night song.

An **impromptu** is supposed to convey the spontaneity its name suggests. A **fantasia** or **fantasie** is a free and imaginative work. The **scherzos** by Chopin are not as playful as those by Beethoven. Instead, they are longer and more serious, although the typical triple meter and fast tempo of the scherzo are retained. **Nocturne** was the name given by the Irish composer John Field to his piano pieces with a songlike melody. Chopin adopted the title from Field and wrote many beautiful, lyrical nocturnes.

Another type of character piece consisted of stylized dance forms such as the mazurka, polonaise, and waltz. What Romantic composers did was essentially the same as what Bach had done with his Baroque keyboard suites. The Romantic composers, however, used different dances and wrote in a very different style from their Baroque and Classical predecessors. They expanded the forms so that each dance became a separate piece rather than just one part of a larger suite.

> Chopin was known to spend as much as six weeks on a single page of music, changing note after note, stomping around in frustration, and breaking pens. Sometimes he would return to exactly what he started with.

These character pieces were often intended to convey an air of improvisation as if they were an inspiration—a momentary feeling that had been rendered in sound. The impression of improvisation is an illusion, however, because Chopin and his contemporaries labored carefully over each measure they wrote. They worked hard at sounding spontaneous.

There is a feature of Romantic music that cannot be seen in music notation but is used frequently in performing the music. It is known as **rubato** ("roo-*bah*-toh"). Rubato is a style of performance in which the performer deviates slightly from the exact execution of the rhythm. A fraction of time is borrowed from one note to lengthen another. Chopin was occasionally criticized as a performer for his use of rubato. Some listeners charged that he could not keep a steady beat. Undoubtedly he could, but he sometimes chose not to. He wanted the music to have the free expression that the Romanticists admired.

Rubato originally meant "robbed" in Italian.

CHOPIN'S NOCTURNE IN D-FLAT

Chopin composed about twenty nocturnes. Most of them have an introspective, delicate, lyric quality. The Nocturne in D-flat, Op. 27, No. 2, is one of the most voluptuous and passionate of these works. It contains rich harmonies and many musical "sighs"

FRÉDÉRIC CHOPIN
Nocturne in D-flat Major, Op. 27, No. 2 (1835)

GENRE: **Character piece** Piano

CD 4 Tracks 23–24
5 minutes 55 seconds

Form: Rondo (*A B A C A B*)

0.00 **23** 0:00 Accompaniment begins and is soon followed by a tender melody (A):

0:42 **24** 0:00 B melody begins and is repeated and varied several times.

1:14 A melody returns.

1:57 B melody line resumes and is extended, leading to a climactic moment.

2:42 A melody returns. Much use of decorative figures.

3:16 B portion returns and grows more passionate.

3:53 Coda begins with a descending, "sighing" interval.

4:12 Sighing figure repeated.

5:13 Nocturne closes with a simple cadence after an ascending, fading scale.

consisting of descending intervals and delayed resolutions of phrases and harmonic progressions. The left-hand part is made up of six continuously moving notes for each beat. The notes are actually chords that are sounded in a broken style. The right hand plays a songlike melody that is decorated with grace notes and other melodic figures. Although the music notation makes the rhythm look steady and regular, pianists almost always take liberties with the rhythm, as Chopin himself did in his own playing.

Pianists also use the pedals a great deal in playing Romantic music. The *Ped.* marking in the notation tells the pianist to depress the damper pedal, which lifts the dampers and allows the strings to resonate freely. Richness is added to the music when the dampers are raised. Proper pedaling also contributes to smooth, lyric phrasing. The composer and

Broken style means that the notes of a chord are sounded neither together nor in succession.

Grace notes are printed in half the size of other notes and have no prescribed rhythmic value.

Frédéric Chopin

© The New York Public Library

BEST-KNOWN WORKS

orchestra:
- Piano Concertos Nos. 1 and 2

piano—character pieces:
- Études (24), including "Black Key," "Winter Wind," and "Revolutionary"
- Fantasies, including *Fantasie-Impromptu,* Op. 66
- Nocturnes (21)
- Preludes (24, one in each major and minor key)
- Scherzos (4)

piano—stylized dances:
- Polonaises, including Op. 53
- Mazurkas
- Waltzes, including "Minute Waltz"

piano—sonatas (3)

Frédéric Chopin ("*Show*-pan," 1810–1849) was the son of a French father and a Polish mother. He exhibited much talent at an early age and received his musical education at the Conservatory in Warsaw. Before he was twenty, he was on his own in the world. He left Poland and traveled awhile before settling in Paris. Shortly after his departure from Poland, the Poles revolted against the Russians and their czar. In time the Russians crushed the revolt, which caused Chopin much anguish.

His abilities as a composer and pianist made him a sought-after musician in Paris. Soon he acquired a circle of artistic friends—the painter Eugène Delacroix, musicians Franz Liszt and Hector Berlioz, writers Victor Hugo, Honoré de Balzac, Alphonse de Larmartine, Alexandre Dumas (père), and Heinrich Heine. Through this group of friends, Chopin met George Sand, and they lived together for nine years.

George Sand was the pen name of Amandine Aurore Lucie Dupin, Baroness Dudevant, who was one of the outstanding writers of the time with more than a hundred books to her credit. She favored novels in which love transcended the obstacles of convention and social class. She had liaisons with a number of famous men, but her most lasting relationship was with Chopin.

Chopin's loyalty to Poland remained strong throughout his life.

When they first met, Chopin, who had always been drawn to beautiful women and loved the polished and elegant life, was repelled by her: She had adopted a number of masculine attitudes and habits, including wearing men's clothes and smoking cigars. And she was not physically attractive. Yet in time he was drawn to her. Her fame as a writer and her strong personality seemed to be a good balance for his not very forceful ways. When they separated, she did not seem to be affected. But Chopin lived only another two years before his death from tuberculosis.

Liszt wrote of the separation: "In the breaking of this long affection, this powerful bond, he had broken his life."

Most composers before Chopin wrote well in a variety of types of music. Chopin was different. He was one of the first composers to limit his writing to one or two areas. He wrote almost exclusively for the piano, and it is this music that made a place for him in the world of music. He is often referred to as "the poet of the piano."

performer must plan carefully for the use of the pedals because unwanted notes that are allowed to sound create a blurring effect.

As you listen to the Nocturne, notice the effect of the long note in the melody and the accompanying notes in the fifth and sixth measures of the opening theme. You can sense that the long note is going to move up a half step, which it finally does. But Chopin makes listeners wait what seems like an extra long time for it to resolve. He is a master at such toying with listeners' expectations.

ThomsonNOW

Learn more about how Chopin works with listeners' expectations in "Hear It Now: A Composer's Dilemma," in *ThomsonNOW,* **Chapter 24.**

VIRTUOSO MUSIC

Another type of piano music was for the virtuoso performer. Audiences during the nineteenth century were fond of dazzling, showy music and stunning performances by musical idols such as the pianist Franz Liszt and the violin virtuoso Niccolò Paganini.

LISZT'S *LA CAMPANELLA*

Liszt admired the virtuoso skills of Paganini on the violin. This admiration led to Liszt's transcribing six of Paganini's violin works for piano under the title *Transcendental Études after Paganini. La Campanella* (*The Little Bell*) is the third of these pieces. Liszt retains the bell effect by sounding a high D-sharp repeatedly throughout the piece.

Transcriptions were popular in the Romantic era. They offered the new public audience the opportunity of hearing technically stunning variations on operatic melodies and other works not originally written for piano. Because there were no recordings and few orchestras, a piano recital was often a listener's only contact with concert music.

La Campanella is a typically Romantic composition, for several reasons:

- It is virtuoso music; even a good professional pianist does not undertake it lightly.
- It demands of the player the full range of techniques developed in the Romantic period.
- It is an attempt to make the piano more orchestral in sound and concept. The very name of the piece suggests that the piano is to be descriptive of something more than itself.

Even though *La Campanella* is technically awesome, it is musically rather simple. It is a set of scintillating variations on a simple melody in which the opening two-measure phrase is stated and then repeated twice with a concluding phrase. After the main theme is presented again, there is a contrasting section. It, too, is composed of short, repeated phrases. The piece has a form of *a a b.*

The technical devices of piano playing are too numerous to cover fully here. A few examples provide an idea of what Liszt did in the way of virtuoso display. One involves rapidly repeated notes, which Liszt used often. It may seem that the pianist is simply rapping his or her finger repeatedly on the key with tremendous speed. Not so. It is much easier to play notes rapidly in succession if the key is struck with a different finger for each sound. Here is an example of where that technique is used:

Liszt arranged many of the transcriptions in the form of duets for two persons playing at the same keyboard.

There were no orchestras that toured in those days.

A CONTEMPORARY CARICATURE of Liszt lampoons his extraordinary virtuosity.

Liszt also calls for very fast playing of the chromatic scale:

The *8va* sign tells the performer to play the notes one octave higher than written.

Alternating hands gives the pianist more speed and power:

FRANZ LISZT

La Campanella (1851)

GENRE: Virtuoso piano work   Piano

CD 2 Tracks 9–10
4 minutes 17 seconds

Form: Theme and Variations (*a a b*)

0:00	**9**	0:00	Introduction based on motive from the theme.
		0:09	The *a* theme with a few decorative notes.

		0:25	The *a* theme repeated with more decorative notes one octave higher.
0:40	**10**	0:00	The *b* portion of theme built on a sequential figure; leads to a fragment of *a* in sequence.
		0:36	The *a* theme played in high notes that alternate an octave apart; then repeated.
		1:04	The *b* theme with rapidly repeated notes; leads to sequence on *a* theme with trill on high notes.
		1:59	The *a* theme returns softly and is repeated with many fast, high notes.
		2:29	The *b* theme returns with a freer tempo and much contrast between high and low notes.
		3:06	Coda begins as *a* theme is repeated at a faster tempo.
		3:37	*La Campanella* closes with a soft but accented chord.

Niccolò Paganini & Franz Liszt

Niccolò Paganini (1782–1840) and **Franz Liszt** (1811–1886) had much in common. First, they were the supreme virtuoso performers of the nineteenth century on their respective instruments: Paganini on the violin and Liszt on the piano. Second, they both came from modest circumstances. Third, for what it's worth, both successfully pursued many women over the course of their lives.

Paganini had a more interesting reputation. Part of his fame was the result of his appearance and character. He had a pale, long face with hollow cheeks and thin lips that seemed to curl in an evil smile, and his eyes had a piercing quality. There were also popular suspicions that he was influenced by the devil.

———◆———

Paganini was even forced to publish letters from his mother to prove that he had human parents!

———◆———

His ability to play the violin was legendary, and he added a new dimension to the playing of the instrument. He developed a repertoire of violin tricks and technical maneuvers that he guarded jealously, refusing to have much of his music published for fear that others might find out exactly what he was doing.

———◆———

One of Paganini's violin pieces is the basis for a work by Rachmaninoff that is presented in Chapter 29.

———◆———

On the night of March 9, 1831, Liszt attended a recital by Paganini. The dazzling virtuoso left an indelible impression on the nineteen-year-old Liszt, who became consumed with the idea that he could do for piano technique what

Paganini had done for the violin. Liszt canceled all his concerts for two years and began to retrain himself. He spent hours practicing techniques such as octaves, trills, scales, and arpeggios (playing notes of a chord successively rather than simultaneously). He returned again and again to hear Paganini and take notes on what he did. He even imitated some of the visual effects of Paganini's appearance: his black, tight-fitting clothes, tossing hair, and facial expressions.

Traditionally, pianists had performed with their backs to the audience and played with the music in front of them. Liszt was one of the first to turn the piano to its familiar sideways position and to memorize his music. His chiseled profile fascinated the audience, especially the women, as he crouched over the keys, alternately caressing and pounding them.

Behind the image of the sensational artist, which Liszt did not discourage, there was a musician of depth and a man of generous heart who helped many young musicians. There was also a prolific composer. Although he is especially known for his piano music—and many more piano transcriptions—he also composed many works for orchestra as well as about sixty religious works.

———◆———

Toward the end of his life, Liszt took minor religious vows and had the title Abbé Liszt.

———◆———

NICCOLÒ PAGANINI

FRANZ LISZT

BEST-KNOWN WORKS OF LISZT

orchestra:
- *Hungarian Rhapsodies* Nos. 2 and 14
- *Les Préludes*
- Piano Concertos Nos. 1 and 2
- *Totentanz* for Piano and Orchestra

piano:
- *Harmonies poétiques et religieuses*
- Sonata in B Minor
- *Transcendental études* (6)

Liszt's exploitation of the range of the piano can be heard in the long trill on the high D-sharp, only a few notes from the top of the keyboard.

Perhaps virtuoso compositions may not be as intellectually challenging as other types of musical works. But most of them—and *La Campanella* is certainly one—contain some really imaginative writing. The high notes of the piano are used in a way that is not found in Mozart or Beethoven sonatas or other piano music. And the variations are fresh and attractive. One must be a virtuoso pianist to play these works well. Technical virtuosity, or any artistic endeavor, whether achieved by an Olympic figure skater or a fine pianist, demands exceptional dedication and talent. It is a pleasure to observe such performances, especially if the observer has tried some skating or piano playing and therefore can appreciate better the skill demanded.

Robert Schumann & Clara Wieck Schumann

Photograph of Clara & Robert Schumann, Musée d'Orsay, Paris. Reunion des Musées, Nationaux./Art Resource, NY

BEST-KNOWN WORKS OF ROBERT SCHUMANN

chamber music:
- Piano Quintet

orchestra:
- Piano Concerto
- Cello Concerto

piano, many character pieces, plus:
- *Carnaval*
- *Fantasia in C*
- *Kinderscenen*

song cycle:
- *Frauenliebe und Leben*

BEST-KNOWN WORKS OF CLARA WIECK SCHUMANN

piano:
- Romances
- Soirées Musicale

violin and piano:
- Three Romances

Robert Alexander Schumann (1813–1856) and **Clara Wieck Schumann** (1819–1896) were husband and wife. Robert's father was a bookseller and writer, who encouraged his son's musical interests. Robert entered law school at the University of Leipzig in Germany but gave it up to pursue his ambitions to become a piano virtuoso. However, he permanently injured his hands in an attempt to develop finger strength with a mechanical device. His interests moved on to the founding of an important music magazine and to composing. Besides a great deal of piano music, he wrote chamber music, concertos, and symphonies. He composed about 150 songs, many of them written the year after he married Clara.

Clara Wieck was the daughter of Robert's piano teacher, and he fell in love with her when she was sixteen. At that time she was already well on her way to becoming an outstanding concert pianist. Her father strongly opposed their marriage, so the couple had to wait until she was twenty-one (minus one day) before getting married. Their marriage was a happy one, and they had eight children. In spite of Robert's bouts with mental illness, Clara continued her career as a concert pianist, although her family demanded more and more of her time.

In nineteenth-century Germany, children seldom could or would go against their father's wishes.

Two years before his death, tormented by hallucinations, Robert leaped into the Rhine River. He was saved, but he spent the remainder of his life in an asylum. Those were difficult years for Clara. At the age of thirty-seven, she lost her husband, to whom she was devoted. She later found herself attracted to the twenty-two-year-old protégé of her husband, Johannes Brahms. Brahms remained a bachelor and Clara never remarried, but they did remain close friends and admirers.

For the last forty years of her life, Clara continued to teach and give concerts. Although she was a promising composer, she was not able to devote much time to this aspect of her great talent. She did write a few works for piano and a piano trio, however. Throughout her adult life, she promoted Robert's music through her performances.

Clara went on tour again after Robert's death. She gave the last of her thirteen hundred public concerts at the age of seventy-two.

CLARA SCHUMANN'S SCHERZO, OP. 10

As seems true of many recognized composers in the eighteenth and nineteenth centuries, Clara Schumann wrote successful musical works before the age of twenty. Her Op. 10, a scherzo for piano, was written when she was nineteen. It reveals her inclination toward virtuoso music with its tempo marking: *Presto, Scherzo con passione* (Very fast, Scherzo with passion). And audiences at that time liked such music.

The form is clear: a scherzo and two trios that are not quite as passionate as the scherzo. Sudden accented chords and trills help make the music dramatic. In true virtuoso style,

Clara wrote to her husband, Robert, from Paris: "It is extraordinary to me that my Scherzo is so well liked here. I always have to repeat it."

LISTENING GUIDE

CLARA SCHUMANN
Scherzo, Op. 10 in D Minor (1838)

GENRE: **Character piece**   Presto (very fast)   **Piano**

CD 4 Tracks 25–27
4 minutes 59 seconds

Form: Scherzo with two trios

0:00	**25**	0:00	Introduction.
		0:08	Scherzo begins; very rhythmic with accented chords.

		0:36	Scherzo repeated.
		1:04	Scherzo varied, growing softer leading to trio.
1:30	**26**	0:00	Trio 1; slower and smoother.

		0:42	Scherzo returns forcefully.
2:41	**27**	0:00	Trio 2; melody in clearly marked style but gentler than scherzo.

1:32		Scherzo returns and builds to fiery ending.

the notes come in rushes of sound, which build to a climactic point. The two trios are more melodic. It is a work worthy of her outstanding abilities as one of the finest pianists of her day.

CODA

Composers such as Chopin, Liszt, and Clara Schumann demonstrated the high quality of music written for the piano. But they did more than show off the vast potential of the instrument. They also created a wealth of music that has withstood the test of time.

Program *and* Ballet Music

25

Program music and ballet music have several things in common. The most significant similarity is their association with something not musical—a story, event, or place. The fact that the stimulus for the music was something nonmusical meant that composers did not need to follow the forms that had prevailed in the Classical period. Although the result might be the general pattern of a form, composers of program and ballet music were more interested in writing imaginative music.

NATURE OF PROGRAM MUSIC

Instrumental works that composers consciously associate with nonmusical ideas are called *program music*. The particular associations are often indicated in the title, or in some cases by an explanation included in the score—the "program." Works that have been named by a publisher or other person are not really program music.

Program music became especially important in the nineteenth century. It provided one type of "form" for a major work. Some program works, however, actually follow one of the traditional forms, even if the composer does not admit doing so. And the opposite may also be true: A composer may compose a work with a title such as Sonata No. 2 that was sparked by some nonmusical association.

Musical sounds cannot really tell specifically about an event or a person. Only a song and its words can do that in music. Musical sounds can, however, convey an atmosphere, a general feeling. Listeners may hear some massive chords and assume that they signify something great or big—the coronation of a king or a large animal walking. The idea of largeness or importance is there, but not the specifics. It is possible to make up a story to go with a musical work, of course, but that story may not be what the composer had in mind. Furthermore, instrumental music that tries to tell a story in detail becomes almost comic. It loses its value as musical expression and becomes something closer to sound effects.

Identifying the nonmusical association is not really all that important anyway. Good program music has substance in and of itself; it can stand without the story because of its musical qualities.

> The term *program music* refers only to instrumental music. Vocal music usually has specific references through its words.
>
> Publishers and others sometimes give a work a name, because names are easier to remember than numbers.

TYPES OF PROGRAM MUSIC

There are several types of program music: concert overtures, incidental music, tone poems (also called symphonic poems), and program symphonies.

Concert Overture

An **overture** to an opera is an instrumental introduction that incorporates programmatic ideas from the story that follows. A **concert overture** is similar, but it is an independent one-movement work that is not associated with an opera. Sometimes it is in sonata form. Several overtures of this type were composed in the nineteenth century. Examples include Felix Mendelssohn's seascape *Hebrides* (*Fingal's Cave*) and Piotr Ilich Tchaikovsky's *Festival Overture "1812."*

> Tchaikovsky's overture celebrates the victory of the Russians over Napoleon in 1812. The score calls for six cannon, and some performances of it include fireworks.

Incidental Music

Early in the nineteenth century, composers were often asked to write **incidental music** for a drama or play. They would compose an overture and five or six other pieces to be performed during the play or between various acts. Although strictly instrumental music, these works are associated with a particular drama. Beethoven wrote a number of incidental works, including some of his better-known overtures, such as *Egmont* and *Coriolan*. Mendelssohn composed incidental music for Shakespeare's *A Midsummer Night's Dream*. Georges Bizet wrote *L'Arlésienne* for a drama, as did Edvard Grieg (1843–1907) for Ibsen's drama *Peer Gynt*.

Tone Poem

The most important type of program music is the **tone poem,** or **symphonic poem.** It is a rather long, complex orchestral work in one movement that develops a poetic idea, creates a mood, or suggests a scene. It differs from the concert overture in that it is much freer in its structure. The symphonic poem was developed by Liszt and Berlioz and expanded by Richard Strauss (1864–1949).

One of the best-known tone poems is *Les Préludes* by Liszt. Its programmatic association is a philosophical poem by Alphonse de Lamartine. The poem begins:

> *What else is life but a series of preludes to that unknown song*
> *whose first solemn note is intoned by Death?*
> *Love is the enchanted dawn of all existence;*
> *but what destiny is there whose first delights of love*
> *are not interrupted by some storm?*

In this work Liszt developed the technique of theme transformation, which Berlioz uses so well in his *Symphonie fantastique*.

PROGRAM SYMPHONY

The main difference between a tone poem and **program symphony** is the presence of more than one movement in a program symphony. Some of the themes usually appear in more than one movement.

BERLIOZ'S *SYMPHONIE FANTASTIQUE*

Berlioz's *Symphonie fantastique* (*Fantastic Symphony*) is a program symphony. And what a program it has! Berlioz had become infatuated with the actress Harriet Smithson. To ease his pain and indulge his fantasies, he decided to compose a symphony. He wrote this about the music:

> *A young musician of morbid sensibility and ardent imagination in a fit of lovesick despair has poisoned himself with opium. The drug, too weak to kill, plunges him into a heavy sleep accompanied by strange visions. The sensations, feelings, and memories are translated in his sick brain into musical images and ideas. The beloved one herself becomes for him a melody, a recurrent theme that haunts him everywhere.*

This recurrent theme is a **fixed idea,** or in French **idée fixe,** that becomes a melodic fragment associated with a particular person or object. The fixed idea, then, is subject to changes in rhythm, harmony, tempo, meter, and elaboration with other tones, but its characteristic pattern of intervals is retained. This technique is called **theme transformation.**

AUDIENCES OF BERLIOZ'S
TIME were sometimes taken
aback by the power of his musical vision. This cartoon satirizes
Berlioz's willingness to expand
the orchestra and experiment
with new instruments, such as
the saxophone and English
horn. The cannon is meant
here as an outrageous joke.

Cliché/Bibliothèque nationale de France, Paris

Theme transformation should not be confused with theme development or theme and variations. Variation involves keeping the theme intact to some extent and arranging the variations so that they contrast with one another. Development involves retaining the theme but manipulating it, often by breaking it into fragments.

Transformation is a looser concept in which a few characteristic intervals are preserved, sometimes with new material interspersed. The retained intervals give the music a sense of unity, and the transformations provide variety. Composers in addition to Liszt and Berlioz exploited this technique; Brahms was masterful in its use.

What are the strengths of Berlioz's music, especially his *Symphonie fantastique*? At least two features stand out:

- His fertile and vivid imagination. Not only is the program associated with the work a bit far out and exaggerated but the music also builds on those sometimes bizarre scenes into a wonderfully imaginative "soundscape." No one can accuse Berlioz of composing run-of-the-mill music!

- His masterful use of instruments. Berlioz's expertise in orchestration shows in his ability to get the best out of each instrument and combine their sounds to get the effects he wants to achieve.

Symphonie fantastique contains five rather long movements. Berlioz provided descriptive commentary for each movement.

ThomsonNOW
"Hear It Now: What Is Transformation?" in *ThomsonNOW*, Chapter 25.

LISTENING GUIDE

HECTOR BERLIOZ

Symphonie fantastique, Op. 14, Fifth Movement (1830)

GENRE: **Program music** Orchestra

CD 2 Tracks 11–15
9 minutes 44 seconds

0.00	**11**	0:00	Muted strings and eerie music give impression of unearthly sounds.
		1:21	Clarinet shrilly plays distorted version of *idée fixe*.
1:38	**12**	0:00	Woodwinds, then orchestra, play loud, grotesque version of *idée fixe*.

		1:17	Funeral bells sound three times interspersed with a fragment of the music used for Witches' Dance.

Dies irae

3:22	**13**	0:00	Dies irae sounds in low brasses.

		0:22	French horns and trombones play Dies irae with note values cut in half (diminution). Funeral bells interspersed throughout this section.
		0:32	Woodwinds play fast, distorted version of Dies irae.
		0:38	Second phrase of Dies irae played by French horns. Then woodwinds play fragments of fixed idea while brasses play the chant.

Witches' Round Dance (Fugato)

5:15	**14**	0:00	Theme enters four times in low strings and woodwinds. A short episode follows.

		0:48	Theme enters three more times in woodwinds, low strings, then orchestra. Another episode containing the "laughing motive" follows.
		1:45	Low strings play fragments of Dies irae. Then portions of the Witches' Dance build slowly to a climactic moment with syncopated chords.
8:00	**15**	0:00	Violins play Witches' Dance as low brasses sound Dies irae.
		0:32	Woodwinds play Witches' Dance again.
		1:05	Dies irae returns in low brasses and percussion as music begins to build.
		1:44	Movement ends in a burst of sound.

RICHARD STRAUSS

Another major nineteenth-century composer of program music was Richard Strauss. His tone poems are monumental in size and sound. At least four or five are performed frequently: *Don Juan, Death and Transfiguration, Till Eulenspiegel's Merry Pranks, Don Quixote,* and *Also Sprach Zarathustra.*

Strauss also composed three successful operas, plus songs and two concertos for French horn and orchestra, but today he is best remembered for his programmatic works.

A portion presenting majestic chords from *Also Sprach Zarathustra* achieved popularity from its use in the sound track of the film *2001: A Space Odyssey.*

BALLET AND BALLET MUSIC

Ballet is an art form in which music and the visual aspects of body movement, costumes, and scenery are combined for the psychological and artistic satisfaction they provide. Ballet is to dance as concert music is to music—an intellectually and emotionally satisfying creation.

There is no clear distinction between concert music and ballet music. Composers originally wrote music specifically to be danced to. But in the past one hundred years, every style of music has also featured ballets. Some ballet music is heard more often today as concert music than in conjunction with a ballet.

Traditionally, the music for a ballet was the result of a collaboration between a composer and a choreographer. Sometimes the choreographer is quite explicit about the type of music desired; at other times only a vague outline is provided for the composer. In a few instances in this century, the dance has been created first, and then the composer has written the music to fit the dance. But the opposite procedure has probably happened more often, when a ballet was created for an existing piece of music.

Like opera, early ballet stories were based on mythological subjects. During the nineteenth century, many plots of ballets had a fairy-tale quality, which is true of Tchaikovsky's *Swan Lake, Sleeping Beauty,* and *The Nutcracker.*

Composers often arrange ballet scores as orchestral suites.

TCHAIKOVSKY'S *NUTCRACKER*

Tchaikovsky was already a famous composer by the time he composed the music for *The Nutcracker* in 1891, only two years before his death. It is the shortest and best known of his three ballets, consisting of fifteen musical works and an overture. A suite of eight pieces from the ballet was organized and presented in 1892, the same year that the ballet itself was given its premiere performance at the Maryinski Theater before the czar and his court.

The story is filled with fancy and magic, as are many ballet stories. At a Christmas party, Clara receives a gift of a Nutcracker from the eccentric Drosselmeyer. Her brother, Fritz, breaks her new gift. Sadly, she cradles the broken Nutcracker and puts it to sleep in a toy cradle before she goes to bed.

After everyone has fallen asleep, she sneaks back into the room to look at the Nutcracker. Magically, the Christmas tree begins to grow to enormous size. Large mice appear from the corners of the room and challenge the toy soldiers, who are led by the Nutcracker. The soldiers are about to lose the fight when Clara throws a shoe at the Mouse King, and the invading mice flee. The Nutcracker is then transformed into a handsome Prince. The Prince invites her go with him to his kingdom. On the way, they stop in a snow-covered pine forest and then go to the Kingdom of the Sweets, where Clara is treated to a lavish banquet, complete with entertainment and dancers from several different lands—Arabia, China, Spain, Russia—as well as by the Reed Flutes.

The Nutcracker ends as Clara awakens to find that she has had only a vivid dream.

© Michael S. Hamashita/Corbis

THE NUTCRACKER looks like an old-fashioned soldier in dress uniform. A lever in its back caused the jaw to move up and down. It would crack a nut that had been placed in its mouth.

The Development of Ballet

Classical ballet began in the courts of Europe, especially France, about three hundred years ago. Its main goal was to achieve grace and courtliness, not artistic expression. Deportment and etiquette were supreme virtues among the aristocracy. In the court of Louis XIV of France, for example, everyone took dancing lessons, and this dancing was not a type in which they just shuffled around. One feature of such dancing was proper ballet posture; another was a balance of footwork and elevation—the ability to rise on the toes and to leap gracefully. Ballet posture was based on a straight and quiet spine; a stiffened, straight knee; and a level hip line. The hips were not to lift, thrust out, or rotate, and the shoulders were not to ripple.

From such principles and practices there developed a systematic set of positions and steps that are basic in classical ballet. From these and other movements, which often carry French names, the **choreographer** (the designer of dances) plans routines and sequences for a complete scene. The choreography is carefully designed to fit with the music and its story, if there is one. (Not all ballets are developed around a story.)

The first truly Romantic ballet was *La Sylphide* (1832) by Jean Scheitzhöffer. Its story was one of love between a supernatural being and a human. If not remembered for its music, this ballet can make two claims to fame: (1) The female lead wore a tight-fitting costume with a short, flared skirt that became the standard for women in all Romantic ballets. (2) It was the first ballet in which the leading ballerina danced on the points of her slippers, which created the technique for dancing on the toes, referred to as *en pointe*.

Other ballets that followed in the Romantic tradition are *Giselle* by Adolphe Adam, *Coppélia* by Leo Délibes, and the three ballets by Tchaikovsky mentioned in this chapter.

The art of ballet remained relatively unchanged until the twentieth century. Ballet is a beautiful art form, but it is also artificial. The first reaction against these artificialities occurred near the turn of the twentieth century, when Isadora Duncan threw off her corset and shoes and danced barefoot throughout Europe. She believed that dancing should be harmonious and simple, with no ornaments. Although she devised no new techniques, she gave ballet a more natural look. Her ideas were adopted by Michel Fokine, Ruth St. Denis, Martha Graham, Agnes de Mille, and others. To some extent the separation between classical ballet and modern dance still exists.

The music for ballet also changed greatly in the twentieth century. One of the most important landmarks in ballet is *The Rite of Spring*, with music by Stravinsky, which is presented in Chapter 32. Other well-known twentieth-century American ballets are *Rodeo*, *Appalachian Spring*, and *Billy the Kid*, all with music by Aaron Copland.

The music for the ballet is not heavy and serious; that would not be in the character of the story. All of it is beautiful and very listenable. The eight parts of the *Nutcracker Suite* are:

1. Miniature Overture
2. March
3. Dance of the Sugar Plum Fairy
4. Russian Dance, "Trepak"
5. Arab Dance
6. Chinese Dance
7. Dance of Reed Flutes
8. Waltz of the Flowers

The "Waltz of the Flowers" is danced in tribute to Clara by the Sugar Plum Fairy's attendants.

PIOTR ILICH TCHAIKOVSKY

"Waltz of the Flowers" from *The Nutcracker* (1891)

GENRE: **Ballet music   Waltz tempo (3/4)   Orchestra**

CD 4 Tracks 28–30
6 minutes 52 seconds

Form: Rondo (*A B A B C A B*)

0:00	**28** 0:00	Woodwinds and harp open with fragment of A theme.
	0:21	Harp cadenza.
	1:08	A theme played by French horns with flowing notes in clarinet.

1:24	A theme repeated.
1:40	B theme enters in violins and then repeated.
2:12	A theme played by French horns and clarinets.
2:43	B theme played by violins and then repeated.

3:14	**29** 0:00	C theme enters in oboe, with contrasting line in violins.

	0:17	C theme repeated.
	0:31	C theme extended by cellos, then violins with contrasting line in woodwinds.
4:40	**30** 0:00	A theme returns played by the French horns as violins play flowing notes.
	0:30	B theme returns in violins and is repeated one octave higher.
	1:10	Coda begins softly but then starts to build as fragments of B are heard.
	1:41	Music suddenly becomes softer with a short passage in two-beat meter.
	2:12	"Waltz of the Flowers" concludes with full-sounding chords.

LISTENING GUIDE

Piotr Ilich Tchaikovsky

Library of Congress

Best-Known Works

ballet:
- *The Nutcracker*
- *Sleeping Beauty*
- *Swan Lake*

opera:
- *Eugene Onegin*

orchestra:
- Piano Concerto No. 1
- Violin Concerto
- *Romeo and Juliet*
- Festival Overture "1812"
- Symphonies Nos. 4, 5, and 6

Until early adulthood **Piotr Tchaikovsky** ("Chy-*koff*-skee," 1840–1893) seemed destined to follow in his father's footsteps by working in a government position. At the age of twenty-three, however, he decided to become a musician, resigned his job, and entered the newly founded Conservatory of Music in St. Petersburg. He did well, and in three years he had finished his course of study. He was recommended for a teaching position in the new Conservatory in Moscow, where he taught harmony for twelve years.

Throughout his life Tchaikovsky was plagued by the fact that he was a homosexual. He once described his existence as "regretting the past, hoping for the future, without ever being satisfied with the present." He married a Conservatory student, a rather unstable girl who was madly in love with him. The marriage was a disaster. Finally, on the verge of a complete mental breakdown, he went to live with his brothers in St. Petersburg.

---◆---

Tchaikovsky visited New York City in the early 1890s and conducted at Carnegie Hall.

---◆---

Nadezhda von Meck entered his life at this point. She was a wealthy widow who, though a recluse, successfully ran her inherited business empire and the lives of her eleven children. She was impressed by the beauty of Tchaikovsky's music and decided to support him financially. There was, however, one unusual stipulation: So that she could be sure she was supporting a composer, not a personal friend, she required that they should never meet. And so it was. For thirteen years they carried on an intense and devoted relationship—all by letters.

In 1893 while in St. Petersburg to conduct his Sixth Symphony, Tchaikovsky contracted cholera and died. Although he was born and lived in Russia, his music is not particularly nationalistic, especially in contrast to the music of some of his contemporaries, who are discussed in subsequent chapters.

CODA

Both program and ballet music explore the imaginative side of Romanticism in a way that is entertaining and fascinating. What else can one say about a work based on the images of a young man's beloved dancing around him as a cackling witch or a young girl's dream about a nutcracker? But what matters most is the music that such scenes inspired.

Romantic Opera

26

Italian opera dominated the opera world until the nineteenth century. But that situation was about to change. Several other distinct styles of opera developed during the Romantic period. One was the German style, followed later in the century by the French and Russian styles. Italian opera also changed, but less dramatically.

THE ITALIAN STYLE

At the beginning of the nineteenth century, Italian opera was still in the style of Mozart's *Don Giovanni,* discussed in Chapter 17. Gioacchino Rossini (1792–1868) even based his opera *The Barber of Seville* on the characters in Mozart's *The Marriage of Figaro.*

With Vincenzo Bellini (1801–1835) Italian opera reached a high point of interest in melody. The arias in his operas, such as *Norma,* emphasize beautiful singing through technically demanding melodic lines, cadenzas, and ornamentation. This style of opera is termed **bel canto,** which means "beautiful singing" in Italian. Gaetano Donizetti (1797–1848) also contributed to the bel canto style of opera. Although these early operas often lack convincing dramatic qualities, the brilliance of the soloists' lines and the beauty of the melodies make them highly enjoyable listening.

The two most important names in Italian opera in the nineteenth century were Giuseppe Verdi and Giacomo Puccini. Both wrote operas that contained the beauty of bel canto melodies, but they added much more to their music.

There are some differences in the two operas. Figaro is a valet in Mozart's opera, not a barber as he is in Rossini's.

In Europe, especially Italy, opera was very popular. Its appeal reached well beyond the upper classes.

VERDI'S *RIGOLETTO*

Rigoletto is hardly the typical hero—he is a hunchbacked court jester. And he isn't even a nice guy. His one redeeming virtue is his love for his daughter, Gilda. Rigoletto's master, the womanizing Duke of Mantua, has been able to get Gilda to fall in love with him while he pretended to be a poor student. He manages to seduce Gilda, which motivates Rigoletto to plot the Duke's murder. But Gilda really loves the Duke, even when she finds out that he is a liar and a cheat. In the end she sacrifices her own life to save his. As often happens in Romantic opera, evil overcomes good.

The Duke's aria "La donna è mobile" ("Woman is fickle") expresses the Duke's pleasure-seeking personality. It also shows Verdi's ability to compose rousing music. He knew that the aria would be a hit, and he didn't want it to leak out of rehearsals and have everyone singing it before the opera opened. Therefore, he waited until as close as possible to the premiere to give the music to the tenor who had the Duke's role.

"La donna è mobile" achieved a popular status in the United States in the 1950s as recorded by a tenor named Mario Lanza.

PUCCINI'S *LA BOHÈME*

La bohème (*The Bohemian*) is a story of the artsy, hippie life on the Left Bank of the Seine in Paris. The curtain rises on the run-down garret where four young men live: the poet Rodolfo, the painter Marcello, the philosopher Colline, and the musician Schaunard. It's Christmas Eve, and they can't afford fuel for a decent fire. Colline and Schaunard

A *garret* is an unfurnished space just under the roof.

LISTENING GUIDE

GIUSEPPE VERDI

"La donna è mobile" from *Rigoletto* (1851)

GENRE: Aria, opera   Soloist and orchestra

CD 4 Track 31
2 minutes 4 seconds

Form: Strophic

0:00 **31** 0:00   Orchestra plays short introduction.

0:13	La donna è mobile	Woman is fickle
	Qual piuma al vento,	Like a feather in the breeze,
	Muta d'accento	She changes her words
	E di pensiero.	And her thoughts.

0:22	Sempre un amabile	Always a lovable
	Leggiadro viso,	And beautiful face,
	In pianto o in riso,	Crying or laughing,
	é menzognero.	Is lying.
0:31	La donna è mobile, ecc.	Woman is fickle, etc.
1:08	é sempre misero	The man's always miserable
	Chi a lei s'affida,	Who believes in her,
	Chi le confida	Who carelessly trusts
	Mal cauto il core!	His heart to her!
	Pur mai non sentesi	And yet one who never
	Felice appieno	Enjoys love on that breast
	Chi su quel seno	Never feels
	Non libra amore!	Really in love!
1:27	La donna è mobile, ecc.	Woman is fickle, etc.
2:04	Aria concludes with tenor singing high note and decisive chords by the orchestra.	

The young men's break comes when the landlord brags about his virility with women, and they threaten to tell his wife.

come back and flourish some of that rare item—money. The landlord, who seems to have heard of their good fortune, soon comes to ask for the rent. By the use of a little trickery, they are able to get rid of him. They decide to celebrate at the Café Momus, and everyone except Rodolfo leaves; he is finishing some writing and plans to join them shortly.

Soon there's a knock at the door. It is Mimi, who has not met Rodolfo before. Her candle has gone out, and she can't see to get up the stairs to her apartment. She is also weak and out of breath, so Rodolfo gives her a little wine and offers her a chair. As he helps her search for the key she has dropped on the floor, a draft of wind blows out their candles. They grope in the dark for her key. He finds it and, thinking quickly, slips it into his pocket without telling her. As they continue feeling along the floor, Rodolfo's hand meets hers and he exclaims, *"Che gelida manina!"* ("How cold your little hand is!") Then begins one of those glorious arias and a duet that show off Romantic opera at its best.

How fortunate for the plot that the wind just happened to come along at that moment!

Giuseppe Verdi & Giacomo Puccini

Giuseppe Verdi ("*Vair*-dee," 1813–1901) was born in a small town in northern Italy, the son of a poor innkeeper. He probably would not have had a musical education had it not been for the support of a prosperous merchant who paid for two years' study in Milan. When Verdi returned, he fell in love with the merchant's daughter. The marriage was a happy one, but misfortune struck. His two children and his young wife died within a three-year span.

Although Verdi's first opera had been moderately successful, the next one was not. That failure, coupled with the tragedies in his family, caused him to give up composing for a year. He was finally persuaded to write another opera on the story of Nebuchadnezzar, the biblical king of Babylon. It was an immediate success and it launched Verdi on a career that spanned more than fifty years. Part of his success lay in his selection of high-quality libretti. He was also an excellent dramatist and sensed what would be effective onstage.

Verdi's career was helped by the strong nationalistic feelings of the Italians, who were attempting to free themselves from the control of Austria. Cries of "Viva Verdi" rang out in Italian opera houses, both in admiration of Verdi and in allegiance to Italy. To many patriots the letters of his name represented "Victor Emmanuel, *Rex d'*Italia."

The phrase means "Victor Emmanuel, king of Italy." He was Italy's first king.

In spite of his fame, Verdi remained a simple man who preferred the quiet of his farm to the pressures of society. His second wife was a sensitive and intelligent woman who encouraged him in his work. Verdi was able to produce one masterpiece after another. He wrote his last operas when he was nearly eighty years old.

Giacomo Puccini ("Poo-*chee*-nee," 1858–1924) was a generation younger than Verdi and perhaps not so sophisticated a composer. He possessed a wonderful gift of melody, however, and an instinct for successful theater. These attributes made his operas very popular.

Verismo operas have no mythological queens or gods.

Puccini belonged to a group of opera composers who stressed *verismo* (realism). Their characters came from everyday life, and they rejected heroic or exalted themes from mythology and history. In *La bohème*, for example, four young men occupy a shabby, cold apartment and have trouble meeting the rent and finding enough to eat.

© Archivo Iconografico, S.A. /CORBIS

BEST-KNOWN WORKS OF VERDI

opera:
- *Il trovatore*
- *La traviata*
- *Rigoletto*
- *A Masked Ball*
- *Aïda*
- *Otello*
- *Falstaff*

© The New York Public Library

BEST-KNOWN WORKS OF PUCCINI

opera:
- *La bohème*
- *Tosca*
- *Madame Butterfly*
- *Turandot*

First Rodolfo tells Mimi about himself and his lonely life as a poet. Mimi responds with an equally beautiful aria. In it she describes her simple life and the flowers she embroiders.

Rodolfo's friends return to the courtyard outside, urging him to get going. He goes to the window and tells them to return to Momus and reserve a table. As his friends leave,

Mimi and Rodolfo break into a duet in which they speak of the newfound love that binds them together. Some of the melodies previously introduced in the arias are heard again.

In good operatic tradition, Mimi and Rodolfo fall in love very quickly. Musically, it all works very well, even if it isn't quite realistic. The scene would not be effective opera if their relationship were allowed to grow more naturally over several hours.

The rest of *La bohème* is equally beautiful and not long, as least by the standards of nineteenth-century opera. Act II is a delightful scene at the Café Momus in which Musetta, Marcello's former love and a notorious flirt, sings a tantalizing waltz. In Act III,

LISTENING GUIDE

GIACOMO PUCCINI

La bohème, excerpt from Act I (1898)

GENRE: Opera   Soloists and orchestra

CD 2 Tracks 16–17
4 minutes 8 seconds

0:00   **16**   0:00   Rodolfo is entranced with the sight of Mimi as she stands in the moonlight.

The 8 below the clef indicates that the pitches Rodolfo is to sing are one octave lower than written.

0.39   **17**   0:00

3:29 The curtain falls, and the music for Act I ends as Mimi and Rodolfo leave the stage arm in arm.

THE FINAL ACT OF LA BOHÈME ends with the death of Mimi in the arms of Rodolfo. Often the duet is staged so that it is sung with a soft spotlight shining on the couple.

Mimi and Rodolfo have had a falling out. There is a hint of impending doom because of Mimi's deteriorating health from tuberculosis.

In Act IV the setting is again the garret, and there are several musical dramatic parallels to the first act. This time Musetta enters, saying that Mimi is downstairs, too weak to climb up them—an ironic parallel to the events of the earlier act. Mimi is helped into the room, and the friends leave quickly to get medicine and a doctor. Rodolfo and Mimi recall their first meeting. The old themes are heard, but the music is no longer robust. It is weak and shattered. The friends return. They talk quietly among themselves, hoping Mimi can sleep. Suddenly, they realize that she has died. "Mimi! Mimi!" Rodolfo cries out. The orchestra strikes the same chords heard in the love music from Act I. This time, however, the music is heavy with grief. The curtain falls.

Romantic operas usually end tragically. It's more dramatic that way.

THE FRENCH STYLE

The French did not develop quite as distinct a style of opera as the Italians or the Germans did. Yet their operas do sound different. The more distinctive French quality would flourish at the turn of the century in the impressionistic music of Debussy and Ravel.

Three French opera composers merit attention. One is Charles Gounod ("Goo-*noh*," 1818–1893). His best-known work is *Faust*, in which a man named Faust sells his soul to the devil in exchange for eternal youth. The Faust legend, which exists in a number of different versions, fascinated the Romantic poets and musicians. Another composer of French opera was Jules Massenet ("Mass-en-*nay*," 1842–1912). His best-known operas are *Manon* and *Thaïs*; the "Meditation" from that opera is often heard as a solo for violin or singer.

Although *Carmen* takes place in Spain and contains much Spanish-sounding music, it is in French and was composed by a Frenchman.

The opéra comique was more a family theater, and probably the femme fatale role of Carmen was disturbing to its patrons.

The opera that nearly everyone has heard about, and most people find very attractive, is *Carmen* by Georges Bizet. Actually, *Carmen* was first presented at the opéra comique with spoken lines instead of sung recitatives. It is not as long and serious as the operas usually presented at the Opera House in Paris. Ironically, it was not initially very well received, which broke Bizet's spirit, and he did not live long after its premiere. Today *Carmen* is the most popular opera in the Western world.

THE GERMAN STYLE

German opera differs from Italian opera in a number of ways. To begin with, the languages are very different. Italian words end in one of the five vowel sounds of the language. German words often conclude with consonants, many of them with hard *t*'s and *k*'s. The subjects are no longer ancient Greek gods but rather the Nordic gods of northern Europe. And the music is different, too. German opera tends to sound heavier and less lighthearted than that of Italy or France.

In 1821 the German composer Carl Maria von Weber ("*Vay*-ber," 1786–1826) wrote *Der Freischütz* (*The Freeshooter*), an opera based on German folklore. The story involves a marksman who receives from the black huntsman seven magic bullets. Six of the seven do as he wills, but the seventh does as the devil wills. The devil also gets the soul of the one who is hit by the bullet. Besides mysticism, the opera features peasants, rustic scenes, and hunting horns.

The black huntsman is the devil.

Weber completed two more operas before his early death. Although they are seldom performed today, they exerted a significant influence on Richard Wagner, one of the musical giants of the nineteenth century.

WAGNER'S MUSIC DRAMAS

More than any previous opera composer, Richard Wagner consciously tackled the dilemma of balance between music and drama. In his lengthy philosophical discourses, he often indicated his belief that poetry and music should be one. To meet his artistic goals, he created a different kind of opera, one that he called **music drama.**

Each of his operas has a score the size of a large book.

Music dramas required a new and different approach to the concept of libretto, so Wagner wrote his own texts. The topics were mythological because he felt that such stories appealed best to the emotions. Wagner's favorite libretto themes were also rich with philosophical overtones—the struggle between good and evil, the contest between the physical and the spiritual, and the idea of redemption through love. Because these overarching themes are present, the characters in the music dramas are not personalities but more like symbols or pawns being pushed about by uncontrollable forces. In this respect, Wagner approaches the drama of the ancient Greeks.

Wagner frequently associates a musical motive with a particular character, emotion, or idea. In his music such a motive is called a **leitmotiv,** or leading motive. As soon as various leitmotivs are established, Wagner weaves them in and out of the music at appropriate times to enhance the intrigue of the plot and to provide unity in the work. Such use of motives permits the orchestra to assume a much more vital role in the music drama, because it can expand on the people and ideas referred to in the text.

Because the division of music into recitatives, arias, and choruses interrupts the forward motion of the drama, Wagner eliminated these forms as independent sections. Instead, he created a flowing, melodious line to serve as an unending melody. The vocal line emphasizes the expression of the words being sung. With its continuous interweaving of motives, the orchestra contributes to the impression of never-ending motion.

To increase the impression that a musical work is seamless, Wagner used much chromatic harmony. By making half-step alternations in the chords, he weakened the magnetic pull of the harmony toward the tonic. The absence of a strong tonic means that the music seldom arrives at a cadence point, so the feeling of key is somewhat nebulous.

Portions of his music dramas are often performed as concert pieces without singers.

Wagner did not treat the orchestra as mere accompaniment for the singers onstage. The importance of the orchestra in his works equals, or perhaps exceeds, that of the

THE TWILIGHT OF THE GODS ends with flaming death, flood, and utter destruction. But because of the power of love, a new world will emerge.

In Romantic operas the course of events often hinges on curses or magic potions.

singers. In a real sense, his orchestra is symphonic, both in size and in its ability to stand almost without the vocal parts.

Wagner's most ambitious achievement was a cycle of four complete operas titled *Der Ring des Nibelungen* (*The Ring of the Nibelung*). The four operas in the cycle are *Das Rheingold* (*The Gold of the Rhine*), *Die Walküre* (*The Valkyries*), *Siegfried*, and *Götterdämmerung* (*The Twilight of the Gods*).

The story of the cycle revolves around gold that had been fashioned into a ring and is guarded by the Rhine maidens in the Rhine River. The gold is stolen and a curse put on it. The curse states that if the possessor will renounce love, he will rule the world. The result is a chain of misfortunes affecting all the characters in the drama.

WAGNER'S GÖTTERDÄMMERUNG

In an earlier opera in *The Ring* cycle, Wotan, king of the gods, made his favorite daughter, Brünnhilde, mortal because she disobeyed him. She falls into a deep sleep, surrounded by a wall of fire. Siegfried passes through the flames and awakens her. Siegfried and Brünnhilde fall in love and become husband and wife.

While on one of his adventures, Siegfried gains possession of the ring. Unfortunately for him, he does not know about the curse. He is subsequently murdered by the evil Hagen, who lusts after the gold.

The immolation scene occurs very late in *Götterdämmerung*. It takes place in front of a castle on the Rhine River. In this scene Brünnhilde sings her farewell before joining Siegfried in death by riding her horse into his funeral pyre. Before ending her life, she takes the ring from Siegfried's finger and puts it on. She also bequeaths it to the Rhine maidens upon her death. After she disappears into the flames, a flood engulfs the stage. The flood is followed by a fire. Valhalla, the home of the gods, is destroyed, along with its inhabitants. *Götterdämmerung* ends in tragedy for all except the Rhine maidens.

The immolation scene is presented in the Listening Guide. The stage actions appear in parenthetical statements. The text is provided in the original German and in English.

As you listen to this scene, pay careful attention to Wagner's use of the leitmotivs. Notice how they not only enhance the text but continue the story, even after the characters have died.

Although *Götterdämmerung* ends tragically, the final leitmotiv is "Redemption by love." The philosophically minded Wagner was saying through this leitmotiv that the most powerful force of all is love and that, in spite of all that had happened, a new world will emerge through its power.

RICHARD WAGNER
Immolation scene from *Götterdämmerung* (1874)

GENRE: Opera   Soloist and orchestra

CD 4 Tracks 32–40
7 minutes 54 seconds

0:00 **32** 0:00   The trumpets and trombones play the leitmotiv for "Law" at a loud dynamic level.

Brünnhilde, the ring on her finger, takes a torch from one of the men.
She then sings to a pair of ravens, which are Wotan's messengers.

0:13   Fliegt heim, ihr Raben! raunt eurem Herren,   Fly home, you ravens! Tell your master
       was hier am Rhein ihr gehört!   what you have heard here on the Rhine!

0:25 **33** 0:00   The orchestra plays the "Magic fire" and "Loge, god of fire" leitmotivs.

Brünnhilde continues singing to the ravens.

An Brünnhildes Felsen fliegt vorbei: Fly past Brünnhilde's rock,
der dort noch lodert,   where Loge is still burning,
weiset Loge nach Walhall!   and tell him to go to Valhalla!
Denn der Götter Ende dämmert nun auf: Because the end of the gods now is dawning.

She throws the torch onto the pyre. The two ravens fly into the background.

so—werf' ich den Brand   See—I throw the torch
in Walhalls prangende Burg.   into Valhalla's glorious fortress!

0:56   Strings play many notes to represent fire.

The pyre bursts into flames. Brünnhilde turns to her horse.

1:30 **34** 0:00   Grane, mein Ross.   Grane, my steed,
                   sei mir gegrüsst!   Greetings to you!

0:17   The French horns and other instruments sound the "Ride of the Valkyries" leitmotiv.

Weisst du auch, mein Freund,   My friend, do you know
wohin ich dich führe?   where I am leading you?
Im Feuer leuchtend.   Into the blazing fire.

1:56 **35** 0:00   The flute and Brünnhilde sound the "Redemption by love" leitmotiv.

liegt dort dein Herr, Siegfried, mein   Your master lies in there, Siegfried, my
   seliger Held.   blessed hero.
Dem Freunde zu folgen,   Are you eager to follow your friend?
wieherst du freudig?   Are you neighing?
Lockt dich zu ihm die lachende Lohe?   Are you attracted by the laughing flames?

0:37   Fühl' mein Brust auch, wie sie entbrennt;   Notice my breast also, how it is burning;
       helles Feuer das Herz mir erfasst.   bright flames consume my heart.
       Ihn zu umschlingen, umschlossen, von ihm,   To hold him, to be held by him,
       in mächtigster Minne vermählt ihm zu sein!   to be united with him by the power of love!

(continued)

1:14	Hei-a-ja-ho! Grane! Grüss deinen Herren!	Hei-a-yo-ho! Grane! Greet your master!
	Siegfried! Siegfried! Sieh!	Siegfried! Siegfried! See!
	selig grüsst dich dein Weib!	Joyfully your wife greets you!

1:36   The brasses play the "Ride of the Valkyries" leitmotiv.

Brünnhilde mounts her horse and rides it into the flaming pyre.

3:38   36   0:00   The orchestra plays the "Magic fire" leitmotiv at a loud dynamic level.

Flames engulf the area in front of the castle, which also soon catches fire.

The "Magic sleep" leitmotiv is heard.

When everything seems to be burning, the glow is extinguished. Soon only a cloud of smoke is seen. The Rhine begins to rise, and its waters pour over the fire. Three Rhine maidens ride the waves and appear by the funeral pyre. Hagen, Siegfried's murderer, panics when he sees them. He tosses down his spear and shield, and then plunges into the waters, crying:

1:09   Hagen: Zurück vom Ring!   Away from the ring!

Two Rhine maidens grab Hagen and drag him down under the water. Another Rhine maiden triumphantly holds up the recovered ring.

A descending pattern played by the strings suggests Hagen's drowning.

1:26   The oboes and clarinets play the "Rhine maidens" leitmotiv.

5:12   37   0:00   The brasses sound the solemn "Valhalla" leitmotiv.

The Rhine gradually returns to its banks, and the Rhine maidens play with the ring in its calm waters.

0:12   An interweaving of leitmotivs is heard. The oboes and clarinets play the "Rhine maidens"; the violins play "Redemption by love"; the brasses sound "Valhalla." That leitmotiv grows more prominent as the music progresses.

5:39   38   0:00   "Rhine maidens" motive and "Redemption by love" motive are played together. Brasses play "Valhalla" motive.

From the ruins of the burned castle, the men and women see the red glow in the heavens. In that glow appears Valhalla, with gods and heroes sitting together.

7:04   39   0:00   The music grows louder as the brasses sound the "Siegfried" leitmotiv.

Flames overcome Valhalla. The gods disappear in the flames.

7:24   40   0:00   Strings sound "Redemption by love" leitmotiv.

1:09   The curtain falls with a long chord.

Richard Wagner

Richard Wagner Museum, Bayreuth

Richard Wagner ("*Ree*-card *Vahg*-ner," 1813–1883) was an artistic phenomenon. Born in Leipzig, Germany, he was the son of a minor police official who died when Richard was still an infant. His mother married an actor and playwright, who encouraged his stepson along similar lines. For most of his career, Wagner was largely self-taught. At the age of twenty, he became a chorus master in a small opera house in Leipzig and produced his first operas.

Success was slow in coming, and for the next ten years it seemed that Wagner would spend his life hovering on the edge of poverty. His first successful opera was *Rienzi*, which earned him a position as conductor for the king of Saxony. Other successful operas followed in the 1840s.

In 1848 Wagner became associated with the political uprisings that were taking place in Europe. He even published two articles in a magazine that advocated anarchy. A revolution broke out in Dresden in 1849, and the king and his court fled. Wagner was forced to escape to the home of his friend Franz Liszt in Weimar. Because there was a warrant out for his arrest, Wagner soon fled over the border into Switzerland. At that point he seemed a ruined man. But he was helped by some willing patrons, and the years in Switzerland were some of his most productive. During this time he began work on *The Ring of the Nibelung*.

---◆---

Bavaria, now part of Germany, was an independent state at that time.

---◆---

Wagner became estranged from his wife, who had grown unsympathetic to his artistic aims and desires. He became involved with a succession of married women. In 1864 again all seemed lost. At that point fate seemed to step in. A nineteen-year-old admirer of Wagner's music ascended to the throne in Bavaria. He was Ludwig II, known as "Mad Ludwig." He summoned Wagner to Munich, where he resumed work on *The Ring of the Nibelung*.

By 1876 Wagner had reached the top of the operatic world. That year he opened his first Bayreuth ("By-royt") festival. Later he built an opera house there, and the Bayreuth festivals continue today. It is the only theater in the world devoted exclusively to the music of one person. He is buried at Bayreuth, which in a sense is his monument.

BEST-KNOWN WORKS

opera:
- *The Flying Dutchman*
- *Tannhäuser*
- *Lohengrin*
- *Tristan and Isolde*
- *The Meistersingers of Nuremberg*
- *The Ring of the Nibelung*

CODA

Although the Italian, French, and German styles of opera differed from one another in the nineteenth century, they were similar in their fondness for expansive emotion—especially feelings associated with tragedies—and glorious, sensuous music. Romantic operas reach out over the footlights and capture the emotions of the audience.

27 Late Romantic Music

The composers of the Romantic period never completely abandoned the forms used by Mozart and Haydn in the Classical period. In fact, some composers, especially in the last half of the nineteenth century, used traditional forms extensively. Most of these compositions were for orchestra, although quite a few of them involved piano, chamber music, and choral groups.

The works created in the century after the Classical period do not sound at all like their predecessors. They are noticeably different, for the reasons mentioned in Chapter 24.

BRAHMS'S SYMPHONY NO. 4

Brahms composed only four symphonies, but each has a prominent place in the repertoire of the symphony orchestra. By the second half of the nineteenth century, composers were treating symphonies as monumental efforts. Brahms was so awed by the symphonies of Beethoven that he waited to complete his first symphony until he was forty-three years old. An earlier aborted attempt at writing a symphony became his First Piano Concerto. He completed his Fourth Symphony nine years later in 1885.

Of all the Romantic composers, Brahms liked to use traditional forms the most. In fact, during his lifetime he was considered by many musicians to be an outmoded conservative. But conservative, Romantic, or whatever, he composed much music of extraordinary quality.

First Movement

The first movement is in sonata form. It begins with a theme that has the sweeping, Romantic quality of many of Brahms's melodies:

The theme is worked with and manipulated throughout much of the movement. For instance, in the next few measures the same idea appears at *twice* its original speed—**diminution**. The notes don't follow the theme exactly, but the general idea is present:

At the end of the development section, the same idea appears at *half* its original speed—**augmentation.** At this point in the movement, Brahms retains the melodic line but alters the rhythm:

At another place, the theme is varied and exchanged between the first and second violins:

Elsewhere it is exchanged between the strings and woodwinds:

One could go on for pages showing the many ways Brahms fragments, varies, develops, and transforms the theme. Almost from the time the theme appears, he is developing it and blending it into the structure of the music in such a way that throughout the symphony he maintains the warm sounds of the Romantic style. From it he extracts two motives, circled in the Listening Guide, that appear often in the movement.

The second theme combines two melodic ideas. One is played by the horns and a few woodwinds. It sounds somewhat like introductory music—and perhaps it is, because soon a passionate melody starts in the cellos and horns. A portion of the theme, including the triplets, is also used as a unifying motive in the movement. Sometimes it is exchanged with the first motive.

A third theme appears later in the movement, but it is not developed extensively.

ThomsonNOW™

"Hear It Now: Development in Music," in *ThomsonNOW*, Chapter 27.

LISTENING GUIDE

JOHANNES BRAHMS

Symphony No. 4 in E Minor, First Movement (1884–1885)

GENRE: Symphony   Orchestra

CD 2 Tracks 18–22
13 minutes 22 seconds

Form: Sonata

Exposition

0:00   **18**   0:00   First theme, which contains two motives (circled), played by violins.

        0:37   First theme repeated.

        1:03   Transition.

1:39   **19**   0:00   Second theme, also containing a motive, begins in woodwinds.

(continued)

0:06   Second part of second theme sounded by cellos and French horns with a rhythmic accompaniment. Violins repeat theme in high notes.

0:44   Violins and woodwinds exchange fragments of first theme.

1:11   Third theme introduced by French horn and flute, then oboe.

1:19   Modified second theme returns in woodwinds.

2:23   Codetta begins in woodwinds with fragments of first theme.

Development

4:19 **20** 0:00   First theme played by violins; then motive from it modulates several times.

0:47   Three accented notes from first theme are exchanged among strings.

1:25   Motives from second and first themes played softly by woodwinds.

1:59   First part of second theme played forcefully by strings and French horn.

2:19   Second theme played by woodwinds as violins play fragments of first theme pizzicato.

2:34   Motive from first theme alternates between violins and woodwinds.

3:18   First theme returns in augmentation in woodwinds.

Recapitulation

8:05 **21** 0:00   First theme returns in violins at the original tempo.

0:30   First theme repeated accompanied by rippling notes in woodwinds.

1:13   Second theme returns in woodwinds and French horn, followed by cellos over rhythmic accompaniment.

1:32   Violins repeat second theme.

1:57   Motive from first theme exchanged between woodwinds and violins.

2:22   Third theme played by oboe and French horn.

2:49   Motive from second theme played softly by woodwinds, then loudly by strings.

11:58 **22** 0:00   Coda contains two-note fragment from first theme played in imitation between strings and French horns; intensity of music increases.

0:31   Violins continue playing two-note fragment from first theme as intensity of music increases.

1:22   Movement concludes after five abrupt chords and final cadence of two long chords.

Four qualities stand out about Brahms's music in general and his Fourth Symphony in particular:

- The sheer beauty of the music. Listening to the rich sounds of its melodies and harmonies could be compared to eating a piece of a perfectly baked German chocolate cake.

- The skill with which themes are organized and developed. This is much more than sensual pleasure in listening to this symphony. Brahms is masterful in working with themes and utilizing forms.

- The quality of optimism and good feeling. This is a subjective element, of course, but there is something about Brahms's music that gives the feeling that things are right and will continue to turn out right. There is no sense of hand-wringing or self-pity in the music.

- The noble quality of the music. The word *noble* doesn't do justice to the music of Brahms and many other composers, but it comes as close as any. It means "possessing outstanding or superior qualities." There is something extraordinary about the music of Brahms and many other composers, something that is beyond or better than what we usually encounter in everyday life.

You can listen to Brahms's music with your heart, or your head, or both, which is the best way.

A listener's score for the first movement of Brahms's Symphony No. 4 is available for downloading.

Second, Third, and Fourth Movements

Brahms is especially gifted in writing melodious second movements, and his Fourth Symphony is no exception. It is built around two themes. The first consists of a short pattern that is immediately followed in inversion and repeated several times. The second theme is a warm, flowing melody first played by the cellos.

The third movement is filled with an optimistic, jovial spirit. Its theme appears in two versions at the same time, with one being the inversion of the other.

The slur marks (⌢) cause the rhythmic emphasis to occur off the beat in the first and third measures. Portions of the melody appear throughout the movement.

The fourth movement is one of the most unusual and musically interesting found in the symphonies of the nineteenth century. It is a massive **chaconne,** which is a set of variations on a short theme. The theme for this movement is only eight measures long with only one note per measure. It is very plain and solid.

Thirty-five variations and a coda follow. At the beginning of the thirteenth variation, the speed of the notes of the theme is slowed to one-half their original speed. During this middle section of the movement, the theme is only implied in the harmony. It is easy to tell when the theme returns, because it is played forcefully again, as it was at the opening of the movement. The return of the original theme gives the movement an overall three-part form in addition to the variations of the chaconne. The continually repeated pattern provides unity to the music, while the variations provide contrast.

Brahms's *A German Requiem*

One of Brahms's greatest accomplishments is *Ein Deutsches Requiem* (*A German Requiem*), which he composed early in his career in 1868 after the death of his mother and his teacher-friend Robert Schumann. It carries the name *German Requiem* because

Johannes Brahms

BEST-KNOWN WORKS

chamber music:
- Clarinet Quintet
- Trio in E-flat for Horn, Violin, and Piano

choral:
- A German Requiem

orchestra:
- Concerto for Piano No. 2
- Concerto for Violin
- Symphonies Nos. 1, 2, 3, and 4

Johannes Brahms (1833–1897) was the son of a rather shiftless double bass player in Hamburg, Germany. Johannes started his musical career by playing piano in the notorious waterfront area of the city. He was highly talented and by the age of twenty-five became the accompanist for one of the finest violinists of the day. He studied composition with Robert Schumann, and the Schumanns took the shy young man into their home. Brahms grew fond of Clara, and he was much help to the family during Robert's illness.

Brahms was aware that he had extraordinary talent as a composer and, for this reason, never accepted a position that made heavy demands on his time. Unlike Beethoven, he left no rejected versions of his music for posterity to find. He wanted the world to know only his best work, so his rough sketches were deliberately destroyed.

It was said that Brahms burned as many of his works as he allowed to be published.

Brahms never composed an opera or a tone poem. His coolness toward opera may be due to the overblown competition between his admirers and those of Wagner. The division concerned artistic philosophy as much as it did personalities. The Wagnerites believed that music was a means for communication of emotions and ideas. The admirers of Brahms viewed music as an end in itself and therefore favored absolute music. Brahms ignored the controversy as best he could and went about his composing. Because there is some truth in both views, the dispute has never been resolved.

it did not involve the traditional Latin Requiem text of the Roman Catholic Church. Rather, it is a personal statement of faith based on German verses from the Old and New Testaments.

This profound and monumental hour-long work consists of seven movements for bass and soprano soloists, chorus, and orchestra. There are connections between Part I and Part VII, with Part VII ending with a much more positive outlook than Part I. There are also musical similarities between the second and sixth parts, and between the third and fifth parts.

Part IV, "How Lovely Is Thy Dwelling Place," is therefore in a pivotal position in *A German Requiem*. Its text is based on Psalm 84. The first two lines of the psalm are heard three times, separated by two contrasting sections presenting other music and lines of the psalm. This gives Part IV an overall *A B A C A* form. The A section has a serene quality, and the B section is also rather even and restrained. The C section, with the words "die loben dich immerdar" ("where they praise Thee evermore"), moves more quickly and vigorously in polyphonic texture. There is also much extension on the word "evermore" before the opening music returns.

The work is a testament to Brahms's ability to compose music for voices as well as instruments. His vocal output includes about two hundred songs for solo singer and almost the same number for various combinations of voices. It also reminds us that many other nineteenth-century composers wrote excellent choral works that are often performed today—Schubert, Mendelssohn, Liszt, Berlioz, and Gabriel Fauré, to name a few.

Part VII begins with the words "Blessed are the dead, which die in the Lord, from henceforth."

JOHANNES BRAHMS

A German Requiem, Part IV, "How Lovely is Thy Dwelling Place" (1867–1868)

GENRE: Oratorio/Requiem   Chorus and orchestra

CD 4 Tracks 41–43
5 minutes 46 seconds

Form: Rondo (*A B A C A*)

0:00 **41** 0:00	Woodwinds softly play a peaceful melody in major.	

0:09	Sopranos sing melody as other sections of the chorus sing harmony parts.	

	Wie lieblich sind deine Wohnungen,	*How lovely is Thy dwelling place,*
	Herr Zebaoth!	*O, Lord of Hosts!*
0:48	Tenors repeat text, and other sections follow in imitation.	
1:30	Chorus sings phrase in minor. Then imitation begins first in basses with many words repeated.	
	Meine Seele verlanget und sehnet sich	*My soul longs and thirsts*
	nach den Vorhöfen des Herrn;	*for the courts of the Lord;*
1:53	Chorus sings soft, sustained chords.	
2:07 **42** 0:00	Chorus sings with orchestra strong accents at the beginning of several measures.	
	Mein Leib und Seele freuen sich	*My body and soul rejoice*
	in dem	*in the*
	lebendigen Gott.	*living God.*
0:34	Orchestra plays opening music in major, and chorus sings with a reassuring quality.	
	Wie lieblich sind deine Wohnunger	*How Lovely is Thy dwelling place,*
	Herr Zebaoth!	*O, Lord of Hosts!*
1:33	Chorus continues.	
	Wohl denen, die in	*Blessed are they who dwell*
	deinem Hause wohnen,	*in Thy House,*
3:54 **43** 0:00	Music takes on martial character as chorus sings in imitation with many words repeated.	
	Die loben dich immerdar!	*Where they praise Thee evermore!*
0:50	Opening music and text return.	
	Wie lieblich sind deine Wohnungen,	*How lovely is Thy dwelling place,*
	Herr Zebaoth!	*O, Lord of Hosts!*
1:53	Orchestra quietly closes with a sustained chord.	

Dvořák's American String Quartet in F Major

This was the twelfth quartet that Dvořák had published.

The quartet Op. 96 (No. 12) by Antonín Dvořák is often called the *American Quartet* because he wrote it in the town of Spillville, Iowa. For three years in the 1890s, Dvořák was director of the Conservatory of Music in New York City. He was homesick for his native Bohemia, so he spent his summers living among the Czech-Bohemian people of that town. But this quartet is largely Bohemian in character, not American.

The *American Quartet* contains the traditional four movements, with the same pattern of forms and tempos found in most symphonies, concertos, and chamber works of the Classical and Romantic periods. And because the Romantic period is noted for its large works, it is worth remembering that nineteenth-century composers also wrote much excellent chamber music. Dvořák's *American Quartet* is only one example of this type of music.

First Movement

The first movement of this quartet is in the traditional sonata form. The first theme is built around four one-measure phrases. These one-measure phrases become the germinal ideas for much of the movement. Dvořák uses many dotted-note figures in his music.

Several features stand out about Dvořák's music, specifically the first movement of this string quartet:

- The energy and vitality of the music
- The good-natured quality of the music
- The skill with which Dvořák worked with the four melodic ideas that make up the first theme
- The songlike beauty of the second theme

Antonín Dvořák

© SF PALM/StageImage

Best-Known Works

chamber music:
- String Quartets Nos. 10, 11, and 12

orchestra:
- Concerto for Cello
- Concerto for Violin
- *Slavonic Dances*
- Serenade for String Orchestra
- Symphonies Nos. 8 and 9

Antonín Dvořák (1841–1904) was born into the family of a Bohemian innkeeper and amateur musician. He grew up listening to the folk music of his native land. After several years of conflict between Dvořák's music teacher and his father, an uncle provided him with the funds needed for a year of music study in Prague. When the money ran out, he earned his living playing in café bands and the National Opera Orchestra.

When Dvořák was about forty, his fortunes changed. He submitted a composition to the Austrian Commission. Although the prize he won was small in monetary terms, it gained for him the devoted friendship and unsparing help of committee member Johannes Brahms. Brahms opened many doors to publishers and conductors for Dvořák, who was genuinely grateful.

By 1885 Dvořák was recognized throughout the world. A few years later, he accepted the directorship of the Conservatory of Music in New York at a salary twenty times what he was earning in Prague. While in America he was introduced to African American music by his pupil Harry T. Burleigh. He also became acquainted with the music of the Native Americans. He was the first composer, native or foreign born, to recognize these musical treasures.

Dvořák once expressed his gratitude in a letter to Brahms: "All my life [I] owe you the deepest gratitude for your good and noble intentions toward me, which are worthy of a truly great artist and man."

After three years in the United States, Dvořák returned to Bohemia, where he became director of the Prague Conservatory. When he died, a national day of mourning was declared in his honor.

LISTENING GUIDE

ANTONÍN DVOŘÁK
American Quartet, First Movement (1893)

GENRE: **Chamber music   String quartet**

CD 5 Tracks 1–5
7 minutes 12 seconds

Form: Sonata

Exposition

0:00 **1** 0:00   First theme played by viola, then repeated by first violin.

0:20   Transition based on measures 3 and 4 of first theme.

1:33 **2** 0:00   Second theme played softly by first violin.

0:27   Transition using first three notes of second theme.

0:55   Codetta based on measures 1 and 2 of first theme begins softly.

Development

2:37 **3** 0:00   Viola plays altered version of first theme.

3:48 **4** 0:00   New melodic idea played by second violin is imitated by first violin, viola, and cello.

Recapitulation

4:22 **5** 0:00   First theme played by viola and repeated by first violin.

0:19   Transition begins based on measure 4 of first theme.

0:22   Cello plays short countermelody.

0:35   Violins play fragments from first theme.

1:37   Second theme played by first violin, then repeated by cello as music begins to build.

2:33   Coda begins with first part of first theme.

2:48   Movement closes with loud chords.

Second, Third, and Fourth Movements

The second movement is in a three-part form. The main melody is flowing and sentimental. The middle section of the movement is also melodious, with the first and second violins playing three notes apart.

The notation for the viola part in the Listening Guide uses the alto clef, the normal clef for the viola. Middle C is on the middle line of the clef. It eliminates the extensive use of ledger lines.

The scherzo is discussed in conjunction with Beethoven's music in Chapter 21.

The third movement has a scherzolike quality. It contains five brief sections in an *A B A B A* pattern.

The fourth movement is a rondo, with the pattern of *A B A C A B A*, which is sometimes termed *sonata rondo*. It has a lively character. It also contains many dotted-note patterns, which Dvořák was fond of using.

TCHAIKOVSKY'S SYMPHONY NO. 4

Much music of the Romantic period is luscious and beautiful, but some of it is vibrant and fiery. The fourth movement of Tchaikovsky's Fourth Symphony is such a work. It begins with a flurry of notes, which are then contrasted with a simple Russian folk song melody called "The Birch Tree." The folk melody contains only four lines in an *a a b b* form and has a range of only the first five notes of a minor scale. How different can two themes be? The movement also cycles back in the development section the stirring introductory music to the first movement. Other characteristics of Tchaikovsky's style can be heard, especially the rapid exchanges of notes among the sections of the orchestra and the gradual buildup to climactic points. It's a real attention-grabbing piece of music.

LISTENING GUIDE

PIOTR ILICH TCHAIKOVSKY

Symphony No. 4 in F Minor, Op. 36, Fourth Movement (1871)

GENRE: Symphony   Orchestra

CD 5 Tracks 6–9
9 minutes 12 seconds

Form: Sonata

Exposition

0:00 **6** 0:00   First theme with its many fast notes is played forcefully by strings in a major key.

0:16   Second theme (Russian folk melody) introduced by oboe in a minor key.

0:30   Woodwinds and violins exchange two-note figure.

0:50   First theme in major repeated by violins.

1:03   Transition played by brasses and woodwinds.

1:38 **7** 0:00   Second theme played softly by oboe in minor.

0:16   Woodwinds repeat second theme.

0:30   Second theme played vigorously by French horns.

0:46   Second theme repeated by trombones as violins play swirling notes.

1:01   First half of second theme played quietly by oboe.

		1:16	Sections of orchestra rapidly exchange melodic figures.
		1:49	First theme played by violins, followed by transition in basses and strings.

Development

4:13	8	0:00	Second theme played by violins in minor.
		0:17	Second theme repeated with flute adding contrasting line, then theme repeated in major.
		0:49	First part of second theme leads to several rapid exchanges between sections of orchestra.
		1:14	Fragments of second theme played by trombones and imitated by trumpets.
5:46	9	0:00	Portion of introduction to first movement played by brasses. French horns and then strings follow as music grows softer.
		1:39	Transition begins in French horns with rapid exchanges among woodwinds and violins as music gradually grows louder and higher.
		2:12	Rapidly moving notes exchanged between violins and woodwinds.

Recapitulation

	2:18	First theme returns in violins.
	2:29	Transition played energetically by brasses and strings.
	2:45	Second theme played loudly by brasses.
	2:58	Coda with many fast passages and tremolos in violins.
	3:26	Movement concludes with timpani and a long, solid chord.

CODA

As Brahms, Dvořák, and Tchaikovsky demonstrate, much of the music of the nineteenth century retained many of the formal practices of the eighteenth century. Sonata form with its development of themes continued, as well as techniques such as theme and variations. What these composers poured into the forms of the Classical period was very different, however. The flowing melodies, rich harmonies, and expansive character are attributes that mark Romantic music.

28 Nationalism

It should be noted that almost no Romantic composers *lived* as peasants. They admired the simple life from a distance.

Romanticism exalted the inherent goodness of humankind in its natural condition. Eighteenth-century intellectuals had considered common folk to be untutored and rough; the Romantics admired them. They thought the life of the simple folk to be good and right because it was largely uncorrupted by society. Furthermore, the life of the common people was a source of subject matter that composers and artists had seldom tapped before.

CHARACTERISTICS OF NATIONALISM

Many nationalistic works are also programmatic.

When associated with the arts, **nationalism** refers to a deliberate, conscious attempt to develop artworks that are characteristic of a particular country or region. Often nationalism involves specific subject matter, such as a painting of a national event or an opera about a historical character.

During the nineteenth century, this search for nationalistic expression was mainly an attempt to break away from the prevailing German-Austrian style. Bach, Mozart, Beethoven, Schubert, Liszt, Schumann, Brahms, and Wagner had long ruled the musical world. To men such as Modest Mussorgsky in Russia, Bedřich Smetana in Bohemia, and Edvard Grieg in Norway, it was time for something different. They knew that Russians and Bohemians and Norwegians were as capable of composing music as were the Germans! And they set about proving it.

There was an additional reason for nationalism in the arts during the nineteenth century: It was a time of rising patriotism. Italy and Germany were finally formed as nations. Unfortunately, wars were frequent. In such conflicts a nation's efforts involved the average citizen to a degree unknown in previous centuries. No longer were wars fought largely by professional soldiers for a king. Now the cause was one's country. In short, the times were a good incubator for nationalism in the arts.

The language of the directions does not affect the actual sounds, but it offers an idea of the composers' outlook toward their music.

In their efforts to assert their independence from foreign influences, some composers indicated the tempo markings and other musical directions in their native language rather than the more internationally accepted Italian. So Debussy wrote *Vif* instead of *Vivace*, Wagner wrote *Schnell*, and some American composers in this century wrote *Lively* or *Fast*, to cite a few examples.

THE RUSSIAN FIVE

Until well into the nineteenth century, Russia had little musical tradition of its own. The czars imported French and Italian opera as well as French ballet. Michael Glinka (1804–1857) was the first Russian composer to write an opera on a Russian theme. Today he is generally considered to be the father of Russian music.

More important was a group of five Russian composers, known as the Russian Five, who lived in the latter half of the Romantic period. The leader of the informal group was Mily Balakirev ("Bal-*lah*-kee-ref," 1837–1910). He himself was not a talented composer. Instead, he had a different but important role: to persuade other Russian composers that they didn't need to imitate the German style in order to compose good concert music. He urged them to draw on the musical resources in traditional Russian music. Four composers, especially, listened to Balakirev's advice: Modest Mussorgsky, César Cui (1835–1918),

Aleksandr Borodin ("*Bor-o-deen*," 1833–1887), and Nikolay Rimsky-Korsakov (1844–1908).

Most of the Russian Five had little formal training in music. Balakirev was self-taught. Cui, an engineer, was not a particularly successful composer.

Borodin was a celebrated chemist and an excellent composer. Had he been able to devote more time to composing, his name would be far better known in the music world than it is today. His Second Symphony is performed often, as are *In the Steppes of Central Asia* and String Quartet No. 2. His greatest work was an opera, *Prince Igor*, which was completed after his death by Rimsky-Korsakov and Alexander Glazounov (1865–1936).

Rimsky-Korsakov represents a phase of Romanticism called **Exoticism.** Like many other Romantic composers, he felt drawn by the mystery and splendor of Eastern cultures. For example, his best-known work is *Scheherazade*, a tone poem based on the Persian legends in *A Thousand and One Nights*. His "Song of India" from the opera *Sadko* and "Hymn to the Sun" from *Le Coq d'Or* (*The Golden Cockerel*) are other works that reveal his keen interest in Asia. Rimsky-Korsakov also wrote nationalistic music and worked avidly to advance the cause of Russian music.

Steppes **are the treeless tracts of land in southeastern Europe and Asia.**

For a while Rimsky-Korsakov was a sailor in the Russian navy, during which time he visited many foreign countries.

MUSSORGSKY'S *BORIS GODUNOV*

Of the Russian Five, the most original was Mussorgsky. He was also perhaps the least skilled technically of the five, but he is the one whose music best represents Russian character and culture. His most significant work, his opera *Boris Godunov*, is derived from a play by the great Russian writer Aleksandr Pushkin. It does not follow a sequential plot, as do most operas. Pushkin's play contained twenty-four scenes. Mussorgsky adapted the libretto himself, using only seven scenes and changing them extensively.

The story is about Czar Boris, who ruled from 1598 to 1605. The plot assumes that Boris had the young Prince Dimitri murdered in order to gain the throne, and the murder is presumed to have taken place before the opera begins. Boris's feelings of guilt are central to the plot, and they finally lead to his death. There is a scheming Polish princess, who with an ambitious pretender to the throne seeks to capture the Kremlin, the huge Moscow fortress from which the czars ruled.

The scene of Boris's death is one of the most moving in opera. The original final scene has a simpleton beggar alone on the stage, having been tricked out of his most valued coin by a gang of ruffians. He seems to symbolize that the real losers are the Russian people, who suffer from the greed and ambition of those who want to be czar.

Later research has indicated that Boris was innocent of the crime.

A SCENE FROM BORIS GODUNOV

LISTENING GUIDE

Modest Mussorgsky

Coronation scene from *Boris Godunov* (1870–1872)

Genre: Opera   Bass singer, chorus, and orchestra

CD 5 Tracks 10–13
9 minutes 17 seconds

Form: *A B A*

0:00	🔟	0:00	Gong and tuba sound two long, low notes; brasses play long chords.
		0:16	Woodwinds and strings play pizzicato a steady series of notes.
		0:50	After a silence, gong and brasses repeat opening music.
		1:00	Woodwinds and strings repeat steady series of notes.
		1:36	Trumpets herald Prince Shuisky, who sings:

> *Long live and reign, Czar Boris Feodorovich!*

Chorus   *Long live our great and noble Czar!*

Shuisky   *Praise him!*

1:56	1️⃣1️⃣	0:00	Chorus sings melody based on Russian folk song.

> *As the sun lights all heavens*
> *So reigns our great and noble Czar Boris!*
> *Hail to Boris, lord of Russia,*
> *Hail to our sovereign Boris!*
> *Long live our Czar!*
> *Czar, our father, hail.*
> *We hail thee, our father,*
> *Our gracious Czar, thou our gracious Czar!*
> *Great and glorious will thy reign be,*
> *Father of Russia!*

0:54	Music changes often between two- and three-beat meter to fit text.

> *Sing, rejoice ye, people!*
> *Sing, rejoice ye, Russian people!*
> *Sing, rejoice ye, faithful people!*
> *Sing, rejoice ye, people!*
> *Come, exalt our Czar!*

1:16	Trumpet heralds the words of the Boyars.

Boyars   *Hail to thee Czar Boris Feodorovich!*
          Long life to thee!
          As the sun lights all heaven,
          So reigns our great Czar, glory!

1:28	Pattern of steady notes from opening of scene is played as chorus continues, with some phrases in imitation.

> *Czar, our father beloved!*
> *Long life to thee!*

2:08	Russian folk song melody returns.

> *As the sun lights all heaven,*
> *So reigns our great Czar, glory!*
> *Sing the glory of the Czar of Russia, glory!*
> *Glory! Glory!*

4:43	1️⃣2️⃣	0:00	Music becomes quiet as horns hold a long note. Boris sings of his torment:

> *My soul is sad!*
> *Against my will strange tremors and evil premonitions oppress my spirit.*
> *O saint long dead,*

O thou my royal father!
Thou see'st in heaven the faithful servant's tears!
Look down on me and send a blessing from on high upon my kingdom!
May I be true and merciful, as thou,
And justify my people's praise.

1:58 Boris decides to proceed with his coronation.

Now let us go and kneel in prayer before the tombs of Russia's kings.
And then the people all shall feast.
Come, ev'ryone from nobleman to serf;
All shall find room, all find an honored welcome!

2:36 After a flurry of sound played by orchestra, sopranos sing.

Long live and reign our great and noble Czar!

7:29 **13** **0:00** Church bells ring freely.

0:07 Opening music returns. Sections of chorus sing "Thou our gracious Czar!" in imitation.

Long life to thee, Czar Boris Feodorovich!
Hail to thee!
As the sun lights all heaven,
So reigns our great Czar of Russia,
Glory and long may he reign!

1:00 Chorus vigorously sings in three-beat meter as low brasses play in two-beat meter.

Glory! Glory! Glory!

1:46 "Coronation Scene" concludes after chorus sings a final "Glory" and two closing chords played by orchestra.

The music reveals Mussorgsky's innate musicianship and his flair for the dramatic. The prologue features the Russian people. Afraid for their future after the death of the czar, they pray for a ruler for their land. To encourage a public clamor for himself, Boris sends one of his lieutenants (Prince Shuisky) to tell the crowd that he still refuses to become czar. A chorus of religious pilgrims approaches and sings before the curtain falls.

The coronation scene, which follows the prologue, is one of the best-known scenes in the operatic repertoire. It takes place in a courtyard in the Kremlin; the Cathedrals of the Assumption, Annunciation, and the Archangel flank the stage.

In several ways Mussorgsky was ahead of his time, musically speaking. Twice in the coronation scene a scale containing only whole steps is implied. The scale (called the **whole-tone scale**) would be used quite often twenty-five years later in the music of Impressionistic composers. In addition, there are places in the coronation scene in which two-beat against three-beat meter is implied. Again such combination of meters (called **polymeters**) would become much more common in the twentieth century. At several places in the orchestral portions of the coronation scene, Mussorgsky has adjacent chords harmonically as far apart as possible. For example, a C major chord is followed by one built on F-sharp. Again, this portends the breaking away from tonal harmony by twentieth-century composers.

The coronation scene from *Boris Godunov* has several notable features:

- The music has a virile, masculine quality. It exudes the rugged, hardy character that one associates with the peasantry of Russia at the beginning of the seventeenth century. Mussorgsky's admiration for the vigor of the Russian people has found its way into his music.

- The words, music, and drama fit together very effectively. Boris's solo is expressive and flexible. It suggests an aria and recitative in which the union of words and music fits perfectly. His prayer sounds somewhat like a chant, which is appropriate because chant is a feature of Russian Orthodox worship.

A generation later Debussy, who first heard Mussorgsky's music while in Russia, used whole-tone scales in his music.

Archivo Iconografico, S.A. /Corbis

Modest Mussorgsky

Best-Known Works

opera:
- *Boris Godunov*
- *Khovanschina*

orchestra:
- *A Night on Bald Mountain*

piano:
- *Pictures at an Exhibition*

During his lifetime **Modest Mussorgsky** (1839–1881) was considered the least accomplished and important of the Russian Five. Today, because of his innovative style and the rugged Russian quality of his music, he is considered the greatest of the five.

He was born into a prosperous landowning family. He showed much talent at the piano at an early age, but he refused to practice and did not seem headed toward a musical career. Instead, he entered a military academy. Soon he began drinking heavily, but his skill at the piano and good singing voice made him popular at parties. While still in the military, he met Borodin and Balakirev. They sparked his interest in composing, and he soon left the army.

Mussorgsky's musical genius was not recognized at the time, partly because of his own personality. First, there was the heavy drinking and occasional bizarre behavior in public. His drinking led to delirium tremens and his death at the age of forty-two. Second, he was undisciplined about his work and rarely finished anything he started. Much of his music was finished and revised by Rimsky-Korsakov, and the twentieth-century Russian composer Dmitri Shostakovich (1906–1975) revised his opera *Boris Godunov*.

- The resonant sound of Boris's bass voice gives the impression of a mighty man, the leader of all Russia, a man who can bend steel with his bare hands.
- The scene is filled with color, both visually and musically. A coronation is an impressive event to see.

A listener's score for the coronation scene from Mussorgsky's *Boris Godunov* is available for downloading.

Mussorgsky's innovations and fresh, nationalistic approach were almost too much for the audience in 1872; even his friends and admirers had trouble understanding *Boris Godunov*. It was rejected twice for performance by the Imperial Opera. Only after two revisions and a performance of three of its scenes at a benefit concert was all of *Boris Godunov* performed.

BOHEMIA

There is no country of Bohemia today, although at one time it was a distinct area of central Europe with its own language and cultural identity. Today most of it lies in the Czech Republic. This rather small area produced two important composers who promoted its music: Antonín Dvořák and Bedřich Smetana. Throughout most of the nineteenth century, Bohemia was part of the Austrian empire, so the style of Dvořák and Smetana does not differ all that much from the prevailing Romantic style of the time. But its nationalism is expressed in the use of folk melodies and native subject matter.

SMETANA'S *MOLDAU*

The Moldau is the best known of Smetana's series of tone poems called *Má vlast*. The program that Smetana placed in the score reads:

> *Two springs pour forth in the shade of the Bohemian forest, one warm and gushing, the other cold and peaceful. Coursing through Bohemia's valleys, it grows into a mighty stream.*

Through thick woods it flows as the gay sounds of the hunt and the notes of the hunter's horn are heard ever closer. It flows through grass-grown pastures and lowlands where a wedding feast is being celebrated with song and dance. At night, wood and water nymphs revel in its sparkling waves. Reflected on its surface are fortresses and castles—witnesses of bygone days of knightly splendor and the vanished glory of martial times.

The stream races through the St. John's Rapids, "finally flowing on in majestic peace toward Prague and welcomed by historic Vysehrad," the legendary castle of ancient Bohemian kings. "Then it vanishes far beyond the poet's gaze."

BEDŘICH SMETANA
The Moldau from *Má vlast* (1874)

GENRE: **Tone poem**   Orchestra

CD 5 Tracks 14–18
12 minutes 43 seconds

0:00 **14** 0:00 *Source of river, two springs:* Rippling sounds in flutes, then clarinets.

1:07 **15** 0:00 *River theme:* Strings play flowing melody.

1:53 *The hunt:* Brasses play fanfare figures.

4:06 **16** 0:00 *Wedding dance:* Strings and woodwinds play happy dance music.

6:00 **17** 0:00 *Nightfall and water nymphs in moonlight:* Slow, high notes in violins with rippling sounds in flutes.

2:39 *River theme:* Violins

3:30 *St. John's Rapids:* Brasses and timpani play turbulent music.

4:45 *River theme:* Orchestra plays theme faster and louder.

11:44 **18** 0:00 *Historic castles:* Brasses play choralelike melody.

0:19 *River fades away:* Long decrescendo depicts river fading into distance far beyond poet's gaze.

1:32 *The Moldau* concludes with two forceful chords.

© Scheufler Collection /Corbis

Bedřich Smetana

Bedřich Smetana (1824–1884) was born in a small town in Bohemia, the seventh child of a music-loving brewer. Family activities included playing string quartets at home. Smetana studied for a while in Prague, served as music master for a rich family, and later became pianist for Kaiser Ferdinand, who had abdicated the German throne and was living in Prague. After about ten years, Smetana moved to Gothenburg, Sweden. He earned a good living there, but the climate was bad for his wife's failing health, so he moved back to Prague several years later.

Like Beethoven, Smetana became deaf toward the end of his life. Some of his best compositions were written when he was deaf.

Smetana once said that he simply could not write absolute music. Perhaps his feelings of nationalism were too strong to allow him to think of music in absolute terms.

BEST-KNOWN WORKS

opera:
• *The Bartered Bride*

orchestra:
• *Má vlast (My Fatherland),* which includes *The Moldau*

OTHER NATIONALISTIC COMPOSERS

Norway

Edvard Grieg (1843–1907) was the leading proponent of Scandinavian music. Among his well-known works are the *Peer Gynt Suites,* which were originally composed as incidental music for Henrik Ibsen's play. He also wrote a melodious piano concerto, as well as many shorter piano pieces and chamber works.

Finland

Jean Sibelius ("Yon Si-*bay*-lee-us," 1865–1957) was Finland's most famous composer. Most of his more nationalistic music was composed early in his career. One of the themes from his tone poem *Finlandia* became the national anthem of Finland. He also used native themes as the basis for program works such as *The Swan of Tuonela* and *Pohjola's Daughter.* The themes in many of his symphonies often have a folklike quality, even if they are not actually folk melodies.

England

The music of Edward Elgar (1857–1934) strikes a consonant note in the hearts of English audiences. Although his music is not very different from that of other Romantic composers, nor is it particularly nationalistic, it possesses a distinctively English quality. Elgar is the composer of *Pomp and Circumstance,* the stately march that is played at so many graduations. His best-known work is *Enigma Variations* for orchestra. Elgar wrote on the score the initials of the friend or family member who is associated with each particular variation. Guessing that person's identity becomes the puzzle or enigma. Fortunately, listeners today can enjoy the beauty of the music without the need to figure out who is being represented.

Several English composers in the early part of the twentieth century are also nationalistic. The most important of these is Ralph Vaughan Williams (1872–1958). He helped

His family name is *Vaughan Williams,* not just *Williams.*

revive interest in English folk music and also contributed to the improvement in the music of the Church of England. He selected texts for his many vocal works from England's finest poets and used themes from earlier English composers in such works as Fantasia on a Theme by Tallis. Other important works of Vaughan Williams include Symphony No. 2 ("The London Symphony") and Fantasia on "Greensleeves."

Italy

Italian nationalism in the nineteenth century was largely confined to opera. Nationalism in instrumental works did not become evident until the twentieth century in the music of Ottorino Respighi ("Res-*pee*-gee," 1879–1936). His *Pines of Rome* and *Fountains of Rome* are definitely nationalistic. His style is strongly Romantic, even if the composition dates from the twentieth century.

Verdi's role in Italian nationalism is discussed in Chapter 26.

Spain

Spanish nationalism is found in the music of Isaac Albeniz (1860–1909), Enrique Granados (1867–1916), and Manuel de Falla ("*Fi*-ya," 1876–1946). Each of these composers exploited the rhythms of Spanish dance and the colorful sounds of its music. Although their careers extended into the twentieth century, their music is essentially Romantic in character.

France

As the Romantic era progressed, French composers began to develop a style that was different from the prevailing German style. A truly distinct French style did not appear, however, until the Impressionistic music of Debussy and Ravel, which is presented in Chapter 29.

United States

Nationalistic music was slow to develop in the United States. In fact, very little existed prior to 1900. The nationalistic music that developed in the twentieth century is discussed in Chapter 36.

CODA

Mussorgsky, Smetana, and a host of other nationalistic composers mined the musical riches of their native lands. In doing so, they added much to the world's treasure of music.

29 Impressionism *and* Post-Romanticism

Over the years all artistic movements, even highly successful ones like Romanticism, spend themselves out. A point is reached where they can be carried no further. Eventually, something has to change.

Post-Romanticism and Impressionism represent two types of change from the German/Austrian style that dominated the nineteenth century. Post-Romanticism was an attempt to pump life into Romanticism by doing more—making the works longer and for larger groups. In contrast, Impressionism focused on the subtle, delicate, and fleeting inner impressions of an outer world. It represented a more substantial change in outlook toward works of art and music.

CHARACTERISTICS OF IMPRESSIONISM

Impressionism probably owes its name to painter Claude Monet, who in 1874 exhibited a picture called *Impression–Sunrise*. Critics took up the term to make fun of the new movement.

Impressionism was an artistic viewpoint in which poets, painters, and composers tried to capture something incomplete, of the moment, a sensation. It is based on the belief that experiences in life are largely impressions rather than detailed observations. To achieve this, Impressionists stressed informality and rarely carried a moral or message. They were also fond of nature and commonplace scenes—sunsets, people in casual poses, water lilies in a pond, and the like.

Several Impressionistic painters, for example, tried to catch the atmosphere of a particular time and place by making rough sketches at two or three different times during the day, because the impression of a scene changed with different lighting. The painting would often be finished in the studio. They also avoided hard outlines and used subtle blending of primary colors.

A picture that you see on a website is made up of thousands of tiny dots called *pixels*.

Some painters used a technique called *pointillism* in which dots of paint are placed close together. Seen up close, the picture looks like a newspaper photo when viewed through a magnifying glass; when viewed from a short distance, however, the dots appear to blend.

In his painting of the Rouen Cathedral, Monet (see next page) was not really trying to represent the cathedral. He did not try to show the entire front of the building or to represent the detail of its stonework. Rather, in a manner characteristic of Impressionistic painters, he used its lines and shapes as objects for the interplay of light, shadow, and color. From his vantage point in a window opposite the church, Monet painted at least thirty identical versions of this scene at different times of day and under varying weather conditions.

Impressionistic poetry and drama were highly symbolic. The writers tried to capture fleeting moments by presenting a sequence of images in words. They intentionally kept their poems in an inconclusive and fragmented condition, which left the meaning up to the reader. Impressionistic writer Maurice Maeterlinck wrote in one of his essays, "Beneath all human thoughts . . . there lies the vast ocean of the Unconscious. All that we know, think, feel, see, and will are but bubbles on the surface of this vast sea."

In one sense, Impressionism represented French nationalism, although it was more of a cultural nationalism than the usual political type. Many works by Impressionistic composers are programmatic. What makes Impressionistic music different from most other program music written in the nineteenth century is that the nonmusical associations are with impressions, not stories or characters.

The Impressionistic movement was unique in the extent to which writers, artists, and musicians knew one another and often worked together. And they held similar points of

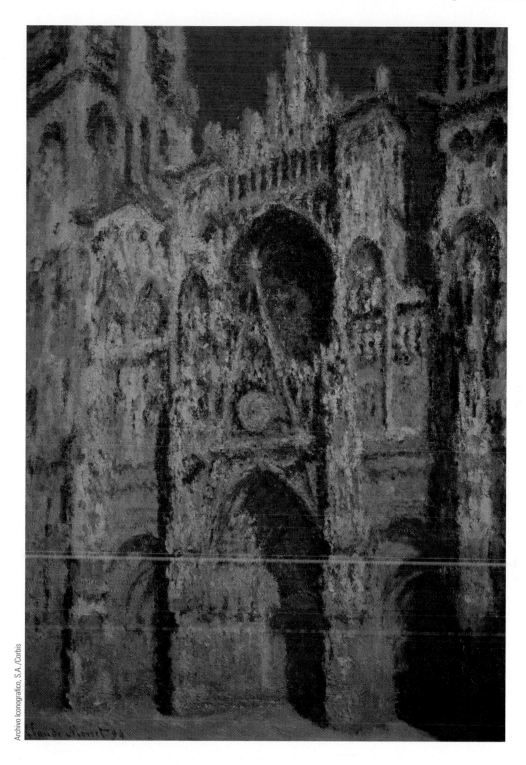

Archivo Iconografico, S.A./Corbis

MONET'S IMPRESSIONIST
PAINTING of Rouen
Cathedral

view about the arts. The painter wanted to capture a fleeting moment on canvas, the author in the printed and spoken word, and the composer in the transitory world of musical sounds. These artists shared a fondness for subtle nuances of light and shadow, vague
contours, and veiled thoughts.

What to Listen For in Impressionistic Music

- A generally lighter timbre and tone than heard in the music of Brahms and Wagner.
  The size of the orchestra is somewhat smaller. The harp and flute are more prominent,
  and less use is made of brass instruments.

- Subtle tonal colors, including chords with notes added simply because the composer wanted that particular sonority. The C E G chord sometimes is a C E G A chord.

- Harmonies with a less functional role in favor of a more tonally colorful role. Sometimes chords move in parallel motion, something that was not allowed in traditional tonal harmony.

- More subtle and blurred rhythm. The metrical pattern is not easily felt.

- A weaker tonal center, especially when a whole-tone scale is used.

- Limited use of the forms developed in the Classical period and little development of themes. Many works are rather short and programmatic.

- Sensual, somewhat subtle music that does not attempt to project any messages. Rather, expect sensitive, subtle musical works that are simply to be enjoyed.

Impressionism partly bridged the change from the Romantic style of the nineteenth century to the music of the twentieth century. It represented a significant break from the predominant Germanic style through its use of added notes in chords, parallel chord movement, and subtle rhythms. But it did not leave all its Romantic tendencies behind. Rather, it exemplified the French love of nuance and color and, in so doing, pointed the way toward the future.

All steps in a whole-tone scale are equidistant, so it has no single tonal center.

Debussy considered the development of themes to be "musical mathematics."

DEBUSSY'S "CLAIR DE LUNE"

"Clair de lune" ("Moonlight") is one of Debussy's best-known compositions. It is part of his *Suite bergamasque* for piano but is usually heard today as a separate piece. It has also been transcribed for orchestra.

LISTENING GUIDE

CLAUDE DEBUSSY

"Clair de lune" (1890; rev. 1905)

GENRE: Character piece   Piano

CD 2 Tracks 23–25
5 minutes 1 second

Form: *A B A*

0:00   **23**   0:00   Opening section (A) begins softly with a gradually descending melody.

Andante, very expressively

pp

0:35   A melody repeated.

1:25   Music becomes somewhat louder and more animated.

2:02   **24**   0:00   Contrasting section (B) begins softly.

pp

0:23   B melody repeated an octave higher as music grows more intense.

0:42   B melody repeated quietly.

3:13   **25**   0:00   Opening melody (A) returns very softly.

0:37   Phrases of A melody repeated several times.

1:14   Music gradually fades as chords are played in harplike manner.

1:49   "Clair de lune" concludes very quietly.

The opening melody has several places in which the last note of one measure is tied to the first note of the next measure. (In music a **tie** is a curved line connecting two notes of the same pitch so that they sound as one long note.) The effect is to blur the meter of the music at those points. At other points he calls for two equal notes to the beat when the rest of the work uses three. At another place he even specifies *tempo rubato*, indicating rhythmic flexibility.

The skeleton of the melody—its basic notes—is quite simple. It is a descending major scale, to which Debussy merely adds a few alternating notes, almost as decoration. It certainly is not the solid kind of melody that Bach and Beethoven favored! Debussy adds other effects, such as rolling out the notes of some of the chords in a harplike manner instead of having them sounded together, which also tends to obscure the rhythm. At other places he doubles notes of the melody an octave higher, which gives the music a more open, almost haunting effect.

The overall effect is luscious and romantic.

RAVEL'S *DAPHNIS AND CHLOÉ*, SUITE NO. 2

About 1910 Maurice Ravel composed a ballet for the famous impresario of Ballet Russe, Sergei Diaghilev, about whom more will be said in Chapter 32. The story concerns a shepherd, Daphnis, and his love for the beautiful Chloé. Today the ballet's music is most often heard in the form of two suites. Suite No. 2 contains some of Ravel's most Impressionistic music, especially the opening section called "Lever du jour" ("Daybreak"). The

---

MAURICE RAVEL

Daphnis and Chloé, Suite No. 2,
"Lever du jour" ("Daybreak") (1910)

GENRE: Ballet music   Orchestra

CD 5 Tracks 19–21
5 minutes 39 seconds

0:00	**19** 0:00	Woodwinds and harps play rippling figures over slow notes in low strings.
	0:29	More instruments join in as music begins long crescendo.
	0:56	Music reaches climactic point, then begins gradual decrescendo.
1:15	**20** 0:00	Violas and clarinet play rich-sounding melody.

	0:25	Flute plays brief contrasting figure; then melody resumes in strings.
	0:45	Clarinet plays brief contrasting figure; then melody resumes.
	1:11	Violins continue melody at higher pitch level; harp and woodwinds take up rippling figures, and chorus enters.
	1:36	Chorus continues singing "Ah" as violins continue melody.
	1:55	Music reaches another climactic point and then begins to grow softer.
	2:06	The tempo becomes faster and more dancelike and soon reaches another climactic point.
4:03	**21** 0:00	Melody begins in lower strings as rippling figures return.
	0:33	Climactic point by orchestra and chorus; then music grows softer.
	1:04	Oboe quietly repeats the same melodic figure several times.
	1:28	Clarinet plays some of the figure in augmentation.
	1:36	The "Daybreak" part of Suite No. 2 concludes quietly.

LISTENING GUIDE

Debussy, Ravel, & Rachmaninoff

CLAUDE DEBUSSY

Claude Debussy ("Deb-yew-*see*," 1862–1918) was born in a small town near Paris. At the age of eleven he entered the Paris Conservatory, where he often revolted again the rules of composition his professors tried to teach him. When he was twenty-two, he won the Prix de Rome, which included study in Italy. Although he did go to Rome, he much preferred the bustle and gaiety of Paris. He also valued the company of painters and writers.

Debussy's early admiration for Wagner faded after a second visit to Bayreuth in 1889, and he developed a dislike for things Germanic. He wrote a number of articles about music, which offered him a chance to vent his feelings. Regarding Wagner, he wrote, "The French forget too easily the qualities of clarity and elegance peculiar to themselves and allow themselves to be influenced by the tedious and ponderous Teuton." He claimed that "beauty must appeal to the senses, must provide us with immediate enjoyment."

The fact that **Maurice Ravel** (1875–1937) followed Debussy both chronologically and stylistically has tended to place him in the background despite his many fine compositions. He was born into the family of a mining engineer who had once aspired to be a musician himself. Ravel studied at the Paris Conservatory and, though highly qualified for the award, was four times passed over for the Prix de Rome. The arbitrary nature of these decisions caused a public furor that

eventually led to the resignation of the Conservatory's director.

A French patriot, Ravel drove an ambulance along the front lines during World War I. After the war he was recognized as France's greatest composer. He died at the age of sixty while undergoing surgery for a rare brain disease that had seriously affected his speech and motor coordination.

One of his best-known works, and certainly the most unusual, is the hypnotic *Bolero,* in which the same melody and rhythm pattern continue throughout the seventeen minutes of the work.

MAURICE RAVEL

Sergei Rachmaninoff (1873–1943) was born in northwestern Russia. His parents were both amateur pianists, and his mother was his first teacher. Later he studied at the conservatory in St. Petersburg and then Moscow. In his younger days he revealed much talent, but he tended to be lazy and spent too much time skating.

He was equally gifted as a composer and pianist, both of which he emphasized at various times in his life. He first toured the United States in 1909, which led to a contract with Edison Records and then RCA Victor. He emigrated to America after the Communist revolution in 1917, but remained homesick for his native land, and felt a loss of inspiration after that time. Nevertheless, he completed his *Rhapsody on a Theme of Paganini* and Symphony No. 3 while in America. He become ill on a concert tour in 1943, and was diagnosed with lung cancer. He died shortly thereafter.

SERGEI RACHMANINOFF

BEST-KNOWN WORKS OF DEBUSSY

opera:
- *Pelléas et Mélisande*

orchestra:
- *La Mer*
- *Nocturnes*
- *Prelude to the Afternoon of a Faun*

piano:
- *Images,* Sets 1 and 2
- *Suite bergamasque*

BEST-KNOWN WORKS OF RAVEL

orchestra:
- *Bolero*
- *Daphnis et Chloé,* Suite No. 2
- *Ma Mère l'Oye* (Mother Goose)

piano:
- *Gaspard de la nuit*
- *Le tombeau de Couperin*

BEST-KNOWN WORKS OF RACHMANINOFF

piano:
- *Preludes*
- *Concertos Nos. 2 and 3*

orchestra:
- *Symphonies Nos. 2 and 3*
- *Vocalise for Soprano*
- *Isle of the Dead*

woodwinds and then the strings provide a rich accompaniment of rippling notes. One can almost sense the glow of the sunrise in the melody. The recording includes a part for chorus in which the singers vocalize on a neutral syllable.

POST-ROMANTICISM

The Romantic outlook did not go quietly into the night. In fact, elements of it are still found in music being written today—and probably always will be. Some composers who lived near the end of the nineteenth century and into the twentieth continued the Romantic tradition by composing works that were more massive and extensive than those of their predecessors.

RACHMANINOFF'S *RHAPSODY ON A THEME OF PAGANINI*

Rhapsody on a Theme of Paganini is one of the best loved of Sergei Rachmaninoff's compositions. It is based on a theme written by the legendary nineteenth-century violin virtuoso Niccolò Paganini. The work opens with a short introduction and one variation before the theme is presented by the violins. It is essentially a simple melody: The same melodic and rhythm pattern is heard on the tonic or home chord, then the dominant chord, then a return to the tonic, and two concluding notes on the dominant. That portion of the theme is repeated before the second half of the theme appears. This half maintains nearly the same melodic pattern and the same rhythmic ideas presented in sequence.

At first the variations are modest in scope. The piano plays decorative versions of the theme that little by little move farther from it. Variation 7 combines the theme played by the low strings and the Dies irae theme played slowly by the piano. Variation 10 again opens with the Dies irae played by the piano, which is then taken up by the orchestra.

The following Listening Guide and music on the ancillary CD begin with Variation 18 and go to the conclusion of the work.

For a number of reasons, this work represents post-Romanticism well. First, it was composed in 1934, well after the Romantic style had been predominant. Second, the theme is by Paganini, who in some ways was the quintessential Romantic musician. Third, the work includes a quotation of the Dies irae theme, which is associated with death and mystery—favorite topics of Romanticists. Fourth, it is basically a rhapsody containing a free expression of feelings, even though it is in the form of a theme and variations.

Gustav Mahler and Anton Bruckner (1824–1896), an earlier Romantic composer, both exhibit one of the traits of Romanticism: a tendency toward musical elephantiasis.

PART VI

Twentieth- Century Music

	1900		1925
Historical Events	First airplane ●	Russian Revolution ●	Great Depression
		World War I	
		● Panama Canal finished	
Visual Arts	▶ Munch, *The Scream* (right)	Mondrian's Cubism	
	Kandinsky's work		
		Picasso, *Three Musicians* ●	
		Rivera's work	
			Braque's work
		Lipchitz's work	
Literature and Theater		Kafka's work	
		Joyce's work	
Philosophy and Science	Freud, key works		
	B. Russell's work		
		Einstein's theories	
Music	Mahler		Rodrigo's work
		Berg's work	
	Sibelius's work		Britten's work
	Stravinsky, *Rite of Spring* (top) ▲		
	Rachmaninoff		
		Webern's work	
	Schoenberg's work		
		Prokofiev's work	
	Bartok's work		
		Villa-Lobos's work	
		Shostakovich's work	
		Varèse's work	
		Hindemith's work	

1950	1975	2000

● India becomes nation

World War II   ● United Nations founded   ● Man lands on moon   ● Gulf War
● Soviet Union dissolves
● Korean War   Vietnam War   War in Iraq ●

Chagall, *Snowing*   Op art

Pop art

H. Moore's work

● Orwell, *1984*   J. K. Rowling, *Harry Potter*

Solzhenitsyn's work

Sartre's work   ● Computers and Internet

Atomic energy ●   Organ transplants   ● First animal cloned

Camus's work

Penderecki's work

Crumb's work

Cage's work (right) ▶

30 Music *in the* Twentieth Century

Twentieth-century music may at times be confusing and difficult to understand, but dull it is not. It's as fascinating and challenging as twentieth-century life was.

THE TREMENDOUS AND TUMULTUOUS CENTURY

The twentieth century was not for the faint of heart, either socially or artistically. It witnessed two world wars and numerous lesser conflicts, a great economic depression and general prosperity, and thousands of discoveries and inventions ranging from organ transplants to computers to exploration in space.

Most of these changes had both benefits and liabilities. For example, as the peoples of the world seemed to be drawing closer together, at the same time they seemed to be becoming more aware of their differences, and in many regions various groups of people worked to assert their particular identities.

Nor did the marvels of technological progress make people any happier. Information is passed along in milliseconds to almost any place in the world, but the quality of what is said often is no better than what hundreds of years ago was written with a quill pen and delivered by hand. Astronauts traveled into space, but they returned to Earth and its many problems.

As was pointed out in Chapter 1, there is a big difference between just hearing music and really listening to it.

As the twenty-first century begins, the pervasive influence of technology grows stronger in many areas of life. It has had a major impact on the amount and type of music people hear, as well as how they think about music. It has also played a very important role in the production and reproduction of music. But, again, it has had both positive and negative results. People today hear much more music than ever before, but they seem to listen to it less and less carefully.

Diverse and complex factors also existed in twentieth-century concert music. It seems to be divided into numerous camps. Some of these subgroups are designated by words that end with *ism*, such as Neoclassicism, Serialism, Primitivism, Expressionism, and Minimalism. Other types are folkloric, experimental, avant garde, and what is considered mainstream. Each of these types represents a view about music and played a role in the development of twentieth-century music.

If twentieth-century music is marked by diversity, dramatic change, and expansion, those same qualities mean that it is also musically very rich. For instance, some twentieth-century music:

- Expanded musical elements in earlier music
- Was influenced by new sources of music, such as Africa and Asia
- Was the result of sophisticated intellectual efforts
- Was a revival of musical practices that were in fashion several centuries earlier
- Was a repudiation of nineteenth-century music
- Probed new and largely untested ways of creating musical works

TWENTIETH-CENTURY ART

For much of history, artists played the role that cameras do today. That is, they tried to create an accurate rendition of a person or a scene. But with the invention of photography in the nineteenth century, and especially with its widespread use in the twentieth, the goal of artists changed. Instead of producing images of what was seen, artists became more interested in interpreting what they saw and creating visual objects that are of interest solely for their visual properties. Their use of shape and color became somewhat like composers' use of sounds in music. This change led to a wide variety of types of artworks.

As the twentieth century saw the return to certain techniques used in musical compositions written in earlier centuries, painters also revisited techniques of artists centuries earlier. Pablo Picasso's *Three Musicians* is a type of Cubism called "collage Cubism," in which the impression is given that the portions of the painting are pasted up like pieces of paper (which is what the word *collage* means in French). The separate pieces are fitted together firmly as little architectural blocks. More than pattern concerned Picasso in *Three Musicians*, however. He tried to project the image of musicians as traditional figures of the comedy stage. Their humanness is sensed behind the screen of costumes and masks.

In spite of its title, Piet Mondrian's *Broadway Boogie Woogie* is not an attempt to represent Manhattan. Mondrian developed a completely nonrepresentational, abstract style. He restricted himself to horizontals and verticals and a few simple colors with no shading. In this way it would be virtually impossible to paint a picture of something. In spite of these limitations, Mondrian succeeded in creating a lively, attractive painting. At first glance it may look easy to imitate Mondrian's style successfully, but the limitations actually make it very difficult.

An important current in twentieth-century painting was fantasy. Many painters became interested in "the inner eye"—the introspective look at imagination and feeling. Such a view seems to be the artistic counterpart to Freudian psychology and its interest in dreams and the subconscious. Marc Chagall appeared never to lose the memories and dreams of his childhood in a Jewish commu-

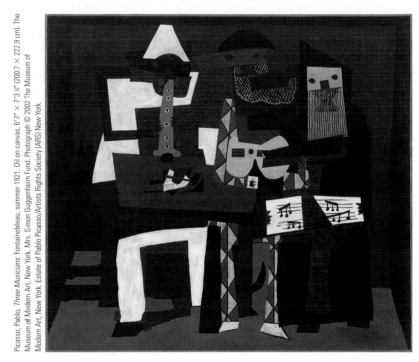

THREE MUSICIANS by Pablo Picasso, 1921. The twentieth century no longer saw the grandiose works of art and music that marked the Romantic period. Instead, smaller and more playful works such as those of Picasso in art and Stravinsky in his Neoclassical compositions replaced them.

BROADWAY BOOGIE WOOGIE by Piet Mondrian. In a simple painting, Mondrian captures the playfulness of jazz and its particular style for piano called "boogie woogie."

nity in Russia. His painting *Snowing* depicts some of that personal mystery and fantasy. Does it contain shades of the highly successful Broadway musical *Fiddler on the Roof?*

DESCRIBING TWENTIETH-CENTURY MUSIC

There is an old saying about "not being able to see the forest for the trees."

With the Baroque, Classical, and Romantic periods, it is possible to describe their main intellectual and artistic features. That is a much more difficult task with twentieth-century music. Perhaps part of the problem is the lack of perspective; we are simply too close to it.

Part of the reason for the lack of cohesion in twentieth-century music is probably due to the diversity and fragmentation in twentieth-century society itself. Core values and beliefs that prevailed in the Classical and Romantic eras no longer seemed to be in effect.

Stravinsky's *Rite of Spring* is presented in Chapter 32.

Equally important is the fact that there is so much music to consider. No longer can an understanding of music be confined to concert music of Europe and America. Music from every part of the globe became available, as well as all types of folk and popular music. Also, more universities and conservatories offered instruction in composition, so more people wrote and made music than ever before. What's more, ever since the Romantic period, composers consciously tried to avoid writing music that sounded too much like any other composer's style. Imitating someone else flew in the face of the idea of creativity as conceived over the past two centuries.

Another reason that it is hard to name one set of standard features for music in the twentieth century is its ever-changing character. For instance, Stravinsky's *Rite of Spring* was modern and novel when it premiered in 1913, but that certainly was not true for long. In fact, it was not even true for Stravinsky a decade later; he had moved on to another style. And Stravinsky was not alone among composers in changing styles.

Some labels are helpful in understanding twentieth-century music, just as period labels such as *Baroque* and *Romantic* are useful in learning about the music of earlier centuries. But such designations should be used with care when discussing twentieth-century music. Composers usually do not like being categorized. They consider their pieces unique works that should be evaluated on their own merits, which is only fair. Still, the use of classifications—the *isms,* for example—can aid in looking at and thinking about the concert music of the twentieth century.

SNOWING by Marc Chagall. Twentieth-century artworks, ranging from Berg's opera *Wozzeck* to plays by Tennessee Williams and this painting by Chagall, probed the world of fantasy and psychology.

The Saint Louis Art Museum. © 2002 Artists Rights Society (ARS), New York/ADAGP, Paris

WHAT TO LISTEN FOR IN TWENTIETH-CENTURY MUSIC

Rhythm

Rhythm is a much more important element in twentieth-century music than it was in previous centuries. Some (not all) of the music composed in the twentieth century broke away from the idea of regular metrical patterns. The "tyranny of the bar line" had long since gone. Composers felt free to mix meters, either by actually changing the signature or by displacing the accents. At one point in Stravinsky's *Rite of Spring,* the meter changes with each measure: 3/16, 5/16, 3/16, 4/16, 5/16, 3/16, and so on.

Measures traditionally contained two, three, or four regular beats. New asymmetrical patterns are found in some twentieth-century works. Measures with five or seven beats per measure are used, as well as measures in which the beat pattern is not regular, as in this 8/8 pattern:

♩. ♩. ♩ = 3 + 3 + 2

Furthermore, musicians felt free to have more than one rhythmic pattern sounding at the same time, what is termed *polyrhythm*.

Some composers consciously tried to return to rhythmic devices found in folk/ethnic music, such as rhythmic ostinatos — the persistent repetition of short rhythm patterns.

The increased attention given to rhythm had a corresponding increase in the importance of percussion instruments. More percussion instruments were used, and they were featured more prominently. In fact, some works were composed for percussion ensembles; others featured percussion instruments.

Polyrhythms are also presented in conjunction with African music in Chapter 42.

Melody

The concept of melody expanded far beyond potentially singable melodies in the traditional major and minor tonalities. Melodies were often no longer warm and flowing as in the preceding century. In fact, melody as such seemed less important in twentieth-century works. Melodies were often conceived nonvocally in their use of wide, awkward leaps and irregular phrases. Sometimes no actual melody can be found in a work. Yet some beautiful melodies exist in the music of the previous century.

Twentieth-century composers broke away from the balanced patterns of phrases found in Baroque and Classical music. No longer were four measures complemented by another four measures. The clearly defined structure of melodies was loosened considerably.

Harmony and Counterpoint

Romantic harmonies are rich and colorful, and chords were built around the traditional pattern of thirds. Twentieth-century composers frequently broke away from that pattern and wrote chords in fourths, fifths, and seconds. More often, however, they added notes to chords just because they wanted that particular sound at that particular place in the music.

Chord progressions in traditional harmony provide a syntax that helps organize the music. Twentieth-century composers did not completely abandon traditional tonal progressions, but they certainly were far less concerned about following them. In fact, not only were they much less interested in tonal centers but some composers also deliberately composed music with no tonal center whatsoever.

Some twentieth-century composers wrote music in two or more keys that sounded at the same time. The term for this technique is **polytonality.** For example, at one point in *Rite of Spring* Stravinsky has an F♭, A♭, C♭ chord in the lower pitches and an E♭, G♭, B♭, D♭ in the upper pitches, a sonority that includes all seven pitches of the C-flat major scale.

Some twentieth-century music was written not in the major/minor keys of the preceding three hundred years but in the modes that prevailed in the Renaissance and earlier periods. This was especially true of music that drew on folk sources.

As the attention given to harmony decreased in the twentieth century, the amount of counterpoint increased. At times the counterpoint sounds like it was written by a resurrected J. S. Bach. Other twentieth-century counterpoint is very different, because it is filled with dissonance.

Examples of chords:
Seconds—C D E F
Thirds—C E G
Fourths—C F B♭
Fifths—C G D

The principle of dissonance resolving to consonance that has prevailed for more than two hundred years is sometimes not followed in twentieth-century music.

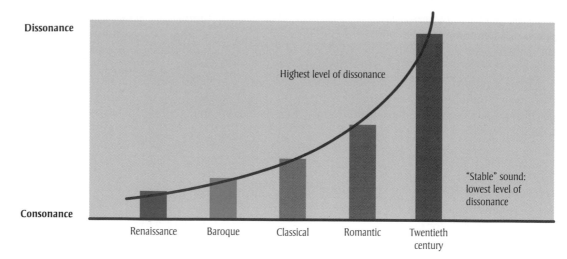

THE INCREASING USE OF DISSONANCE in music through history

Dissonance

The changes in harmony led to one of the things people notice first about twentieth-century music: dissonance. A few composers carried the idea of dissonance to its limit, for example, by asking the pianist to push an elbow down on the keyboard or by specifying a stick that is 14 ⅜ inches long and pushing it down on the keys. Often dissonance is used to add a certain color to the music, not to create or resolve tension, as it had been traditionally employed. In any case, the amount of dissonance in twentieth-century music is much greater than at any other time in history.

Timbre

A synthesizer can produce almost any sound. It is not limited to the standard timbres of instruments.

The technique is called **prepared piano.**

Twentieth-century composers opened up a new world in terms of timbre with the synthesized sounds and effects available through technology. Even without technology, composers freely milked every possible sound from conventional instruments and the human voice—shrieks, babbling, tongue-clucking, banging, squeaking, buzzing, and sounds made with parts of the instrument removed. Some works for piano call for placing thumbtacks, rubber bands, coins, and other objects on the strings to create different timbres.

The idea of timbre became the central element in some works that consist of organized series of tone colors rather than themes and melodies.

Form

Tone rows are presented in Chapter 33, and chance and electronic music in Chapter 34.

A few composers wrote works in sonata and other forms. But formal patterns seemed not to be very important to most twentieth-century composers. Some attempted other approaches to organizing their music, and several of these are described in the following chapters.

Sources

The advent of tape recordings made possible a knowledge of many kinds of music that had not been known before. Also, the field of ethnomusicology has researched many types of music.

Musicians in the twentieth century knew more about music from every historical age and part of the globe than their predecessors did. Ease of communication and improved scholarship into the world's treasure trove of music made this possible. Twentieth-century music is pancultural and panhistorical as no other music has been before. A number of twentieth-century composers drew heavily on elements of music from non-Western cultures, as well as from past times.

CODA

Because of its diversity and richness, twentieth-century music offers something for just about every musical taste. And because of its wide diversity, probably few people like every kind of music that was created in that century. Whether a particular type is for you, all of it merits exploration and explanation.

• It would follow traditional forms. The first movement is in sonata form, the second movement follows a large three-part form, the third is a stylized dance, and the fourth returns to sonata form.

First Movement

The first movement is presented in the Listening Guide.

SERGEI PROKOFIEV

Classical Symphony, Op. 25, First Movement (1917)

GENRE: Symphony   Orchestra

CD 6 Tracks 1–4
3 minutes 43 seconds

Form: Sonata

Exposition

0.00   **1**   0:00   Orchestra plays opening chord loud, followed by violins playing first theme.

0:21   Transition consisting of short melodic fragments begins in woodwinds.

0:48   **2**   0:00   Second theme played lightly by violins as bassoon plays steady, short notes.

0:22   Violins repeat second theme.

0:31   Short codetta.

Development

1:32   **3**   0:00   Silent measure; then violins play part of first theme as music modulates often.

0:19   Transition played by woodwinds and violins.

0:25   Second theme played forcefully by violins followed by other sections of orchestra.

Recapitulation

2:33   **4**   0:00   First theme played by violins.

0:09   Transition begins in woodwinds; other sections follow.

0:31   Second theme played very quietly by violins at a high pitch level.

0:56   Coda begins as woodwinds and violins outline chords.

1:12   Movement closes in a rush of sound.

Second Movement

This movement is quiet and songlike. The main melody seems to be the epitome of delicate, refined beauty.

Third Movement

The third movement is a gavotte—sort of. It does have all the features of the **gavotte** of earlier times, but is actually quite twentieth century in its free use of keys. The form is interesting. The movement opens and closes with the same music. Between the two appearances of that music, there are two sections of contrasting music, each repeated. When the second of these sections is repeated, the oboes add a line of counterpoint.

The stylized dance form used in the symphonies of Haydn and Mozart was the minuet. Prokofiev parted from the Classical tradition a bit in this movement.

Fourth Movement

The movement is marked *Allegro vivace* with a metronome marking of 152 beats per minute. In other words, the notes fly by, especially for the violins. Prokofiev reveals his twentieth-century harmonic thinking with a number of interesting key changes. The codetta presents a third theme, which is used prominently in the development section.

It is hard *not* to like Prokofiev's *Classical Symphony*. It has all the attributes of the music of Mozart and his contemporaries—the tuneful themes, the well-thought-out forms, the neatly balanced phrases, and generous amounts of charm and beauty. But Prokofiev has taken those characteristics and added a richer palette of harmonies and treatment of melodies.

HINDEMITH'S *KLEINE KAMMERMUSIK*

The full title of Hindemith's work is *Kleine Kammermusik für Fünf Bläser*, Op. 24, No. 2, which translated is *Little Chamber Music for Five Winds*. The five instruments are flute, oboe, clarinet, bassoon, and French horn, which constitute the usual woodwind quintet. The work demonstrates Hindemith's Neoclassical tendencies in its sparse use of instruments and in the short, concise format of its movements.

The first movement is cheerful in quality and follows a loose sonata form. The second movement is a subdued and graceful waltz consisting of rather short sections. The third is an elegant slow movement with long melodic lines. The fourth movement is short and fast. It is built around a short, pounding theme that alternates periodically with free-sounding solos for each instrument.

Paul Hindemith

Paul Hindemith (1895–1963) was born in Hanau, Germany, and his Neoclassical works have a certain Germanic, "academic" quality. As a teenager he played in dance bands and then became a member of the Frankfurt Opera Orchestra. For a while he played viola in the Amar-Hindemith Quartet. He became professor of composition in Berlin, but his modernistic music was banned by Hitler in 1934. He left Germany, lived in Turkey for a few years, and then came to the United States and taught composition at Yale University until 1953. He returned to Europe and taught at the University of Zürich until his death.

Hindemith composed sonatas for virtually every instrument. He also wrote a large amount of chamber music and a number of motets and choral works. A few of his works were large in scope, including his program symphony *Mathis der Mahler* (*Matthias the Painter*), inspired by three paintings by Mathis Grünewald on the altar at Isenheim, Germany. He also wrote two books on music theory in which he promoted his views about consonance and dissonance.

B. Schott's Söhne, Mainz

The fifth movement is very fast, with a symmetrical form: *A B C B A*. The differences among the themes are as much rhythmic as melodic. The first theme has accents falling logically on the beat. In the second theme the accents occur off the beat, while a bass line sounds on the beat. Also, when the pitches of the second theme ascend, the bass line descends in contrary motion, and vice versa. The melodies are not flowing ones but, rather, are cohesive fragments more in the style of the Classical period. Irregular meter can be seen in the first two themes. In fact, Hindemith changes it so often that he doesn't bother with meter signatures. And he uses chromatic notes so freely that he doesn't bother with a key signature either.

LISTENING GUIDE

PAUL HINDEMITH

Kleine Kammermusik für Fünf Bläser, Op. 24, No. 2, Fifth Movement (1922)

GENRE: Chamber music   Woodwind quintet

CD 6 Tracks 5–6
2 minutes 52 seconds

Form: Rondo (*A B C B A*)

0:00   **5**   0:00   Lively A theme played by flute, oboe, and clarinet.

0:13   B theme has oboe playing off the beat as bassoon plays a line in contrary motion.

0:24   French horn enters with contrasting part.

0:37   All except French horn play figure based on B theme.

0:49   Transition introduced by oboe.

1:03   **6**   0:00   Wide-ranging C theme begins in flute, then repeated with rhythmic accompaniment.

0:36   B theme played quietly by oboe, then repeated with flute as music grows more intense.

0:47   Music becomes more dissonant as French horn enters.

0:55   A theme returns in flute, oboe, and clarinet, then French horn.

1:18   Coda begins with clarinet and bassoon playing softly.

1:25   B theme returns forcefully with much dissonance.

1:46   Movement closes with three solid chords.

OTHER NEOCLASSICAL WORKS

Prokofiev was by no means the only composer attracted to Neoclassicism. Stravinsky has already been discussed; the milestone Neoclassical work by him was his Octet for Wind Instruments, which he composed in 1923. Other works by Stravinsky that reveal strong Neoclassical tendencies include the ballet *Apollo* (*Apollon Musaagète*), *Jeu de cartes* (*Game of Cards*), *Oedipus Rex*, *Pulcinella*, Suites Nos. 1 and 2 for Small Orchestra, and *Symphony of Psalms*.

Although known first for his compositions on Jewish themes, Ernest Bloch (1880–1959) composed two concerti grossi and a number of suites. Several twentieth-century French composers adopted the Neoclassical approach as well. Among them were Jacques Ibert (1890–1962), Francis Poulenc, and Darius Milhaud. A number of American composers also took a Neoclassical approach. They are discussed in Part VII.

TONE ROW MUSIC

It had worked for almost three hundred years. Music from popular songs to symphonics had a tonal center around which it functioned. The key of a work may have strayed and for a time become lost, but inevitably it was there and the music returned to it. This principle of a tonal center and the movement of chords in relation to that tonal center seemed as necessary to music as the law of gravity seems to us.

But was it? Arnold Schoenberg did not think so. He and other composers initially wrote works (mostly Expressionistic ones) that centered around no particular key. In short, that music was **atonal.** But Schoenberg was not satisfied. He felt the need to develop a new system for composing. About 1923 he devised a means of "composing with twelve tones," as he termed it.

The heart of Schoenberg's system is its **tone row.** The basic row, which the composer determines before writing the composition, includes the twelve different pitches of the chromatic scale, with no pitch being repeated before the row is complete. In this way no tonal center can be implied, because all the notes in the chromatic scale are treated equally.

Tone row music is linear, although it does contain some chords. The predetermined row is treated in four ways: (1) the *original*, (2) the **retrograde** (backward, in reverse order), (3) the **inversion** (all intervals reversed from their original direction), and (4) the **retrograde-inversion** (reverse pitch direction and reverse order). Any of the forms of the row can be transposed.

Although at first glance the idea may seem limited, it has been calculated that there are more than 479,001,600 rows available!

SCHOENBERG'S VARIATIONS FOR ORCHESTRA

As its title implies, the work is a set of variations on a theme. There certainly was nothing new about that. What was new was the use of the tone row theme and the ways in which it is varied.

The overall plan for Variations for Orchestra consists of an introduction, the theme, nine variations, and a finale. The introduction contains a series of sounds including tremolos in the violins and *flutter tonguing* by the flute. It also includes a time-honored motive built around the notes B-flat, A, C, and B-natural, which in German spells B A C H. Bach himself used this pattern of notes to spell his name as a fugue subject in his last composition, *The Art of the Fugue*.

The variations are short, sometimes only twenty-three measures long. They often feature small groups of instruments, not the entire orchestra. The finale is longer than any of the variations. The work closes after a final statement of the B A C H motive.

Flutter tonguing is actually created by a fluttering motion of the tongue.

In Germany the musical note *H* is B-natural, and *B* is B-flat. Therefore, the four notes of Bach's name in music are B-flat A C B-natural. Several composers have since written works based on his name as a tribute to him.

Here is the basic tone row for Variations for Orchestra:

The structure of the music is very carefully planned. For example, the chords are derived from one version of the row, and the number of notes in the melodic phrases corresponds to the number of notes in the chord.

Tone row compositions present problems for listeners not familiar with this type of music. The concept of the row is not hard to understand, but the row itself can seldom be heard in the composition. Furthermore, its chromatic nature makes it difficult to remember. Actually, the row is mainly a compositional technique or approach for composers; hearing the row as such is not necessary for listeners.

The idea of manipulating timbre also fascinated Schoenberg and other Expressionist composers. He devised a technique for doing that, which he gave the German name **Klangfarbenmelodie.** It involves changing the timbre along with the pitch changes. This is accomplished by giving different instruments various notes of the melody so that even though the melody is present, it is not heard in its complete form played on just one instrument.

Schoenberg vigorously denied that his music was cold and intellectual. When the requirements of tone row composition are considered, that denial may seem inaccurate. His music does contain much activity crammed into most of its measures. It seems as if

The German word Klangfarbenmelodie literally means "manufactured tone color melody."

© The New York Public Library

Arnold Schoenberg

BEST-KNOWN WORKS

chamber music:
- *Pierrot Lunaire*
- Trio for Strings

orchestra:
- Chamber Symphony No. 1
- Variations for Orchestra
- *Verklärte Nacht*

Arnold Schoenberg ("*Sh(r)n*-bairg," 1874–1951) was born in Vienna. He began studying violin when he was eight and became an avid participant in amateur chamber music performances. After his father's early death, he went to work as a bank clerk. He had little formal training at an advanced level.

For many years he had shown an interest in composing, and that interest increased until he decided to make it his life's work. He spent two years in Berlin as music director for a cabaret and then returned to Vienna. He served in the Austrian army for two years during World War I. In 1925 he was appointed professor of composition at the Berlin Academy of Arts, where he remained until Hitler came to power. Because of the anti-Semitic actions of the new regime, he decided to leave Germany for the United States, where he taught at the University of California at Los Angeles (UCLA) until his death.

Schoenberg is important in the world of music as much for his leadership and innovative ideas as for his compositions. Prior to 1908 he stood in the tradition of Wagner and composed large Romantic works. About 1908, however, he started turning to music for smaller groups. His music became more contrapuntal and much more chromatic. Over a period of time, he began to write music that had no tonal center. He also moved even further toward Expressionism.

About 1923 he devised the tone row system, which he followed for most of the remainder of his life. This was a system that was to leave its mark on the world of music.

ARNOLD SCHOENBERG
Variations for Orchestra excerpt (1928)

GENRE: **Tone row** **Orchestra**

CD 6 Tracks 7–8
1 minute 2 seconds

Form: Theme and variations

0:00 **7** 0:00 Cellos begin with original version of the row.

0:13 Retrograde-inversion of the row begins on a different note from original.

0:31 **8** 0:00 Retrograde of the row begins on same note as original.

0:11 Inversion of row begins on same note as retrograde-inversion.

0:30 Theme concludes quietly.

he compressed the dimension of time, causing what happens to the sounds to be much more concentrated than in previous music. Schoenberg obviously did not conceive of music in the rambling dimensions of the Romantic period.

SERIALISM: BEYOND TONE ROWS

Since 1950 a number of other composers have turned to tone rows. This movement can be attributed primarily to the influence of a quiet student of Schoenberg's: Anton Webern (1883–1945). Although he composed in the same style as Schoenberg, Webern's music is more austere and economical. Of his thirty-one compositions, the longest is just ten minutes, and all his music can be performed in less than three hours! His dynamic levels are often very soft, and his frail tone row melodies are subtly passed from one instrument to another. If he had written more sparsely, it seems that the music would disappear completely.

Articulation refers to tonguing, slurring, and the style with which notes are played.

Webern expanded the concept of tone row music with the introduction of **Serialism.** In it the principles of tone row music are carried further with the development of one or more series of pitches within the row. The idea was subsequently extended to rows or series of articulations, dynamic levels, and rhythmic values. Serialism represented additional intellectual control over musical sounds.

Consider the basic row for Webern's Concerto for Nine Instruments:

Brackets have been placed over the four subrows.

The row can be divided into four subrows. In turn, each of these subrows can be divided into three segments, each consisting of two adjacent notes and one that is either a line or a space farther away. The first three notes can be thought of as a miniature row, followed by its transposed retrograde-inversion, retrograde, and inversion.

The Concerto for Nine Instruments begins:

A STYLE OF PAINTING that features total intellectual control can be seen in Kasimir Malevich's *Suprematist Composition: White on White.* Painted in 1918, the work is devoid of anything except what is absolutely necessary.

In this example the groups of three notes are retained, although with **octave displacement,** which is the technique of sounding a pitch in an octave higher or lower from most of the others in the row. The first group is played by the oboe, the second by the flute, the third by the trumpet, and the fourth by the clarinet. In addition, a different rhythm is associated with each three-note group, and different articulations are specified.

A number of composers, including Stravinsky, have been attracted to the principles of tone row and serial music and have used them in some of their compositions. Other composers made tone row or serial music their dominant style.

CODA

Neoclassical and tone row music both represent an intellectual approach to music. The Neoclassical, "Back to Bach" compositions employ some of the forms of earlier times, but what is included in the music is definitely from the twentieth century. Tone row music and its extension into Serialism are truly mind over music. Some people enjoy working crossword puzzles for intellectual challenge and enjoyment. The analogy is by no means perfect, but the element of intellectual enjoyment is present in both.

New Sounds *and* New Techniques

With the end of World War II in 1945, the world moved into a new era. In a faltering manner, the nations and peoples of the world started to rebuild in both a physical and an emotional sense. Most people realized that whatever might happen in the future, things would never be the same again.

Along with the monumental changes that have come about in the more than six decades since that time, new generations of composers have been active. New ways of making music have become available through technological advances, and different attitudes about music and music listening have evolved.

From about 1945 to 1960, the competition for leadership in the world of concert music was between those who favored strict control of musical sounds through Serialism and those who favored only a few specifications through chance music and improvisation.

EXTENSIONS OF SERIALISM

Although Schoenberg devised the tone row system in the 1920s, until about 1950 only a few of the major composers were attracted to it. The tone row approach began to find more favor after 1945, partly because of the influence of Webern.

As mentioned previously, Webern extended the idea of a row beyond pitches to include series of articulations, dynamic levels, and rhythmic values. The leading proponents of what is described as **total Serialism** were the French composers Pierre Boulez (b. 1925) and Olivier Messiaen (1908–1992). In one of his works, Messiaen uses one series for the melody, another for the dynamics, and another for the rhythm; each of the series is a different length.

Other composers who favored highly controlled works in the 1950s were Luciano Berio (1925–2003) in Italy, Milton Babbitt (b. 1916) in the United States, and Karlheinz Stockhausen (b. 1928) in Germany. The music they created during those years is very complex, so it is difficult for listeners to perceive and performers to render accurately. Over the years some of these composers have changed their approaches to composing.

Tone row music may have been originally rejected because of its association with Expressionism.

CHANCE MUSIC

The American John Cage (1912–1992) was a major promoter of **chance** or **aleatory music.** In such music the sounds are partly the result of chance, so they are unpredictable. A player might be instructed to play anything that comes to mind or just rest. Or the notes can be the result of throwing dice or dropping pages of music on the floor.

At first glance, such musical practices may seem like a put-on, but they are not. They are the application in music of an existential outlook on life. For centuries Western civilization believed in progress, the idea of moving toward a goal. Through increased knowledge—which in turn led to such practical outcomes as improved medical care, more food, and increased leisure—it was thought that the human race was progressing. However, the idea of progress came under attack in the twentieth century from proponents of existential philosophy and from advocates of Asian religious beliefs. The idea of progress is false, they maintained. There is only change, not progress.

The implications of the only-change, no-goal-toward-which-to-progress philosophy are enormous. It is like removing the goal lines and uprights on a football field and

© Hulton-Deutsch Collection/Corbis

COMPOSER JOHN CAGE said of his music, "I have nothing to say and I am saying it."

The term *aleatory* comes from a Latin word meaning "dice" or "gambler," which in the ancient world signified chance.

ROY LICHTENSTEIN'S **WHAAM!** has no message. According to Lichtenstein, "Stylistically, my work is devoid of emotional content. And it's what I want." He and his musical counterpart, John Cage, created works that were so obvious that they invite no interpretation. They represent a complete rejection of the nineteenth-century belief in art as the conveyor of great ideas that need to be studied and pondered.

The epitome of Cage's views was his work 4' 33", which premiered in 1955. The pianist simply sits at the piano that long but never plays a note!

ceasing to keep score or time: The game just happens. About the only assumption that can be made is that the players will eventually tire and stop playing.

This philosophical position rejects the idea that works of art must have meaning. As Cage said, "My purpose is to eliminate purpose." Depicting a can of Campbell's soup or creating a painting that looks as if it came from a comic book is not, as some people believe, a comment on the vulgarity of contemporary civilization. The content of such works is so obvious that it no longer encourages interpretation by the viewer, which is the way the artist wants it. A picture is a picture—and that's all.

In his book *Silence*, Cage urges the composer to "give up the desire to control sound, clear his mind of music [in the usual sense] and set about discovering means to let sounds be themselves rather than vehicles for man-made theories or expressions of human sentiments." Using chance devices to determine sounds is one way in which Cage and others try to get listeners to just consider the sounds and not attempt to read meaning into them.

These ideas have been attempted by a number of composers, including Karlheinz Stockhausen. In a complete change from his electronic works of the 1950s, Stockhausen's *Originale* (1961) is based on a series of simultaneous, incoherent "happenings." In one scene the directions are "Pianist and percussionist put on clothes brought in by cloak-room attendant. The pianist takes off his cultic robes and puts on Oriental female costume. . . . When he is ready, he begins to brew up tea at the piano."

ELECTRONIC MUSIC

As music moved into the 1960s, both serial and chance music faded and electronic music began to receive much more attention. Prior to that time, technologically created and produced music had been confined to a few expensively equipped studios. When the cost of such equipment dropped enough in price, many more composers started to work with computers and synthesizers.

The term *musique concrète* means "concrete music" in French.

There are two general types of electronic music. One is ***musique concrète***. Recordings are made of actual sounds—parts of human speech, the buzzing of an insect, the soothing sound of water running, the shrill sound of a whistle, and so on. Then the recording, which in the 1960s was on magnetic tape, is manipulated by the composer:

- It can be speeded up or slowed down.
- It can have other sounds added by splicing or editing.

- Some of the partials of a sound can be filtered out.
- The order in which sounds appear can be arranged and altered.

An American advocate of *musique concrète* was Vladimir Ussachevsky (1911–1990), who was one of the founders of the Columbia–Princeton Electronic Music Laboratory in New York City. *Musique concrète* has been used successfully as background music for movies, plays, and ballets, especially when eerie music is appropriate.

Another type of electronic music consists of sounds produced on electronic equipment such as synthesizers and computers. Such music had its beginning in the Studio for Electronic Music of the West German Radio in the 1950s but today is actively pursued throughout the world.

Technology offers a composer total control over the music, for several reasons:

- There are no performers to alter the music, either intentionally or unintentionally by making mistakes. Once the right button is pushed, the equipment plays exactly what the composer entered into it. Therefore, there is no longer any need for music notation.
- Any pitch is possible, including ones so high that most humans cannot hear them, as well as **microtones,** which are intervals closer than the half steps found on keyboards and many instruments.
- Any combination of pitches is possible.
- Any rhythm is possible, no matter how complex, including multiple rhythms occurring at the same time.
- Any timbre is possible. Electronic devices can filter out or increase partials in a sound to achieve any tone quality the composer wishes.
- Any dynamic level is possible. The sounds can be almost inaudibly soft or so loud that they cause physical damage to the loudspeakers (and listeners' eardrums!). Crescendos and decrescendos can be regulated exactly.
- Any electronically created sound can be combined with any recorded sound in any way the composer desires. Actual sounds of instruments can be *sampled* (recorded) and incorporated into electronic compositions.
- The computer can be programmed in conjunction with other electronic equipment to make some of the decisions in the creation of music. When this happens, the creator of the program becomes to some extent the "composer of the composer."

The world of electronic music has changed rapidly, and it has been around only a few decades in anywhere near the form in which it is found today. No solid repertoire of such music exists. Each new work is to some degree an experiment.

LE CORBUSIER'S PAVILION at the Brussels World Fair

The line between *musique concrète* and electronic music is by no means clear-cut.

VARÈSE'S *POÈME ÉLECTRONIQUE*

Poème électronique by Edgard Varèse comes as close as any work to being a masterpiece of this type of music. It was created in 1958 for the Brussels World Fair and was a part of the pavilion designed by the Swiss architect Le Corbusier for the Philips Radio Corporation. Not only did Le Corbusier design the exterior but he also used a planned sequence of colored lights and images to be projected on the interior walls while Varèse's three-track tape was played through 425 loudspeakers.

The interior of the pavilion contained many different shapes and angles. When visitors walked through the building, they were greeted with different colors, images, and musical sounds. Varèse realized that people would not go through the pavilion according to an established path; they were free to move about as they wished, which meant

EDGARD VARÈSE

Poème électronique, beginning (1958)

GENRE: Electronic music   Synthesizer

CD 2 Track 34
2 minutes 50 seconds

Form: Rondo

0:00	**34**	0:00	Sounds of a large bell, wiggling sounds, and sirens.
		0:43	Driplike sounds, followed by something sounding like squawks.
		0:56	Three-note pattern ascends three times.
		1:11	Low sound sustained along with rattling sound, then siren, and more squawks.
		1:28	Siren sounds are played again and followed by more squawks. Soon more chirping sounds are heard.
		2:04	Sound of percussion instruments, as well as siren.
		2:35	Large bell sound, along with sustained tones.
		2:50	Recording fades.

There was a consensus that it was really *very different*!

that there was an element of chance in what they encountered. The reactions of the visitors in 1958 to what they saw and heard ranged from anger and fear to curiosity and awe.

Varèse's work certainly represents a break with traditional music. It has no melody, harmony, beat, or meter. Instead, it is a series of organized sounds, mostly of a *musique concrète* nature. They pop in and out of a soundscape that is either interesting or confusing, depending on one's individual inclinations.

The use of electronic music in conjunction with visual images has fascinated both concert and popular composers. The potential of electronic music has barely been

Edgard Varèse

© Corbis-Bettmann

BEST-KNOWN WORKS

electronic:
• *Poème électronique*

flute:
• *Density 21.5*

instrumental:
• *Ionization*

Although he was born in France, **Edgard Varèse** (1883–1965) lived most of his life in America. Appropriately, his first composition after he moved to his new country was entitled *Amériques*. It called for an orchestra plus an unusual combination of percussion instruments: drums of different types and sizes, siren, rattle, sleigh bells, castanets, glockenspiel, and xylophone. Ten years later he composed a work that is better known today — *Ionization* — which uses thirty-seven different percussion instruments played by thirteen musicians.

Varèse came to music via a different route than most composers. He was trained in engineering and mathematics. His scientific leanings led to his contact in 1927 with engineers at the Bell Telephone Company laboratories to urge them to create machines that would synthesize musical sounds.

Notice the year that he made his request to Bell Telephone and how far ahead of his time Varèse was.

When magnetic tape recorders became available in the 1950s, he was the first to explore their potential for music making. Those efforts led to *Poème électronique* in 1958.

tapped. It offers vast possibilities for working with sounds and images, and many composers today are exploring this new medium.

ECLECTICISM

Although contemporary music is very pluralistic, with composers writing in widely divergent styles, some composers use what they think is the best of each style. They take various elements from different styles and synthesize music that is uniquely their own, a practice known as **Eclecticism.** They owe allegiance to no musical system or viewpoint, and their compositions are not easily classified. Whether or not Eclecticism is successful depends on the abilities of the particular composer.

CRUMB'S *NIGHT OF THE FOUR MOONS*

George Crumb's series of four songs, entitled *Night of the Four Moons*, contains elements of a number of styles and demonstrates aspects of several types of twentieth-century music. It was composed during the *Apollo 11* moon flight, July 16–24, 1969. Crumb writes of the work:

> *I suppose that* Night of the Four Moons *is really an "occasional" work, since its inception was an artistic response to an external event. The texts—extracts drawn from the poems Federico García Lorca—symbolize my own rather ambivalent feelings vis-à-vis Apollo 11.*

It was commissioned by the Philadelphia Chamber Players and uses a chamber ensemble consisting of an alto singer, alto flute (doubling on piccolo), banjo, "electric" cello (that is, a cello amplified through a speaker), and one percussionist playing a number of instruments: large drum, crotales (metal shells strung together), cymbals, tambourine,

George Crumb

George Crumb (b. 1929) is a truly eclectic composer. He grew up in Charleston, West Virginia. His music studies include a bachelor's degree from Mason College, a master's degree from the University of Illinois, advanced study in Berlin, and a doctorate from the University of Michigan. He recently retired after teaching composition for thirty years at the University of Pennsylvania.

His compositions are almost entirely for soloists or chamber groups, and many

of them involve the use of electric or amplified instruments. His music juxtaposes contrasting styles, ranging from the Western concert music tradition to folk/ethnic music and hymns. Much of his music contains mystical, symbolic, and theatrical elements. He has been the recipient of many awards and grants, including a Pulitzer Prize, a Grammy, and six honorary degrees.

Bettmann/Corbis

BEST-KNOWN WORKS
- *Ancient Voices of Children*
- *Black Angels*
- *Music for a Summer Evening*

PART VII

Music *in the* United States

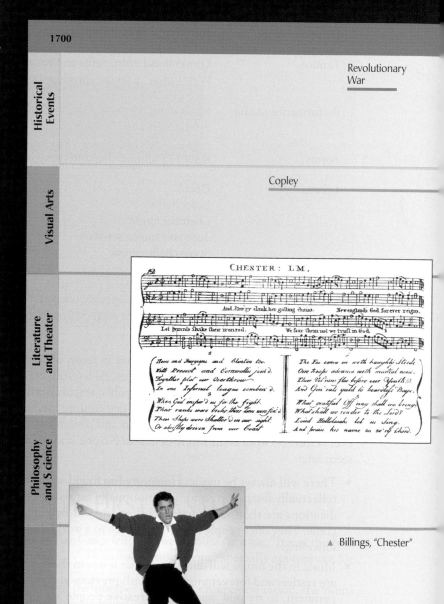

	1700				
Historical Events					Revolutionary War
Visual Arts					Copley
Literature and Theater					
Philosophy and Science					
Music					▲ Billings, "Chester"

CHESTER: L.M.

And Slav'ry clank her galling chains.   New-england's God for ever reigns.

Let tyrants shake their iron rod,   We fear them not we trust in God.

Howe and Burgoyne and Clinton too.
With Prescot and Cornwallis join'd.
Together plot our Overthrow
In one Infernal league combin'd.

When God inspir'd us for the fight,
Their ranks were broke their lines were fix'd
Their Ships were Shatter'd in our sight.
Or swiftly driven from our Coast.

The Foe comes on with haughty Stride,
Our troops advance with martial noise.
Their Vet'rans flee before our Youth D.
And Gen'rals yield to beardless Boys.

What grateful Off'ring shall we bring?
What shall we render to the Lord?
Loud Hallelujah's let us Sing,
And praise his name on ev'ry Chord.

1800   **1900**   **2000**

• Louisiana Purchase   World War I   Terrorist attacks •

     • War of 1812   Westward expansion   Great Depression

           Civil War   World War II   Iraq Wars

        • Transcontinental railroad   Korean War •   Vietnam War

---

Eakins's work   Wood, *American Gothic* (top right) ▲   Saarinen's work

Stuart's work   • Homer, *Breezing Up*   • Lichtenstein, *Wham!*

           Cassatt's work

             F. L. Wright's work   Pei's work

       Poe's work   Sandburg's work   T. Williams's work

Cooper's work   Longfellow's work   O'Neill's work   Mailer's work

                                           M. Graham's work

      • Hawthorne, *The House of Seven Gables*   Lewis's work

Whitman, *Leaves of Grass* •   Frost's work   • A. Miller, *Death of a Salesman*

        Twain's work   Hemingway's work   Baldwin's work

• First steamboats   Dewey's work   • TV   Internet •

      • Reaper invented   • Automobiles   • Atomic energy

        Lightbulb, phonograph •   • Airplanes   • DNA discovered

           James's work   • Radio   • Satellites

     Gottschalk's work   Jazz •   Swing •   • Soul   Glass's work

       Foster's work   Sousa's work   Gershwin's work   Bernstein's work

                    Copland's work   W. Schuman's work   • Zwilich, *Concerto Grosso*

                  Country •   Barber's work   J. Williams's work

       A. C. Beach's work

        MacDowell's work   Ives   Cage's work   Adams's work

              Hanson •   ◄ Rock (bottom left)

35 American Music before 1920

New York was once called New Amsterdam, Louisiana was named for King Louis of France, and *Florida* comes from a Spanish word referring to "the land of flowers."

There were no democratic nations in the seventeenth century. The belief in the equality of all people was a revolutionary idea that developed in America.

The first edition of the *Bay Psalm Book* published in 1640 had no music. Music was not included until the ninth edition in 1698.

Until well into the twentieth century, it was believed that an aspiring artist, composer, or performer should spend some years studying in Europe.

The United States of America has a unique history. North America was only thinly populated by Native Americans until the arrival of Europeans in the early part of the seventeenth century. And when Europeans did arrive, they came to stay, not just to take the gold and other treasures and head back home, as happened in Central and South America. For the first century and a half after the first settlements, the question was not whether America would be a colony, but whose colony it would be. The English, Dutch, Spanish, and French all laid claims to it at one time or another.

America represented a fresh start, a chance to develop a new country that was largely unfettered by ties to the past. It was a circumstance that has rarely happened in history. This situation led to the fruition of ideas that today we take for granted—ideas such as all people are created equal and government should function democratically.

Even though the American experience was good for democratic government and the common good of its citizens, it was not so helpful in the development of the arts. They had a slow start in America and did not really flourish until the twentieth century.

Why were the arts slow to develop in America? There are several reasons:

- For much of the first three hundred years of its history, its people were occupied with practical matters related to settling a new land. Except for a tiny number of prosperous families on the eastern seaboard, they had little time for the arts.

- Rightly or wrongly, the Puritans, who were among the earliest settlers, thought that art and theater were undesirable. At best, they considered them worthless diversions; at worst, they were products of the devil. The only music permitted in church was the unaccompanied singing of psalms and hymns. Not surprisingly, the first book published in America was the *Bay Psalm Book*.

- America had almost no titled families to patronize the arts. This fact contributed much to the development of a democratic society, but it removed an important source of patrons for composers and artists.

- Initially, Americans brought their language and arts with them from their former lands. They thought that European art and music were superior to whatever might be developed in the colonies or in the young nation. For hundreds of years, the attitude was one of transplanting the superior culture from Europe, not of developing a culture that was distinct and indigenous. In short, Americans suffered from a cultural inferiority complex, a condition that has not entirely disappeared even today.

ART IN AMERICA

American artists were affected by the factors just mentioned. As a result, they developed a simpler, more down-to-earth style than that of European artists. Instead of painting members of the nobility, they painted common people doing common activities. And until the twentieth century their works were not noticeably influenced by intellectual theories about art.

Winslow Homer's *Breezing Up*, painted in 1876, suggests mood, feeling, and atmosphere in a vivid way. The picture of three small boys and a fisherman in a sailboat evokes the pleasure of sailing in a nice breeze. It's a simple, straightforward work of art.

Grant Wood's *American Gothic* is one of the most famous American paintings (page 286). It has graced doormats and T-shirts and has been seen in cereal commercials on

Homer, Winslow, *Breezing Up (A Fair Wind)* 1876. The National Gallery of Art, Gift of the W. L. and May T. Mellon Foundation, 1943. Photograph © 2002 The National Gallery of Art, Washington, D.C.

BREEZING UP by Winslow Homer, 1876

television. It depicts something very American in its matter-of-fact representation of life. It celebrates the homely, simple virtues of rural life, of America as it once was. The use of the term *Gothic* is intended as an ironic comparison with the massive and complex structures found in the European Gothic tradition. The pointed-arch window of the dwelling in the background is an example of what is sometimes called "carpenter Gothic," which is the American version of a European style carved ornately in stone.

In spite of its slow start, American music is a rich and rewarding type of music to know and understand, especially, of course, for Americans. It is an essential part of a course that covers music listening today.

American music can be divided into three broad categories: folk, popular, and art. American folk music is discussed in Chapter 40. The latter two types are presented in the following chapters.

THE EIGHTEENTH CENTURY

The most sophisticated music written in the American colonies before the Revolutionary War was the product of the Moravian communities around Bethlehem, Pennsylvania, and Winston-Salem, North Carolina. These people had come from what is today part of the Czech Republic, bringing with them a rich musical heritage. Besides music for church services, they also wrote chamber works. There were several active composers among the Moravians, but John Frederick Peter (1746–1813) was the most skilled. He immigrated to America in 1770.

Probably the first native-born American composer was a musical amateur, Francis Hopkinson (1737–1791), a friend of George Washington and a signer of the Declaration

Washington was humble in his response to Hopkinson:

I can neither sing one of the songs, nor raise a single note on any instrument to convince the unbelieving, but I have, however, one argument which will prevail with persons of true estate (at least in America)—I can tell them that **it is the production of Mr. Hopkinson.**

The model for the man was Wood's dentist.

AMERICAN GOTHIC by Grant Wood, 1930. This portrait of an Iowa farm couple contains some of the simple but strong elements found in Copland's *Fanfare for the Common Man*.

Billings was not modest in making claims about fuguing:

[Fuguing] is twenty times as powerful as the old slow tunes. Each part striving for mastery and victory. The audience entertained and delighted. Now the solemn bass demands their attention; next the manly tenor. Now here, now there, now here again! O ecstatic! Rush on, you sons of harmony.

of Independence. In 1788 he published some songs, for which he also wrote the words. He dedicated the book to Washington. Hopkinson's most famous song was "My Days Have Been So Wondrous Free."

William Billings (1746–1800) was a tanner by trade and later one of a talented number of singing-school masters. He had an insatiable drive to write music and was a firm believer in American music for Americans. He explained in his first collection, *The New England Psalm Singer* (1770), that he would follow his own rules for composition. One of the techniques he used in his hymns was "fuguing," which was an impressive name for simple imitation.

Whatever Billings lacked in training was offset by his natural musical ability. Despite some rough places, his music possesses a vigor that continues to fascinate many musicians and listeners. A number of Billings's tunes are still performed today. The tune

As is true of a great deal of American culture, much of its patriotic music consists of songs with European roots. The origin of "Yankee Doodle" is unknown, but it was introduced in the colonies by a British doctor named Shackburg about twenty years before the Revolutionary War began. It was first sung by the British to ridicule the New Englanders, who promptly took it over as their own song by adding new verses.

The melody of "The Star-Spangled Banner" was adapted from a popular English drinking song, "To Anacreon in Heaven." This song to an ancient Greek poet was probably composed by John Stafford Smith (1750–1836). The words were written by an American lawyer, Francis Scott Key. During the War of 1812 between the Americans and the British, Key went aboard a British ship in Chesapeake Bay to negotiate the release of a Dr. William Beames, who was being held prisoner by the British. On September 13, 1814, the British fleet sailed up the bay to bombard Fort McHenry, which guarded Baltimore harbor. Before the battle began, Key, Beames, and a companion were transferred to a small boat behind the fleet.

All night Key paced the deck, wondering if the American flag would still be there in the morning. If it were, it would mean that the fort had withstood the challenge and that Baltimore had been saved. "By the dawn's early light" Key could see the Stars and Stripes still flying and he was moved to begin the poem that is sung today. By that afternoon he had finished it, and a week later it appeared in the *Baltimore American*. The words were sung for the first time by an actor in Baltimore. It was not officially made the national anthem until 1931.

"My Country 'Tis of Thee" ("America") is sung to the same melody as the British national anthem, "God Save the King (or Queen)," which was written by the English composer Henry Carey (1685–1743). The words sung in this country were written in 1832 by the American Samuel Francis Smith (1808–1895), somewhat by accident. Lowell Mason was searching for music to arrange for children to sing in church. He had been given a collection of songs used in German schools. Not knowing German,

Mason had asked Smith, a student at Andover Theological Seminary, to set English words to them in his spare time. It took Smith only half an hour one February day to write his words to the tune, which he did not realize at the time was "God Save the King."

"America, the Beautiful" is sung to a hymn tune, "Materna" ("O Mother, Dear Jerusalem"), by Samuel A. Ward, an obscure organist from Newark, New Jersey. The words were the creation of Katherine Lee Bates (1859–1929), a professor of English at Wellesley College and author of a number of books and poems. She was so impressed by her first visit to the summit of Pike's Peak in Colorado that the opening lines of the poem seemed just to come to her. They were printed in a magazine called *The Congregationalist* on July 4, 1895, and were subsequently set to several different tunes, but the "Materna" melody is the only one heard with the poem today.

John Philip Sousa's "The Star and Stripes Forever" is discussed later in this chapter. "Hail Columbia!" is another patriotic march. Feeling the need for a song to help unify the young nation, in 1798 Joseph Hopkinson wrote the words and set them to a melody that had been written as an inaugural march for George Washington nine years earlier. The composer of the march is generally believed to be Philip Phile. In those days America was often referred to as Columbia (the feminine form of Columbus), as can be seen in the designation *District of Columbia* for the national capital area.

"God Bless America" was composed by Irving Berlin (1888–1989), an emigrant from Siberia who came to America at the age of five. He was a prolific composer of musicals but today is best remembered for his songs. The original version of "God Bless America" was composed for a musical in 1918, but Berlin decided that its solemn quality didn't fit the comedic elements of the show. In 1938 he decided to write a "peace" song, and he recalled his song from twenty years earlier. Singer Kate Smith introduced the slightly revised version in a radio broadcast that December. It was an immediate sensation and has become the unofficial national anthem.

"Chester" is one of his best known. A version of it from Billings's *Singing Master's Assistant* is shown on page 288. The melody is in the tenor part, which is the third line from the top. The music has a plain and direct quality.

During the eighteenth century, music in America was not confined to religious situations; a folk music tradition was also developing. Much of this music, as is pointed out in Chapter 40, consisted of adaptations of music from England and much of it was not published.

"Chester" was the theme for one of the movements in William Schuman's *New England Triptych*, which was written in 1956.

THE NINETEENTH CENTURY

When the nineteenth century began, the former colonies had been the United States of America for little more than a decade. Its population was just over 5 million people, who lived almost entirely east of the Appalachian Mountains. Most of its goods were still imported from Europe, and there were serious doubts that the young nation would survive. The arts were still in a largely embryonic state. Over the next hundred years, these conditions would change dramatically.

The name *Mason* is an important one in American music. Lowell Mason (1792–1872) wrote many hymns, including "Nearer, My God to Thee," and conducted the Handel and Haydn Society in Boston. Two of his sons founded the piano-manufacturing company of Mason and Hamlin, and a third son became a famous music teacher. Mason led a campaign against some of the religious music of his day, which came into being after the decline of Billings's "fuguing tunes." As part of this effort, Mason published a large number of music collections.

Not only did America import much of its music, it also imported musicians. European virtuosos found it profitable to tour the United States. The most sensational of these was the singer Jenny Lind, who was advertised by her brilliant promoter, P. T. Barnum, as "the Swedish Nightingale."

An early American piano virtuoso was Louis Moreau Gottschalk (1829–1869). He was a handsome man who cultivated some of the mannerisms of Liszt. He often left his white gloves on the piano for his female admirers to fight over. He wrote sentimental pieces with such tear-jerking titles as "The Last Hope" and "The Dying Poet." "The Banjo," which is based on American rhythms and melodies, became very popular in Europe in the 1850s.

Louis A. Jullian (1812–1860) chose a different approach. He kept his white gloves on as he conducted with his jeweled baton. He played some high-quality music, including some by American composers. But his biggest success was a number titled *Fireman's Quadrille*, during which, as flames burst from the ceiling, the local fire department would rush into the hall to dramatically quench the blaze.

For sheer spectacle no one equaled Patrick Gilmore (1829–1892), a bandmaster who organized supercolossal extravaganzas. One was the Great National Peace Jubilee in Boston in 1869. The performers included a chorus of ten thousand and an orchestra of a thousand, with cannons and a hundred firemen pounding anvils in the "Anvil Chorus" from Verdi's *Il Trovatore*! The only way for Gilmore to top that was to organize a World

Peace Jubilee, which he did. For this event he brought Johann Strauss from Vienna to lead his *Blue Danube Waltz*. Although the orchestra was restricted to one thousand players, the chorus was increased to twenty thousand singers!

From Jullian's orchestra came a young German violinist named Theodore Thomas (1835–1905), who organized his own orchestra in 1862. Thomas maintained high standards of performance and tried to educate his audiences. In so doing he laid the foundation for the symphony orchestras of today. He traveled widely throughout the United States and for a time was the conductor of the New York Philharmonic. Later he organized the Chicago Symphony and was its conductor for many years.

The political upheavals in Europe, and especially Germany, in the mid-1800s brought thousands of immigrants to the United States. Some were musicians who soon became affiliated with orchestras and opera companies throughout the country. The European immigrants constituted an audience for the German symphonic music that Thomas's orchestras performed for them.

Late in the nineteenth century, several American composers began to write longer and more-sophisticated works. Most of these composers lived around Boston, and almost all of them had studied in Germany at one time or another. For this reason most of their music sounded similar to works of European composers. The "Boston" or "New England" group included George W. Chadwick (1854–1931), Horatio Parker (1863–1919), Arthur Foote (1853–1937), John Knowles Paine (1839–1906), and Amy Cheney Beach (1867–1944), who was the first American woman to write a symphony. She is probably the best known of these composers today.

Edward MacDowell (1861–1908) had excellent musical training. He studied at the Paris Conservatory when he was eleven years old. After his return to America, he became a professor of music at Columbia University. Most of his works are for piano, including the often played "To a Wild Rose" from *Woodland Sketches*. He also wrote four piano sonatas and two piano concertos. His Suite No. 2 ("Indian Suite") is a landmark because of its early use of Native American music.

In a letter home, Strauss described his feelings of terror as he stepped before the huge aggregation.

Amy Beach followed the custom of using her husband's first and last names. She signed her works "Mrs. H. H. A. Beach."

MacDowell was a classmate of Debussy's at the Paris Conservatory. Later he played for Liszt at Weimar.

THE EARLY TWENTIETH CENTURY

Soon after the turn of the century, the popularity of German Romanticism began to recede in America, only to be replaced by attempts to imitate French Impressionism. The best-known American who wrote in this style was Charles Tomlinson Griffes (1884–1920). He started out composing in the German tradition but later switched to the Impressionistic style of Debussy and Ravel. "The White Peacock" from his *Roman Sketches* is frequently performed. Charles Martin Loeffler (1861–1935) also wrote Impressionistic-sounding music.

Sousa and Wind Band Music

Not all music at the turn of the century in America was heard inside concert halls. Some of it was band music that was enjoyed while relaxing on the grass in a park or town square on a warm summer's evening. In the early 1900s, most Americans lived on farms or small towns. Most small towns had a bandstand from which local bands performed, often with more enthusiasm than skill.

The popularity of the band as a concert ensemble—very much an American musical institution—encouraged the development of a number of virtuoso performers, such as Arthur Pryor on trombone and Herbert Clarke on trumpet. It also resulted in a number of composers who wrote marches and overtures for wind bands.

Sousa thought out "The Stars and Stripes Forever" on a ship while returning from Europe. He then wrote it down verbatim when he reached shore. The march follows the traditional march form, except for the addition of a **break**,

© Bonnie Kamin

JOHN PHILIP SOUSA on the cover of his most famous work. Sousa wrote more than ninety marches, which are still widely performed today. Much of his music was patriotic.

LISTENING GUIDE

JOHN PHILIP SOUSA

"The Stars and Stripes Forever" (1896)

GENRE: March   Wind band

CD 6 Tracks 11–13
3 minutes 6 seconds

Form: *a a b b c d c d*

| 0.00 | **11** | 0:00 | March opens with a few introductory measures. |

First Strain

| | | 0:04 | Melody for first strain contains syncopation and features brasses followed by a drum roll. |
| | | 0:17 | First strain repeated. |

Second Strain

| 0:30 | **12** | 0:00 | Melody for second strain is more energetic. |
| | | 0:14 | Second strain repeated. |

Trio

| 0:58 | **13** | 0:00 | Music changes key and becomes softer and more songlike. |

		0:27	"Dogfight" featuring low brasses playing repeated notes in sequence.
		0:48	Trio repeated with lively countermelody played by the piccolo.
		1:17	"Dogfight" repeated.
		1:38	Trio repeated with brasses playing melody loudly as piccolo plays countermelody.
		2:09	"The Star and Stripes Forever" ends with a short, abrupt chord.

Dogfight is a term band directors often use to describe a part of a march in which there is a rapid exchange of musical material among sections of the band.

or **dogfight,** before returning to the main melody of the trio. This march is also famous for the decorative countermelody played by the piccolo when the melody of the trio reappears after the dogfight.

Although the melody of the trio may seem simple, it is not. It consists of two sections that are each sixteen measures long. These are further divided into four smaller phrases. The rhythm of two notes on the upbeat leading to one longer note pervades the melody. Other than one instance of syncopation, the melody is rhythmically quite straightforward.

Sousa's bands were not large, ranging between forty-eight and fifty-two players. They consisted of about twenty-five clarinet and saxophone players, sixteen brasses, six percussion, and one string bass. Sousa did not perform his marches at as fast a tempo as some directors take them today. He gave them a dignified, not a harried, sound.

John Philip Sousa

The person most recognized for his contributions to band music is **John Philip Sousa** (1854–1932). Sousa was born in Washington, D.C., of a Portuguese father and a Bavarian mother. The first ten years of his career were spent as a violinist in a theater orchestra. In 1880 he became leader of the U.S. Marine Corps Band. After twelve years he left that position to form his own band. It was very popular (and financially successful) and toured extensively until his death forty years later. He helped develop the sousaphone, a version of the tuba that can be carried over the shoulder while marching. Despite his busy schedule, Sousa found time to compose operettas and marches, as well as write novels and an autobiography. He is remembered today only for his marches and is often referred to as "the March King."

© Corbis

IVES'S SYMPHONY NO. 2

Ives composed his Second Symphony between 1897 and 1901. It is a rather early work and is somewhat conservative for Ives. Except for having five movements, it is a relatively standard symphony.

FIRST MOVEMENT   The movement has a moderate tempo and consists mostly of music for strings. In several respects it is a long introduction, including the fact that it is attached to the second movement without a break.

SECOND MOVEMENT   This is a lively movement that features quotations from two old American hymns: "Bringing in the Sheaves" and "When I Survey the Wondrous Cross." The latter of these tunes is played in long note values (augmentation), sometimes with portions of the other themes serving as counterpoint. The hymn tunes are two of the four themes used in the movement.

Sheaves are bundles of grain stalks; but in the song, bringing them in is a metaphor for saving souls.

THIRD MOVEMENT   The third movement is slow and melodious.

FOURTH MOVEMENT   This movement is slow and majestic.

FIFTH MOVEMENT   In this movement Ives quotes from American folk and patriotic songs, in contrast to the second movement and its quotations from hymns. One of the songs is Stephen Foster's "Camptown Races," and another is "Columbia, the Gem of the Ocean." Another song sounds a bit like Stephen Foster's "Old Black Joe," but it is not. Instead, it is from a work titled *The American Woods* by Brookfield. A fragment of the bugle call "Reveille" is also used. The use of segments of other pieces is often referred to as **quotation music.**

Stephen Foster is discussed in Chapter 37.

LISTENING GUIDE

CHARLES IVES
Symphony No. 2, Fifth Movement (1897–1901)

GENRE: **Symphony   Orchestra**

CD 6 Tracks 14–18
9 minutes 7 seconds

Form: *A B A B C*

0:00	**14**	0:00	Opens with violins scurrying through notes rapidly.

	0:23	French horns play fragment of Stephen Foster's "Camptown Races."

	0:45	Snare drum and piccolo take up short segment of "fife and drum" music.
	0:57	Trombone plays fragment of "Camptown Races."
	1:14	Strings play opening theme as French horns play fragments of "Camptown Races."

1:47	**15**	0:00	French horn plays a quiet, tender melody that sounds like a Stephen Foster song.

	0:48	French horn repeats songlike melody.
	1:17	Woodwinds and violins play a transitional figure that begins somewhat like "Joy to the World." Then trombones play fragments from slow melody.
	2:04	Violins play scurrying theme again.
	2:22	French horns loudly play fragment of "Camptown Races."

4:31	**16**	0:00	Snare drum and piccolo play short section of "fife and drum" music.
		0:12	Trombones and bassoons play fragment of "Camptown Races."
		0:29	Violins play opening scurrying music and are soon followed by woodwinds and low strings playing fragments of "Camptown Races."
		0:54	Trombones begin portion of "Columbia, the Gem of the Ocean." Other instruments follow.

5:52	**17**	0:00	Cello plays songlike melody as flute plays contrasting figures.
		0:49	Cello repeats songlike melody.
		1:17	Orchestra plays transition.
		1:30	French horns forcefully play part of songlike melody.
		2:13	Trombones and then trumpets play phrase of "Columbia, the Gem of the Ocean."
		2:26	Trumpet plays part of the bugle call "Reveille."

8:22	**18**	0:00	Trombones play very loudly "Columbia, the Gem of the Ocean" while orchestra provides vigorous accompaniment.
		0:26	Series of closing chords.
		0:48	Movement ends after "Reveille," followed by portion of "Columbia, the Gem of the Ocean" and dissonant chord.

Charles Ives

Library of Congress

Charles Ives (1874–1954) was born in Danbury, Connecticut, the son of a bandmaster. His father was no ordinary town bandleader. He encouraged his son to listen carefully and to experiment with different tonal effects. "Stretch your ears" was his advice. So Charles tried such things as retuning the piano and writing for two bands playing different pieces of music while marching toward each other.

Ives attended Yale University as a music student. After graduation he went to New York City, where he made a fortune in the insurance business. He composed his music alone and had little contact with other musicians. Because he had no need to make money, he did not try to have his compositions published and sold. For this reason, for many years almost no one knew about them. Many of them sat in the barn at his country home in Connecticut. Partly because of health problems, he stopped composing around 1915, almost forty years before his death.

Shortly after the turn of the century, Ives was writing novel harmonies and rhythms that did not appear in Europe for another decade. He experimented with

Ives studied composition with Horatio Parker at Yale, but the conservative Parker and the experimental Ives had quite different ideas about what music should be!

such techniques as polytonality, dissonant counterpoint, atonality, polyrhythms, chords with added notes, unusual melodic intervals, and *sprechstimme*. Ives was also fond of weaving fragments of familiar tunes into his works. He seemed to thrive on the element of surprise and what was novel.

Ives's Symphony No. 3, composed between 1901 and 1904, was awarded the Pulitzer Prize in 1947. The insurance man Ives took the seed of American music planted by the tanner Billings a century before and made it flourish. But until the 1940s, no one knew it.

BEST-KNOWN WORKS

orchestra:
- Symphonies Nos. 2 and 3
- *Three Places in New England*
- *The Unanswered Question*

organ:
- Variations on "America"

piano:
- Sonata No. 2 ("Concord")

songs:
- "The Cage"
- "Lincoln, the Great Commoner"

CODA

Although World War I was to leave the United States a world power, the country was still timid about realizing its musical potential. Nevertheless, American music had come a long way from Hopkinson and Billings and would soon assume a leadership role in the world of music.

36 Concert Music since 1920

What changes took place in American concert music in the decades following World War I? In a word, *plenty*! To begin with, American composers and American performers came of age. Over the years, they shed their feelings of musical inferiority and gradually assumed a leadership role in the world as performers and as composers.

Part of the reason for the rise of American music was the nation's good fortune in coming out of both world wars with its land virtually unscathed. True, in both wars thousands of American young men died in combat, but their numbers were nowhere near those of Europe and Japan, and the battles took place thousands of miles away from the shores of the then forty-eight states. America did not become exhausted in a struggle for survival or have its cities decimated, as was true of England, Germany, Japan, Russia, and a host of smaller countries.

Stravinsky, Hindemith, and Schoenberg were but three important composers who came to America.

In addition, a number of outstanding musicians fled to the safety and freedom of the United States prior to and during World War II. These musicians and composers provided America with an enormous musical infusion.

Over the years, America's training of musicians also became better, until it reached a point where it was no longer necessary to study in Europe to achieve success. Of the three composers featured in this chapter—Aaron Copland, Ellen Taaffe Zwilich, and John Adams—only Copland studied overseas for any length of time, and he was almost two generations ahead of Zwilich and Adams. In fact, today thousands of students from Asia and Central and South America, plus some from Europe, come to the United States to study music at American universities and music schools.

The quality and quantity of concert music in the United States have also been advanced by the National Endowment for the Arts (NEA), which was established in 1965. The NEA represents the first promotion of the arts by the federal government. A sizable portion of the NEA's funds are passed on to state arts councils, which in turn cooperate with and support arts efforts in large and small communities throughout the nation. A number of major foundations have also continued or increased their support of music.

The United States and Japan have led the world in the development and use of technology for music making and listening. Starting with the phonograph invented by Thomas Edison in 1877 through radio, television, tape, long-playing records, compact-disc players, and now CD-ROM and DVD, with their music and images, the procession of technological advancement has significantly affected, and continues to affect, the music that people hear and how they listen to it.

Although it is impossible for any three works to give the total picture of the wonderfully rich and diverse conglomeration of American concert music since 1920, Copland, Zwilich, and Adams each represent important aspects of its rich musical fabric.

NATIONALISM

Although Nationalism was one of the features of nineteenth-century Romanticism in Europe, it did not appear in American music until well into the twentieth century. Besides, until then only a small amount of concert music was being composed in America, and those few composers were attempting to emulate European models. The greatest interest in nationalistic music occurred from the 1930s through the 1950s. Composers most associated with this movement were Samuel Barber (1910–1981), Howard Hanson

Courtesy the Kennedy Center for Performing Arts, Washington, DC

A PERFORMANCE AT THE KENNEDY CENTER in Washington, D.C. The center has contributed to the growth of American music at the national level, as has the Public Broadcasting System (PBS).

(1896–1981), Roy Harris (1898–1979), William Schuman (1910–1992), and especially Aaron Copland (1900–1990).

Barber composed *Knoxville: Summer of 1915* and Adagio for Strings. Hanson wrote an opera, *Merry Mount,* and promoted American music as director of the Eastman School of Music for forty years. Harris composed Symphony No. 4 ("Folksong Symphony"). Schuman wrote *New England Triptych* and an opera, *The Mighty Casey.*

Although Charles Ives revealed strong nationalistic tendencies in Symphony No. 2, his music was almost unknown until the 1940s.

COPLAND'S *FANFARE FOR THE COMMON MAN*

A **fanfare** is usually a rather short work for brass instruments, sometimes with percussion included. It's the kind of music associated with the appearance of royalty. But Copland had a more democratic idea. When asked to compose a fanfare for the Cincinnati Symphony Orchestra to play in its 1942–1943 season, during which the United States was involved in World War II, he decided to recognize the common people. Copland sought to honor the people who may not do heroic deeds or carry a royal title but who struggle daily to lead useful, productive lives. This fanfare certainly achieved his goal.

The art of twentieth-century America sometimes expressed a social or political message consonant with the ideals of Copland's *Fanfare for the Common Man. Four Piece*

Aaron Copland

Fanfare for the Common Man (1942–1943)

Genre: Fanfare   Brass and percussion

CD 6 Tracks 19–20
3 minutes 12 seconds

0:00   **19** 0:00   Bass drum, gong, and timpani sound notes followed by rests.

Very deliberately (♩ = ca. 52)

f

0:22	Trumpets play theme.
0:49	Bass drum and timpani.
0:53	Trumpets and French horns play theme.
1:26	Bass drum, gong, and timpani play some of opening music.

1:38   **20** 0:00   Trombones play theme, which is imitated by timpani.

0:41	Trombones, with horns and trumpets imitating, forcefully play theme.
1:06	Trombones and trumpets play theme in augmentation.
1:35	*Fanfare for the Common Man* concludes with a large crescendo.

Orchestra, by the New York painter Ben Shahn, is a political allegory showing a worker, a farmer, and a boss "harmonizing." Notice the simplicity and charm of the painting. It is based on no theories of art; instead, it seeks to project its democratic, egalitarian message in an imaginative way.

Photograph © Scala/Art Resource: © Estate of Ben Shahn/Licensed by VAGA, New York, NY

Four Piece Orchestra by Ben Shahn

A SCENE FROM Copland's ballet *Appalachian Spring*, with Martha Graham dancing the bride's role

COPLAND'S *APPALACHIAN SPRING*

Copland composed *Appalachian Spring* in 1943–1944 for the outstanding choreographer and teacher Martha Graham. It is about the courtship and wedding of a couple in rural Pennsylvania in the 1800s. Copland writes some very American-sounding melodies for it, in addition to using the Shaker song "Simple Gifts." The overall spirit of the ballet is calm and its music often hymnlike, which suits the character of the people being portrayed.

Copland provides this synopsis of the score:

Today *Appalachian Spring* is heard in an orchestral suite that Copland himself arranged.

1. Very slowly. Introduction of the characters, one by one, in a suffused light.

   The bride enters, then the groom, a neighbor, and a revivalist and his flock. The music is built around a motive derived from a major chord. Soon a hymnlike melody emerges.

The interval between the notes of the theme is often four or five steps, which adds to the open, simple sound of the music.

2. Fast. A sudden burst of unison strings in A major arpeggios starts the action. A sentiment both elated and religious gives the keynote of this scene.

   The theme is a lively one that sounds like it could have come from no other country than the United States.

Copland soon combines the high, rapidly moving part with the long notes in the trombones and basses as the flute plays a contrasting line.

3. Duo for bride and her intended—scene of tenderness and passion.

4. Quite fast. The Revivalist and his flock. Folksy feeling—suggestions of square dance and country fiddlers.

5. Still faster. Solo dance of the bride—presentiment of motherhood. Extremes of joy and fear and wonder.

   The music of this section is particularly sensitive and tender.

6. Very slowly (as at first). Transition scene to music reminiscent of the introduction.

   Some of the music of this section is derived from the second section.

7. Calm and flowing. Scenes of daily activity for the bride and her farmer husband. There are variations on a Shaker tune.

   This section of *Appalachian Spring* is presented in the Listening Guide.

   Variation 5 of the preceding section was for many years the theme music for CBS News.

8. The bride takes her place among her neighbors.

   This section is a quiet coda that balances the introduction. The neighbors depart, and the newlyweds remain "quiet and strong in their new house." The music closes with a serene passage for strings, which sounds, in Copland's words, "like a prayer."

   Copland succeeded in writing music that sounds very American. In it he captures the simplicity and strength of a part of American life from its past.

LISTENING GUIDE

AARON COPLAND

Appalachian Spring, Section 7 (1943–1944)

GENRE: Ballet music   Orchestra

CD 2 Tracks 35–37
3 minutes 11 seconds

Form: Theme and variations

| 0:00 | 35 | 0:00 | "Simple Gifts" melody played by clarinet. |

		0:33	Variation 1: Oboe and bassoon.
1:02	36	0:00	Variation 2: Violas play melody in augmentation. Strings follow in imitation.
		0:49	Variation 3: Trumpets and trombones play melody.
2:16	37	0:00	Variation 4: Woodwinds, slowly and softly.
		0:18	Variation 5: Full orchestra in a majestic style.
		0:56	Section 7: Concludes with a full-sounding chord, followed by sustained note by French horn leading to next section.

NEOCLASSICISM

In the decades following World War II, a number of composers in America moved toward a more intellectual, Neoclassical style of music. Most of them composed absolute music. The major composers in this group include Roger Sessions (1896–1985), Elliott Carter (b. 1908), and Ellen Taaffe Zwilich (b. 1939).

ZWILICH'S *CONCERTO GROSSO 1985*

Ellen Taaffe Zwilich's *Concerto Grosso 1985* was commissioned by the Washington Friends of Music to commemorate Handel's three hundredth birthday. Accordingly, she composed a work expressly with Neoclassical elements, including the use of a theme from Handel's Sonata for Violin and Continuo in D Major. Her admiration for the work is clear from what she has said about it. "I performed [it] many years ago, and I especially love the opening theme of the first movement. . . .Throughout [*Concerto Grosso 1985*] I found myself using compositional techniques typical of the Baroque period, including terraced dynamics, repeated phrases . . . techniques I would not normally use, but I felt inspired to do so because of the fact that this piece was based on Handel." Adhering to Neoclassical practice, Zwilich wrote for a small orchestra and includes a harpsichord. She also gives solo instruments, especially the violin and oboe, prominent roles.

The five movements of *Concerto Grosso 1985* follow a symmetrical pattern, with the last one similar to the first, and the fourth matching the second. The first and fifth use passages from Handel's sonata, with the other movements using shorter quotations.

The first movement contrasts majestic-sounding music in twentieth-century style and its angular melody with Handel's theme. Both the old and new lines have one aspect in common: a repeated rhythmic pattern of short-short-long and a similar melodic outline. Zwilich also adds a long pedal tone in the bass that contrasts with the more dissonant lines above it.

Ellen Taaffe Zwilich

Ellen Taaffe Zwilich was born in 1939 in Miami, Florida, the daughter of an airline pilot. She studied music at Florida State University and the Juilliard School before playing violin for several years in the American Symphony Orchestra under Leopold Stokowski. She also studied composition with Roger Sessions and Elliott Carter. In 1969 she married Joseph Zwilich, who died ten years later.

Since 1975 her career has been a series of commissions, awards, and performances by major symphonies under highly esteemed conductors. In addition to the Pulitzer Prize for Symphony No. 1, she has been awarded the Elizabeth Sprague Coolidge Chamber Music Prize and the Arturo Toscanini Music Critics Award and has received two Grammy Award nominations. She has received a Guggenheim Fellowship as well as grants from the New York State Council on the Arts, the Martha Baird Rockefeller Fund for Music, and the National Endowment for the Arts.

Photo courtesy Ray Stanyard, Florida State University *Research In Review*

BEST-KNOWN WORKS

chamber music:
- String Quartet

orchestra:
- *Concerto Grosso 1985*
- Concerto for Trombone
- Symphonies Nos. 1 and 2

LISTENING GUIDE

Concerto Grosso 1985, First Movement (1985)

GENRE: **Concerto grosso** Orchestra

CD 2 Tracks 38–39
2 minutes 43 seconds

Form: *A B A B A B*

0:00	**38**	0:00	Orchestra sounds three sustained notes in unison.
		0:18	Violins play several angular short-short-long figures as opening note continues.

0:35	**39**	0:00	Violins play Handel's theme while low strings and harpsichord play the continuo part.

	0:21	Violins interrupt Handel's theme and play short-short-long figure over a long, low note.
	0:40	Oboe continues Handel's melody accompanied by continuo part.
	0:57	Short-short-long figure returns in violins and alternates with woodwinds.
	1:16	Violins play Handel's melody.
	1:29	Short-short-long figure returns in violins over a sustained low note.
	1:39	Dissonant chord is held while fragments of short-short-long theme appear.
	2:06	Chord grows louder as the movement concludes.

MINIMALISM

At times, twentieth-century composers seemed intent on seeing how *much* they could work into their compositions in terms of techniques and musical ideas. **Minimalism** is a reaction against the technical complexities and highly charged emotional content in much of the concert music of the previous centuries. Minimalist composers are intent on seeing how *little* they can do in their music and yet create something interesting and satisfying to listen to. They take a small amount of musical material and repeat it again and again, usually with small modifications.

The effect on listeners of the continual repetition of Minimalist patterns is almost hypnotic. And with good reason. Minimalist music changes very little and does so at a slow rate. These conditions also contribute to the considerable length of most Minimalist music. Minimalist musicians do not think of their musical works as finished products, but rather as processes. What happens during the music is considered more important than the final result.

Minimalism in music has been largely confined to America. Composers associated with this type of music include Philip Glass (b. 1937), Steve Reich (b. 1936), and John Adams (b. 1947). Glass, who attended the Juilliard School, worked in New York for two years before moving to Paris. While there he was employed copying music for Ravi Shankar, the well-known sitar player. Shankar's Indian music gave Glass an appreciation of the idea of "change within repetition."

Minimalism is sometimes referred to as "trance music," a name that is rejected by Minimalist composers.

Although both Javanese and African music contain much repetition of musical material, Minimalism has been almost exclusively developed by American composers.

Minimalism didn't exactly take off with audiences and critics. Glass had to drive a cab in the daytime and rehearse his group of six players at night. But success did come over time, including music for the award-winning movie *The Thin Blue Line* (1988) and a song collection, *Songs from Liquid Days* (1986) with Paul Simon and Linda Ronstadt. Rock star David Bowie also made a Minimalist pop album called *Low* in 1977.

ADAMS'S *SHORT RIDE IN A FAST MACHINE*

Short Ride in a Fast Machine exudes energy and fun. It is a short work for orchestra and two synthesizers. When asked about the title, Adams responded, "You know how it is when someone asks you to ride in a terrific sports car, and then you wish you hadn't." Appropriately, he uses the descriptive term *delirando,* meaning "frenzied," for the work.

The work was composed in 1986 for the Great Woods Festival in Mansfield, Massachusetts.

Adams shows his Minimalist approach to music by having the brasses play a very rhythmic pattern that evolves as the music flies along:

changes to

changes to

changes to

changes to

JOHN ADAMS
Short Ride in a Fast Machine (1986)

GENRE: **Program music   Orchestra**

LISTENING GUIDE

CD 6 Tracks 21–22
4 minutes 2 seconds

0:00 **21** 0:00   Wood block begins insistent pattern; synthesizers and woodwinds soon join in with faster pattern. Brasses enter with irregular pattern that evolves through several different versions.

0:33   Brasses play even notes; music grows more uneven and dissonant.

1:02   French horns enter with uneven rhythm pattern punctuated by bass drum.

1:43   Brasses play even-note pattern as music gradually grows louder and more dissonant.

2:53 **22** 0:00   Solo trumpet enters. Lower brasses play slow notes in contrast to orchestra.

0:29   Brasses continue long notes as music sounds more majestic; horns play persistently repeated notes.

0:57   Earlier portion of music returns.

1:05   Music grows more frenzied until it abruptly concludes.

John Adams

BEST-KNOWN WORKS

opera:
- *The Death of Klinghoffer*
- *Nixon in China*

orchestra:
- *Harmonielehre*
- *Harmonium*

piano:
- *China Gates*
- *Phrygian Gates*

John Adams was born in 1947 in Worcester, Massachusetts, and grew up in Vermont and New Hampshire. He majored in composition at Harvard, earning both his bachelor's and master's degrees there. In 1971 he accepted a position at the San Francisco Conservatory of Music. From 1978 through 1985 he was composer-in-residence for the San Francisco Symphony. Adams has spoken of himself as "a minimalist who is bored with minimalism."

He has written for a wide range of media: orchestra, opera, video, film, and dance. His most widely seen stage events are his two operas, *Nixon in China* (1987, which was telecast on PBS) and *The Death of Klinghoffer* (1991). The former is about President Richard Nixon's historic visit to China after nearly a quarter century of no formal contact between the two nations. The latter concerns the murder of an elderly New York businessman when a Mediterranean cruise ship is taken over by Palestinian terrorists.

Adams may feel bored with Minimalism, but he gives his music tremendous vitality.

The repetition of rhythmic motives, which mutate as the music moves along, are the basis for the work. Then there are the insistent sounds of the wood block. The music tends to propel itself to its frenzied conclusion.

CODA

And, best of all, listeners can return as often as they wish to the banquet!

Listeners considering the American concert music scene are like people standing in front of a magnificent buffet table filled with interesting and attractive foods. Which delicious foods should they put on their music plates today? The Neoclassicism of Zwilich, the quotation music of George Crumb (b. 1929), the Postminimalism of Adams, the experimental music of Cage, the electronic music of Varèse (b. 1933), the nationalistic music of Copland, or the Neo-Romantic works of Howard Hanson and Samuel Barber? What an abundance! What wonderful musical opportunities are waiting to be enjoyed!

Popular Music *and* Jazz *to* 1950

37

Music critic Sigmund Spaeth has asserted that the history of popular music "is an index to the life and history of a nation." All music is an index to some extent, of course, but the popular and folk types seem more closely attuned to experiences of a majority of the people of a nation than music created for the concert hall. In any case, popular music merits investigation.

The term **popular music** implies music that is widely known, usually through commercial enterprises such as sheet music publishers, record companies, and radio and television. In contrast, folk music is passed among the people on an informal basis with little or no commercial involvement. Furthermore, popular music is much more closely involved with business and economics than is concert music. Although money certainly plays a role in concert music, that role is not nearly as important as it is in popular music.

The popular music discussed here is mostly secular. Large amounts of religious music existed as well, but in white churches the traditional music inherited from Europe prevailed. A rich musical tradition also developed in black churches, but only recently have scholarly investigations been conducted in this area. A definite relationship existed between religious and secular music in both black and white churches, which is what one would expect, but there were also noticeable differences.

> The terms *popular music* and *folk music* are general. There are always exceptions to these generalizations.

POPULAR MUSIC BEFORE 1850

The popular music of colonial America and the early days of the new nation was heavily European in character. Its dances were originally the same ones found in Paris and London. After the Revolutionary War, these dances fell out of favor because of their association with European monarchies, and country dances largely replaced them. For example, a dance imported from France, the cotillion, became the quadrille. It eventually developed into the square dance, which became very popular in nineteenth-century America and is still danced today.

Not much is known about the popular music in the early days of America. Secular songs were not published with words and music together until nearly 1700. Prior to that time, song sheets contained only words. The people then must have been guided by an oral tradition regarding which tunes to sing with which set of words, because often the sheets did not indicate a tune. Even if a tune was indicated, that information is of limited usefulness to researchers today, because sometimes the same tune was known by different names.

> As discussed in Chapter 41, the words to popular songs were printed on sheets of paper called *broadsides*.

The **parlor song** was an important type of popular music in early nineteenth-century America. These songs were purchased in sheet music form and sung in the homes of the rapidly expanding middle class. They generally required only modest music-making skill. All of them were in major keys—even the sad songs. The accompaniments, which were usually played on the piano or small pump organ, were rather easy. Many of them were based on Irish folk melodies, which can partly be explained by the large number of Irish immigrants who came to the United States during those years.

The texts and moods of parlor songs were usually sentimental and filled with nostalgia, and they often dealt with death. One well-known song of this type was "The Ocean Burial," which began with the words "O! Bury me not in the deep, deep sea." Later this song was transformed into "O! Bury Me Not on the Lone Prairie," and it became one of the more popular cowboy songs.

> It is hard for us today to understand the appeal of sentimental music, just as it would be difficult for people who lived in the nineteenth century to understand why songs today often have so little sentimental quality.

A few popular soloists or groups toured America prior to the Civil War. One was the Englishman Henry Russell (1812–1900). Although he spent only about seven years in the United States, he greatly influenced Stephen Foster and the Hutchinson Family Singers.

The Hutchinson family consisted of three brothers and their sister, and they reached the height of their popularity in the 1840s. Many songs sung by Russell and the Hutchinsons promoted social causes. One song, "The Maniac," drew attention to the terrible conditions in mental asylums at the time. Other songs dealt with women's rights, the abolition of slavery, and the evils of alcohol. Sometimes the music of the Hutchinsons and similar performers was presented in melodramatic scenes that included acting.

> People today would find such melodramatics comical, but audiences at the time were impressed.

FOSTER'S "BEAUTIFUL DREAMER"

"Beautiful Dreamer" is a good example of the sentimental parlor song that was popular in the nineteenth century. Its gentle, quaint text seems to us to come from another age, which in fact is the case. The song nevertheless has a tender charm and beauty that is still appealing.

LISTENING GUIDE

STEPHEN FOSTER
"Beautiful Dreamer" (1863)

GENRE: Parlor Song **Soloist and piano**

CD 6 Track 23
3 minutes 28 seconds

Form: Strophic

0:00 **23** 0:00 Short introduction played by piano with a cello.

0:16 Singer begins:

Moderato

Beau - ti - ful dream - er   wake un - to   me, _____

> *Beautiful dreamer, wake unto me,*
> *Starlight and dew drops are waiting for thee;*
> *Sounds of the rude world heard in the day,*
> *Lull'd by the moonlight have all pass'd away!*

0:49 Contrasting section:

> *Beautiful dreamer, queen of my song,*
> *List while I woo thee with soft melody;*

1:06 Opening melody returns:

> *Gone are the cares of life's busy throng*
> *Beautiful dreamer, awake unto me!*
> *(last phrase repeated)*

1:32 Introduction played again.

1:47 Second verse:

> *Beautiful dreamer, out on the sea*
> *Mermaids are haunting the wild lorelie;*
> *Over the streamlet vapors are borne,*
> *Waiting to fade at the bright coming morn.*

> *Beautiful dreamer, beam on my heart,*
> *E'en as the morn on the streamlet and sea;*
> *Then will all clouds of sorrow depart,*
> *Beautiful dreamer awake unto me!*
> *(last phrase repeated)*

3:28 Song closes with a few measures played by piano and cello.

Stephen Foster

© Foster Hall Collection: Center for American Music, University of Pittsburgh

The most popular composer of his time was **Stephen Collins Foster** (1826–1864). He was the ninth child in a prosperous family that lived near Pittsburgh, Pennsylvania. He revealed his sensitive, artistic nature as a boy, but his interest in music was discouraged by his family, who simply could not understand it. In 1846 he went to Cincinnati to work as a bookkeeper for his brother. In his spare time, he wrote songs. About half of them were for the popular minstrel shows, and the other half were the more sentimental parlor songs. In 1848 Foster sold "Oh! Susanna" for one hundred dollars. It quickly became a hit with the forty-niners on their way to the goldfields of California.

"Oh! Susanna" was so popular that soon twenty editions of it appeared, nineteen of them pirated!

Foster's music is generally associated with the South, even though he lived for only a few months in Bardstown, Kentucky, about forty miles south of

Foster never saw the Suwannee River in northern Florida. He liked the sound of its name, which he changed slightly to "Swannee."

Louisville, and made only one boat trip to New Orleans. But something about the African American songs he heard along the Ohio River and around Bardstown must have made a great impression on him. Some of his songs idealized life in the South, but his attempts at black dialect in some of them can at times obscure their melodic charm.

By 1860 Foster seemed to lose his ability to compose attractive songs. He moved to New York to give his career a boost, but the move did not help. He began drinking heavily, and his wife left him. He died in 1864 at the age of thirty-eight after an accident in a Bowery flophouse. A piece of paper with the words "Dear friends and gentle people" was found in his pocket. Perhaps it was an idea for another song by the composer of some of America's favorite music.

BEST-KNOWN WORKS

songs:
- "Beautiful Dreamer"
- "Camptown Races"
- "Hard Times"
- "Jeannie with the Light Brown Hair"
- "My Old Kentucky Home"
- "Oh! Susanna"

Hoping to cash in on Foster's death, his publisher claimed that this song was his last, which it was not. The publisher had bought the song from Foster and had the plates engraved a year or so before he died, but for some unknown reason had not yet released it.

By the time of the Civil War (1861–1865), a popular music–publishing industry was in place. Sheet music was to popular composers at that time what recordings are to popular music today. Without sheet music, it would have been impossible for most people to know the music of Foster or other songwriters.

The Civil War spawned quite a few new songs, or old songs with new words. A few of these, especially Julia Ward Howe's "The Battle Hymn of the Republic" and Dan Emmett's "Dixie," are still sung today.

Some Civil War songs had two sets of words, one for the Union and the other for the Confederacy. Even the melody of "The Star-Spangled Banner" had different words set to it.

TOWARD TIN PAN ALLEY AND RAGTIME

Following the Civil War, America witnessed rapid territorial and economic expansion. It was also a time of social unrest and of social causes such as the antisaloon movement. During these years there was much victimization of Native Americans, and the robber barons who built the railroads amassed their fortunes. For the first twenty-five years following the Civil War, popular songs looked to the past more than to the future.

The transcontinental railroad linking the east and west was completed only four years after the end of the Civil War.

Tin Pan Alley

Tin Pan Alley started at 28th Street, then moved to 42nd Street, and finally to the Brill Building on 47th Street.

Beginning about twenty years before the end of the nineteenth century, popular music changed with the emergence of a nationwide music industry for the promotion and publication of songs. The center of this industry was New York City, which dominated both musical theater and popular music. The origin of the term **Tin Pan Alley** has never been clearly determined, and neither has its location. Essentially, it referred to the popular music industry, much as the word *Hollywood* refers to the motion picture industry today.

It was (and still is) the nature of the commercial music industry to issue a huge number of songs, most of which had very short lives. Most of the songs barely paid their printing costs. But every so often, a song came along that made its composer and publisher wealthy. The first to reach into the millions in sales was the early 1890s song "After the Ball" by Charles K. Harris.

"After the Ball" sold 10 million copies at about fifty cents a copy.

The payment to performers was an early version of a now illegal practice later known as *payola*.

To amass large numbers of sales, publishers hired "pluggers" to go into music and department stores to play and sing the publisher's music for the customers. A number of well-known songwriters began as pluggers—Irving Berlin, Jerome Kern, George Gershwin, and others. In addition, publishers made outright payments to performers, who were then mostly in vaudeville, to perform particular songs.

The decade of the 1890s was termed the *Gay Nineties* because it was relatively prosperous and trouble-free.

The lyrics of "The Bowery" tell of the naughty things people say and do there. It is said that the song reduced property values in that part of lower Manhattan for a while.

Tin Pan Alley songs of the 1890s were remarkably similar to one another. They were set in 3/4 waltzlike meter, had a form that consisted of a lead-in verse and a chorus in thirty-two-measure form (*a a b a*, each with eight measures), and simple harmony. Some of these Gay Nineties songs include "Meet Me in St. Louis" (a song promoting the World's Fair there in 1904), "In My Merry Oldsmobile," and "The Bowery." There were some songs about women betrayed ("Only a Bird in a Gilded Cage") and some Irish American songs ("My Wild Irish Rose" and "Who Threw the Overalls in Mistress Murphy's Chowder?").

Ragtime

Ragtime existed in two related forms. One form consisted of popular songs; it was popular between 1890 and 1920. The other form was for piano and was a forerunner of jazz. Ragtime songs were usually peppy tunes in 2/4 meter with a lot of syncopation. Some of

© Corbis-Bettmann

Scott Joplin

Scott Joplin (1868–1917) was born near Texarkana, Texas. He showed much musical talent, learning to play the banjo, and to some extent the piano, on his own. He then studied with a local classically trained teacher and began a career as an itinerant pianist. He settled for a number of years in Sedalia, Missouri, where he played at the Maple Leaf Club, which provided the name for his most successful ragtime piece. In 1899 "Maple Leaf Rag" sold 1 million copies.

In 1900 Joplin moved to St. Louis to work more closely with his publisher, John Stark. Two years later his first major composition was a ballet suite that included ragtime music. An opera, *Guest of Honor*, followed, but the music for it has

since been lost. In 1907 Joplin moved to New York and wrote an instruction book on ragtime music, which over time earned him the informal title "King of Ragtime." After his contract with Stark ran out in 1909, he made many piano rolls. Joplin also devoted much of his attention to an opera, *Treemonisha*, for which he wrote both the libretto and the music and planned the choreography. It was not successful and was performed only once during his lifetime in 1915. The opera's failure contributed to his failing health. By 1916 he had to be institutionalized, and he lived less than two more years. *Treemonisha* was published and staged in 1972 and awarded the Pulitzer Prize in 1976.

the better-known titles include "Hot Time in the Old Town," Irving Berlin's "Alexander's Ragtime Band," which is basically a march instead of a rag, and "Way Down Yonder in New Orleans."

Rags have balanced phrasing and key centers, two beats to the measure, and catchy melodies with lots of syncopation accompanied by steady, even chords in the bass. They are sectional in form.

Although many ragtime songs were written, today rags are known almost exclusively as solo piano music. The most recognized composers of piano rags were Ben Harney (1871–1938), Tom Turpin (1873–1922), and, most notable of all, Scott Joplin.

The rise of piano rags paralleled the rapid increase in the sales of pianos in America between 1890 and 1920, after which a decline began. Piano rags also benefited from the development of the mechanical player piano, which was operated by small holes punched in rolls of paper that were pulled across pneumatic tubes connected to the keys. In fact, some rags existed only on piano rolls and not on sheet music. The performance of "Maple Leaf Rag" on the ancillary CD was originally a piano roll made by Joplin himself.

Ragtime did not follow the path through Tin Pan Alley to the public, as did most popular music. Instead, its home was the large and small cities of the Midwest—St. Louis, Sedalia, and Kansas City, Missouri; Moline, Illinois; New Albany, Indiana; Oskaloosa, Iowa; as well as Memphis and Indianapolis.

Three major developments in the 1920s brought an end to ragtime and major changes in the popular music industry:

1. The rapid demise of sheet music and piano roll sales and a corresponding rise in the sale of recordings.

2. The advent and development of commercial broadcasting. In January 1922 there were twenty-eight broadcasting stations; by December of that year there were 570.

3. The introduction of sound motion pictures in 1927. Within two years of that date, 320 songwriters and composers were working in Hollywood.

> "Hot Time in the Old Town" is reported to have been based on a song heard in a famous St. Louis bordello.

> Piano rags, as many a pianist has discovered, are not easy to play well. Both Harney and Joplin wrote instruction books for playing them.

SCOTT JOPLIN
"Maple Leaf Rag" (1899)

GENRE: Ragtime music   Piano

CD 6 Tracks 24–27
2 minutes 38 seconds

Form: *a a b b a c c d d*

0:00	24	0:00	The section (or *strain*) begins in major with steady chords and syncopated melody.

		0:19	The strain repeated.
0:36	25	0:00	The strain begins higher and descends.
		0:18	The strain repeated.
		0:36	The strain returns.
1:29	26	0:00	The strain begins in a new major key.
		0:17	The strain repeated.
2:03	27	0:00	The strain returns in original major key.
		0:17	The strain repeated.
		0:35	"Maple Leaf Rag" ends with two solid chords.

LISTENING GUIDE

Another musical phenomenon affected American popular music in a profound way in the 1920s and 1930s: the popularization of jazz.

BLUES

The **blues** began as folk music (their musical characteristics are discussed in Chapter 41), but a few words listing musical features can't provide the true flavor of the blues. Beyond their lowered notes in the scale and *a a b* pattern of lines covering twelve measures, there is something about a singer's tone quality, small shadings of intonation, and basic melancholy feeling that makes the blues sound "blue." The vocalist always sings alone of his or her personal and usually unhappy feelings; blues songs are not for a vocal ensemble.

The first publication of blues dates back to 1912, but the high point of their popularity came in the 1920s and early 1930s with performances by vaudeville singers. The best-known blues singers were Ma Rainey (Gertrude Pridgett, 1886–1939) and Bessie Smith.

Bessie Smith is often referred to as the "Empress of the Blues."

SMITH'S "LOST YOUR HEAD BLUES"

Bessie Smith recorded "Lost Your Head Blues" in 1926. She is joined on the recording by two other jazz greats: Fletcher Henderson on piano and Joe Smith on trumpet. Although each *a* line is repeated, Smith varies it slightly.

LISTENING GUIDE

BESSIE SMITH
"Lost Your Head Blues" (1926)

GENRE: Blues   Soloist, piano, trumpet

CD 6 Track 28
2 minutes 52 seconds

Form: Strophic, *a a b*

0:00 **28** 0:00   Short introduction.

0:11   The *a* line is based entirely on tonic, or I, chord. Short trumpet break follows Bessie's singing.

I was with you baby when you did not have a dime.

0:22   Repeat of *a* line is mostly based on subdominant, or IV, chord, but returns to tonic at the end. Another trumpet break follows.

I was with you baby when you did not have a dime.

0:32   The *b* line is mostly based on dominant, or V, chord, but concludes on tonic, followed by a trumpet break.

Now since you got plenty money you have throw'd you good gal down.

The rest of the verses follow the same pattern, except for the final verse, when the breaks also occur in the middle of lines.

0:43   *Once ain't for always, two ain't for twice. (Repeat)*
When you get a good gal, you better treat her nice.

1:16   *When you were lonesome, I tried to treat you kind. (Repeat)*
But since you've got money, it's done changed your mind.

1:48   *I'm gonna leave, baby, ain't gonna say goodbye. (Repeat)*
But I'll write you and tell you the reason why.

2:19   *Days are lonesome, nights are long. (Repeat)*
I'm a good old gal, but I've just been treated wrong.

2:52   Song concludes quietly.

Bessie Smith

Bessie Smith (1894–1937) was born in Tennessee but was "discovered" singing in Selma, Alabama. She was contracted by Columbia Records in New York. Between 1924 and 1927 her recordings of the blues sold more than 2 million discs, making her the highest-paid black performer of the time. She died as the result of an automobile accident in 1937.

In popular music, and certainly in the blues, the performer is far more important than the writer of the music; often he or she is hardly mentioned. Smith was successful because she projected a magnetism that comes through even though the recordings of the 1920s lack the fidelity of recordings today. But her success can be attributed even more to her expressive singing voice and style. She adjusted her tone quality and added subtle nuances in pitches to make her singing memorable.

© Getty/Archive

JAZZ

The roots of **jazz** are complex, but certainly some of them reach back to the African heritage of African Americans. Other influences include minstrel show music, work songs, blues, French-Creole and Latin American music, and especially ragtime.

The traditional beginning of jazz lies with the brass bands that played for funerals in New Orleans. As a part of the procession to the grave site, the band played solemn versions of hymns like "Nearer My God to Thee." After the burial, the band would assemble a couple of blocks away from the cemetery and break into a ragtime version of a hymn or tune like "Didn't He Ramble." The bands were competitive in their ability in *cutting* or *bucking*, the terms for such playing. The style eventually moved to the red-light district and the bordellos of New Orleans.

Like folk music, jazz was created by generally untrained musicians who could not have written down what they played or sang, even had they wanted to. But it differs in two ways: (1) It sprang up in the cities, so its roots are urban; and (2) only a few people perform jazz, while many listen.

> These bands were small by today's standards.

> The "jazz funeral" is still practiced in New Orleans today.

> Some of the early jazz musicians didn't want to learn to read music because they claimed it might hinder their creative abilities.

Elements of Jazz

MELODY   The most notable feature of jazz melodies is the **blue notes.** These notes are created by altering the major scale by lowering the third, fifth, or seventh steps. The chords that accompany these notes are not altered, however, so there is a dissonance between the lowered melody note and the note in the chord. The result, however, is not so much dissonance as it is a particular tonal effect.

HARMONY   Traditional jazz harmony is as conservative as a church hymn. Most chords consist of the three primary triads used for harmonizing most simple songs: tonic (I), dominant (V), and subdominant (IV). As jazz matured, however, its harmonic palette became much richer and more sophisticated.

RHYTHM   Jazz assumed many of the rhythmic characteristics of ragtime—a meter of two beats per measure combined with a countless variety of syncopated melodic figures. Jazz rhythms cannot be written precisely in traditional notation. Jazz musicians make small deviations in timing and emphasis, which most trained musicians cannot execute without guidance and practice.

JOE "KING" OLIVER'S CREOLE JAZZ BAND

Bettmann/Corbis

The plunger mute was originally a rubber sink plunger.

TIMBRE Jazz has its own tonal colors. Certain instruments and certain styles of playing have become associated with jazz. The saxophone was intended to be a concert instrument, but jazz players took it up and produced a different timbre. Brass instruments in jazz often use mutes. Some of these mutes have distinctive names, such as *cup, wah-wah,* and *plunger*.

The style of singing jazz is quite different from that used for singing an art song or a folk song. Jazz singers employ more colors and "bend" the pitch for expressive effect.

The idea of "note bending" was a vocal technique derived from field hollers. It was picked up by instrumentalists and used in jazz.

FORM Jazz has no overall form that applies to all its styles. The form generally consists of a series of variations on a simple harmonic pattern. As mentioned previously, the blues have a traditional pattern of three lines set in an *a a b* pattern. Sometimes the singer does not sing all the way through a section, and an instrumentalist fills in with a short solo called a *break*.

IMPROVISATION Making up music on the spot is fundamental to jazz. Traditionally, jazz was not written down, but, as it developed, it was often arranged with at least some of the music notated. The extemporaneous creation of music gives jazz an ever-fresh quality. Improvising in jazz is based on the chords of the tune. Players are not confined to just the notes of the chords, especially as jazz has evolved, but they are aware of them and make up their music accordingly.

The key can be decided in a few seconds. Jazz musicians are usually "easy" about such things.

Typically, the players in a jazz performance agree that they will play a certain piece in a particular key. They also agree on an order in which each player is featured, although it can be changed during the performance by a nod of the head. Each player in turn improvises a chorus while keeping in mind the harmony of the song. Often for the final time through the piece, everyone joins in simultaneous improvised counterpoint. Only the musical instincts and good ears of the players, as well as the basic chord patterns of the piece, keep the music together.

Often during jazz improvisation, the melody can no longer be detected in the mosaic of sound. This happens because players sound many notes in addition to the former melody, and the tune becomes pretty well obscured.

Types of Jazz

The U.S. Navy had Storyville shut down because it was concerned about its impact on the physical and moral health of the servicemen.

Until the end of World War I, jazz had been mostly confined to the South, especially New Orleans. A number of factors led to the movement "up the river" to St. Louis, Chicago, and other cities in the North. One was the closing of Storyville, the red-light district in New Orleans. Many jazz musicians who worked in the bordellos lost their jobs and had to seek work elsewhere.

In addition, during World War I many young men, who had previously never thought they would see much more than the area where they grew up, were assigned to military camps and bases all over the United States. Furthermore, travel between cities by train was easy and not too expensive, if one was willing to ride coach class. If a jazz piano player lost his job in New Orleans, he could buy a ticket and head for St. Louis or Chicago. One of the best-known bands to make such a move was Joe "King" Oliver's Creole Jazz Band.

DIXIELAND   The predominant type of jazz in the 1920s was **Dixieland.** It consisted of music in two beats to the measure with a strong upbeat and a "busy" quality when several players were improvising at the same time. The bands were small, usually four to seven players. Originally, they did not include drums; keeping the beat was the piano player's job. Drums were added in later years. Dixieland bands loved to describe their music as being "hot," which meant that it was somewhat faster and louder than people were accustomed to at the time.

The song "Come Back, Sweet Papa" is a good example of Dixieland style. The tune was written by Paul Barbarin and Bob Russell, but in jazz what the players do with a tune is much more important than the original tune. If a recording had been made of "Come Back, Sweet Papa" a day or even a few minutes after the version on the ancillary CDs, it would be similar but not exactly the same, because the players make up some of what they play as they go along.

"Come Back, Sweet Papa" was recorded by Louis Armstrong and his Hot Five in Chicago on February 22, 1926. On the recording Armstrong plays cornet. Other instruments heard on the recording are trombone, sax/clarinet (the same player doubling), piano, and banjo. The recording has a twangy quality, due largely to the inadequacies of recording equipment in 1926. It could be remastered today to sound "warmer," but why? Part of its charm lies in its original timbre.

Scat singing was an instrumental style of singing introduced by Armstrong in a recording of a song called "Heebie Jeebie." It sets syllable sounds without meaning to an improvised vocal line. The sounds are usually sung quite quickly.

> What was "hot" in the 1920s seems rather tame to most listeners today.

> Notice that there are no drums in the Hot Five.

> The most famous scat singer was Ella Fitzgerald.

LOUIS ARMSTRONG
"Come Back, Sweet Papa" (1926)

GENRE: Dixieland jazz   Trumpet, trombone, sax/clarinet, bass

CD 6 Track 29
2 minutes 32 seconds

Form: Variations on tune

0:00	29	0:00	Short introduction played by trumpet and saxophone.
		0:08	Sax plays chorus.
		0:28	Sax repeats chorus.
		0:48	Trumpet takes up chorus as trombone adds melodic figures.
		1:08	Trumpet repeats chorus.
		1:27	Trombone plays sliding notes (glissando), and trumpet continues as clarinet improvises contrasting part.
		1:49	Piano plays chorus.
		2:08	Clarinet, trumpet, and trombone play chorus together.
		2:32	Piece concludes with characteristic rhythm figure.

© Corbis-Bettmann

LOUIS ARMSTRONG

Louis Armstrong & Duke Ellington

Louis Armstrong (1900–1971) was born on the Fourth of July into a poor and unstable New Orleans family. As a boy he became involved with street life and at the age of twelve was sentenced by the juvenile court to the Colored Waifs' Home. It was there that he learned to play the cornet. After two years in the home, he was released; he did odd jobs and played whenever the opportunity presented itself.

Good fortune struck when Joe "King" Oliver took an interest in Armstrong, including sending him jobs that he couldn't accept himself. In 1919 Oliver moved to Chicago, and Armstrong was recognized as the best trumpet player in New Orleans. Two years later Oliver telegraphed Armstrong to join him in Chicago. Two years after that, Fletcher Henderson offered him a job with his outstanding band in New York.

Armstrong's first name is pronounced "Loo-ie," which indicates the French tradition in his native New Orleans. He also acquired the nickname "Satchmo" for "satchel mouth."

After leaving Henderson's band some years later, Armstrong led several groups of his own, including the Hot Five. By the 1940s he was featured on many radio shows and appeared in a number of films. His last movie was *Hello, Dolly!* In his later years, he sang as much as he played. He served as a goodwill emissary for the U.S. State Department on a number of worldwide tours.

Armstrong was once asked to define jazz. He replied to the effect that "If you don't know, I can't explain it."

Armstrong is considered the first great improvising soloist. He established a high standard of performance that has lasted for generations. In so many ways, he caught the elusive quality and joy of jazz.

Octave tremolos are the rapid alternation between two notes an octave apart.

BOOGIE-WOOGIE After the Great Depression hit in 1929, for economic reasons people often hired only a piano player rather than a six- or seven-piece band. This situation encouraged the development of a type of jazz piano playing called **boogie-woogie.** It features a persistently repeated bass figure over which the player improvises trills, octave tremolos, and other melodic figures. Boogie-woogie was often called "eight to the bar," because the repeated bass part has eight notes per measure.

SWING By 1935 jazz had progressed from small groups improvising in Dixieland style to intricate arrangements for bands of twelve to nineteen players. Much of their music was written down. Many pieces were played in four rather fast beats per measure, and the

DUKE ELLINGTON

Edward Kennedy "Duke" Ellington (1899–1975) lived a very different life from that of Louis Armstrong. Ellington was born in Washington, D.C., into the middle-class family of a butler. He studied both art and music when he was young, and his piano lessons included instruction in the popular ragtime style of the day. Although he was successful in his art studies, he decided on music and formed a band that played at social events in the Washington, D.C., area.

Ellington's interest in art is reflected in a number of his song titles that mention colors, including "Mood Indigo" and "Black, Brown, and Beige."

In 1923 he joined a five-piece combo called The Washingtonians and went to New York. Success didn't come easily, but three years later he was playing at the Cotton Club, which at that time was the most expensive nightclub in Harlem. It catered to white audiences who wanted to hear good jazz.

Over the years, Ellington's band was responsible for many musical innovations, including echo chambers in recordings to increase reverberation (which became standard practice later), the flatted fifth, the amplified bass, and the baritone saxophone. By the 1950s his group seemed to be declining after twenty years, but a stunning performance at the Newport Jazz Festival in 1956 revived it. He composed a number of sacred works in his later years and made goodwill tours for the U.S. State Department.

Ellington's compositions were partially group efforts. He would begin playing a musical idea on the piano, and other members of the band would join in and add ideas. He would then massage these ideas into a final composition. Duke Ellington and his band left a legacy of elegant jazz.

Jazz bands were noted for a high turnover rate. Not so with Ellington. For example, Harry Carney, his baritone sax player, was with him for forty-seven years!

---

chords were far more complex than they had been in earlier jazz. The term **swing** may well have come from the bouncy quality of the music.

The Swing Era was a time when audiences danced. Its concert halls were such places as the Roseland Ballroom in New York and the Palladium in Hollywood. It was also a time when the more successful bands had regular broadcasts over national radio networks.

Improvisation was still an important part of swing. Arrangers marked places for a soloist to *ad lib*—to improvise at liberty or at will. And there were many outstanding soloists: Gene Krupa on drums, Harry James on trumpet, Coleman Hawkins on saxophone, Artie Shaw and Benny Goodman on clarinet, and others. It was also the era of outstanding bands: Glenn Miller, Paul Whiteman, Les Brown, Count Basie, Woody Herman, and especially Duke Ellington. These bands had outstanding arrangers who had as much to do with the musical results as the composers of the tunes. Ellington's "Take the 'A' Train" is typical of swing music.

The Swing Era was also known as the Big Band Era.

LISTENING GUIDE

DUKE ELLINGTON
"Take the 'A' Train" (1941)

GENRE: Big band jazz   Large jazz band

CD 2 Tracks 40–41
2 minutes 26 seconds

Form: *a a b a*

40 0:00   Short introduction, then saxes play first part (*a*) of the tune.

0:17   Saxes repeat first part of the tune.

0:29 **41 0:00**   Saxes play a contrasting section (*b*).

0:11   Saxes play *a* part again.

0:22   Saxes play *a* variant of the tune as a muted trumpet improvises contrasting part.

0:33   Variant of *a* section is repeated.

0:46   Muted trumpet continues with *b*.

0:57   Trumpet and saxes repeat variant of *a*.

1:08   Modulation to new key.

1:14   Saxes embellish variant of *a* as trumpet improvises. Then variant is repeated.

1:37   Trumpet and saxes play variant of *b*, concluding with a cascading chord sounded by trumpets and trombones.

1:48   Saxes play original *a* tune against lively rhythmic pattern in trumpets.

1:59   Saxes quietly repeat part of *a* several times as music slowly fades.

2:26   "Take the 'A' Train" concludes quietly with a long chord.

CODA

From the broadsides of colonial days, to the parlor songs of the nineteenth century, to the piano rags at the turn of the century, to the big-band arrangements of jazz in the middle of the twentieth century, American popular music has paralleled the changes in American society. It has indeed been an index of life in the United States.

Popular Music since 1950

38

In many ways America today is not all that different from America in 1950. Its governmental structure and economic system are virtually unchanged, and most of its core beliefs and values are still somewhat intact. But in other ways, America has moved far from what it was in 1950.

A number of these changes have had a major impact on music, and especially on popular music.

- The population of the United States has almost tripled since 1950. Therefore, several segments of it easily became large enough to draw the attention of the media and make the marketing of specially oriented products, including music, well worthwhile.

- The decade of roughly 1947–1956 saw a huge increase in the number of children born, partly because veterans of World War II had to delay having families until after the war.

- The general economic level of the United States reached new heights. Most teenagers are able to buy recordings, movie tickets, and clothes and other products especially created for them as never before.

- Television replaced radio as the prime form of mass-media entertainment. Network radio, which in the 1930s and 1940s had been an extremely important cultural force, almost disappeared except for its news function. Instead, hundreds of local radio stations sprang up, many of which catered to audiences of a particular age level or ethnic group. Most of these stations survived (and often thrived) by playing recordings of popular music interspersed with spot commercials.

- Recordings could be produced and marketed by small companies, which greatly reduced the influence of the few large record companies that had controlled the industry in the previous decades. These small companies were much more innovative and responsive to changes in audience tastes than the established companies. Without these new companies, many of the developments in popular music would have happened much more slowly, if indeed at all.

- America's minority populations became much more conscious and proud of their particular identities. For quite a few years, most whites could not understand the feelings that the "Black is beautiful" slogan and the words of Malcolm X evoked in African Americans. The awareness of ethnic and racial identity greatly influenced people's choices in popular music.

Baby boomers are a very large and significant age group in the population of the United States.

THE POPULAR MUSIC INDUSTRY

The years since 1950 have witnessed a major expansion of the mass marketing of commercial popular music. The industry continued to produce a large number of songs, very few of which would be successful. But the few that became "hits" made huge amounts of money for the recording company, publisher, and performer.

One of the causes for the expansion was increased economic prosperity, which meant that more money was available for the products that the under-twenty-one market wanted, including music. Another factor was the sizable increase in population of the United States. By the turn of this century there were more than 30 million teenagers, and it is estimated that they were able to spend more than 150 *billion* dollars.

The sales of popular music are mostly to young people under the age of twenty-one, and the industry focuses almost all its efforts on them.

ROCK BAND KISS PERFORMING IN COSTUME Bass player Gene Simmons of KISS sticks out his tongue as he jams with guitarist Paul Stanley.

The years since 1950 have also been a time of rapidly increased means of hearing music. From the long-playing records in the 1950s to CDs to the downloading of songs from the Internet on handheld devices, music became far more available. In addition, it has became even more pervasive in society, as music is heard nearly everywhere one goes, a fact that was pointed out in Chapter 1.

Only a few recording companies exerted control of much of the popular music industry prior to 1950. That situation ended, and soon many different record labels and types of popular music became available. Over the years the industry and performers learned that bad publicity is better than good publicity, and certainly better than no publicity. For example, to keep her name before the public, the performer Madonna (Madonna Louise Ciccone) tried to alter her "bad-girl" image to a "good-girl" image in a matter of just a couple of years. Others wore bizarre clothing or makeup when performing. Some performers resorted to sensationalism or repulsive acts such as biting off the head of a bat during a concert.

> What matters to Madonna and other performers is that people are aware of them, even if it's not in a positive way.

Although popular music is more of a sociological and economic phenomenon than it is musical, a small number of popular performers and musicians have created some truly imaginative pieces of music. Some of the time these works represent crossovers between popular and concert music. In other cases popular performers have demonstrated much creativity and originality. Whatever the case, popular music is a fascinating mix of many kinds of music that have been influenced by a number of factors. No discussion of it, even one the size of an entire book, can do it justice.

BLUES AND SOUL

Two of the main types of American popular music were born in the rural South. And just as the South was segregated on the basis of race until a few decades ago, its popular music also had strong racial associations. The *blues* is the music of the blacks, and *country* is the music of the whites.

Blues began as a type of folk music, as described in Chapter 41. As many African Americans migrated over the years from the South to the cities of the North, the blues moved with them. It spoke of the harsh life that they encountered in the northern cities.

The acoustic guitar was replaced by the electric guitar, and piano, drums, and other instruments were added to accompany the singers. The music became louder than before, and blues singers often adopted a shouting style, even though they usually used a microphone. The style of piano playing was similar to what was used in boogie-woogie, with its heavy left-hand repeated patterns. Drums were eventually added as well.

Rhythm and Blues

By the 1950s saxophones and backup vocal ensembles had completed the migration of the blues from the country to the city. And it had acquired a new commercial name: **rhythm and blues.** Entertainers such as Chuck Berry (b. 1926) and Bo Diddley (Elias McDaniel, b. 1928) created a music that became the basis of rock and roll, which began to appear in the mid-1950s.

Motown Records was a major force in promoting rhythm and blues. It was founded in Detroit in 1958 by then auto worker and part-time songwriter Barry Gordy, with seven hundred dollars he borrowed from his credit union. At first success was limited. The real breakthrough happened in 1964 with a recording of "Where Did Our Love Go?" by the Supremes.

Motown Records carefully developed its stars and their recordings, including choreography and arrangements slicked up for white audiences. In addition to the Supremes, its major stars were Smokey Robinson, The Temptations, Stevie Wonder, and Michael Jackson, who began as a boy singing with his brothers but later moved to solo appearances during his three-decade-long career. In 1988 Motown Record Corporation was sold to MCA, Inc., for $61 million.

The name *Motown* is a contraction of "Motor Town," a nickname sometimes given Detroit. Gordy once described the Motown sound as "rats, roaches, struggle, talent, guts, love."

That's 87,142 times the value of Gordy's initial investment!

CHUCK BERRY, THE SUPREMES, STEVIE WONDER, AND MICHAEL JACKSON

Soul

Rhythm and blues gradually gave way to a more general concept of African American music: **soul.** This term is somewhat nebulous, but it is strongly associated with the racial and cultural identity of African Americans and is created primarily for them. Musically, it is a synthesis of blues, jazz, and gospel. On the surface its prominent musical characteristics are not all that different from those of rock. But underneath there lies a wealth of subtle tonal and rhythmic nuances that make soul distinctive and highly expressive.

RAP

In *"Cop Killer"* rapper Ice-T bragged about slitting a policeman's throat and watching his family mourn. A few years later he was playing a detective in the TV series *Law and Order: Special Victims Unit.*

Rap became the popular music phenomenon of the 1990s. It is half spoken, not sung in the usual sense of the word, with strong, persistent rhythm. The most notable feature of rap is its messages, which contain simple rhymes. They often talk about violence, resentment, and aggression in harsh and unvarnished terms. Favored topics include guns, drugs, murder, sex, and hatred of authority, as can be seen in these lines referring to what some police believe:

> They have the authority
> To kill the minority

Some rap is plain ugly, with displays of racism and homophobia, and demeans women, who are often referred to as "bitches" or "ho's" (whores). The result: The sales of rap CDs boomed. By 2003 rap had more than a 13 percent share of the recording market, which is nearly double its share only eight years earlier.

In its rather short history rap has tended to divide into two categories. One is "gangsta rap" with its angry, violent messages, heavy rhythm, and little melody or harmony. The other, sometimes called "pop rap," speaks about unity and has more melodic interest. Queen Latifah's (Dana Elaine Owens) "Unity," for example, talks about respect and community.

COUNTRY MUSIC

Country music was (and still is) the "people's music" among the whites in the South. It began as folk music but evolved into a national phenomenon and a huge commercial enterprise.

Characteristics of Country Music

SINGING STYLE The style of singing is a direct carryover from the style used for folk songs. It has a lonesome quality and is sung with a clear tone and no vibrato. It tends to be nasal and slightly tense or strained. Often singers let their voice "break" to add emotion to a moment in a song. Yodels are sometimes added, especially in the West. Above all, the singing projects sincerity, or it is just not country music.

Often fiddlers perform tricks, such as playing the instrument behind their backs, holding the bow between their legs while moving the fiddle with their hands and arms, and similar antics.

INSTRUMENTS Country music is traditionally played on stringed instruments—the fiddle, dulcimer, guitar, banjo, and mandolin. The *fiddle* is a violin played in a distinctive way with a straight, penetrating tone, short and rapid bow strokes, and much sliding from one note to another. Some country music festivals have fiddling contests. The *mandolin* is associated with Italy but became widely used in some types of country music.

MELODY AND HARMONY Country music is simple and direct. As it became more popular, major and minor scales replaced the extensive use of the older modal scales. Its songs are mostly harmonized with the three primary chords found in so much music in the Western world: tonic, dominant, and subdominant.

RHYTHM The rhythm is simple, with only a little syncopation. Most of the songs are two beats to the measure.

TEXTS The texts of country songs are an interesting blend of realism and sentimentality. Topics include death, drinking, nostalgia, loneliness, and, the perennial favorite, broken love.

Development of Country Music

The move of country music away from its folk status to the world of popular music coincides with the widespread use of recordings and radio in the 1920s. Record companies realized the commercial potential of what was then called *hillbilly* music. They recorded singers such as Uncle Dave Macon from Tennessee, the Carter Family from Virginia, Gid Tanner and his Skillet Lickers from Georgia, and especially Jimmie Rodgers from Mississippi.

Radio broadcasts were vital to the growth of country music, because a large part of its audience lived in remote, rural, mountainous areas. The radio show that eventually became the Grand Ole Opry started in 1925 on WSM in Nashville with two unpaid performers and no commercial sponsor!

> The lack of a sponsor seems unbelievable today.

The first major country music star was Jimmie Rodgers (1897–1933) from Meridian, Mississippi, who was known as the "Singing Brakeman." His career was short — only six years. But during those years, he recorded 111 songs and sold 20 million records, an amazing feat for that time. He was quite eclectic in the music he performed, which included work songs, white blues, love songs, and melancholy ballads.

> A brakeman was one of the crew on a locomotive.

Country music had a close cousin in country-western music. Part of the commercial success of this music was due to the popularity of movies about cowboys and the music performed in them. Some performers became well known in these films: Gene Autry, Ernest Tubb, Maurice "Tex" Ritter, and the Sons of the Pioneers, which at that time included Roy Rogers (Leonard Slye).

Country music grew rapidly after World War II. The most important name in country music from the early 1950s was Hank Williams (1923–1953), who, like Jimmie Rodgers, had a short career. He and his band, the Drifting Cowboys, recorded such perennial favorites as "Your Cheatin' Heart," "I'm So Lonesome I Could Cry," and "Hey, Good Lookin'." Other important names include Johnny Cash, Tennessee Ernie Ford, Merle Haggard, Patsy Cline, and Loretta Lynn, whose life story was made well known in her autobiography and subsequent movie, *Coal Miner's Daughter*.

> Notice the use of a western name for Williams's group.

LISTENING GUIDE

HANK WILLIAMS

"Your Cheatin' Heart" (1953)

GENRE: Country music   Vocalist and string band

CD 6 Tracks 30–31
2 minutes 40 seconds

Form: Strophic (*a a b a*)

0:00	**30**	0:00	After short introduction, singer sings first verse.
			Your cheatin' heart will make us weep, *Etc.*
		0:37	Singer sings second verse.
			When tears come down like fallin' rain, *Etc.*
1:08	**31**	0:00	Band plays short interlude, and then singer sings third verse.
		0:29	*Your cheatin' heart will pine someday,* *Etc.*
		0:49	Repeat last half of first verse.

COUNTRY GREATS HANK WILLIAMS, AND LORETTA LYNN

"Your Cheatin' Heart" was recorded very near the end of Hank Williams's short life. It is a remarkably simple song. The four lines of the song follow the usual *a a b a* pattern of popular songs (and many church hymns) of the time. The third and fourth lines in the second verse are an exact repeat of the first verse. Pairs of words rhyme: *weep/sleep, through/you,* and so on. The melody can be accompanied using only the three primary chords, I, IV, and V, although the accompanying instruments add a few more on the recording. Its easygoing rhythm is straightforward and steady.

Types of Country Music

The success of country music led to several variants in its style. *Rockabilly,* as its name suggests, was strongly influenced by rock. It was mostly the product of Sun Records and was represented by Carl Perkins (1932–1998), Elvis Presley (1935–1977), and Jerry Lee Lewis (b. 1935).

Another variant is sometimes referred to as *honky-tonk.* It centered around Austin, Texas, and its most recognized performer is Willie Nelson (b. 1933).

A third variant, **bluegrass,** attempted to return country music to its traditional roots. Only acoustic (nonelectric) instruments are used, and its song topics return to the less commercial ones of early years. Bluegrass music can largely be credited to one man, Bill Monroe (1911–1996), who grew up in Kentucky. Monroe was a virtuoso performer on the mandolin.

Country music's growth has made Nashville "Music City, USA," complete with a new Grand Ole Opry House in 1975, television and recording studios, publishing houses, agents, and amusement parks. Names such as Dolly Parton, Faith Hill, Barbara Mandrell, Tim McGraw, Kenny Rogers, and a host of others are familiar to the many millions of people who enjoy country music today.

ROCK

It would be easy to say that **rock** is the musical progeny of a union between blues and country music, because it contains important elements of both. But it is much more than that.

Rock often vents strong feelings of revolt. As one writer has said, rock "expressed a visceral impatience with sociopolitical norms." Although rock first appeared in the mid-1950s, it did not begin to dominate the popular music scene until the mid-1960s. The fact that these years also witnessed the emergence of the baby-boomer generation as college-age young people at the same time as the turmoil over the Vietnam War can hardly be a coincidence.

Rock had its start with a Cleveland disc jockey named Alan Freed, who played rhythm and blues. He probably coined the term **rock and roll,** as it is used today, as he

Hank Williams died at the age of twenty-nine from a combination of alcoholism and barbiturates prescribed by a con-man doctor.

"Your Cheatin' Heart" was No. 1 on *Billboard* magazine's country chart in 1953 and was No. 7 in 1962 with Ray Charles's recording.

Bluegrass has no songs about truck drivers or urban situations.

"Rock around the Clock" was the theme song for the 1955 motion picture *Blackboard Jungle,* in which rebellious students smashed the teacher's valuable collection of jazz records. Later it was the theme for the popular television show *Happy Days.*

called his radio program "Moondog's Rock and Roll Party." Later Freed moved to New York City as a disc jockey for WINS, which soon became that city's leading popular music station.

At about the same time, white groups began recording their own versions of rhythm and blues. The first such hit was Bill Haley's (1925–1981) "Rock around the Clock." Elvis Presley was soon to follow with songs such as "Heartbreak Hotel," which in 1956 succeeded in both the black and white segments of the market—something that rarely happens.

Presley is easily the most remembered country-rock star. His dynamic singing and personal magnetism greatly enlarged the audiences for both country and rock music. His recordings have sold an astounding 1 *billion* worldwide, with 111 albums or singles going gold, platinum, or multiplatinum. In addition, he appeared in thirty-three films and sang hundreds of concerts. The public's fascination with Presley continues. His home, Graceland, in Memphis is the second most visited home in the United States; only the White House exceeds it.

ELVIS PRESLEY, THE KING In the years since his death, he is reported to have been seen in hundreds of different places.

Characteristics of Rock

RHYTHM The heart of rock is its strong beat. Often the beat is incorporated in a simple melodic figure played in the bass parts. Another feature of rock rhythm is its prominent *backbeat*. The backbeat is what audiences clap along with: 1-**2**-3-**4**, 1-**2**-3-**4**. In some types of rock, this backbeat is incorporated with other rhythm patterns to create a complex combination of rhythms.

MELODY AND HARMONY The melodies and harmonies of rock are strongly influenced by folk music. It has an elemental simplicity. Rock has more songs written in the modes than other types of music, which again reveals some of its folk heritage.

As described in Chapter 41, modes are scale patterns other than major or minor.

TIMBRE The tonal qualities of rock depend on the particular style. "Hard" rock is very loud with distorted sounds, which is not true of "soft" or "pop" rock. Rock's sounds are almost always amplified electronically, which affects the timbre of the music. The style of singing can vary from raucous, almost shouted sounds of undetermined pitch to energetic but tuneful. Singers work hard at developing individual styles that listeners can easily identify.

LYRICS The form of a rock song is usually built around its lyrics. Songs are often strophic and have more verses than traditional Tin Pan Alley songs. Often lines of text are freer in phrase lengths than the usual thirty-two measures in *a a b a* form. Some rock music uses sophisticated lyrics in terms of rhyme schemes and frame of reference, and sometimes the lyrics do not follow metrical patterns.

PERFORMANCES Most rock musicians are very conscious of visual effects. Some have experimented with subjective mental states in concerts and on videos, or what has often been termed "psychedelic" rock. Some of these images have been fantasy, some subliminal, and some probably influenced by drugs. Because of the enormous amount of money that top rock stars earn, they can afford the best in terms of lighting and other visual and sound effects. Rock concerts are usually more than just music. They include stunning lighting and dramatic effects to captivate their audiences.

THE BEATLES: GEORGE, JOHN (TOP), PAUL, AND RINGO

FOLK-ROCK POET AND PER-
FORMER BOB DYLAN

Developments in Rock since 1965

BRITISH INFLUENCE The close relationship between British and American popular music has a long history. Therefore, it was not surprising when two British groups, The Beatles and the Rolling Stones, became very influential in the American rock music scene. In fact, after the mid-1960s the rock music styles of the two countries became almost indistinguishable from each other.

FOLK ROCK Rock had its urban folk form in the music of Bob Dylan (Robert Zimmerman, b. 1941), who was associated with Greenwich Village in New York City. He infused his music with both folk qualities and social protest lyrics. Other singers of folk rock included Judy Collins and Joni Mitchell.

Some rock groups vary their style quite a bit, which blurs their classification.

FUSION The combination of two or more different musical styles is called **fusion.** The fusion of rock with other styles was inevitable, given its enormous popularity. One fusion occurred between rock and jazz. Several groups successfully blended these two types of music. Blood, Sweat and Tears and Chicago perform a variety of types of rock music. The combination of styles is heard particularly in the treatment of rhythm. Some of these works were considerably longer than the usual rock song.

Another fusion involved the influence of classical music in rock. Three British musicians or groups achieved recognition for this type of music: Keith Emerson, the Bee Gees, and Deep Purple. Emerson, with Greg Lake and Carl Palmer, also produced popular versions of music by such composers as Copland and Mussorgsky.

George Harrison and The Beatles were among the first, if not *the* first, to include elements of Asian music in their rock works. Indian music especially attracted Harrison.

An art form has evolved to a more mature state when it can poke fun at itself.

SATIRE AND PUNK One piece of evidence regarding the maturing of rock was its increasing use of satire. Frank Zappa (b. 1940) and the Mothers of Invention engaged in theatrics and put-ons that caused audiences to wonder about the seriousness of it all. Zappa himself kept interviewers guessing about the nature of his artistic intentions with his rambling and unclear statements.

While Zappa may have been having fun with audiences, *punk* rock was deliberately being rebellious. The feelings of rebellion were directed at both the norms of society and the rock establishment, which these performers thought had sold out to commercial interests. The musical impact of these groups was probably less than their social impact, as they sometimes engaged in repulsive behavior in their performances.

Punk rock groups did not lack for interesting names, including Weirdos, Sex Pistols, the Lewd, the Mutants, the Ghouls, Flesheaters, Slash, Search and Destroy, Circle Jerks, Crime, Damage, and Destroy All Music.

MUSIC VIDEOS

The present generation of young people is sometimes described as "the Video Generation." It has grown up with visual images provided by television and other technology. And these images are not just pictures or designs, but frequent, often rapid-fire moving images that flash across a screen.

Even on network television, one shot is almost never maintained for more than four seconds. The time span is shorter yet in music videos.

It was only a matter of time before popular music began to combine music and visual images. This effort led to the establishment of MTV (Music Television) in the early 1980s. Initially, the purpose of the videos was the promotion of recordings. One of the early and most widely recognized music videos was Michael Jackson's "Thriller," which was taken from his 1983 album of the same name.

Music videos can be divided into four main types:

- Videos that present a performer in a concert format
- Videos that present music in a dance format
- Videos that present a story, which may or may not relate directly to the lyrics of the song
- Videos that present fantasy images, often on the premise of a dream

Music videos rely heavily on the manipulation of images, using computers and other technological equipment.

Any survey of a musical style is limited in the amount of information it can provide and in the conclusions it can draw. This seems especially true of rock, because it changes so rapidly and because it is a complex social-psychological-musical phenomenon. Whatever else may be said of rock, it is truly a fascinating topic and a creative type of music.

OTHER TYPES OF POPULAR MUSIC

Although soul, country, and rock cover much of the popular music scene since 1950, they certainly do not account for all of it. Several other types of popular music were influential as well.

Latin American

Latin American music has influenced the popular music of the United States since at least the 1920s, when the husband-and-wife team of Vernon and Irene Castle popularized the tango. By the 1930s the *rumba* had become a popular dance. Cuban music soared in popularity as "The Peanut Vendor" recorded by Don Azpiazú became the first Cuban hit record. Also, Xavier Cugat, who was born in Spain but lived most of his life in Cuba, and his band were appearing in a number of motion pictures.

A *rumba* is a dance in a rapid two-beat meter with an intricate contrasting part played by the percussion. It is Afro-Cuban in origin.

Interest in Latin American music reached a high point in the 1950s and 1960s with the popularization of the *mambo*. The person most responsible for the interest in this dance music was Tito Puente (1923–2000), who was born in New York City of Puerto Rican parents. His most successful recording from this period was "Dance Mania."

© Mike Alans/AP Photo

TITO PUENTE

Salsa means "sauce" or "spice."

The 1970s saw the advent of a "hot" style of Latin American music called *salsa*. It originated in the Cuban nightclubs in the 1940s, from where it spread to the rest of the Caribbean and then on to the United States. Three cities became known as the "salsa triangle": San Juan in Puerto Rico, Miami, and New York.

Another type of Latin American music is associated with the American West. Austin, Texas, became the center for an amalgamation of Mexican and country music called *Tex-Mex*. The best-known singer of Latin American music in the 1970s was Linda Ronstadt. She grew up in Tucson, Arizona, the daughter of a part-Chicano father.

Although *reggae* originated in Jamaica in the 1960s, it did not become widely known in the United States until fifteen or so years later. Reggae features accents on the back-beat with simple melodies and few chord changes. Bob Marley (1945–1981) and the Wailers presented colorful sounds that became popular with the 1976 song "Roots, Rock, Reggae."

The interest in Latin American music is very strong. In 1992 Puente recorded "Numero 100," his one hundredth recording. The Miami Sound Machine with Gloria Estefan is another example of Latin American music that appeals to a wide audience.

Modern Jazz

The share of the radio and record market occupied by jazz slipped to about 2 percent.

Jazz reached a turning point in the 1950s: It became more sophisticated—gone was the strong beat that people could dance to. In its place was a music that began for the first time to be considered seriously as concert music by its audiences and many of its performers. No longer was it music for the players; instead it became music for listeners. In the process, jazz lost its appeal to the young people, who moved to rock and rhythm and blues.

Dizzy Gillespie defined bop by saying that in bop you go *Ba*-oo *Ba*-oo *Ba*-oo *instead of Oo*-ba *Oo*-ba *Oo*-ba.

The change began with a style of jazz called **bebop** or, more common, **bop.** It was the product mainly of Charlie "Bird" Parker (1920–1955) and Dizzy Gillespie (John Birks, 1917–1993). Bop contains nearly continuous syncopation, dissonant chords, and freely developed melodies. Bop groups were usually small combos, not the big bands of the 1940s. The string bass was often responsible for maintaining the beat. Some of its musical passages were played in unison, often with lots of notes.

Miles Davis (1926–1991), Dave Brubeck (b. 1920), and the Modern Jazz Quartet turned toward a "cool" style of jazz. Their music was more intellectual and well ordered, and it was also performed by small groups.

BRUBECK'S "BLUE RONDO A LA TURK"

Dave Brubeck's "Blue Rondo a la Turk" reveals its more sophisticated nature in its title. First, it alludes to rondo form in which the same music returns several times with other music interspersed between its appearances. Second, it refers to Turkish music and its frequent use of asymmetrical rhythm patterns. Appropriately, the first section of the piece opens with nine rapid beats per measure arranged in a 1 2, 1 2, 1 2, 1 2 3 pattern. "Blue Rondo a la Turk" also has a "cool," intellectual quality, especially in its long sax and piano solos.

DAVE BRUBECK

© Dat's Jazz/Corbis

LISTENING GUIDE

DAVE BRUBECK
"Blue Rondo a la Turk" (1959)

GENRE: Modern jazz   Drums, bass, saxophone, piano

CD 6 Tracks 32–33
3 minute 53 seconds

Form: Rondo

0:00	**32**	0:00	Piano, bass, and drums play nine fast notes in a 2 + 2 + 2 + 3 pattern, with every fourth measure in a 3 + 3 + 3 pattern.
		0:11	Saxophone joins in.
		0:22	Piano, bass, and drums continue without saxophone.
		0:43	Saxophone enters as piano drops out.
		1:08	Saxophone plays main thematic idea again.
		1:19	Piano begins transition based on main theme.
		1:53	Music suddenly changes to four-beat meter with a more leisurely character. This is briefly interrupted three times by the opening music.
2:14	**33**	0:00	Saxophone begins lengthy improvised solo accompanied by bass and drums.
		1:39	Recording fades.

A less well-understood type of jazz is called **free jazz.** It was first developed by Ornette Coleman (1926–1967) about 1960. Other practitioners of this style include John Coltrane (1926–1967) and Cecil Taylor (b. 1933). Free jazz usually involves collective improvising, no predetermined chord progressions or tonality, playing deliberately out of tune, and expanded forms that are longer than those usually encountered in jazz.

Some jazz composers, notably Miles Davis, moved to electronic sounds and changes that made their works jazz-based compositions. Davis's "Bitches Brew," created in 1969, uses a number of electric instruments and an almost rocklike rhythm pattern that is ornamented with Latin American figures. In 1995 Wynton Marsalis (b. 1961) and his

© Zack Seckler/Corbis

WYNTON MARSALIS at Lincoln Center in New York City

Septet followed in Davis's footsteps with "Citi Movement," a thirty-seven-minute-long ballet. These compositions represent high artistic aspirations. Jazz has indeed moved far from what its founding fathers back in New Orleans had started early in the twentieth century.

CODA

Popular music in America has come a long way in five decades. It has developed new and different types of styles and has acquired much economic and social importance as well. Because the various types of popular music are continuously evolving, they are as fascinating and complex as American society itself.

Music *for* Stage *and* Film

39

Music for stage performances and films is somewhat different from concert music. Such music does not stand alone. It always involves a visual element and usually drama. Composers therefore face somewhat different requirements when writing for stage or film. They need to create music that is effective in tandem with the action and story with which they are working. In spite of this apparent limitation, this requirement has produced a body of beautiful and interesting music.

EARLY CONCERTS

Public performances of music in the 1700s were mostly confined to four cities: Philadelphia, New York, Boston, and Charleston. These performances were hardly concerts in the current sense of the word. They included songs, dances, recitations, card tricks, and even balancing acts. Audiences were noisy, and performers often had to request them to be quiet. In fact, for many years some of the audience was allowed to sit onstage.

On bad nights the audience threw nuts, fruit, and even bottles at the performers!

No clear division existed between popular and concert music in stage productions, a situation that lasted until about 1830. Songs were almost always included in early public performances, but few of those songs have survived.

A few types of musicals existed. Most of these had skeletal plots around which composers created some songs, but most of the music for these stage productions has been lost.

MINSTREL SHOWS

An indigenous American type of stage show is the **minstrel show,** which developed in the decades before the Civil War. These shows enjoyed enormous popularity and existed well into the twentieth century.

Minstrel shows featured the exaggerated portrayal of black people by white performers wearing blackface. The shows consisted of songs, dances, jokes, skits, and satirical speeches. Originally, there were only four performers seated in a semicircle. They didn't sit still for long, however; they were almost constantly in motion, even when sitting. Banjo and fiddle players occupied the middle two seats. The other two performers were logically called "end men." They played the bones and tambourine and engaged in entertaining horseplay. The music for minstrel shows was generally in a major key, had a lively tempo, and contained much repetition of short motives.

After the Civil War, blacks became the main performers in minstrel shows.

The *bones* were two small clappers played with the fingers. They were originally animal bones but were later made of hardwood.

Two names are especially associated with minstrel shows: Stephen Foster, who was discussed in Chapter 37, and Dan Emmett (1815–1904). Emmett composed "Dixie" while working with a minstrel show company.

The well-known song "Dixie" has each of these characteristics.

VAUDEVILLE

Late in the 1800s, a new and important form of stage entertainment appeared: **vaudeville.** It descended from minstrel shows, the English music hall, and the "burlesque" type of entertainment offered in saloons. Vaudeville usually consisted of a succession of

0:57   The Jets urge Tony to be present for the anticipated fight.

> We're counting on you to be there,
>   tonight.
> When Diesel wins it fair and square,
>   tonight.
> That Puerto Rican punk'll
>   go down,
> And when he's hollered "Uncle,"
> We'll tear up the town!

1:14   Maria sings "Tonight," and the Sharks keep urging Tony to be there.

> *Tonight, tonight*
>
> *won't be just any night*
>
> *tonight there will be no morning star.*

> So I can count on you, boy?
> (Tony) All right.
> We're gonna have us a ball!
> (Tony) All right.
> Womb to tomb!
> (Tony) Sperm to worm!
> I'll see you there about eight.
> (Tony) Tonight.

1:27   The Jets sing about the anticipated fight as Maria continues.

> *Tonight, tonight*
> *(Anita) Tonight,*
>   *I'll see my love tonight*

> We're gonna rock it tonight!

1:33   Anita enters singing about her date with Bernardo.

> *(Anita) Tonight, late tonight,*
>   *we're gonna mix it tonight.*
> *(Maria) and for us,*
>   *stars will stop where they are.*

> They're gonna get it tonight.

3:06   **44**   0:00   Tony joins Maria in singing "Tonight" as Anita, the Jets, and the Sharks sing in anticipation of events to come.

>   *(Tony and Maria) Today the minutes seem like hours,*
>
> *Anita's gonna have her day*
>
> They began it
> They began it,
>
> *Anita's gonna have her day*
> *Anita's gonna have her day*
> *(Sharks) They began it*
>   *the hours go so slowly*
> *(Anita) Bernardo's gonna have his way*
>   *tonight, tonight!*
> *(Sharks) They began it!*
>
> They began it,
>
> and we're the ones
>
>   *and still the sky is light.*
>
> to stop 'em once and for all
>
> *We'll stop 'em once*
>   *and for all*
>   *Oh moon, grow bright!*
>
> *The Sharks are gonna have*   The Jets are gonna have
>   *their way,*   their way,
>   *and make this endless day*
> *The Sharks are gonna have*   The Jets are gonna have
>   *their day,*   their day,
> *(Anita) Tonight, this very night,*
>   *endless night,*
> *We're gonna rock it tonight,*   We're gonna rock it tonight,
> *tonight!*   *tonight!*   tonight!

0:31   Singers and orchestra end on a long, brilliant chord.

Leonard Bernstein

Hulton /Deutsch Collection /Corbis

Leonard Bernstein (1918–1990) was born in Lawrence, Massachusetts, of Russian-Jewish parents. His businessman father moved the family to Boston shortly after Leonard's birth, and he graduated from the Boston Latin School and Harvard University. Later he studied at the Curtis Institute in Philadelphia.

During his career he developed a number of successful television programs on musical topics, appeared as a piano soloist, and composed a variety of types of music. For a decade he was conductor of the New York Philharmonic Orchestra.

BEST-KNOWN WORKS

ballet:
- *Fancy Free*
- *On the Town*

musical:
- *West Side Story*

orchestra:
- *Candide: Overture*

OPERATIC MUSICALS

A noteworthy trend in music for the stage in recent years is a growing number of the successful musicals that are virtually operas—every word in them is sung. Three examples of this trend are *Phantom of the Opera* by Andrew Lloyd Webber and *Les Misérables* and *Miss Saigon* by Claude-Michel Schonberg. There are, however, several differences between them and the operas of Mozart, Verdi, and other composers as performed by the major opera houses of Europe and the Americas.

- The style of singing is more like what is heard in musicals.
- The singing is amplified, although no microphones are visible and the sound levels are not particularly loud.
- The vocal parts are technically less demanding; no virtuoso singing ability is required.
- The accompanying orchestra is rather small.
- They are sung in English in English-speaking countries.
- They contain one or more humorous sections and characters.
- The action onstage moves at a faster pace.

These musicals have international roots; they are no longer just Broadway musicals. Lloyd Webber is British and Schonberg is French. Furthermore, these musicals opened in London and Paris, respectively, and came to New York after having enjoyed much success overseas.

Phantom of the Opera is based on a story about a phantom (who is actually a man with a terribly scarred face) who haunts the Paris Opera House. It has been made into at least two movies and a stage play. The plot revolves around the love of the phantom for a beautiful young soprano. He sabotages the efforts of the opera managers to promote her place in the company. He also tries to win her affection

Claude-Michel Schonberg and Arnold Schoenberg are not related genetically or musically.

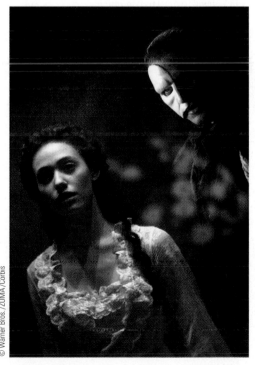

© Warner Bros. /ZUMA /Corbis

PHANTOM OF THE OPERA Actors Emmy Rossum as Christine Daae and Gerard Butler in *The Phantom of the Opera*

Les Misérables used a rotating stage. It made sixty-three turns in each performance.

Les Misérables is probably the world's most popular musical, with an audience approaching 40 million. It has been translated into fourteen languages and has won thirty-one awards.

A Listening Guide for the finale of *Les Misérables* is included in the *Study Guide*.

Miss Saigon contains many parallels to Puccini's opera *Madame Butterfly*, the story of an American naval officer who fathers a child with a young Japanese woman while on tour in Japan and then abandons her.

A Listening Guide for the duet "I Still Believe" from *Miss Saigon* is included in the *Study Guide*.

and keep her from her fiancé. Fortunately, he fails. *Phantom* is quite theatrical, and at times it contains elements of old-style film music, with its sinister theme and crashing chandelier.

Schonberg's *Les Misérables* and *Miss Saigon* were both originally written in French with the text by Alain Boubil. English translations were carefully prepared later.

Les Misérables is based on the great novel by the French writer Victor Hugo. It tells of a man, Jean Valjean, who while young committed a petty crime for which he spent several years in jail. Although initially bitter after his release, his feelings change after being befriended by a kindly priest. He eventually adopts a new name and becomes a factory owner and mayor of his town but is still pursued by an unrelenting police inspector. One of his good deeds is to raise as his own an illegitimate girl, Cosette. Her mother had worked for a while in Valjean's factory, but she had fallen on hard times and died while Cosette was quite young.

Times are hard in France in the 1830s, and Valjean joins a band of students who hope to bring about another revolution to better the lives of the poor. The revolution fails because the people do not rise up as they did in 1789. Valjean saves Cosette's fiancé, who was one of the revolutionaries, by carrying him unconscious through the sewers of Paris to safety. The young man recovers, and the couple marry. Finally, they learn the truth about all that Valjean has done for them. *Les Misérables* closes with Valjean being escorted into heaven by Cosette's mother and the stirring marching song of the revolutionaries.

Miss Saigon is a much more contemporary story about Chris, a U.S. Marine in the war in Vietnam, who falls in love with a Vietnamese girl named Kim. Despite his best efforts, he is forced to leave her behind when the Americans withdraw. Two years later, now married to an American woman, Chris learns that Kim is alive and that he has a young son in Vietnam. He returns to see her and the child. Kim, realizing that the best hope for her son's future is with his father in America, decides to give him up to Chris. In her grief-stricken state, she commits suicide, dying as Chris bends over her in anguish as the curtain falls.

Each of the three musicals mentioned here is filled with memorable music. All are well worth knowing.

AMERICAN OPERA

In the late 1800s and early 1900s, many American cities had "opera houses," but they were used mostly for concerts and other events, not operas.

The Medium uses only five singers and an actor who plays the role of a person who is deaf and cannot speak. Its orchestra is very small, there is no chorus, and it lasts for less than an hour.

Opera has never been as popular in America as it has in many European countries. Some of the reasons for this are mentioned in Chapter 12, but certainly the lack of operas in English is significant. Another probable reason is the lack of an American aristocracy to fund and support opera.

It is not that American composers have failed to write several first-rate operas. Rather, it is that only a few of them seem to have achieved a permanent place in operatic repertoire. One candidate for this permanent status is Howard Hanson's *Merry Mount*, which is based on a story by Nathaniel Hawthorne set in New England.

Another candidate is *The Medium* by Gian-Carlo Menotti, who was born in Italy but immigrated to the United States when he was seventeen. *The Medium* is based on a grisly story of a devious old lady who claims to communicate with the dead in fake séances. Eventually, her conscience begins to bother her, and she imagines that something clutched her throat during a séance. Disaster follows. Menotti's *Amahl and the Night Visitors* was one of the first operas composed for television. After its premiere on the *Hallmark Hall of Fame* in 1951, it became an annual Christmas telecast for nearly two decades.

GERSHWIN'S *PORGY AND BESS*

The opera that has secured for itself a solid place in American operatic repertoire is not a true opera but rather, in the composer's words, a "folk opera." *Porgy and Bess* by George Gershwin is based on a story by DuBose Heyward set in Charleston, South Carolina. It is about a beggar named Porgy, who cannot walk and must get around in a goat cart. Gershwin could see the dramatic possibilities in the story and decided to compose an opera based on it.

To make the story as real as possible, Gershwin has the characters speak many of their lines instead of singing recitatives. He also incorporates the music of the black people of Charleston—the blues and features of jazz—into the opera. Although he does not include actual folk songs, the music has a folklike quality. Its jazz elements are written down rather than made up on the spot.

The story of *Porgy and Bess* is filled with tragedy. Porgy leads a lonely life; Bess, a loose-living woman, comes to town with her lover, Crown. Neither Bess nor Crown is accepted by the people of Catfish Row. Crown kills a local man in a fight, and Bess takes refuge from the police in Porgy's shanty. Their relationship grows into genuine love.

When Crown learns of Bess's love for Porgy, he sets out to kill him. In the fight between the two men, Crown is stabbed and dies. Porgy is taken off to jail on suspicion of murder.

Now is the moment the character Sportin' Life has been waiting for. He represents the easy, evil life that Bess left behind when she moved in with Porgy. Because Porgy may never be freed from jail, Sportin' Life is able to persuade Bess to go back to New York

The U.S. Department of State has on several occasions supported overseas tours of *Porgy and Bess*.

George Gershwin

Bettmann /Corbis

George Gershwin (1898–1937) was born and educated in Brooklyn, New York. His family was poor but was able to afford piano lessons for him. At the age of sixteen, he was employed as a song-plugger by a Tin Pan Alley publisher, and his career in music began. He often collaborated with his brother, Ira, who wrote the lyrics for many of George's songs.

Although successful and now financially well off, Gershwin was ambitious about composing concert music. His first big success came with *Rhapsody in Blue* in 1924. He originally composed it for piano and jazz orchestra; later he asked Ferde Grofé to arrange the orchestral parts. Whatever he lacked in developing musical ideas he more than made up for in his sparkling tunes and moving melodies.

George Gershwin died in Hollywood of a brain tumor after unsuccessful surgery to save his life.

BEST-KNOWN WORKS

orchestra:
- *American in Paris*

orchestra and piano:
- Concerto in F
- *Rhapsody in Blue*

opera:
- *Porgy and Bess*

musicals:
- *Of Thee I Sing*
- *Girl Crazy*
- *Strike Up the Band*

OPERA SINGERS IN PERFOR-MANCE Opera singers Simon Estes and Grace Bumbry in a New York City Opera production of *Porgy and Bess*.

© Jacques M. Chenet/CORBIS

with him. But Porgy is released, and when he returns home, he finds Bess gone. "Where is she?" he asks. "New York," answer his neighbors. *Porgy and Bess* closes with the pathetic scene of Porgy climbing into his goat cart to go to New York to find Bess.

The song "Summertime" appears near the beginning of the opera and helps establish the opera's setting. The mood is lazy and relaxed as the mother sings her baby to sleep. The accompaniment suggests a gentle rocking motion. The song includes some vocal devices such as a slide, or glissando, and a little catch on the word *cry*.

LISTENING GUIDE

GEORGE GERSHWIN

"Summertime" from *Porgy and Bess* (1934–1935)

GENRE: Opera   Soprano and orchestra

CD 6 Track 34
2 minutes 28 seconds

0:00   **34**   0:00   Introduction soon falls into a gentle rocking sound between two notes.

0:25   Soprano begins:

Moderato

p Sum - mer - time_____ an' the liv - in' is eas - y,_____

Summertime an' the livin' is easy,
Fish are jumpin',
an' the cotton is high.
Oh yo' daddy's rich,
an' yo' ma is good-lookin',
So hush, little baby,
don't yo' cry.

1:21   Song continues with much the same melody as singers join in accompanying part.

> *One of these mornin's*
> *You goin' to rise up singin',*
> *Then you'll spread yo' wings*
> *an' you'll take the sky.*
> *But till that mornin'*
> *there's a nothin' can harm you*
> *With Daddy an' Mammy standin' by.*

2:28   After a long note on the word *by*, during which the accompaniment plays some chromatic harmony, the song ends quietly.

MUSIC FOR FILMS

In a sense, commercial movies have almost never been silent. In the small, low-priced theaters a pianist pounded out music at appropriate places as the film flickered by on the screen. In upscale theaters small- to medium-sized orchestras played music especially composed for the film. This body of theater music has now been largely forgotten.

Role

Today, of course, music is an integral part of almost every commercial film, even showings of old silent movies. Why? Because music contributes to a film in a number of ways.

- It creates a more convincing atmosphere of a particular time and place. A scene with a ship sailing through the seas calls for one kind of music, and a scene in a crowded western saloon requires another.

- It gives the viewers cues about the unspoken thoughts of the characters or the yet unseen implications of a situation. If a man is looking at a woman and he is filled with feelings of love and desire, the music can project his feelings.

  In many ways music can express such feelings better than words.

- It provides neutral filler or background sound. Although such music is of little interest in itself, it does fill the empty places in a film.

- It helps build a sense of continuity in a motion picture. This is done by associating certain music with a particular character or situation.

- It supports and contributes to the buildup of a scene, including giving the film a solid ending.

  Almost no movie ends in silence, even if it lacked much of a musical score.

Development

It wasn't much of a beginning back on October 6, 1927, with *The Jazz Singer*, the first motion picture with music. The sound portion consisted of just five songs, including Irving Berlin's "Blue Skies." Its sound quality was vastly inferior to what we are used to today. To help the picture succeed, Warner Brothers picked a well-known vaudeville performer, Al Jolson. Impressive by today's standards or not, *The Jazz Singer* opened the door, and soon "all-talking, all-singing, all-dancing" films would follow.

It was as though a great divide had been reached that separated silent movies from films with sound. Within a few years of *The Jazz Singer*, Hollywood was attracting top musical talent for its productions. Many of the best Broadway composers and arrangers worked there—George Gershwin, Jerome Kern, Irving Berlin, Cole Porter, and Harold Arlen.

At first glance, composing some music to serve the five purposes described earlier would seem to stifle creative quality. After all, the music must match the film to the sec-

© 20th Century Fox /ZUMA /Corbis

STAR WARS EPISODE III: REVENGE OF THE SITH Actors Natalie Portman as Senator Padme Amidala with C-3PO (Anthony Daniels) and Hayden Christensen as Anakin Skywalker in *Star Wars: Episode III Revenge of the Sith*.

Both Miklos Rozsa and John Williams have pointed out that music for a film has to be immediate in its effectiveness. Musical ideas cannot be introduced gradually.

ond, so little development of musical ideas is possible. Either because or in spite of these limitations, a number of excellent composers established their professional reputations through their film music—Miklos Rozsa, Erich Korngold, Henry Mancini, Alfred Newman, Dimitri Tiomkin, James Horner, Max Steiner, Jerry Goldsmith, Maurice Jarre, Bernard Herrmann, and John Williams, among others. Some of their music has found a life apart from the movie for which it was made in terms of commercial recordings. Some of it has almost assumed a folklore status, such as the shrieking sounds from the violins that Herrmann wrote for the soundtrack for Alfred Hitchcock's *Psycho* and Williams's ominous throbbing sounds for the shark in *Jaws*.

WILLIAMS'S MAIN TITLE FROM *STAR WARS*

The Main Title from *Star Wars* was presented in Chapter 1. Listen to it again, and notice how your understanding of music has increased in view of the information in the preceding thirty-eight chapters.

Also notice the following features:

- The sensuous, richly Romantic character of the music; its roots go back to nineteenth-century Romanticism. The fact that the music for a space-age epic is Romantic may seem to be a bit of a contradiction in a film filled with technology and futuristic scenes. But love and conflict exist, whether the actors are wearing jeans and riding a horse or wearing spacesuits and floating through space.

- The attraction of the music lies in its overall massive and colorful sounds and timbres and its energetic rhythms.

The movement titled "Mars" in Holst's *The Planets*, which was composed about 1915, is quite similar to parts of the Main Title from *Star Wars*.

- Something is happening in the music almost all of the time. Something in addition to the themes can be heard—a rhythm pattern, swirling notes played by the violins, points of tonal color added by the harp, and so forth. It contains elements of the English composer Gustav Holst (1874–1934) and several other composers.

- The form of the music is rather sectional. It is not music that takes a theme and works with it in the manner of Beethoven or Zwilich. Nor does the music feature much counterpoint in the manner of Bach or Palestrina. The reason for the sectional character of this music is the need to fit with the different scenes and characters of the film.

MUSIC AND VISUAL IMAGES

Technology is opening up an easy union of music with visual images. One attempt at doing this is MTV, which was discussed in Chapter 38. Sometimes the role of movies in the promotion of music, especially popular music, has been overlooked. The film versions of Broadway musicals did much to further that type of music, which is also true of Latin American music and some of the big-band music of the Swing Era. But videotape and DVD now offer even more intriguing possibilities.

CODA

The situations presented on a stage or in film have often inspired composers to create music with much emotional impact. The challenge of integrating the music with dramatic scenes seems to have been a good incubator for many inspirational and beautiful works of music.

PART VIII

Music
around
the
World

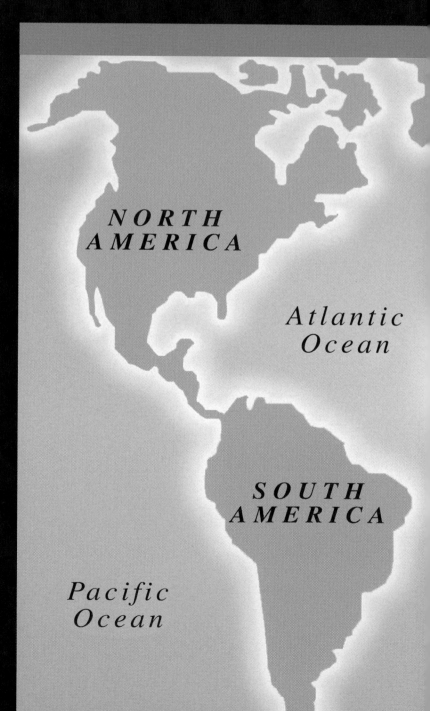

NORTH
AMERICA

Atlantic
Ocean

SOUTH
AMERICA

Pacific
Ocean

Index

Performers List CDS 1 AND 2

CD ①

1 J. Williams: Main Title from *Star Wars*
John Williams and the Boston Pops
℗ 1990 SONY BMG MUSIC ENTERTAINMENT

4 Bizet: *Farandole* from *L'Arlésienne* Suite No. 2
Toronto Symphony; Andrew Davis, conductor
℗ 1981 SONY BMG MUSIC ENTERTAINMENT

7 arr. Copland: "Simple Gifts" from *Old American Songs*
William Warfield, baritone; Columbia Symphony Orchestra;
Aaron Copland, conductor
Originally Released 1963 SONY BMG MUSIC
ENTERTAINMENT

9 Rodrigo: *Concierto de Aranjuez*, II
John Williams, guitar soloist; Philadelphia Orchestra;
Eugene Ormandy, conductor
℗ 1974 SONY BMG MUSIC ENTERTAINMENT

13 John Rutter/Lancelot Andrewes:
"Open Thou Mine Eyes"
The Cambridge Singers
℗ 1984 Collegium Records
Courtesy of Collegium Records

15 Anonymous: Dies irae
Schola Cantorum Amsterdam; Vim Van Gerven, conductor
℗ 1973 SONY BMG MUSIC ENTERTAINMENT

16 Palestrina: "Sicut cervus"
Westminster Cathedral Choir; James O'Donnell, conductor
℗ 1991 Hyperion Records Ltd.
Courtesy of Hyperion Records Ltd.

19 Weelkes: "As Vesta Was from Latmos Hill Descending"
Consort of Musicke; Anthony Rooley, director
℗ 1988 Hyperion Records Ltd.
Courtesy of Hyperion Records Ltd.

Handel: *Messiah*

21 "The Voice of Him That Crieth in the Wilderness"

22 "Ev'ry Valley Shall Be Exalted"

24 "Hallelujah Chorus"
Le Grand Ecurie et la Chambre du Roy; Jean-Claude Malgoire,
director
℗ 1980 SONY BMG MUSIC ENTERTAINMENT

27 Bach: "Zion Hears the Watchmen" (Section 4)
from Cantata No. 140
American Bach Soloists; Jeffrey Thomas, conductor
℗ 1996 Koch International L.P.
Courtesy of The American Bach Soloists

29 Vivaldi: "Spring" from *The Four Seasons*, I
St. Paul Chamber Orchestra; Pinchas Zukerman,
violin and conductor
℗ 1974 SONY BMG MUSIC ENTERTAINMENT

34 Bach: Toccata and Fugue in D Minor
Peter Hurford
℗ 1979 Decca Music Group Limited
Courtesy of Decca Music Group Limited under License
from Universal Music Enterprises

38 Mozart: Symphony No. 40, I
Cleveland Orchestra; George Szell, conductor
Originally Released 1970 SONY BMG MUSIC
ENTERTAINMENT

43 Haydn: Concerto for Trumpet in E-flat, III
Chamber Symphony of New York; Gerard Schwartz,
trumpet soloist and conductor
℗ 1983 Delos International, Inc.
Courtesy of Delos International, Inc.

46 Mozart: *Don Giovanni*, excerpt from Act II, Scene V
Kiri Te Kanawa, soprano; Ruggero Raimondi, bass; Chorus
and Orchestra of the Paris National Opera Theater; Lorin Maazel,
conductor
℗ 1979 SONY BMG MUSIC ENTERTAINMENT

CD ②

1 Beethoven: Symphony No. 5 in C Minor, I
Cleveland Orchestra; George Szell, conductor
Originally Released 1964 SONY BMG MUSIC
ENTERTAINMENT

6 Schubert: "Der Erlkönig"
Dietrich Fischer-Dieskau, baritone; Karl Engel, piano
℗ 1995 ORFEO International Music GmbH
Courtesy of Qualiton Imports Ltd.

9 Liszt: *Grandes Etudes de Paganini*,
No. 3 in G-Sharp minor, *La Campanella*
André Watts, piano
Originally Released 1971 SONY BMG MUSIC
ENTERTAINMENT

11 Berlioz: *Symphonie fantastique*, V,
"Dream of the Witches Sabbath"
New York Philharmonic; Leonard Bernstein, conductor
Originally Released 1969 SONY BMG MUSIC
ENTERTAINMENT

16 Puccini: *La bohème*, excerpt from Act I
Renata Tebaldi, soprano; Franco Corelli, tenor; Chorus and
Orchestra of the Academy of St. Cecilia; Tulio Serafin, conductor
Courtesy of Decca Music Group Limited under License from
Universal Music Enterprises

18 Brahms: Symphony No. 4 in E minor, I
Cleveland Orchestra; George Szell, conductor
Originally Released 1967 SONY BMG MUSIC
ENTERTAINMENT

23 Debussy: "Clair de lune"
Philippe Entremont, piano
Originally Released 1961 SONY BMG MUSIC
ENTERTAINMENT

26 Bartók: Concerto for Orchestra, IV
New York Philharmonic; Pierre Boulez, conductor
℗ 1973 SONY BMG MUSIC ENTERTAINMENT

29 Britten: Dies irae from *War Requiem*
Atlanta Symphony Orchestra and Chorus; Robert Shaw, conductor
℗ 1989 TELARC
Courtesy of the Telarc International Corporation

31 Stravinsky: *The Rite of Spring,* excerpts from Act I
Cleveland Orchestra; Pierre Boulez, conductor
Originally Released 1969 SONY BMG MUSIC
ENTERTAINMENT

34 Varèse: *Poème électronique*
Realized on Electronic Tape
Originally Released 1960 SONY BMG MUSIC
ENTERTAINMENT

35 Copland: *Appalachian Spring,* Section 7
London Symphony Orchestra; Aaron Copland, conductor
Originally Released 1971 SONY BMG MUSIC
ENTERTAINMENT

38 Zwilich: *Concerto Grosso 1985,* I
New York Philharmonic; Zubin Mehta, conductor
℗ 1989 Recorded Anthology of American Music, Inc.
Courtesy of New World Records

40 Ellington: "Take the 'A' Train"
Duke Ellington and His Famous Orchestra
Originally Released 1941. All rights reserved by BMG Music

42 Bernstein: "Tonight" (Quintet) from *West Side Story*
Original Cast Recording
Originally Released 1957 SONY BMG MUSIC
ENTERTAINMENT